PHILOSOPHY
OF KNOWLEDGE

Selected Readings

FELIX M. CLEVE

FRANCIS H. PARKER

YVES R. SIMON

NELSON GOODMAN

CLARENCE I. LEWIS

A. I. MELDEN

JACQUES MARITAIN

WILLIAM P. MONTAGUE

EDWARD D. SIMMONS

BENJAMIN L. WHORF

HENRY B. VEATCH

GERALD B. PHELAN

F. H. HEINEMANN

FELIX KAUFMANN

ERNST CASSIRER

ELIZABETH FLOWER

ANTHONY NEMETZ

RALPH B. PERRY

J. O. WISDOM

A. CORNELIUS BENJAMIN

ETIENNE GILSON

HANS U. VON BALTHASAR

Edited by

ROLAND HOUDE
St. John's University
Jamaica, N. Y.

JOSEPH P. MULLALLY
Queens College
Flushing, N. Y.

PHILOSOPHY

OF KNOWLEDGE

Selected Readings

J. B. LIPPINCOTT COMPANY
Chicago · Philadelphia · New York

truth is its own value

and is to be accepted

irrespective of its source

To PH and MJM

PREFACE

IT is clear to the serious student of philosophy that his science is not a dogmatic, *a priori* discipline, but a discourse, a search. It was perhaps inevitable that at some point in this "conversation of the ages" the question of the truth value of knowledge itself should be raised. We are now at a point in history where the question has been posed, its ramifications explored, and a branch of philosophy founded to seek what can be known about knowledge itself. Whether we call this study epistemology, critique, criteriology, gnoseology, or simply philosophy of knowledge, there can be no doubt that it has emerged—with logic and psychology—as the most important area of modern philosophic thought.

If we regard Descartes as the first to raise the epistemic question, it becomes obvious that only in recent times have philosophers concerned themselves with the philosophy of knowledge itself; that is, with the very "tools of the trade," whose adequacy the pre-Cartesians had never seriously questioned. Indeed, it was not until the nineteenth century that the problem became urgent. But even then, skepticism concerned itself primarily with the knowability of religious truths and the abstractions of metaphysics; the certainty of experimental data was not doubted. The problem in the twentieth century has apparently reached its ultimate crisis, for, as James Conant points out in *Modern Science and Modern Man,* experimental data themselves are not the hard core of knowables that the nineteenth century thought them; or, as Percy W. Bridgman, in *The Way Things Are,* has remarked, *a propos* the limitations of man's power of comprehending his universe, "It is the nature of knowledge to be subject to uncertainty."

The questions that confront the theorist of knowledge today are thus of the greatest urgency, not only in the area of conception, or metaphysical formulation, but also in the process of sense perception itself. Unfortunately, the philosophy of knowledge has not kept pace with the need of investigators in other fields to determine the value of their intellectual constructs. For the physical scientist himself, the problem may appear to be a pseudoproblem; in their research the nuclear physicist and the astronomer bypass the issue and are content with hypotheses which they regard as implements merely. Their truth value does not concern them. But for the philosopher, as for the man of common sense, it is impossible to refrain from asking the eternal questions of the human intellect: "What?" and "Why?" The alternative to satisfying the epistemological problem is intellectual despair.

For an introduction to the study of the philosophy of knowing, the present editors have adoped the anthology method in the belief that it is by far the best. Especially is this true in a science like epistemology, where the "rules of the game" themselves are not agreed upon. A formal presentation of the subject would inevitably be slanted toward the author's own philosophy of knowledge. An historical survey would lack the immediacy of the sources themselves. The present method lends itself to what we regard as the ideal situation: the original texts, the teacher, and the students—with a minimum of interference from too-zealous editors or biassed authors.

If the anthology principle be granted, there still remains the matter of selection. Here, the editors can only point to the table of contents and ask the reader to judge for himself. But the editors would like to call attention to the fact that there is little abridgement of the items in this work. Several of the pieces, such as the essays by Professor Parker and that by Professor Simon, were written especially for this anthology. Professor Gilson's essay on realism has here been given its first English translation. The other selections are either entire articles appearing in journals or else they form integral units in the books in which they appear. The editors thus feel that they have avoided the pitfall of the "snippet" type of anthology.

The order of parts in this book is of necessity loose rather than tight; the volume is designed to cover the major aspects of epistemology. The introductory chapter surveys in depth the birth and scope of philosophic inquiry and summarizes in breadth the problem of knowledge; it introduces notions which the later parts amplify and particularize. Part II, it will be seen, treats sense knowledge and Part III intellectual knowledge. This order is based upon the recognition of the two basic types of human knowledge. Part IV deals with the human judgment, its types and properties. It is the view of the editors that the matter dealt with in Part III and IV constitutes the very heart of epistemic study. Part V contains a grouping of statements of some basic epistemological positions. It affords a conclusion in the sense that it brings together some of the broader problems which grow out of the basis upon which one's thinking rests.

The bibliographical items have a two-fold purpose: some constitute provocative commentaries upon the material of the texts; others are intended to be guides to lead the student through problems posed by the texts.

The editors here wish to express their sense of indebtedness to Henry B. Cushing and John M. Green of Villanova University. Beyond their competence in the special field of their research and teaching, they have evidenced a grasp of both the data and the significance of other areas of knowledge and of the interrelationships of disciplines of thought. Their suggestions, cooperation, and friendship have helped greatly in making this volume possible.

The editors are deeply indebted to all the contributors of original essays. Grateful acknowledgment is due the authors who have kindly granted permission for the reprinting of their material in this book; the editors of *The Journal of Philosophy, Mind, International Journal of American Linguistics, The Thomist, Philosophy of Science, Philosophy and Phenomenological Research,* and *The Philosophical Review;* and the Pontifical Institute of Mediaeval Studies, Yale University Press, Librairie Pierre Téqui, George Braziller, Inc., The Newman Press, Pantheon Books, Inc., George Allen & Unwin Ltd., and Marquette University Press. The source of each reading selection is stated in the editorial presentations which constitute an extension of these acknowledgments.

For specific criticisms, suggestions, and advice, the editors are indebted to Professors Elizabeth Flower, University of Pennsylvania; Y. R. Simon, University of Chicago; L.-M. Régis, O.P., Université de Montréal; Robert Lechner, C.P.P.S., Saint Joseph's College, Indiana; D. Gallagher, Villanova University; and E. C. Garvey, C.S.B., Assumption University of Windsor. The editors bear responsibility for whatever shortcomings the book may have.

R. H.
J. P. M.

Lac Chat
27 August, 1959

CONTENTS

xiii *Contents*

Part I : THE PHILOSOPHY
OF KNOWLEDGE

F. M. Cleve : SOURCES AND MOTIVES OF PHILOSOPHY

Dʀ. *Felix M. Cleve, Professor of Metaphysics and Ancient Greek Philosophy at The New School for Social Research in New York City, in this essay both probes to the historical and psychological roots of philosophic speculation and delineates the major problematics of such speculation. In this and the succeeding essays, the role of philosophy and the specific divisions of criteriology are established—as an introduction to the particularized studies of epistemic problems. This essay is taken from Dr. Cleve's forthcoming work:* THE GIANTS OF PRE-SOPHISTIC GREEK PHILOSOPHY.

• Philosophy was not always philosophy. The word repeatedly changed its meaning.

"Philosopher," "philosophical man," is an expression to be found for the first time in Heraclitus (floruit ca. 504–501 B.C.). One of his aphorisms runs:

> Philosophical men, namely, shall have knowledge of a great many things.

Strangely enough coinciding with modern usage, "philosopher" means here a man searching for ultimate truth.

Apart from this solitary instance, however, "philosophy" was originally equivalent to, and interchangeably used for, "science," "research," "intelligence," "education," "intellectual culture," "mathematics," "geometry," "art of a sensible conduct in life," and "wisdom."

According to Herodotus' narrative (I, 30), King Croesus says to his guest, Solon: "I have heard about your having traveled in many lands philosophizing for the sake of knowledge." Here, by "philosophizing" is obviously meant: "out of ethnographic, geographic, sociological interest." —Or take that famous oration in Thucydides (2, 40) where Pericles declares about himself and the people of Athens: "We love luxury without wastefulness and we philosophize without effeminacy." Also here, "to philosophize" does not mean philosophize. Pericles merely wants to say: We are striving for intellectual culture, we are refined people, but without getting effeminated by that.—In Plato's dialogue *Theaetetus,* there is a passage (143 D) about "geometry or some other philosophy." The word is here synonymous with theory in general, geometry being the "philosophy" of space.

From the broad range of meaning a small part was separated as "first philosophy" by Aristotle. This "first philosophy," or introductory science, was supposed to be "the science of the philosopher" proper (cf. *Metaphys.,* III, 3. 1005a21). In contrast to the various special sciences, the "so-called particular sciences" (cf. *Metaphys.,* III, 1. 1003a22), this introductory science is to deal with "being as such " (*ibid.*), while the subject-matter of zoology, e.g., would be dog-being, horse-being, lion-being, etc.

This division is an historical fact. Whether it makes sense, and whether "being as such," the Aristotelian subject-matter of the philosopher proper, means anything at all, these are questions to be answered in due time.

Later on, when philosophy had become denominational, with Jewish or Christian or Moslem orientations, the term assumed the sense of "worldly science" (*Weltweisheit*) as contrasted to theology. It came to designate such theoretical knowledge and such practical wisdom as could be obtained through the *lumen naturale,* the "natural light of reason" alone, as distinguished from cognitions of the supranatural and from those rules of life which were possible through Revelation only. Thus any knowledge belonged to *Weltweisheit,* and also philosophy insofar as it did not appeal to Revelation.

Actual modern usage distinguishes *theoretical philosophy* from *practical philosophy.*[1]

The two fields have very little in common. Theoretical philosophy consists, on the whole, of constructions, conclusions, conceptions, hypotheses, theories. It is a mental beholding and building, the making of a world picture. The philosophy of practice, also called ethics or philosophy of morals, wants to teach how to conduct a sensible life. No doubt, to construct hypotheses is one thing and to live reasonably another. The one is an art of living, the other, speculation. And there are those who even maintain that the better artist of life is he who speculates as little as possible. But at any rate, of practical philosophy one speaks only where there is involved some formation of a way of life, some estimation and evaluation, some regulation of the conduct in life by approval and disapproval.

In other words, theoretical philosophy aims at the formation of a world picture that we behold, practical philosophy, at the formation of a life that we live. It may be wise, therefore, not to labor to bring the theoretical and the practical fields under one notion and not to claim for the word "philosophy" the same meaning in each of the two terms.

Theoretic philosophy has got a supplement: epistemology, or the theory of cognition.

In former times, philosophy was considered a cognition beyond experience. Naturally, some day one could not help asking whether such "philosophical" cognition—cognition beyond experience, that is—was possible at all. This question was indeed the impulse to the origin of epistemology.

And so, from a certain period on, philosophy has had epistemology as a companion, while in the naive stage philosophers take it unquestioningly for granted that they "cognize."

Therefore, epistemology is not itself a philosophical activity. It is rather an inquiry into, and a criticism of, the feasibility of such philosophical activity, a criticism, however, that presupposes a claim of that activity to be cognition.

Several disciplines have separated from philosophy.

Psychology, e.g., has become a descriptive science. It describes the facts of consciousness, such as facts of sensation, facts of inner perception, facts

[1] Both expressions are rather awkward. Properly speaking, there is no such thing as "practical philosophy." What is meant is "philosophy of practice": practice is made a topic of philosophizing. And "theoretical philosophy" would mean "theoretical theory." Yet, the terms are traditional.

of dreaming, etc. These facts are of all realities the most real ones anyway (if such a superlative were permitted) and cannot be doubted by any "theory of cognition."

Yet, psychology contains also an hypothetical admixture. Other people's consciousness and one's own so-called "unconscious"—whatever this term may in fact mean—cannot be reached as such by introspection. And so, the psychology of the "I" being an exact science, the psychologies of the "Thou" and the "It" are already philosophy, strictly speaking.

Logic, too, has become independent. The historical fact that persons occupying themselves with logic were usually the same as those interested in philosophy would seem almost a mere accident. They could have been mathematicians as well, and even he who cultivates any science whatsoever is implicitly also a logician.

But it could be that there is a reason why things have come to be as they actually are. In this field, there have been and still are many such problems as can be clarified and solved only when approached from the side of psychology, and particularly psychology of language. Until not so long ago, however, psychology was one of the basic disciplines of philosophy.

Logic, at any rate, is a prerequisite to every science, and it is much too narrow to call it, as has been usual, philosophical propaedeutics, or introduction to philosophy. It is the "propaedeutics" to any science.

The so-called philosophy of art is another field that has got on its own. Today, if to be taken seriously, it is no longer a normative aesthetics, a "prescribing science of the judgments of taste." It has changed partly into history of the arts, partly into physiology and psychology of artistic production and artistic enjoyment. An aesthetics proper, in the old-fashioned manner, seems to have been losing ground.

Theoretic philosophy, then—to return to what here will be the main topic—is meant as the making of a world picture that would have to reach beyond the frontiers of experience in some way or other: by way of certain cognitions, in the opinion of many; or, according to others, through some sort of revelation; or, as still others believe, by means of artistic imagination.

In the course of the history of philosophy, quite a number of such world pictures have been made. To study them with regard to their contents is, of course, indispensable. But it need not be the only thing to do. In addition, those pictures could also be scrutinized with a view to the motives. One could try to find out, not merely what this or that philosopher says, but also why and also out of which psychological motive and source.

Such quest may not seem to be new. Common opinion has it that at least one of the psychological roots was unearthed by Plato and Aristotle who are said to have stated that the root of philosophy was amazement.

It will be worthwhile looking into this matter more closely. Painful experiences give warning not to place implicit confidence in philosophical quotations. Inexactness is epidemic in this field.

The Plato passage about amazement allegedly being the source of "philosophy" is in his dialogue *Theaetetus;* the Aristotle passage, in the *Metaphysics.*

Says Plato:

This feeling of amazement, namely, is very much peculiar of a philosopher: for there is no source of philosophy other than this.

This is in *Theaetetus* 155D. But in a very near neighborhood, 143D, Plato speaks of *geometry or some other philosophy.* Should it not seem obvious that as in 143D so also in 155D "philosophy" is not what we mean by this term, but is used in that broader sense of "science" and "scientific investigation"? [2]

And now the passage in Aristotle (*Met.* I, 2. 982b12):

For by way of amazement people began to philosophize nowadays as well as in olden times,

But this is not yet the end of the sentence, and the very continuation after the comma clearly shows that here, too, "philosophize" does not mean philosophize:

first, by getting amazed about the nearest of the startling things; later, by thus making progress little by little and getting puzzled about those bigger things, such as *the phases of the moon and the (various problems) concerning the sun and about the stars and the origin of the universe.*

That is to say, it is astronomical, physical, cosmological problems that Aristotle has in mind. Here by "philosophy" he obviously means natural science, hypotheses about nature, at any rate, special sciences.

Thus it seems to have been overlooked that in both passages not philosophy is meant but various special sciences, in Plato such as are in the neighborhood of geometry, and in Aristotle astronomy and the like. Both apparently considered amazement the root of the "sciences in particular," a finding that can readily be adopted as correct.

But even if reference to those passages were justified, one still would have to remember: *amicus Plato, amicus Aristoteles, magis amica veritas.* For, in fact, never was amazement the root of philosophy.

[2] See also v. Wilamowitz, *Platon,* I, 2nd ed. (1920) p. 108: *"Diese Philosophie macht dann Platon zu dem, was wir Wissenschaft nennen."*

7   *F. M. Cleve*

There are other and entirely different roots of theoretical philosophizing.

An artistic bent for building and moulding is one of the roots.

As long as man is not stunted (by too much one-sided scientific activity, e.g.), as long as he is a *whole* human being and not yet senile and decrepit, there is in him an artistic bent for building. This he gratifies in various ways and also by complementing the given piece of reality to a whole.

The real as given us is indeed a fragment; it is finite in space, finite in time. We do not know what was before us, we have not seen it. We do not see what will be later, after us. Nor do we see things far away in space, any more than we can see the finest textures. The real as offered us gives an impression of being a fragment of something, and that is a stimulation, a challenge for our building-drive. It provokes it to completing, to building up something whole, in the style of that fragment.

Such completion of the world fragment is performed without any desire for redemption or solace or hope. It is neither in favor of religion nor against it. It is a purely theoretical philosophy, stemming from a purely artistic attitude. If Thales teaches all things consist of water, the consequence is neither hope nor solace. Here, only one thing matters: that it be the simplest possible.

But why on earth should it matter whether one assumes one primordial stuff or a hundred? From the practical point of view it does not matter at all. Yet, it certainly is artistic to develop something very complex from something very simple.

Or take those endeavors to arrive at the utmost simplicity of the laws of motion or even, if any possible, one sole such primordial law. This, too, is an artistic ideal, properly. In both instances there is a correspondence with the building style of nature as we see it, and an artistic urge it is to complete a fragment in true style.

Now, what is meant by "building style of nature"?

There is, e.g., a great number of species of animals and plants, and a small number of elements of which they consist. That means: a few elements and a great many combinations. This clearly is a building style. And it is then gratification of an artistic urge to build even all things out of one element, for instance one primordial matter. (Which is possible in imagination only, of course.)

That the number of properties diminishes ever more, the more one goes down the levels of organization, is another example of building style in nature. Birds fly, fish swim—with their whole organisms. That is the topmost level of organization. But a single bone, a single muscle cannot run or spring or swim or fly any more. On the way from tissue to cell the loss continues, and when coming to the molecule there has been still more loss. A single gas molecule, e.g., cannot fall down, but when within an aggregate it can. And the really ultimate particles of material things, finally, have even neither plasticity nor elasticity nor hardness nor heat any more. Such an ultimate particle cannot transform "internal movement of its particles" into heat—just because it is only one, single particle. Neither is it plastic nor elastic nor hard, since here there are no particles (in the plural) to shift their positions toward each other. All this gets lost for an ultimate particle. The more one steps down, the smaller becomes the number of properties.

This, too, is a building style of nature that stimulates imagination into assuming for the ultimate particle only one property and into having all the rest originate from the very aggregation as such. So that even gravitation would not be taken for a primary property, but would have to be constructed as resulting from gravity-less, though moving, particles by way of having them push each other in such a manner as to produce the outward appearance of attraction.

An artistic drive, then, is being gratified by dint of imagination.

Yet, here imagination is not free. It is bound to the building style of nature. Or else no artistic effect will be accomplished. The flashes must come the same way they come to the artist. But then anything that would not conform must be eliminated.

This type of theoretical philosophy, therefore, holds an intermediate position between art and science. Science must not contradict the facts directly. Philosophy must not contradict the facts indirectly, in its consequences.

Accordingly, here inductive inference is not a serviceable method. Here one has to guess. When, e.g., constructing the finest textures, one must not merely reduce in size; one also has to simplify. After the discovery by Anthony van Leeuwenhoek (1632–1723) of the spermatozoa, Hartsoeker and Swammerdam believed themselves to see in protoplasm a tiny human being, an *homunculus*. That was induction. And it was wrong, of course.

Likewise, if we are forced—as in fact we are—to assume a plurality of consciousness-units, this too is no induction. From induction the result would always be restricted to one's own world, one's own consciousness-unit. Imagination it is and a gift for construction, bridled by the facts.

Hence, the outcome is no system of cognitions, but a piece of art.

If one thinks it is cognition, the end is disappointment. If, however, theoretic philosophy is gratification of an artistic bent for building, then a demonstration to the effect that it offers no cognitions cannot inflict any harm to it. For only under the presupposition that it be a system of cognitions has metaphysics been crashed by Kant.

Yet, there is one basic difference between a work of philosophical artistry and any other work of art: We do not believe in a work of art, while philosophical constructions are expected to make us believe in them.

This concomitant belief is indeed indispensable. It arises by way of a psychological and physiological compulsion if a philosophical construction punctiliously follows the style of sense-given reality.

If a philosopher is an artist in spite of himself, he will attach all value to that belief and do all he can to force it by logical operations. In this way, the theoretical philosopher becomes the criticized object of the epistemologist. If, however, the philosopher is aware that he is building in the manner of an artist, then he will calm down in the gratification of his bent and accept that concomitant belief as a welcome additional boon, without laboring to force it by means of logical operations and without talking too much about it. Such belief cannot be forced by any logical operations. But neither can logical operations suppress it.

There are, then, purely theoretic philosophies. For this type of philosophy that, without ulterior motives, merely wants to behold and then, in the style of what had been beheld, build up a whole world picture, there is no current name as yet. The Greek word for "spectator" is *theoros*. Hence, a philosophy arising from the frame of mind of such a spectator may fittingly be called a *theorogon* philosophy.[3]

The foremost organ to furnish building material for this type is the eye, the "great sense," as it was called by Anaxagoras, the "king of the senses," according to Leonardo da Vinci.

Many such world pictures have been made, and very different ones. But since they are works of art, and not cognitions, this is not harmful.

The number of those many systems has been diminishing. They have been converging in the long run. In the beginning, there was less science, less factual knowledge, hence less possibility of checking with the facts, and so there was more room for fancy. The greater the number of established facts, the more easily can flashes be checked. As a consequence, from each system something is taken away, and so they come closer and closer to each other. Today they are still widely apart, but obviously much less than, e.g., in 500 B.C.

Thus it could come to pass at some future time that only one such work of philosophical artistry may be feasible and survive. Which then could look like cognition and give the wrong impression as if only one such world picture had been admissible. And yet, it would still not be cognition.

Theorogon philosophy is one type. Its root is definitely not amazement. Here amazement must have already been overcome. Otherwise one would not even have the courage to build and mould.

There is another type. Its source is confusion.

[3] Cf. A. Stöhr, *Psychologie*, 2nd ed. (Vienna, 1922), p. 535.

According to the German philosopher, Johann Friedrich Herbart (1776–1841), all philosophy arises from the confusion of notions and consists in their clarification. This is certainly not true. But it does apply to a very large group.

Speech is earlier than thought. Only when a person forms a word by himself is talking subsequent to thinking. But whenever a word is accepted ready-made, by a child, e.g., or a pupil, talking precedes thinking. That is why human thinking is to such an extent intermingled with thoughtless talking. A great many people are indeed but pure talking automatons with a minimum of concomitant thought. Thinking can even be downright overpowered by speech.[4] Then thinking stops completely and talking continues by dint of the brain's being still innervated in a motory way. And for quite a while what has the outward appearance of thinking is mere talking and not thinking at all. On the other hand, when man has to think intensively he stops talking.

Substitution of speech for thought can be, and in fact mostly is, an advantage even, a beneficial arrangement of nature. For if, whenever people are talking, everything had to be clearly and plastically imagined all the time, man would wear himself out prematurely and, besides, what otherwise takes a quarter of an hour would require a whole day. But what usually is an advantage turns into a disadvantage when the mill is running empty.

And so language can become a source of trouble. Messed-up grammar, misused metaphors, mistaking metaphors for adequate expressions, taking purely linguistical forms for forms of thought, and the like—all such things make for confusion.

When a man has become confused in this way, he will do all he can to get rid of his confusion—only to get still more confused. Then he will also make other people confused, in order to have somebody to converse with. And as soon as a sufficient number of equally disturbed, "congenial" persons have gathered around such a man, they form a new philosophical school.

It will be a mere word philosophy. By thinking one cannot get into confusion. Nonsense comes into the world by way of speech. A circular quadrangle can only be talked.

A word philosopher can, of course, not by any means be made to realize that he is a talking machine. One just has to leave him alone. But it is easy to learn his language. All one has to do is listen attentively and find out those words, those "technical terms," at which he obviously does no longer think at all, and then use those terms in the same associations and concatenations as he does. . . .

[4] Cf. Ossip Lourié, *Le Langage et la verbomanie,* Paris, 1912, and *Le Langage et la graphomanie,* Paris, 1922.

F. M. Cleve

To this type, the *glossogon*[5] type, belongs an enormous part of Western philosophy. (Indian philosophy seems to suffer from the same disease to a considerably lesser extent.) The history of theoretic philosophy in Western civilization, as far as not the theorogon type is concerned, is in the main the history of a battle being fought between talking and thinking.

The domain of glossogon philosophy is gigantic; its menace to culture, horrifying. Cultural progress would require a steady diminishing of this type of philosophy until, due to man's increased capacity for thinking, it might by self-dissolution eventually disappear.

Of theorogon philosophy the opposite holds true. Here to stop philosophizing would mean to stop being an artist and to become but a shriveled scholar.

In the course of history, there was first an increase of the glossogon type. Today its culmination may have already been passed, but there is still present a vast lot of it. Whether its complete elimination will ever come true is quite a question. At any rate, it may take some thousands of years until then.

Glossogon philosophy is not aware of its origin. If it were, it would not exist.

It produces a self-delusion of some resemblance to mathematics and geometry. Just as these need neither experiments nor ordinary accidental experience for arriving at their cognitions, so philosophy too, it is contended, requires no empirical contents as a material to be complemented by construction, but allegedly can deduce cognitions from mere notions.

Yet, in mathematics and geometry there is an equivalent for the passively received observation or actively arranged experiment of the natural scientist: intuition that can be constructed anew any time. And besides, there are in mathematics and geometry all kinds of substitutions and other invented operations. The mathematician does not say, as does the mathematizing philosopher: 4 is 4, or 4 is not not — 4. The mathematician says, 2 times 2 is 4, after having invented the operation of multiplying, or the arrangement 1, 2, 1, 2. The mathematizing philosopher has no invented operations for his deductions to refer to. The equations, "A = A" and "A = not not — A," merely formulate the rejection of nonsense, but nothing new is obtained in this way.

Glossogon philosophy does not consider itself sterile and barren. . . .

There is still a third root of philosophy: the fact of suffering.

Every human being suffers from life more or less. This is the most characteristic feature, if not the essence, of human existence. These sufferings are of a vastly variegated nature and spring from different fountains.

[5] "Glossogon" means "arisen from language" (cf. Stöhr, l.c.).

Subhuman nature is one of the sources. The animal world, the vegetable world, and lifeless matter are not only causes of joy. They also are, and even more than today were in earlier periods of mankind, a source of fright and misery, danger and trouble.

Man suffers also from his own nature. His heart is full of enemies playing him nasty tricks, enemies such as foolishness, laziness, ignorance, intemperance, passionateness, and what other names they may have.

An overflowing well of suffering, furthermore, is the fellow-man who so often is the anti-man, the foe in the battle of life. And who can deny that that sentence in Plautus, *homo homini lupus,* is wrong only in so far as a wolf can never be so cruel, so bestial, or rather so human, so humanly vicious and mean, as human beings can be to each other?

Man defends himself against all these sorts of suffering by deeds and omissions. And the so-called progress of mankind is greatly an increasing development of devices for choking those fountain-heads of suffering. Worship of ghosts is the method by which primitive man is seeking protection from the terror of nature. The next step is sorcery: humble and stooped originally, man now stretches his hand out for a share in the power of the ghosts over the powers of nature. And at the end of that same road, there is the modern art of control over nature by means of mathematics, science, and technology. The enemies in man's own heart are being weakened by ever more improved methods of education, by training in the art of self-control and by finding, and keeping to, the middle of the road between the extremes, equally dangerous, of ascetic resignation and excessive indulgence. And also the evils stemming from men's living together are being fought against with all kinds of endeavor for an ever more increasing betterment of human society.

Yet, that list of the sources of suffering is not complete. Supposing man had already won unlimited control over nature—subhuman nature, that is —and it were perfectly pliable to all his wishes and needs; also the inner foe were conquered, and every man's breast were filled with harmony and peace; and relations between men were resembling those ideal conditions of the Golden Age that, according to the poet, *vindice nullo sponte sua sine lege fidem rectumque colebat*—even then there would still remain quite enough of suffering that could not be removed or even only mitigated by any deeds or omissions. There is no invention to eliminate the fact of death, not to mention so many other instances. Already Old Homer distinguishes between suffering beyond fate, *hyper moron algos,* that suffering which can be avoided, and *morsimon algos,* inescapable suffering, unavoidably connected with human nature, imposed by some superhuman might, by an *inevitabile fatum,* no matter whether that *fatum* be thought of as blind or otherwise.

Man defends himself against this *morsimon algos,* too, but not by deeds or omissions, these being of no avail against fate. However, although he cannot diminish that kind of suffering, he wants at least to learn how to bear it better. And that is where philosophy comes in.

At first sight, such suffering appears to be altogether senseless, useless, a matter of sheer accident. Nothing, however, is so torturing and embittering as that. And it is an incontestable fact that no sooner does man believe that he has found out some meaning and aim of his suffering than he feels it less grievous and easier to endure. Hence, unawares procreated by the will to suffer less, there grows in him a desire to guess a meaning behind his suffering, and the result is a philosophy with a sense-giving faith, a world interpretation, by which the fact of suffering, though unchanged in itself, is shifted into a different light, appears meaningful and, just by that, does no longer hurt so much.

Here belong all those systems of philosophy which stem neither from an artistic delight in beholding and building nor from confusion by linguistical troubles not recognized as such. But likewise all religions come under this notion of a system of faith to mitigate suffering from destiny by giving it some meaning. Psychologically, there is no difference. The root as well as the end is the same.

It is the will to suffer less, the will to survive, that here, unconsciously, is forming certain imaginations and symbols beyond experience and also the concomitant faith in those imaginations and symbols.

The Greek word for "suffering" is *pathos;* the word for "will," *boulé.* This third type of philosophy, therefore, could be called *pathogon* or, which amounts to the same, *boulogon* (cf. Stöhr, l.c.).

With the pathogon type, the contents of faith are pronounced without proofs. Arguments are neither offered nor asked for nor missed—originally. Only afterwards grows a wish for argumentation which is usually a sign indicating that that will has been losing strength, and that the boulogon philosophy is going to be shifted upon a new fundament and given the outward appearance of a theorogon or a glossogon philosophy, as the case may be, in the hope thus to prevent the boulogon edifice from crumbling: faith labors to become cognition.

Yet, pathogon philosophy never seeks cognition for the sake of cognition, but for the sake of solace and hope or, at least, tranquillity of mind. Accordingly, any pathogon philosophy develops from the very outset so as to yield somehow such emotional fruit.

These, then, are the three types of theoretic philosophy, with regard to the psychological root.

Theorogon as well as glossogon and pathogon wefts are in the texture of virtually every philosophical system. Yet, almost in any system one of the three wefts is conspicuously predominant, in accordance with the root predominant in any given case, be it the phantasy of the artist, the sentiment of the sufferer, or the tongue of the confused. On the prevalent root depends the over-all character and emotional hue of a philosophy.

But the builder of a decidedly theorogon system may nevertheless become a word philosopher once in a while, whereas another man's philosophy is glossogon throughout, a few plastic images here and there notwithstanding, mostly borrowed from somewhere else.

Of pathogon philosophers, however, there are two sorts. The one operates with visual and plastic constructions as in a theorogon system. Yet, all is in the service of the pathogon goal and appealing to emotion. The other operates with mere words, though, like the spinner of a glossogon yarn. But the difference is unmistakable all the same. It is always easily felt whether a man is a pure word philosopher or whether his dry, "discoursive" verbiage is fraught with sentiment and feeling and, in fact, is merely the garment of a pathogon philosophy.

In the beginning of these introductory remarks, it has been said that theoretical philosophy and practical philosophy, or ethics, are two completely different fields. This statement has now to be somewhat qualified. For in a certain area the two are overlapping.

Practical philosophy and the theorogon sort of theoretical philosophy are indeed two separate things. Whether, e.g., an hypothesis assumes that atoms have the shape of a ball or of a cube, that they are impenetrable or penetrable, or even that atoms do not exist at all, but instead perhaps a continuous filling of space, this has no impact on the conduct of our lives.

Neither has glossogon philosophy. This species of babbling in a sophisticated manner is disastrous for culture, it is true. But it is a private matter, after all, for a person to take pleasure in such verbiage. And if a grown-up man is spending his life on such-like things, he is probably good for nothing better anyway.

At any rate, correct judgment of theorogon as well as glossogon philosophies will be the more facilitated, the more they are separated from ethical problems.

The gist and goal of pathogon philosophy, however, solace and hope, easier endurance of one's fate—these are things that do belong to our behavior in life. For, above all and in the first place, the art of living is the art of keeping us alive.

Every human being suffers from life more or less. But in the course of time, man accumulates experiences about how to diminish those sufferings: the bare fact of living is elevated to an art of living. Not that the art of living would entirely consist of ways and means to diminish suffering. There is also the sum total of endeavors and practices to increase enjoyment. But here we are concerned with that other part only, the negative aim of which is prevention and alleviation of suffering.

Such art of living, or biotics, practiced first instinctively and changing later into conscious maxims, is not yet ethics (just as that other part of biotics, with the positive aim of enjoyment, is not yet culture). It is merely just an art of living that the individual uses for himself, without giving away, let alone recommending, his secret wisdom to another person, except perhaps a beloved son or so. It is not yet ethics, nor does it always have an ethical contents, even, but everybody just strives, in the first place, for such an art of living as is adequate to his individual constitution and his sphere of power. Only if and when such art of living is made the norm and standard for the whole community, biotics changes into ethics.

That part of biotics which is a defense against suffering, and accordingly also ethics later on, has four divisions, in correspondence with those four sources of suffering: subhuman nature, man's own nature, his living together with fellow-men, and superhuman powers.

It is in the fight against suffering from superhuman powers that theoretical philosophy and practical philosophy are overlapping.

From the desire to bear an inevitable fate in the best and worthiest manner, from the desire for solace and hope, unawares arises either a religion or a pathogon, boulogon philosophy, the one being a mass phenomenon around the strong personality of the founder,[6] the other taking form independently in the individual philosopher.

Not deeds and omissions, but that unwittingly grown faith is here the weapon. The fate of the individual is not changed as such. Yet, it appears in a different light and, just by that, is more easily endured.

Pathogon, boulogon faith is sometimes concerned with another world "beyond": the external world, the metaphysical, that can give this world, the phenomenal, another meaning or even some meaning at all. And sometimes such faith, without metaphysics in the narrower sense, refers to a far distant future in this world, to future conditions of this phenomenal reality. In the latter case, the boulogon trait consists in giving the pictures of the future the nicest possible qualities. What is lacking in exact proof is supplemented by the will.

These two sorts of pathogon faith are frequently in a relationship of mutual competition.

Insofar as such a faith—as basis of an art of suffering in dignity and beauty under an inevitable fate—refers to a so-called metaphysical contents, this part of practical philosophy virtually coincides with the pathogon sort of theoretical philosophy.

That is also why, when treating history of philosophy, one cannot separate the two fields completely. For otherwise one would either have to eliminate from theoretical philosophy all the pathogon components and,

---

[6] Religion belongs to both ethics and culture. As a faith yielding hope and solace, it is a pathogon alleviation of suffering and, therefore, ethics. Since it is connected also with positive constructions, it is culture.

by that, deprive it of one of its most interesting parts, or one would have to restrict practical philosophy to nature control, self-control, and social problems.

Such restriction of ethics is possible, though. There are indeed certain modern schools of thought that on principle would reject any ethics of faith, as if ethics were without remainder resolvable into those three parts or even into social ethics alone.

But such elimination would at the same time also block the road to any deeper understanding of the facts involved.

Suffering from fate is a fact, and man's shifting of such suffering into a meaningful light is a fact. That such shifting is done in more than one way, and that each of these ways means an alleviation, is another fact as well as that each of them has the tendency of becoming normative. As a consequence, there then arise conflicts of *Weltanschauung,* clashes of the faiths, and religious wars. These conflicts, these clashes, these wars, however, are the most embittered and hottest of all. For what is involved here, affects man most intimately. All these are indubitable facts.

To ignore these facts, by eliminating faith from the field of ethics, would mean to be blind to human passions, to be of a dull, insensible nature oneself, and to presuppose that in this respect all men are equally insensible and dull.

F. H. Parker : A REALISTIC APPRAISAL OF KNOWLEDGE

Dr. *Francis H. Parker, Professor of Philosophy at Haverford College, in a basic essay prepared specifically for this volume, supplements the preceding theme by indicating the phases and aspects of the specific philosophic inquiry of epistemology, the investigation of the act of knowing, its possibility, its terms, its causes and its dimensions. Herein are sketched fundamental areas of chief concern in that most insistent philosophic problem of recent centuries and of today: the subsuming question of if, how, and what man knows, and its corollary question, what is the relation of knower and known.*

• Before trying to look at the nature of knowledge, a prior question may arise: *Is* there any such thing as knowledge? There is little point in attempting to study something which is illusory or non-existent. Buildings really exist, so it is sensible and practicable for men to learn about them. But is there any point in men studying knowledge? Is there really such a thing as knowledge, or is it an illusion?

A. True Knowledge Exists

In the history of men and ideas we have seen the collapse of so many pieces of "real, certain, true knowledge" that we are today, understandably, more than a little skeptical. In the ancient world it was "truly known" that the earth was flat, and that it was in the center of the universe. And not very many years ago most people were convinced that it was impossible to transmit voices, let alone pictures, over long distances. Indeed, so often have we discovered the falsity of widely held ideas that we perhaps tend to think that man progresses rather by the rejection of "truths" than by their discovery. And to increase this skepticism we find even our most deep-seated convictions—such as the belief in an external physical world—being questioned by many of our modern philosophers. So it's little wonder that we're inclined to be skeptical of the existence of true knowledge.

Now there is no denying, of course, that knowledge is a fragile thing, hard won and easily lost, and that we have perhaps less of it than we might like to think. But our present question is: Is there *any* knowledge? Is there *any* truth? If so, can knowledge or truth be attained? And when the question is put in this more radical way, it is not hard to see that the answer must be: "Yes, there is at least some knowledge, some truth." For to deny it—to say: "There is no knowledge; there is no truth"—is to contradict oneself.

If the statement, "There is no knowledge," is *true,* then it is *false,* for the statement itself claims to be a piece of knowledge. That is, the speaker knows that there is *no* knowledge. And if this should cause the speaker to become more wary and to say only, "I don't know whether or not there is any knowledge, any truth," he again claims knowledge of *that*—of the fact that "I don't know. . . ."

The only way, therefore, to maintain such a radical skepticism is by not speaking at all—and indeed, by not even thinking, for thinking is a kind of speaking to oneself; and such a maintenance of skepticism could not of course be a defence of it. Such a skeptic would not be a human being, but rather a vegetable, as Aristotle pointed out (in a slightly different context) more than two thousand years ago. "We can demonstrate negatively that such a view is impossible," he said, "if only our opponent will say something. For in saying something he necessarily pretends to know something. On the other hand, if he will not say anything, there is no use arguing with him. For a man who will say nothing is, as such, no better than a vegetable; and one cannot argue with a vegetable".[1]

There is, then, such a thing as true knowledge. And this statement is necessary, or to contradict it is to contradict oneself. There is at least some true knowledge.

B. Intentionality and Its Bi-polarity

Having now reassured ourselves of the reality of true knowledge, we must return to the topic of the *nature* of that knowledge. What is knowledge? And first of all, what is the broadest and deepest trait of knowledge as it presents itself for our inspection?

Knowledge is most basically characterized by its "intentionality."[2] The most fundamental feature of knowledge—and indeed of all awareness—is that it is always *of* or *about* something other than itself. We have an experience *of* war, a feeling *of* pain, a concept *of* a triangle. We make propositions *about* bodies gravitating, and arguments *about* the interior angles of a triangle equaling two right angles. All awareness, all consciousness, all knowledge is *about* something other than itself. It tends into, or intends, something other than itself. For this reason this most fundamental trait of knowledge is called its "intentionality." All knowledge is "intentional"; every piece of knowledge is an "intention."

It is obvious at once that the word "intention" has here a somewhat different meaning than usual, for we ordinarily use the word to pertain to acts of *will* or *purpose*. Indeed, intentions are the things which, when they are good, pave the road to hell, as Dr. Johnson remarked, and, when they are dishonorable, are what we must warn our daughters against. Yet this does not mean that the word is here being given a meaning which is absolutely different from its usual meaning. Indeed, the moment we stop to think about it, we can see present in acts of will the very same *of-* or *about-* structure which we have noted in instances of knowledge. You have the intention *of* studying, or the purpose *of* making friends, for example. Furthermore, it is not difficult to see that willing and purposing are "intentional" precisely because they contain a cognitively "intentional" element. You can have the purpose of being courteous, for example, only when you have the knowledge of what courtesy is.

Thus the most basic trait of knowledge is its intentionality—the fact that it is always *of* or *about* something other than itself. And this trait sharply distinguishes instances of knowledge from other things. Your concept of a

---

[1] *Metaphysics*, 1006a, 12–15. This is a paraphrase rather than a literal translation.

[2] The next three paragraphs are taken almost verbatim from Francis H. Parker and Henry B. Veatch, *Logic As a Human Instrument*, Harper, 1959, p. 13.

triangle, or your proposition about its interior angles, for example, is *of* or *about* the triangle; but the triangle isn't of or about anything—it is just itself. Thus intentionality is the distinguishing feature of all items of consciousness and the most basic general characteristic of knowledge.

Knowledge contains two poles: the knowledge and the object. Now as soon as we recognize this intentionality of knowledge, we see that it contains two distinct elements or "poles"; the *knowledge-pole* and the *object-pole*. In your knowledge of the world, there is the knowledge and there is the world. In your concept of a triangle, there is the concept and there is the triangle. In short, intentionality (and therefore knowledge) is bi-polar; it is characterized by its bi-polarity. There is what is intended, and there is the intention of it. The former is the object of knowledge—the object-pole, the objective-pole; and the latter is the knowledge of it—the knowledge-pole, the subjective-pole.

In order now to gain some insight into the nature of knowledge, we must turn to a separate consideration of these two poles. The fact that knowledge is bi-polar means, of course, that we cannot consider either of these poles without some reference to the other, that a consideration of the object of knowledge requires some reference to the knowledge of it, and vice versa. But nevertheless let us first consider primarily the object, and then primarily the knowledge of it. What, then, is it that we know when we know? And what is involved in our knowing of it?

II. THAT WHICH WE KNOW: THE OBJECT OF KNOWLEDGE

The object of knowledge is being. What is it, then, that we know when we know? The simplest and most basic answer to this question is that at least it is *something,* of *some* sort. Even if we know nothing else about the object of knowledge we at any rate know that is *something.* Moreover, we know that it *is* something, that it is in some sense something existent. What kind of existence the object has is a more specific question, and the answer differs from case to case. When our knowledge is true, its object exists in the real objective world independently of the knowledge of it. But even in cases of the grossest hallucination, the object has some kind of existence. When the patient suffering from *delirium tremens* says that he sees a writhing snake where you see only a bedpost, it does little good to tell him that there isn't any snake at all. On the contrary, it is rather evident that what he sees is in some sense existent, for it is surely having a very real effect on him. Indeed, it is difficult to imagine any experience at all which is not in some sense an experience of something existent, for if the object were simply non-existent, it would not be an object of experience, and hence there would be no experience.

So whatever else we shall say, and whether the awareness is true knowledge or merely illusion, we must at least say that what we know when we know is something existent. The mind is by its very nature ordered to *being,* and every fulfillment of this ordering in a bit of actual knowledge consists in an actual cognitive contact with something which in some sense exists. Thus the object of knowledge is being.

But granted this much, what more can we say about the object of knowledge? Here two distinct questions arise. In the first place, *what* is the object of knowledge? What is its nature? And in the second place, *where* is the object of knowledge? What is its status, or *"locus,"* in the world? Let us now consider each of these questions in turn, remembering again that their consideration will require some reference to the knowledge of the object.

A. What Is the Object of Knowledge? (The Nature of the Object)

Our first answer to this question is apt to be: "Why, the objects of knowledge are simply the things we observe with our senses—the trees, rocks, men, and other natural things that we see about us." Now if it were not for the word "simply," this answer would be largely true. But the word "simply" indicates a belief, usually tacit, that knowledge consists merely in sense-experience—that the objects of knowledge are merely what we see, hear, touch, taste, and smell, and that any non-sensory elements are nonsensical, or at least mere "theory" or "interpretation." "Seeing is believing," we say; and we are apt to mean also that believing is seeing (or touching or hearing, etc.). Moreover, we often say, "I can't imagine how that could be so," as if true knowledge of the thing in question consisted in our ability to form a sensory image of it. What, then, is the object of knowledge? Our first, unexamined answer is likely to be that it is always what we sense in a sense-image.

But this answer, as it stands, is inadequate. And we can see that this is so if we will but consider carefully the characteristics of sense-images and their objects and compare them with what we mean by an object of knowledge.

Sense-objects are constantly changing and hence unique and unrepeatable. Suppose, for example, that you hold up a penny in front of a group of people and ask them to tell you what they see. At least the unsophisticated members of your audience will at first say that what they see is a penny. But you, wishing to discover the characteristics of sense-objects as such, will insist that they confine their answers to just what they really and literally see, that is, sense. Now, perhaps, one person who is directly in front of the coin will say that what he sees is a circle; one slightly to the side will say that what he sees is an ellipse; and one directly to the side of the penny will say that what he sees is a straight line. Again, someone in the back of the room will say that he sees a small circle; someone seated very close, a big ellipse; and finally, if there should wander into the room someone suffering the results of an overly enthusiastic celebration, he might well say that he sees two circles.

Furthermore, as you yourself look at the penny, you notice that your visual image is a microcosm of ceaselessly seething flux. It vibrates in its position; its color waxes and wanes as the light varies; it becomes more and then less round as your fingers move.

Having conducted this experiment, what will you now conclude? Mustn't you conclude that the objects of sense are constantly changing, and that no two sense-images are ever the same, either from person to person or from time to time? Even if two of your spectators, eager to disprove your conclusion, should bump heads in their attempt to get their eyes in the same location so as to see the very same thing, you would point out to them that the position of their eyes is not exactly the same, that the acuity of their sight differs, that your nervous hand has shaken the penny slightly, that the light has faded a little, and that innumerable other differing factors make it impossible for them to see exactly the same thing. And if one of the two should then claim that he can have the same image twice in a row, you would invite him to try it, as you did, and you would suggest that his own sense-experience from moment to moment is subject to these same fluctuating and therefore unrepeatable conditions.

Indeed, thinking of possible experiments with senses other than sight, you would add that the simple fact that the organs of sense are physical and in space and time is enough to prove that sense experience is a constant flux and that no two sense-objects can ever be the same, for no two places or times are ever the same. So you would conclude that every sense-object is incurably *transitory* and *unique,* and hence *unrepeatable,* either in more than one *mind* or in more than one *moment* or in more than one *object.* Sense-objects are thus the most rugged of individualists.

The objects of knowledge are stable and communicable. And yet the members of your audience will all swear (or affirm) that they see a penny, and that they therefore have the very same object in mind. They will insist that they all understand each other, that they are communicating with each other. But how can this be, you will ask, if the object of knowledge is merely a sense-object, since every sense-object is fluctuating, unique, and unrepeatable? Indeed, it is of the very essence of knowledge that its object be stable, common, repeatable, communicable. What would science, for example, be if there were nothing common and public to be communicated from one person to another and from one time to another? There would evidently no longer be any science, but rather sciences—as many different sciences as scientists. Indeed, you might even say that there would be as many different sciences as different moments in the consciousness of the scientists, for you saw that it is impossible for even one person to have the same sense-image at two different times, for the conditions of his sensing are constantly changing.

So you see that knowledge is communicable from person to person, while the unique and fluctuating character of sense-objects makes them incommunicable. And you therefore conclude that this is one reason why the object of knowledge cannot be merely the object of sense.

Then, furthermore, in thinking back over your experiment you remember that you had kept referring to the object on display as a penny; and you wonder how that could be if the object before your mind were merely a unique sense-object, different from one moment to the next. For what you merely saw at one moment was certainly not the same as what you merely saw at the next, for the place, position, and so on of the penny and of your eyes were different in the two moments. And yet you say that you had the same object in mind, and you applied the same name to "it."

With this thought you see a second reason why the object of knowledge cannot be merely the object of sense. What you know is a penny, and this idea is applicable to many, many sense-images and their objects. But your visual image of this penny now is certainly applicable to nothing save itself. There are many pennies, but there is only one this-penny-now. Your ideas that make up your knowledge are therefore applicable to many different things—to different things at the same or different times and to the same thing at different times—but your sense-images are certainly applicable only to themselves. How then could we classify, if knowledge were not concerned with something applicable to many things? How could we generalize? How could science formulate such laws as "all bodies gravitate," if knowledge consisted merely of sense-images, each of which is applicable only to itself?

So the object of knowledge cannot be merely the object of sense. The absolutely unique and constantly changing character of sense-images therefore presents two reasons why the objects of knowledge cannot be merely the objects of sense: (1) Knowledge and its objects are communicable, while sense-images and their objects are incommunicable. (2) Knowledge and its component ideas are applicable to many things, while sense-images are applicable to nothing save themselves. The incommunicability of sense-objects means that if they were the mind's only objects each mind would be held incommunicado in a private world all its own. The inapplicability of sense-images means that if they were the mind's only window the world would be completely novel for that imprisoned mind at each moment. What it experienced would not be the same as it or any other mind had ever before experienced; its eyebrows would be perpetually lifted in startled amazement.

Such, then, is the world of the senses—a world of utterly fleeting, irrevocable, and incommunicable sights and sounds and tastes and smells and feels. If these, then, were the only facts, there simply would be no knowable reality at all. "Knowledge" would be, to use William James' phrase, "a blooming, buzzing, confusion," and hence not knowledge at all. But there *is* knowledge, as we have seen; and it is communicable and stable. We may therefore conclude that knowledge cannot consist merely in sense-experience, that the object of knowledge cannot be merely a sense-object.

The object of knowledge is the stable object of reason. What, then, can qualify as the object of knowledge? In considering the sense-object as a candidate, we discovered that the qualifications of the object of knowledge are primarily its repeatability, and hence its stability—its repeatability in many minds (its communicability) and its repeatability in many sense-objects (its applicability). Do we find in our consciousness any such stable, repeatable object?

We have already seen that we do. Ideas or concepts are universal. In addition to the unique, fluctuating, unrepeatable sense-objects, we found a common, stable, repeatable object which we referred to as "penny". This object was not restricted to an absolute here and now as was the object of sense. On the contrary, it was present before each and every one of the minds concerned, and it was present in all of the many objects of sense. "This unique object that I now sense is a penny;" etc. but if this stable, common object of knowledge is not the object of sense, it must be the object of some other cognitive faculty. What is this other faculty? It is what we call reason, intellect, or intelligence. The object of stable, communicable knowledge is the stable, common object of reason. It is the object of what we call an "idea" or "concept" as distinguished from an image or sensation, and its hall-mark, as we have seen, is its stability and repeatability. And it is for this reason that ideas or concepts are said to be universal, in contrast to sense-images which are always particular or individual.

Universals are required for any description or explanation. Moreover, it is precisely this universality of the object of reason which qualifies it as an object of knowledge. The unique particular explains nothing. Since it stands only for itself, it obviously cannot explain anything else. To explain anything, or even to describe it, is possible only in terms of universal concepts or ideas. Thus to say that this is a book, or that that man is tall, or that you are studious, is necessarily to speak in terms of universals. For "book" is a universal; it applies not only to this book here before you, but also to any and every book. So also with "tall," "man," "studious," and all such objects. They are universals and, as such, applicable to many, whereas a sense-image is always an image of just one thing and nothing else.

Such reflections, then, should be enough to convince us that the object of knowledge must be the stable, communicable object of reason, that knowledge not only involves particular fluctuating sense-images by which we are brought into contact with the individual and changing aspects of reality, but also involves unchanging, universal ideas by which these changing particulars may be understood.

B. *Where Is the Object of Knowledge?* (*The Status of the Object*)

Having now seen something of the nature of the object of knowledge, we must turn to our second question concerning the objective-pole of knowledge: Where are these stable, unchanging, universal objects of knowledge? What is their status in reality? What is their locus?

A riddle: how can we have unchanging knowledge of changing nature? Our first answer to this question will probably be: "Why, they are just where they seem to be—in the natural world about us." Although we shall see that this natural answer is ultimately the correct one, it presents us at once with a serious problem. For we have seen that since knowledge is communicable and stable, its objects must be universal, stable, and unchanging. Yet we have also seen (and we would naturally maintain) that the natural world is quite the opposite—that it is made up of individual, unstable, and constantly changing things. If this is so, how can the objects of knowledge be located where we naturally think they are—in nature? Indeed, a knowledge of changing nature would seem to be impossible, for to conceive things as stable and universal when they are really changing and individual is not true knowledge, but rather illusion.

Thus if you know that your pen is green when as a matter of fact it really isn't green at all, having already changed and become different at the very instant you "know" it—indeed, if it isn't even any thing at all, not green, not a pen, not a physical substance, not even an "it," but only a continual, unintelligible flux—then certainly to describe it by such stable, universal concepts as "pen," "green," "physical," etc. is not merely futile but grossly false.

It thus seems certain on the one hand that knowledge requires a stable, unchanging object and yet just as certain on the other hand that the natural world is anything but stable and unchanging. Our question therefore seems to force us into the following dilemma: If the objects of knowledge are in nature, then nature isn't changing; and if the objects of knowledge are not in nature, then we can have no knowledge of nature. Hence we seem to be driven to the conclusion that either nature isn't changing or else we can't have knowledge of it. But our common sense would reject both of these alternatives. Yet how *can* it? Evidently it can do so only by solving the following riddle: How can we have unchanging knowledge of changing things? How can the unchanging objects of knowledge reveal the changing things of nature?

This riddle has been the focal point and spring-board for much of the history of philosophy, and the various alternative ways of solving it were seen and propounded in ancient Greek thought. These alternatives are basically four in number, though the first three are not so much solutions of the riddle as declarations that it is insoluble.

Thus in the first place (1) we may say that nature is truly continually changing—even is pure flux—and that we therefore cannot have knowledge of it (since knowledge requires an unchanging object). This was the position of the philosopher, Heraclitus—or at least his position as interpreted by Plato. Or in the second place (2) we may insist that we do have knowledge (because to deny it is to contradict oneself, as we saw earlier), and that the natural world therefore does not change (again, since knowledge requires an unchanging object). This was the position of Parmenides and his Eleatic school of philosophy, especially as propounded by Zeno in his famous paradoxes. Or in the third place (3) we may insist both that we do have knowledge and that nature is constantly changing and then escape the riddle by adding that our knowledge is therefore *not of nature*. This was the position of Plato; for him the objects of knowledge inhabit a realm of forms separate from the natural world, and our awareness of nature is only fluctuating sensory "opinion."

And yet our common sense rejects these three alternatives, and, indeed, our whole lives are based upon such a rejection and upon the conviction that we can have genuine, stable, scientific knowledge about the changing natural world. Indeed, if our knowledge could not be about nature as it really is, but consisted merely of illusory pictures which we human beings paint, the remarkable success that we have had in using this "knowledge" to control nature would be simply fantastic and unintelligible. Conscious control of nature necessarily pre-supposes an understanding of nature as it really is. And finally, it might well be argued that even the denial that our knowledge is of nature as it really is presupposed that we have some such knowledge. For does not the speaker profess to know at least what he means by "nature" and "real"? He is assuming, it would seem, that he knows at least enough about nature to know that we can have no knowledge of it. So here again we run into the same contradiction which we noted earlier in connection with the necessity of there being some knowledge of some sort.

So we do and must reject these three alternative answers to our riddle. Yet how *can* we? What other solution can we find?

The solution: the objects of knowledge are the stable natures of changing things. We mentioned earlier that there is a fourth solution to the riddle, and it would now behoove us to see whether it offers us any hope. This alternative, which is the view first clearly developed by Aristotle, the student of Plato, accepts the riddle and then tries to solve it. It asserts that we *do* have knowledge, that nature *is* changing, and *yet* that our knowledge is *of nature*. This, then, is the alternative which we must accept if we are to avoid the difficulties just discussed. But how can we accept this alternative? The riddle still remains to be solved.

The solution to the riddle lies in the convergence of two different approaches: (1) an "objective" approach, by an understanding of what is involved in change itself, and (2) a "subjective" approach, by understanding the character of our cognitive faculties. Let us consider each of these separately.

Change itself requires unchanging aspects. When you analyze any change,[3] you will see that it is not quite such a "whooshy" flux as you might at first suppose. Indeed, change itself requires unchanging elements, or there would be nothing *to* change, and nothing for it to change *from* or *to*.

Suppose you consider the change, "your walking across the room." There is a flux here—the process of walking. But there is also you—the stable person who walks. You are the same person before, through, and after your walking. Furthermore, the position that you occupied before walking, and the position that you now occupy after walking, are themselves constant and unchanging: each could be given a geographical definition. Hence not everything in this change is changing. On the contrary, at least three items remain the same: you and the two positions.

Or to take another example, if your hair changes from brown to grey, it is nevertheless still hair, and your hair and the colors brown and grey do not change. Again, change by its very nature involves unchanging elements. If there were just sheer flux, there would be no thing which is *fluctuating*, nor anything for it to fluctuate from and to. If there were just sheer process, there would be no thing to proceed, nor anything for it to proceed from and to. By our first, "objective" approach, then, we see that the "all-or-none" assumption—that a thing is either changing in toto or not changing at all—is wrong. We see therefore that changing nature just in order to be changing must contain unchanging, stable features which *could* be the objects of our knowledge.

Reason is revelatory of nature. To turn now to our second, "subjective," approach, we must recall our earlier discussion of the view which identifies knowledge with sense-experience and the object of knowledge with the sense-object. That view, as we saw, maintains that sense-experience alone reveals the world about us, that any non-sensory elements are at worst nonsensical and at best merely interpretive constructions. And since, as we also saw, the objects of sense are notorious for their absolute uniqueness and unrepeatability—in short, for their constantly fluctuating character—it would naturally follow from such a view that the world about us is a sheer flux containing nothing stable and unchanging.

[3] The nature of change and the changing world is the special concern of the philosophy of nature. For an excellent account of the nature and principles of change see John Wild, *Introduction to Realistic Philosophy*, Harper, 1948, Chapters 13–16.

But we have just now seen that the world about us is not, and cannot be, a mere flux, that change itself necessarily involves unchanging features. Consequently it must follow that the sense-experience view by itself is wrong (as we also saw earlier in a different context), that sensation is not our only avenue to the world about us. But what other avenue do we have? We have already seen that we have also the faculty of reason, whose object is the stable, unchanging, communicable object required for knowledge. The obvious conclusion for us to draw, then, is that the *unchanging features present in changing nature and the unchanging objects of reason and of knowledge are one and the same thing.*

In doing this we see that reason, as well as sense, reveals the real world about us. Recognizing that there is, of course, a changing face of nature, and that it is this which our senses disclose to us, we must at the same time recognize that there are certain stable, unchanging aspects of the natural world, and that it is precisely the function of reason (intellect or intelligence) to disclose these.

The stable objects of knowledge are the natures or essences of things. Indeed, when we speak of the "natures" or "essences" of things, what else do we mean but just such stable patterns present in reality itself? For example, we refer to human "nature" or the "nature" of hydrogen, or we say that something is "of the essence," or pertains to the "essence of," something else. What we mean in all such cases is just that aspect of things which is really present in them but which at the same time is free from that ceaseless flux which strikes our senses.

Thus we all recognize that when an individual man is born or dies, human nature itself is not thereby created or destroyed. Or again, if one draws a triangle and then, by adding two sides, makes it a parallelogram, this hardly changes the essence of a triangle into the essence of a parallelogram. On the contrary, the essence or nature of a triangle—its "triangularity"—is still the same, even though that particular, or any particular, triangle has entirely changed its character.

These stable natures are the objects of every science. And thus as soon as we recognize the fact that such unchanging natures are really present in nature—that they *really* underlie the ceaseless flux of things and are no mere creations of the mind—then we can at once see that these are the very same as the objects of knowledge—that it is just these permanent and unalterable aspects of things which are the proper objects of any science. Thus a contemporary biologist says:

The natures of things are in a certain sense unalterable and eternal; between the nature of a thing and the various aspects of its activities there is a fixed, unalterable, necessary relation; which is in its own order the foundation of Science.

Thus, to take a specific example, the substance we call iron has a certain definite specific nature. So long as iron remains itself, its behavior under any definite set of circumstances will remain the same. It will always have the same molecular weight and melt at the same temperature. On the other hand, what we can say about any particular piece of iron has not by any means this specific and unalterable character. The piece of iron may be large or small, round or square, in this place or that. It may lose its identity by combining with some other element. We shall perhaps realize this more fully if we consider that a description, no matter how detailed or complete, of any particular bit of iron— its exact position, size, shape, weight, and color, etc.—would really add nothing fundamental to what chemistry can already tell us about the element iron. The more perfectly the description brings out the individual characteristics of the thing, the more useless it is, from the genuine scientific standpoint; for Science deals, and can deal, only with the general. Nevertheless, in all concrete, real objects, we can realize the existence of these two aspects, the general and the particular, the specific and the individual, or, as Aristotle put it, the formal and the material; or, looking at the matter from yet another angle, the necessary and the contingent. What appertains to the nature of a thing is necessary—must be so—what appertains to the individuality is contingent—may or may not be so.

Science thus has as its object the natures of things and all its effort consists in an attempt to sift out or disentangle from the complex moving current of ephemeral, individual, contingent events, the definitions of the natures involved in the movement and the laws of their interactions, so as to build up a corpus of permanent and immutable truth; a pattern not only acceptable to the intelligence but coincident in its essential points with reality itself.[4]

What, then, is the answer to our riddle? How can we have unchanging knowledge of changing things? The answer is that we have unchanging rational or scientific knowledge of the unchanging aspects of changing things. What and where are the objects of knowledge? They are stable natures or essences, and they are present in the changing things of the world about us. The solution to our problem lies in the fact that the objects of knowledge are the stable natures of changing things.

We must have knowledge of things themselves, not merely of their unchanging aspects. This answer, however, while true as far as it goes, does not yet seem to be complete. For if the objects of knowledge are the unchanging aspects of real things, our knowledge still seems not to be of the real things themselves. The world about us, we say, is made up of changing things; but our knowledge, we have said, is only of certain aspects of these things, not of the things themselves. So apparently we still do not have knowledge of nature itself or natural things themselves, but merely of certain of their traits. And yet, as already stressed, it is nature itself—natural things—that we control with our scientific knowledge; we

---

[4] W. R. Thompson, *Science and Common Sense,* Longmans, Green, & Co., 1937, pp. 22–23. Although Mr. Thompson is a biologist by profession, in this passage he is writing as a philosopher, and his view should therefore be judged on philosophical rather than biological grounds.

do not control merely their natures or essences. Hence we must have knowledge not only of the stable natures of things, but also of those things themselves. How can we account for this?

To account for this we have only to remember that the natures or essences which are the objects of our knowledge are the natures or essences *of* real things. Where are the objects of knowledge, we asked? *In* the natural things that we sense, was the answer. It is only *in* things and as the essences *of* things that these natures exist.

Insofar, therefore, as our knowledge is relevant to what really exists, it must be a knowledge of things through their natures or essences. In other words, while natures or essences are the objects of our knowledge, they are so, in a sense, only instrumentally, since it is by their means that we come to know the real things in which these natures exist.

Things themselves are the material objects, and their natures the formal objects, of our knowledge. In order, therefore, to gain a complete answer to our question concerning the nature and status of the objects of knowledge, we must recognize that the objects of our knowledge are two-fold, or double-phased.[5] First, there are the natures or essences of things, which are the immediate objects of our knowledge. Second, there are the things themselves of which they are the natures, which things themselves are the mediate objects of our knowledge. The immediate objects (natures) are sometimes called the formal objects of knowledge. The mediate objects (things themselves) are sometimes called the material objects of knowledge. The material objects of knowledge are thus the real things which we know, and the formal objects of knowledge are those intelligible aspects (natures or forms) through which we come to know them. Or in other words, the material object of knowledge is what we know, and the formal objects of knowledge are what we know about it. Thus what you know, for example, is this book (material object); and you come to know it through its stable natures such as "book," "epistemology," "difficult," etc. (formal objects).

With this we have now more completely answered our question. We not only have unchanging knowledge of the unchanging aspects of things. We also have unchanging knowledge of those changing things themselves through their unchanging aspects. We know material objects by means of formal objects.

But this more complete answer seems unhappily to raise another question. We saw earlier that the object of sense is the changing, natural thing, and we have just now seen that the material object of knowledge is also the changing, natural thing. If this is so it would seem that the object of knowledge is the object of sense after all, and that we do not need the dis-

[5] The remainder of this paragraph closely follows the footnote on p. 47 of Parker and Veatch, *op. cit.*

tinct faculty of reason or intellect to apprehend what sense already apprehends! Isn't there a needless duplication here?

Sense and reason are both genuine faculties and are closely connected. It is certainly true in the first place that the objects of reason and the objects of sense (and, correspondingly, the faculties of reason and sense) must be understood as interfused in an extremely intimate way. This is denied, as we saw, by the view which regards sense alone as revelatory of the world about us and which confines reason to the "interpretive" task of filing and arranging the data of sense. This is the view of "Empiricism," a school of philosophy which has had a number of famous historical representatives. This view, as we saw, is untenable precisely because it makes stable, communicable knowledge of extramental reality impossible. On this "Empiricist" view the really cognitive part of our experience is incommunicable, and the communicable part is not genuinely cognitive—that is, not revelatory of the world about us. It is the great insight of "Empiricism's" opposite, "Rationalism," that reason is revelatory of reality; and we have seen that reason discloses real aspects of the world just as much as sense does.

But the intimate inter-relation of the objects of sense and reason is also denied by "Rationalism," for it goes to the extreme of regarding reason as the only genuine cognitive faculty. But if this were so, if sense did not genuinely reveal something about reality, then the world of science and common sense would be devoid of flux and fluidity and peopled only by stable, unchanging natures. It is the great insight of "Empiricism" that sense also grasps a genuine aspect of reality.

So while recognizing the truths contained both in "Empiricism" and in "Rationalism," we must avoid the errors of their extremes by recognizing the genuineness of both faculties, sense and reason, and of their intimate relation. But just how are they related?

Sense and Reason bear on the same reality. To see their relation, let us recall our earlier example of the penny. You see the penny, and you also know or understand or conceive the penny. The penny, then, is the object of both sense and reason. But what about the penny do you see? And what about it do you understand or conceive? You see the penny as this unique, particular, elliptical patch, changing gradually but relentlessly as you look. But you understand and conceive the penny as having certain unchanging properties throughout its fluctuations in your vision. You conceive it as a penny, as a coin, as copper, etc.

It should by now be apparent that what we must here recognize is the fact that the object of sense is two-fold, just as we saw the object of rational knowledge to be. Sense has its material object and its formal object, and so does reason. And seeing this distinction enables us to see the closeness and yet the difference between reason and sense and their objects.

Sense and reason have the same material object but different formal objects. The object of reason is materially the same object as that of sense, but is a different formal aspect of it. You now see this page (material object), for example, as a unique, fluctuating conglomeration (formal object). And you understand this page as being made up of all the distinct formal natures or traits—"page," "white," "rectangle," etc.—which are fused or conglomerated in the object of sense. Thus the material object is the thing itself—this page—and it is grasped by both sense and reason. The formal object of sense is the individual and changing aspects of the material object—this unique page here and now. The formal object of reason is the universal and unchanging aspects of the material object—the natures "page," "white," "rectangle," etc. Thus sense and reason both apprehend the same object, but sense apprehends it *insofar as it is unique and changing,* while reason grasps it *insofar as it is made up of universal, unchanging natures.*

The object of sense is thus a confused and fluctuating welter of stable natures, each of which can be abstractly and specifically considered by reason. This process by which we come to know things as having certain stable structures is called *abstraction.* And that from which we abstract to gain this knowledge is the confused, fluctuating object of sense.

And here it is well to be sure that we see that although knowledge does not consist merely in sensation, all knowledge must certainly begin in sensation. From what we see, hear, touch, feel, etc., we abstract the stable natures really present in the things thus sensed and thereby come to know the natures of these things as they really are. Though these stable natures which are the formal objects of reason are really present in the object of sense, the eyes of sense are blind to them. At this point an analogy may help.

Let us suppose that in the midst of a raging battle a messenger is ordered to carry a codified message from the front lines back to headquarters. Since the message is in code, and since the messenger, lest he be captured and tortured, has not been given the key to the code, he cannot read it. Yet he carries it; and when he has carried it to headquarters, the intelligence officer will be able to read the message because he has the key to the code and can therefore decodify it.

The messenger in our analogy is sensation, and the codified message that he carries is the object of sense. The intelligence officer is reason, and the decodified, meaningful message that he reads is the object of reason. Thus sense bears a message (the stable natures which are the formal objects of reason) which is meaningful only to reason.[6] And the decodifica-

---

[6] Cf. Etienne Gilson, *Réalisme Thomiste et Critique de la Connaissance,* Paris: J. Vrin, 1947, p. 218. These two paragraphs are an extension of Gilson's metaphor.

tion of this message by reason is the process called abstraction. But what more can we say about the nature of abstraction?

As we have seen, the natural things which we sense in the world about us always consist of a conglomeration or fusion of different natures or traits. In the world of nature, no nature or characteristic ever exists just by itself. On the contrary, it always exists in union with a whole host of other natures or characteristics which do not have to be connected with it, but which as a simple matter of fact just are conjoined with it accidently and contingently. Before such a nature can be apprehended just as it is in itself, therefore, it must first be extricated or disentangled, so to speak, from that whole context of natures in which it finds itself in a given instance. Now it is precisely this process of extricating and disentangling which goes by the name of abstraction. This is the process of decodifying the message of sense.

Consider, for example, a chemical compound like salt. Salt has a certain nature or essence. Yet no particular existing bit of salt is ever just the essence of salt and nothing else. It has, indeed, the essence of salt. And yet it also has present in it many other characteristics. It is fine or coarse, in the chemist's laboratory or on his dinner table, warm or cool, five grams or ten grams, and so on.

Now all of these other characteristics—texture, place, temperature, etc. —are themselves natures or essences. But we recognize quite readily that they are wholly accidental to the nature or essence of salt, and it to them. There is nothing about the nature of salt that requires that it be in the quantity of five grams, for example. Accordingly, if we wish to understand either the nature of salt or the nature of five grams, then we must first abstract these traits or natures from those other traits or natures with which they are fused in the particular concrete instance. Furthermore, if we were to gain complete knowledge of that particular concrete instance of salt, we would have to abstract each and every one of the traits or natures fused together in it. Fortunately for our human energies, however, such complete knowledge (even if it were possible!) is unnecessary.

This account of the process of abstracting indicates another fact about our knowledge and its objects, namely that we invariably come to know one thing through a multiplicity of its traits. In other words, a single material object of knowledge comes to be known through a number of its intelligible aspects, each of which in being abstracted becomes a formal object of knowledge.

For instance, suppose you form an acquaintance with a given individual, John Doe. Do you come to know him all at once and in a single concept? Hardly. Thus at first you may know little more about him than that he is a student, that he is majoring in chemistry, that he is peculiarly addicted to going to sleep in class, etc. And perhaps after that you desire to know no more. But however that may be, the interesting thing about the situation is that an individual who is truly one being, a real unity, is nevertheless known through the many natures that are present in him.

Nor is it merely individuals in the material world that come to be known through a number of concepts of their several natures. On the contrary, even such a thing as a nature or essence itself we can, in most cases, come to know through a whole multitude of concepts. True, a nature is not itself made up of natures, as is an individual material thing—and it can therefore not properly be called a material object of knowledge. And yet any nature does comprehend or comprise within itself a number of "notes," by which we may take note of it, so to speak, or come to know it.

Thus for example, consider some such thing as human nature. How do we understand this? We recognize man as being a substance, and more specifically a living substance, and still more specifically a living animal substance. We realize, moreover, that man is a particular kind of animal, a rational animal. In short, it is through all these notes such as substance, living, animal, rational, etc. that we come to understand the single nature of man. The same is true, for example, in understanding the nature of hydrogen. Do we not understand this as an element, as a colorless, odorless gas, as inflammable, as lighter than any other known element, etc.? Again we come to know a single nature through many of its notes.

Knowing is a "withdrawal and return." In addition, then, to the fleeting, individual events of nature, there are also present in reality certain enduring and unchanging aspects which we call the essences or natures of things. It is these which are the formal objects of our stable, communicable knowledge, just as it is the changing face of nature which is grasped in our sense-impressions. What we call scientific knowledge, therefore, is a knowledge of things in terms of their permanent, universal natures, rather than in terms of their particular, changing aspects. As Aristotle so constantly reiterated, science is always of the universal and necessary, never of the merely individual and accidental. And these universal and necessary natures are present, in a confused way, in the objects of sense; their understanding, and consequently the understanding of those things whose natures they are, requires that they be abstracted from the objects of sense-experience.

Thus in knowing anything, we complete, so to speak, a full circle, or rather a spiral—a withdrawal and a higher level return. We start with sensation and its object grasped as a fusion of many traits or natures into a fluctuating whole. We then abstract or withdraw certain of these natures and concentrate upon them just in themselves. And then, finally, we return to the whole but now with new light, understanding the whole material object through certain of its stable traits.

What, then, is the object of knowledge? The material object of knowledge is the same as the material object of sense—some integrated thing in the world about us. The formal object of rational or scientific knowledge is the stable structure of this material object, and we grasp it by abstracting from the unique, fluctuating formal object of sense. What, then, do we know when we know? We know the real things in the world about us through their stable, unchanging natures.

We have now examined at some length the nature of the object-pole in knowledge—the nature and status of the objects of knowledge. We have seen that the formal objects of knowledge are the stable, unchanging aspects of things and that these things themselves which we come to know through their stable aspects are the material objects of knowledge. We must now turn our attention to the knowledge-pole—the mind's intention of some object—and try to discover what is involved in it. Just as our examination of the object of knowledge required some discussion of the knowledge of it, so also our consideration of the knowledge-pole will necessarily involve some reference to the object. But nevertheless we shall concentrate primarily upon the knowledge-pole—the intention. What, then, is involved in our knowing of objects?

A. What It Is Not: a Physical or Quasi-physical (Transitive) Action

At the beginning of our inquiry into the nature of the object of knowledge, we examined the common tendency to identify the object of knowledge with what we see, touch, hear, etc. So also now we must first consider a parallel tendency concerning the act of knowing, a tendency, namely, to regard the act of knowing as being just like any natural, physical change or event. What is the act of knowing? Our first answer is apt to be that it is a physical process just like all the physical processes in the world around us.

Thus when you analyze your awareness of this book, for example, you may say that the process goes something like this: First of all, there is the book—a real, physical thing existing in a certain definite spatial location. Then there is the light reflected from this book, waves or particles (or "wavicles") of light passing from the surface of the book to your eye. Upon reaching your eye, you may continue, these particles of light pass through the cornea, aqueous humour, lens, and vitreous humour and then strike the nerve-endings in the retina where they produce an electrochemical impulse. This impulse, you may then say, travels along the optic nerve to the occipital lobe of the brain in the back of your head, whereupon, finally, you say you "see" the book. Thus awareness, you may suggest, is merely a straightforward physical process, just like any other.

But what about this account? How must we evaluate it? In order to evaluate it, let us ask the same two questions which we have asked previously. What and where is the object of knowledge, according to this materialistic account of the process of knowing? Let us take the second question first.

The object "known" is not the object known. Where, then, according to this materialistic account, is the object of your knowledge? Where is the book that you see? You will probably answer at once: "Why, out there, in space, where we said it was." But let us be careful here. Is this true? Is the book that you see (according to this view) "out there"?

Let us look once more at the process involved. The seeing of the book requires all of the steps enumerated above. You do not see the book until after all these steps have occurred, until the end of the process. And when the process is completed, the earlier stages no longer exist. But where is the end of this process? In the back of your brain. Hence it would appear that the physical thing that you physically see is not "out there," separate from you in space, but rather in your head—"under your hat." And for this reason this materialistic account of the act of knowing has sometimes been called the "under-the-hat" theory. It might perhaps be diagrammed thus:

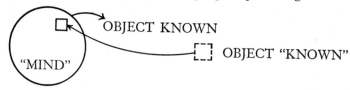

But this answer must seem very strange, to say the least. If the book that you really see is in the back of your brain, behind your eyes, how does it happen that it seems to be "out there," in front of your eyes? The philosopher, Hobbes, one of the main exponents of this materialistic view, tried to answer this question by saying that the brain *projects* the particles back out again—since for every physical action "there is an equal and opposite reaction"—and that such projection accounts for the apparent external location of the object. But even if such projection of sensed objects actually takes place (which is certainly dubious, to say the least), still the book that you actually see would not be the book that you think you see. Even if the projective reaction were *so* equal and opposite as to make the "seen" particles bump into the bundle of particles that originally reflected the light (that is, the book that you think you see), still they would not be the same particles, for no two physical things can ever occupy the same space at the same time—no two physical things are ever identical. So even when the "under-the-hat" theory is given its most favorable interpretation, what you know would still never be what you think you know. To "know" something is therefore not to know it.

If, on the other hand, the particles that you actually see are really in the brain (as seems more plausible), then another disturbing implication arises. Since everything which is known—the objects of all science and common sense—would then be physically contained in human brains, the arduous and painful process of education would seem to be rather inefficient, to say the least, for we ought then to be able to learn everything that is known by the relatively simple process of brain surgery.[7] We would be able to learn a given thing, presumably, simply by opening the appropriate skull, and the brain surgeon should therefore be the wisest of all men. It hardly needs to be mentioned, however, that no brain surgeon will ever find a book in your brain (at least while you are thinking about a book), nor when what you know is the universe will he find the universe in your brain—for this would mean that the whole is contained in a rather small and insignificant one of its parts. Nor would it help for the "under-the-hat" theorist to object that this may be because our present knowledge of the brain is far from complete.

Moreover, the objects known by this wisest of men, the brain surgeon, would in turn be in his own brain. And this would mean, again, that the objects of his wisdom would not be the same as the objects "known by," or present in, his patient's brain. So we are presented with the paradoxical situation in which the wisest man cannot be the wisest man because in knowing other brains he knows only his own brain. Again, to "know" something is not to know it.

Furthermore, to carry this just one step further, the brain surgeon could not after all really be said to be operating on other brains at all, but only his own, for the operation that he knows is in his own brain. And as to how a person can be both brain-surgeon and brain-patient at the same time is mysterious, to say the least.

Finally, having seen that on this view you could never know anything outside your own brain, there is a serious question as to whether you could even know anything in your own brain. For here again the process of "knowing" would be a physical one, whose beginning and whose end are consequently different. If, for example, the object of your knowledge were a certain structure in one of the fissures of your frontal lobe, your knowing of it would consist in a physical series whose last member would be located somewhere else in your brain. If, for instance, your knowledge of that frontal fissure consisted in part in the formation of a visual image of it, that visual image would not occur until the process had terminated in the back of your head, in which case the object of your knowledge is not the frontal fissure at all, but rather something in your occipital lobe. And if you were to know this particle in the back of your head, what you would

[7] The following argument is adapted from A. O. Lovejoy, *The Revolt Against Dualism*, Open Court, 1930, pp. 237–238.

know would be another particle somewhere else. And so on indefinitely.

In short, when we ask the Materialist where the object of his knowledge is, he must, if he is consistent, answer that the object which he *"really knows"* is at best different from the object which he *"thinks he knows"* (the former being under his hat or projected out from under his hat) and at worst no object at all—since his knowing of anything means that he does not know it, but rather something different, ad infinitum. So the Materialistic account of the act of knowing is untenable, in the first place, when we consider the location of its object of knowledge.

The object "known" is merely the object of sensation. And if we ask the Materialist our second question—*What* is the object of knowledge? What is its character?—we see a second reason for the unacceptibility of his theory. Every factor in the Materialistic account of the act of knowing is purely physical, so the object of knowledge is also purely physical. Now every purely physical thing, as we have seen, is a constantly fluctuating, absolutely unique and unrepeatable individual. In short, the object of knowledge for the Materialist is always the object of sensation. But we have already seen that the object of knowledge cannot be merely the object of sense, for the former is stable and repeatable while the latter is fluctuating and unrepeatable. Consequently, the Materialistic account of the act of knowing also breaks down when we consider the nature of its object. The Materialist theory of knowledge inevitably tends to be a sensationist theory of knowledge and is also for that reason unacceptable. It is therefore doubly impossible for the act of knowing to be merely a physical action.

We have now seen that our physical contacts with the world can result (at best) merely in unique, fluctuating sense-images. And yet we have also seen that knowledge absolutely requires a stable, repeatable object. Where then does this object come from, and by what act do we know it?

If in rejecting the Materialistic view we nevertheless continue to think exclusively in terms of physical actions, we shall have to say that these stable objects of knowledge are constructed or created by the mind itself. In other words, if, on the one hand, we (rightly) maintain that our physical contacts with the world can at best produce only sense-images, and if, on the other hand, we believe (wrongly, as we shall see) that our physical contacts are our only cognitive contacts with the world about us, then it will follow that those universal, stable objects which are the *sine qua non* of knowledge cannot come from the world about us. On the contrary, they will have to come from within; they will have to be produced by the mind itself. Now there is no empirical evidence for a brain physically producing physical universal objects—and, indeed, a physical thing is just what cannot be universal. This productive activity of the mind will therefore have to be regarded as non-physical or immaterial. But since the assumption that our only cognitive contact with the world is physical is itself a physicalistic assumption, and since, moreover, this mental production will almost invariably be described in the same way as physical production, the act of knowing is for this view quasi-physical.

Thus if you again analyze your knowledge of this book, you may say that you receive a "blooming, buzzing confusion" of sense-data, chaotic and meaningless in themselves. In order to make them into meaningful knowledge, you may continue, your mind must take this chaotic mass of sense-data and organize it in terms of certain categories or classifications, such as "book," "rectangle," "paper," or such as "substance," "being spatially and temporally located," etc. Since these interpretive categories are universal and unchanging, they cannot, on this view, have been derived from the world about you. On the contrary, they must have lain *"a priori"* in your mind, waiting to be imposed upon masses of sense-data, thereby to create out of these sense-data meaningful objects of knowledge.

And of course you cannot afford to say that it is merely your individual mind which constructs these objects, for then what you know could not be the same as what any one else knows. You would then be locked up in your own little cognitive world—a condition called "solipsism," where "only yourself" can be known to exist. Hence, you must say that the mind which constructs the objects of knowledge is a general or over-all mind, either the human mind as such (a view held by the philosopher, Kant) or the mind of the Absolute (a view held by the Absolute Idealists, e.g. Fichte, Hegel, and others). Knowable reality is then, in any case, constructed or created by the knowing mind with its "ideas." Hence this view which regards the objects of knowledge as constructed by the mind is called Idealism, or better, "Idea-ism." The act of knowing is an act of making. What, then, shall we say of this view?

In the first place, it is at any rate not subject to the second criticism we levied against the Materialistic theory, for the Idealistic view maintains that the objects of knowledge are stable and universal, not merely unique, fleeting sense-impressions.

The Idealistic view is, however, subject to other serious objections. In the first place, since it regards the object of knowledge as being constructed by the mind, we could on this view never know anything as it really is independently of the mind. But would this account permit that scientific knowledge of reality which we have seen is involved in our control over nature? Obviously not, for if we can never know things as they really are, independently of the mind, then we certainly could not possibly exercise any conscious control over them. We may, of course, take the metaphysical leap of Absolute Idealism and extend the mind so that it includes everything, asserting that reality is mental or ideal in its real nature, and that real things therefore are the things that the Absolute Mind constructs in its knowing. But in the first place this sort of view is certainly entirely alien to our deepest common convictions. And in the second place, if the knowing mind is merely one Absolute Mind in many manifestations, as is maintained by Absolute Idealism, what happens to that individual independence and freedom of mind and action which we prize so highly? Academic freedom, for example, would certainly then be merely "academic." And finally, and even more telling, even if real things were the constructs of the Absolute Mind's acts of knowledge, still no human mind could ever know anything as it really is, since for the human mind to know it must construct and alter, and hence it could never know anything as it was really constructed by the cognitive act of the Absolute Mind.

But there is a more serious, and more specifically epistemological, objection to this Idealistic view which regards the act of knowing as a construction of its object. The essence of this Idealistic theory is that the act of knowing changes its object into something new. But let us follow out the implications of this view. In knowing A, you must change or construct it into B, in which case you do not know A at all. Thus in "knowing" A you do not know A—which is a flat contradiction. If you say that it is B which you know, that B is the object of your knowledge, the same thing happens again, for just in knowing B you change B into something else, and hence in "knowing" B you do not know B—again a contradiction. And so on.

Indeed, the Idealistic account reminds one of the story of the donkey and the carrot. The donkey, you will remember, is led on by a carrot held dangling just out of reach in front of him by a pole fixed to his harness. Hence every step that the donkey takes to get the carrot keeps him from getting it; every one of his attempts simply pushes the carrot out of his reach. To "get" the carrot is not to get it. So also, on the Idealistic view of the act of knowing, to "know" anything is not to know it, for to "know" it is to change it into something different. Indeed, how can the Idealist even know his own theory, if to know anything is to change it and hence not to know it? Because of this "always reaching but never attaining" character of the Idealistic theory, we might perhaps diagram it thus:

OBJECTS "KNOWN"

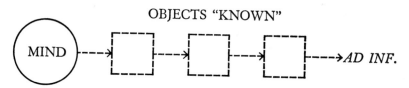

At this point, however, the Kantian Idealist might object that Kant never said that the original thing is known, and hence that there is no contradiction at all. The original thing, according to Kant's terminology, is not itself an object of knowledge at all, but only the material from which the mind produces the proper object of knowledge, the "phenomenon."

Once this object has been constructed by the imposition of mental forms on sensory materials, why then the resulting object, the "phenomenon," is just simply known as it is, intuitively. Now this qualification does indeed avoid the contradiction and infinite regress we have just been discussing—but only by conceding the point at issue, that the act of knowing cannot be a constructive, transitive action. In short: if the proper object of knowledge is transformed transitively, then contradiction and infinite regress inevitably result; and if the theory is qualified so that the act of knowing does not transform its proper object, then, of course, knowing itself is no longer regarded as a quasi-physical transitive action.

The act of knowing cannot be described in physical terms. Hence, we cannot, with Idealism, regard the act of knowing as a quasi-physical act which constructs or produces its object. The Idealistic view is wrong—indeed, it is self-contradictory—for on this view, just as on the Materialistic view, to "know" something is not to know it. In fact, the two theories, in the last analysis, boil down to about the same thing, because they both describe the act of knowing after the fashion of physical actions, and for every physical action "there is an equal and opposite reaction"—Materialism stressing the physical action of the object upon the "mind" and Idealism stressing the quasi-physical action of the mind upon the object. Thus these apparent opposites are at bottom very much alike.

This same situation may also be put in terms of our earlier discussion of the contrast between sensation and reason.[8] The Idealist shares the same false assumption with the Materialist, namely, that our only contact with a world beyond us is sensation. They are both right to this extent: that contact with a world beyond us requires sensation. But they are wrong in assuming that such contact is in sensation alone. The Materialist, wishing above all to save the contact, reduces knowledge to sensation and thus has an object that cannot be known. The Idealist, wishing above all to save the characteristics of permanence and universality in knowledge, makes the object a construct of the mind and thus has a "knowing" without an object.

Is there now any over-all moral to this story of Materialism and Idealism? There is. The moral is this: In order to describe the act of knowing we must stop thinking in physical terms. The act of knowing, and for that matter every act of awareness, is in essence non-physical, and hence we cannot correctly describe it after the fashion of physical actions. This point is all-important, if we are to gain any understanding of the nature of knowledge. Knowing is not a physical action and hence cannot be adequately described as such.

[8] For this way of putting the situation I am indebted to Professor Samuel M. Thompson of Monmouth College.

B. What It Is: An Immanent (Non-physical) Act

So far, however, we have said only what the act of knowing is not—that it is not of the nature of physical actions, with which our experience first and most frequently confronts us and with which we are therefore most familiar. This negative description is legitimate and important, however, for it is through its contrast with physical actions that we come to understand the non-physical nature of knowing. But what, more specifically, is this contrast?

Physical actions are transitive. The basic characteristic of physical action is what is called its *transitivity*—the fact that the action passes across from the agent or actor over into the patient or thing acted upon. Thus as you write, for example, energy passes through your arm over into your pencil to change it, and then from your pencil over into the paper to change it. Or if you cut an orange with a knife, the activity passes over into the orange to produce a real, new property in it—its being cut into halves. Thus every physical action is basically transitive.

IV. THE ACT OF KNOWING IS IMMANENT

But no act of awareness is transitive. Knowing the orange does not change the orange to produce any real, new property in it, as cutting the orange does, for if it did we would change the orange into something different, and hence not know *it*. On the contrary, *knowing* does not act on the orange at all; it acts only on the mind that knows the orange. The orange, it is true, does act on the knower; but this action is not physical or transitive, or we would *be* oranges, or something like them, instead of knowing them. The act of knowing is thus basically characterized by its *immanence,* for the act of knowing remains immanent within the knowing faculty. No act of awareness ever passes transitively over into its object to change it. Quite the contrary; any act of awareness produces its change only immanently, within the mind. Your cutting the orange physically changes both you and the orange. But your knowing the orange changes only you (and then not merely physically); it makes not a whit of difference to the orange.

Here, however, two possible objections need to be forestalled. In the first place, though knowing makes no change in the thing known, it is evident that the physical conditions of knowing do make such a change.[9] Here the Materialist is right. Before you can see this page, for example,

---

[9] The Heisenberg uncertainty principle is a recognition of a particular instance of this general situation. The Heisenberg principle is sometimes wrongly interpreted to mean that the very act of awareness itself changes the position or velocity of the particle.

the page must be illuminated to a certain extent, the medium between the page and your eyes must be transparent, your eyes must possess certain physical properties, etc. All these physical factors do influence what you see, because their actions are transitive. If you blow smoke between your eyes and this page, or if you cross your eyes, what you see will be changed. But your knowing does not itself consist in these various physical actions —as we have seen. Light striking your eyes is not the same as seeing; air vibrations striking your ears are not the same as hearing; and brain-waves are not the same as thinking. And it is these acts of awareness themselves which produce no change in their objects.

In the second place, we realize that once knowledge is acquired it can, of course, be used in action to alter objects. After you understand the nature of atomic energy, for example, you can apply that knowledge in such a way as to make quite a difference in the world—either constructively or destructively. But such practical application of knowledge is quite distinct from the knowledge which is thus applied. And the knowledge itself, just insofar as it is knowledge, makes no difference to the thing known whatsoever.

Thus the act of knowing is an immanent, non-physical act, making no change at all in its object. And from this fact there follow two very important corollaries.

The object of knowledge is independent of and unrelated to the knowledge of it. In the first place, the immanence of the cognitive act means that the things we know are quite independent, in both their existence and their nature, of our knowledge of them. This does not mean, of course, that the things that we know are always independent of any and every act of knowing or consciousness, or independent of mind, for obviously many of the things that we know are mental in character or depend on some mind for their existence and nature—such things as purposes and fictions, for example. But it does mean that anything that we know is independent of that precise particular act by which we know it. Your friend's thoughts, for example, are dependent upon *his* mind, but are quite independent of *your* thinking about them. Now what does this independence of the objects of knowledge mean?

It means that the things that we know are in no way related to us by the fact that they are known. This last qualification is of course necessary, for the thing known may be, and usually if not always is, related to the knower by one or more relations other than the cognitive relation. This page is related to you by a number of real relations such as distance, dissimilarity, etc.; and with respect to these relational properties, it depends on you as it would on any other natural thing. But it is not related to you, and hence does not depend on you, in any of its properties, insofar as you know it. And this is so, we have seen, because the act of knowing is immanent rather than transitive, and hence produces no real property in the page which could give rise to any such relation of dependence. You, of course, are related to it, and you therefore depend upon the page that you know, since that knowledge does change you. But the page is not cognitively related to you.

Thus the cognitive relation is called a *non-mutual* relation. That is, the knower is related to the known, but there is no real, answering, mutual relation from the known to the knower.[10] When you say that what you know has the property of being "known by" you, therefore, you cannot mean that this is a real property of the thing, for if you did knowing would have changed it by producing that real property, and hence you would not know it at all. This peculiar relation, "known by," is not a real property of the thing at all, but only a mental relation set up by your mind when, in reflection, it moves back from the object of the real relation, "knower of," to your knowing mind which really has that relational property.

Thus it follows from the immanence of the cognitive act that its object is not really related to, nor consequently dependent upon, that cognitive act. Knowledge is always a revelation into the lives of things wholly undisturbed by that revelation.

The second very important corollary of the immanence of the act of knowing is a point which we have already constantly referred to in somewhat disguised forms. This is the fact that the cognitive relation is a relation of identity. This means nothing more than the fact that when you know something, you know it, itself, identically—and not something different which your mind has produced. This is not a mere verbalism. It is rather a necessary truth about the nature of knowledge.

This fact that the cognitive relation is one of identity follows from, and only from, the fact that the act of knowing is immanent and non-physical rather than transitive and physical. For if knowing is a transitive action, then it changes its object into something different, and hence is not a knowing of it at all. But as soon as we regard knowing as an immanent act, then it makes no change whatsoever in its object and hence consists really in a knowing of it, identically, as it really is.

Just as the immanence of the cognitive act implies that the cognitive relation is one of identity, so also to regard the cognitive act as transitive implies, as we have seen, that the cognitive relation is not one of identity, but rather, at best, merely one of *similarity*. On this view it has to be admitted that we do not actually know real things themselves, but rather at best only their copies or likenesses. On this view, that is to say, we know only our own ideas (described either Materialistically or Idealistically), and these are at best mere copies of reality.

[10] For an excellent introductory account of the nature and types of relation, see Wild, *op. cit.*, pp. 347–351.

But this copy-theory[11] is self-contradictory in just the same way as its parent, the transitive theory of the cognitive act, was seen to be. For if we know merely copies and not real things themselves, then we cannot possibly know even that there are real things which are such that they are similar to the copies that we know. To know that X is similar to Y, we must first know Y itself, identically, and that it in itself really is similar to X. But this is just what the copy theory denies.

Here it might be objected that although we cannot directly know the "external" real thing itself, we can nevertheless infer the real thing from its idea-copy. But this will not work, for such an inference is impossible unless here again, we grasp, identically, what is inferred. To infer X from Y is to have the mind pass from Y to *X itself,* identically. But this identity is, again, just what the copy-theory denies. Hence it cannot assert that we infer the real thing. The very same is true if it is then suggested that the idea-copy represents or signifies the real thing, for if it signifies it, then we are led by the sign to the thing itself, identically. Thus our conclusion stands: On the basis of the copy-theory we cannot know even that there *is* anything which is copied, nor, consequently, even that there is anything which copies. Thus we are locked within the iron ring of our copy-ideas. This is what has been called the "egocentric predicament."

Furthermore, if we can never know anything itself, identically, then we cannot even know the idea-copy which is declared to be similar to an unknowable real thing. If it is objected that we can indeed know the idea-copy itself, identically, then there is no necessary reason to deny that we can also know the real thing itself, identically. And if it is suggested that, while we cannot know the idea-copy itself directly, we can know it through another idea-copy which is similar to it, then the same difficulty arises again and we are in an infinite regress.

Thus we must conclude that on the basis of the copy-theory, insofar as it is consistent, we can know neither real things nor their idea-copies. In short, on the basis of the copy-theory, insofar as it is consistent, we can never know anything. But such a theory is self-contradictory because, as we have already seen, it asserts that we know at least one thing, namely, that the cognitive relation is merely one of similarity, that ideas are merely copies of things. But, by the argument just presented, this is to assert that we know that we cannot know. And since this theory is self-contradictory, its contradictory—that the cognitive relation is one of identity—is necessarily true. To know something is to know it, identically, and not something else. And this is possible only when the act of knowing is recognized as being immanent and non-physical and therefore as not making any change in its object.

What, then, is the act of knowing? It is an immanent, non-physical act making its change only in the cognitive faculty and not in its object. And

[11] This theory is also often called "representationalism" and "epistemological dualism."

from this principle there follow two corollaries: (a) The objects of knowledge are independent of and not really related to the acts of knowing them; (b) The cognitive relation is one of identity; to know something is to know it.

V. A CONCLUDING ANALOGY [12]

To summarize and conclude, let us liken knowledge to photography. While each element in the photographic process is physical and transitive and therefore in itself very different from the elements involved in the immanent, non-physical act of knowing, the relations among the elements of each process are significantly similar.

Let us imagine a dimly-lit chamber containing people and objects which, because of the poor lighting, shade off into each other so as to be hardly distinguishable in the gloomy shadows, just as the traits and characteristics of things are confused together in sensory experience. Then, when the photographer has everything set, a flashlight suddenly illuminates the shadowy scene just as reason illuminates the "blooming, buzzing confusion" of sense experience. The various features which really inhere in the objects in the room but which are not distinguishable by sense at once become clearly and distinctly visible and are then impressed upon the camera film of the mind.

The impression of the film is in one way quite different from the structure of the room. One is in the camera, the other in the room. But the two patterns are nevertheless the same (formally similar though not identical, since this is a physical process). In just the same way the things that the mind truly knows are identical in nature with real things.

Now think of the elaborate process of developing the film, making the prints, and touching them up to produce the finished picture. All this takes place in a darkroom and studio quite apart from the original objects. It involves various peculiar chemical processes which have nothing to do with anything in the original objects. Yet the fully processed print may be an accurate replica of the original scene—though not identical with it since the print is physical. Think now of the analogous mental processes in which the natures apprehended by our minds are defined in clear concepts and combined in true, demonstrated propositions about things in the real world. All this takes place in the mind quite apart from the original objects. It involves various peculiar processes which are quite unlike the real things. And yet the fully developed knowledge that results may truthfully reveal the original things in the real world. By these processes true knowledge is achieved, not of the processes, but of the real things which lie beyond them.

Finally, the camera does not make the scene what it is; it records what

[12] This analogy is adapted from and closely follows that in Wild, *op. cit.*, pp. 464–467.

it already independently is. The creation of a different scene would contradict the very nature of photography whose function is to reproduce something exactly as it already exists. The camera produces something new only in the camera, not in the room. The things in the room, therefore, do not depend on the camera (they do, of course, in some slight degree, since the camera is physical); the camera depends on them. So also the mind in knowing does not create the things which it knows; it reveals what already exists independently of it. Knowing is an immanent, not a transitive, activity; it makes something new only in the knower, not in the known. The realities which are known therefore do not depend on their being known, in either their nature or their existence; the knowledge depends on the realities known. Human knowing is the immanent, immaterial activity of identifying the very natures of the real, independent, existent things in the world.

BIBLIOGRAPHY FOR PART I

Anderson, F., "The Relational Theory of Mind," *The Journal of Philosophy,* XXXIX (1942), pp. 253–61.

Balz, A. G. A., "Nature, Knowledge, and Myth," *The Journal of Philosophy,* XXXXIII (1946), pp. 253–66.

Brennan, J. G., "Problems of Knowledge," *The Meaning of Philosophy,* Harper & Brothers, New York, 1953, pp. 73–188.

Brunner, A., "Perils of Technological Thought," *Philosophy Today,* I, no. 2 (1957), pp. 114–17.

Cousin, D. R., "Some Doubts about Knowledge," *Proceedings, Aristotelian Society,* 1935–36, XXXVI, pp. 255–72.

De Laguna, G. A., "Being and Knowing," *The Philosophical Review,* XXXXV (1936), pp. 435–56.

Dewey, J., *The Significance of the Problem of Knowledge,* University of Chicago Press, Chicago, 1897.

——, "What is Thinking," *How We Think,* D. C. Heath and Co., New York, 1933, pp. 1–12.

Eaton, R. M., "What is the Problem of Knowledge," *The Journal of Philosophy,* XX (1923), pp. 178–87.

Forest, A., "Essai d'une étude critique de la connaissance," *Revue Thomiste,* XVI (1933), pp. 109–23.

Frondizi, R., "On the Nature of the Self," *Review of Metaphysics,* III (1950), pp. 437–51.

Garrigou-Lagrange, R., "La première donnée de l'intelligence selon S. Thomas," *Mélanges Thomistes,* Le Saulchoir, Kain, 1923, pp. 199–217.

Gény, P., "Sur la position du problème de la connaissance," *Revue de Philosophie,* XIII (1908), pp. 449–60.

Hall, E. W., "Of What Use Is Metaphysics?," *The Journal of Philosophy,* XXXIII (1936), pp. 236–45.

Hallet, H. J., "The Essential Nature of Knowledge," *Philosophy,* XX (1945), pp. 227–43.

James, W., "On the Function of Cognition," *Mind,* X (1885), pp. 27–44.

Kent, J. B., "The Problem and Method of Epistemology," *The Philosophical Review,* XXXIX (1930), pp. 17–35.

Klausner, N. W., "Three Decades of Epistemological Dialectic, 1900–1930," *Philosophy of Science,* XIV (1947), pp. 20–43.

Marvin, W. T., "The Emancipation of Metaphysics from Epistemology," *The New Realism,* The Macmillan Co., New York, 1912, pp. 45–83.

McKian, J. D., "The Metaphysics of Introspection According to St. Thomas," *The New Scholasticism,* XV (1941), pp. 89–117.

Miller, D. S., "Is There not a Clear Solution to the Knowledge Problem," *The Journal of Philosophy,* XXXIV (1937), pp. 701–12; XXXV (1938), pp. 561–72.

Montague, W. P., "The Story of American Realism," *Philosophy,* XII (1937), pp. 140–61.

Morandini, F., "L'épistémologie thomiste," *Revue Philosophique de Louvain,* Tome 49, 1951, pp. 641–51.

Nagel, E., *Sovereign Reason,* The Free Press, Glencoe, Ill., 1954.

Noël, L., "The Neo-Scholastic Approach to the Problems of Epistemology," *The New Scholasticism,* I (1927), pp. 136–46.

Owen, E. T., "The Illusion of Thought," *The Journal of Philosophy,* XXXXV (1948), pp. 505–11.

Parker, F. H., "Realistic Epistemology," *The Return to Reason,* ed. J. Wild, Henry Regnery Co., Chicago, 1953, pp. 152–76.

Phelan, G. B., Anderson, J. F., "Metaphysics of Knowledge," *Proceedings,* American Catholic Philosophical Association, XXI (1946), pp. 106–11.

"Programme d'études sur le problème de la connaissance," *Revue de Philosophie,* XII (1908), pp. 449–62.

Quine, W. V., "On What There Is," *Review of Metaphysics,* II (1948), pp. 21–38.

Raymond, R. P., "Bulletin de Philosophie. Questions de critériologie," *Etudes Franciscaines,* XVIII (1907), pp. 234–58.

Reilly, G. C., "St. Thomas and the Problem of Knowledge," *The Thomist,* XVII (1954), pp. 510–24.

Renard, H., "The Problem of Knowledge in General," *The Modern Schoolman,* XXIV (1946–47), pp. 1–11.

Ruja, H., "On the Possibility of Knowledge," *The New Scholasticism,* XI (1937), pp. 237–46.

Russell, B., *Human Knowledge: Its Scope and Limits,* Simon and Schuster, New York, 1948.

Ryan, J. H., "The Approach to the Problem of Knowledge," *The New Scholasticism,* II (1928), pp. 18–28.

Searles, H. L., "The Revolt Against Epistemology," *Proceedings,* XIth International Congress of Philosophy, II (1953), North-Holland Publishing Co., Amsterdam, pp. 11–16.

Smith, W., "Knowledge," *Mind,* N.S., IV (1895), pp. 489–505.

Toohey, J. J., "The Starting Point of Epistemology," *The New Scholasticism,* VI (1932), pp. 95–107.

Tymieniecka, A. T., "Toward the Formulation of a Fundamental Epistemology," *Philosophy and Phenomenological Research,* XVIII (1957), pp. 88–95.

Wood, L., "Inspection and Introspection," *Philosophy of Science,* VII (1940), pp. 220–28.

Part II : SENSE KNOWLEDGE

Y. R. Simon : AN ESSAY ON SENSATION

PROFESSOR *Yves R. Simon, of the Committee on Social Thought, University of Chicago, presents in his essay written especially for this volume, the mature reflections upon, and long familiarity with the role of senses in the acquisition of knowledge. The relation of object and sense power, the truth of sense knowledge, the role of the senses in scientific observation are here developed.*

• The worst difficulties of the present subject originate in our inability to achieve the experience of a sensation free from association with images, instinctive judgments, memories and thoughts. If it were possible for us to suspend, no matter how briefly, all such associated representations and processes, if it were possible to elicit pure sensations and yet to watch ourselves sensing, the understanding of sensation would, no doubt, be greatly facilitated. But sensation is the center of a complex, and from this complex it cannot be extracted, except by rational analysis.[1] Experientially considered, sensations always exist in the vital unity of wholes. By reason of this unity, we attribute to senses the apprehension of things which are neither sense qualities nor modes of sense qualities. Thus, the proposition, "I see the father of our friend" does not look like falsehood or nonsense. With equal sincerity we would say, "I smell ammonia," or "I touch scar tissue." Yet such a system of relations as "father of a friend," such a natural species as "ammonia," such an effect of accident and nature as "scar tissue," are things in the apprehension of which memory, imagination, instinct, animal intelligence and understanding obviously play decisive roles.

It is good usage to call "perception" the complex act by which these things are apprehended and "sensation" the act, whatever its nature may be, which lies at the core of perception and makes the difference between having and not having things present in sense experience. This difference is of fundamental significance in daily thought and in philosophic consideration as well. I can imagine my mother vividly, remember many events concerning her and achieve—better, perhaps, than when she was alive and present—an intelligent grasp of her personality. But the thing that I am stubbornly denied is the privilege of seeing her, of hearing her voice, of holding her hand; in the words of a poet, "and, oh,/The difference to me!" *The study of sensation is, so to say, the study of this difference.*

Two contrasts will help to express the basic difficulties raised by the immeasurable distance that we experience between sensing an object and merely imagining, or remembering, or understanding it: the contrast of the physical and the psychical and the contrast of cognition and affection.

---

[1] Bertrand Russell, *Journal of Philosophical Studies,* 1 (London: Macmillan, 1926), p. 79: " 'Sensation,' as opposed to perception, is more or less hypothetical. It is supposed to be the core, in the perception, which is solely due to the stimulus and the sense-organ, not to past experience. When you judge that the table is rectangular, it is past experience that enables and compels you to do so; if you had been born blind and just operated on, you could not make this judgment. . . . From an introspective point of view, the elements due to past experience are largely indistinguishable from those due to the stimulus alone. . . . The notion of sensation as opposed to perception belongs, therefore, to the causal study of perception, not to the introspective study."

Is sensation a psychical process? More precisely, is it a *distinct* psychical process? This question has been stated by most modern philosophers in the framework of Cartesian dualism. A negative answer was, accordingly, inevitable, for, in Descartes, whatever is not extension is spirit, and if an operation does not consist in a movement, it is a thought of some kind. Thus, any component of sensation which proves irreducible to local motion belongs to the world of thought, where it occupies a low rank. Sensation, as a psychical reality, is not possessed of a distinct nature. It is a confused and unreliable thought.[2] How this act of thought is related to the mechanistic processes which are said to take place in sense organs is one of the greatest difficulties of Cartesian dualism.

The second contrast is best approached by comparing, among objects of knowledge, those which can stir affection with those which cannot. Mathematical entities cannot stir affection because they involve a condition incompatible with real existence.[3] True, it is possible to bring about in the real world things called circles or cubes, but these are physical things, circular or cubic. Mathematical entities are neither good nor bad, and final causality plays no part in mathematics. It is possible to love mathematical sciences—many people do—and it is possible to hate them. But there is nothing desirable, or undesirable, about the mathematical objects themselves. Knowledge is a system of formal causality which may retain all its meaning and worth when it is, as in mathematics, dissociated from any system of final causes.

On the contrary, where there is affection, some good or evil condition is referred to in an essential manner. Whatever is affected is moved toward its final cause or away from it. The question is whether the sentient, as such, bears this characteristic of the affected subject. Indeed some sensations, viz., physical pleasure and pain, are commonly described as affective, and concerning the other sensations the least that can be said is that they do not exist without an affective tone of great significance. What takes place in me when I watch the sun rising is certainly not of the same affective nature as, say, the pleasure of resting after an exhausting walk; yet the contemplation of the rising sun, taken in its psychological con-

[2] Confused and unreliable if it is expected to let us know what things are, but "sufficiently clear and distinct" (*Meditation* VI), and dependable insofar as it yields information about the useful or harmful effects of surrounding agents upon our bodies. The deceptiveness of sensation is held compatible with the truthfulness of God, "for using the senses in order to know is using them for a purpose that God did not intend them to serve." Etienne Gilson, *René Descartes, Discours de la méthode, Texte et commentaire* (Paris: Vrin, 1939), p. 367.

[3] Aristotle, *Met.* 3. 2. 996a29; 13. 3. 1078a31; St. Thomas, *Sum. theol.* i. 5. 3 ad 4; Cajetan, on this text; John of St. Thomas, *Cursus theologicus* i, disp. 6, a. 2, Ed. Solesme, vol. 1, 532 ff. Although mathematical objects do not admit of goodness, they admit of beauty. Indeed, they are famous for their beauty, and more than ever among contemporary mathematicians. They cannot stir affection, but they do stir admiration.

creteness, involves an affective state which may attain high intensity. We are not asking whether affection is a thing of importance in our sensorial relation to the world: this question obviously calls for an affirmative answer.[4] Rather, we want to know whether the feature by reason of which to see and touch is a thing so much different from imagining, remembering or understanding boils down to a way of being affected or includes irreducibly an act of cognition.

*

* *

Considered in terms of change, sensing is first of all describable as a way of *being acted upon,* a way of undergoing influences from the physical environment, a sort of passion. But let it be remarked at once that a process involving passivity is not necessarily exclusive of activity. To say that the sentient undergoes the influences of stimuli and objects is by no means to suggest that sensation is merely a passion. A subject may well be passive in one respect and in another respect exercise an activity of its own.

Further, "to be acted upon" admits of two meanings. There are two kinds of passivity, which are unequal as well as qualitatively different, for they embody in diverse degrees the essence of undergoing, of being acted upon, of being passive, of being subjected to external influence. There are cases in which the determination received is incompatible with the determination previously possessed. When this occurs, passion has the character of a disturbance; it is a complex event in which the loss of a state is a necessary and essential condition for the acquiring of a new state. Suppose that a sculptor, being short of clay for a bust of Queen Elizabeth, uses the material out of which a bust of Queen Victoria was made: the form that is being induced displaces an actually existent form, and it is by essential necessity, not by accident, that displacement occurs. All over physical nature the law of displacement prevails. Human life does not escape this law, and much can be learned by inquiring into the reasons why men resent it so bitterly. By the law of complex becoming and displacement, a destruction is the price of every new perfection. Choice, in this world, involves sacrifice. Every departure is an image of death. Our lives are spent fighting our way through never-ending series of incompatibilities. The remarkable thing is that we dislike so much a state of affairs which is so obviously natural.

In Aristotle's words the more determinate sense of the expression "to

[4] A. N. Whitehead, *Adventures of Ideas* (New York: The American Library, 1955), p. 182. "It must be distinctly understood that no prehension, even of bare sensa, can be divested of its affective tone, that is to say, of its character of a 'concern' in the Quaker sense. Concernedness is of the essence of perception."

be acted upon" refers to the destruction of one contrary by the other: this remark is strikingly borne out by the fact that in various languages the words meaning passivity generally connote suffering. But the passion involved in sensing is not a destruction; rather, it is the maintenance, the progress, the salvation of the passive subject under the influence of a friendly agent which resembles the patient as act resembles the ability to be in act.[5] When the sense opens to the world of physical appearances, what it receives is its own actualization, its own perfection, its own fulfillment according to its own law. Think of a blind person who recovers sight: his sense is acted upon, indeed, by a host of colored spots; thanks to this welcome invasion, a subject naturally able to be in act of vision, but accidentally prevented from exercising his natural ability, becomes what his nature wants him to be. The possibility of being acted upon by the colors and shapes and the other visible properties of the world gives him a chance to be what he is. In this distinguished way of being acted upon, the passive subject is changed into itself. St. Thomas uses the expression "passion properly so-called" to designate the "being acted upon" which implies a complex change, a displacement of form by form and a destruction. He uses the expression "passion improperly so-called" to designate the "being acted upon" which consists in a simple accomplishment and a pure progress. The passion properly so-called may also be described as heteronomic, and the passion improperly so called as *autonomic*.

The first tenet of Aristotle's doctrine on the senses is that sensation is an *autonomic passion*. To ascertain this proposition, good method demands that inquiry be focussed on the most difficult cases, viz., on situations where a passion of the heteronomic type asserts itself conspicuously and seems to constitute the whole state of affairs. Near the fireplace, cold

[5] *On the Soul*, 2. 5. 417b2. "Also the expression 'to be acted upon' has more than one meaning; it may mean either (a) the extinction of one of two contraries by the other, or (b) the maintenance of what is potential by the agency of what is actual and already like what is acted upon, with such likeness as is compatible with one's being actual and the other potential. For what possesses knowledge becomes an actual knower by a transition which is either not an alteration of it at all (being in reality a development into its true self or actuality) or at least an alteration in a quite different sense from the usual meaning." Tr. by J. A. Smith, *The Basic Works of Aristotle* (New York: Random House, 1941). On the subject of the diverse meanings and degrees of passivity, many references are found in the excellent book of Matthias Meier, *Die Lehre des Thomas von Aquino De passionibus animae in quellenanalytischer Darstellung* (Münster i. W., Aschendorff, 1912, *Beiträge zur Geschichte der Philosophie des Mittelalters*. Bd. XI. Hft. 2). Notice that the division of passion, both in Aristotle and in St. Thomas, is sometimes bipartite and sometimes tripartite. Three members are distinguished by subdivision of heteronomic passion into the case in which the loss does not outweigh the gain—designated by the common expression "passion properly so-called"—and the case in which it does—"passion most properly so-called" in the language of St. Thomas. All emotions are, by reason of the physiological disturbances which are part of their essence, passions properly so-called; but whereas joy is only a passion properly so-called, sadness is a passion most properly so-called (*passio propriissime dicta*).

hands and feet soon become warm, and whichever way we interpret such notions as those of cold and heat, it is clear that a state has been displaced by another state. The presence of a heteronomic passion is obvious, but the relevant question is whether this passion constitutes sensation. Just consider that the same heteronomic passion takes place in the garment, in the dead leather of the shoes, in the dead wood of the chair, and would take place in a corpse. *Sensation begins where heteronomic passion ends.* More precisely, it begins when undergoing the influence of the environment no longer amounts to a mere displacement of forms. In the case of touch, e.g., in sensations of heat or pressure, the concomitant heteronomic passion may be held more conspicuous and, so to say, more voluminous than the autonomic passion itself; yet, the latter is what makes all the difference between, say, what happens in inanimate things exposed to the heat of the fireplace and what happens in the living flesh where the warmth not only displaces the cold but also is sensed.[6]

In the example just considered, the presence of an alteration concomitant to sensation is particularly obvious. The question must be asked whether in all kinds of sensation an alteration, or heteronomic passion of the organ accompanies the autonomic passion of the sense. To this question all our experience suggests an answer in the affirmative. Some ancient philosophers were deceived by the crudeness of their experimental approach. St. Thomas believes that there is no alteration of the sensorial organs in the highest senses, viz., sight and hearing.[7] True, the chemical

[6] The strongly asserted presence of the heteronomic passion in touch has, no doubt, something to do with two well-known characteristics of touch sensations: on the one hand, they are rough, clumsy, generally unable to achieve fine discrimination. On the other hand, they enjoy unique certitude. When we wonder whether what we apprehend is physical reality or illusion, we trust our hands more than our sight or hearing. The remarks of Aristotle about delicate touch as a condition of subtle understanding seem to mean that when discrimination is coupled with certitude the best sensorial conditions of understanding are realized. (*On the Soul,* 2. 9. 421a19.)

[7] *Sum. theol.* i. 78. 3. In this article St. Thomas attempts to explain each external sense in philosophical, i.e., ontological, terms. Thus, sight is defined as the sense which is actuated by a purely spiritual change (*immutatio spiritualis*) without there being any concomitant physical change, either on the part of the organ or on the part of the object; in hearing there is physical change on the part of the object, but still none on the part of the organ. . . . Much can be learned from the failure of this attempt to define ontologically the senses considered in their specific particularity. No doubt, it is possible to define philosophically the external sense and it is possible to express philosophically the division of the external senses into higher and lower. But to achieve further specification, e.g., to define sight or hearing, it seems necessary to use nonphilosophical ways of understanding and conceptualizing. The explanation of the five senses by St. Thomas is a distinguished example of what Professor Maritain called the "philosophical imperialism" of the ancient philosophers of nature. So long as philosophers were insufficiently aware of the possibilities open to the nonphilosophical analysis of nature they were badly tempted to decide by philosophic ways issues which, if decidable at all, have to be treated by the methods of nonphilosophic sciences.

The proposition that there is no physical alteration in sight is also expressed by St. Thomas

changes that light causes in the retina are alterations, no less certainly than the displacement of cold by warmth. But to be aware of chemical changes in the retina philosophers need methods of inquiry more refined than those provided by common experience.

Just as the concept of autonomic passion expresses the difference between sensation and the common ways of being passive, so the concept of immanent action distinguishes the act of sensing from the ways of activity that commonly belong to things of nature.

The opposition between immanent and transitive action[8] is described by Aristotle in an exposition whose context should be carefully noted, for it constitutes the best guaranty against likely misinterpretations. Aristotle is studying the relations of act and potency in terms of priority and posteriority. He has just declared that act is prior to potency from the standpoint of the final cause. Yet, a difficulty arises: the end sometimes seems to lie neither in the potency nor in the act, but in a result distinct from the act. The following text is the historic origin of all that the philosophers ever had to say about immanent action: "For some potencies, exercise is the ultimate thing, e.g., seeing is ultimate for sight, which does not elicit any product distinct from seeing itself. But with other potencies there is production of a thing, e.g., from the art of building there results not only the act of building but also a house. In the first case exercise is [unqualifiedly] the end of potency, and in the second case it is still more of an end than potency is. True, the action of building is in that which is built and it is brought into being, and exists, together with the house that is built. Thus, whenever there is production of a thing over and above the exercise of the potency, the act exists in the thing produced, as building in what is built, weaving in what is woven, and the same in other cases; universally, movement exists in the moved. On the contrary, when there is not production of a thing distinct from the act itself, the act remains within the potency, as vision in the seeing, contemplation in the contemplating, and life in the soul, and happiness also, for it is a kind of life."[9]

in his *Com. on Met.* 1, les. 1 (Ed. Cathala, 6). But in the *Com. on On Sense and Sensible Objects,* les. 4 (Ed. Pirotta, 51), he writes, in a discussion of Democritus, "since vision is not an act of the soul save through a corporeal organ, there is no reason for wonder if it is caused, in some way, by a corporeal passion: this does not mean that the corporeal passion itself is the same as vision."

[8] Aristotle has no names for the two kinds of action. St. Thomas uses paraphrases, *actio quae transit in exteriorem materiam, actio quae manet in agente.* The expression *actio immanens* appears, at the latest, a short time after St. Thomas, in the celebrated *Summa of the Whole Logic of Aristotle* (6. 2), of uncertain authorship and spuriously classified, under No. 48, among the *Opuscula* of St. Thomas.

[9] *Met.* 9. 8. 1050a23. Translation mine, in complete agreement with that of W. D. Ross so far as meaning is concerned.

This text can be summed up in a simple diagram:

Potency	Action	Effect
Sight	Seeing	
Art of building	Act of building	House

Immanent action would be insufficiently defined by saying that it is one whose effect remains within the agent.[10] The core of its definition is expressed, unmistakably though negatively, by saying that it is not related to any further result as a way is related to its end. Following Aristotle's words, the diagram comprises an empty box. And yet an immanent action may have effects. This is plainly the case in the examples used by Aristotle. The act of intellectual contemplation produces a concept. But contemplation does not have the character of a way leading to a concept, it does not exist for the sake of a concept, it does not *consist in* the production of a concept. Rather, it is the concept which exists for the sake of understanding: if we take so much trouble, sometimes over generations or centuries, working out definitions—i.e., unfolded concepts—it is because we want to understand better the object expressed by the concept and the definition. The teleological relation terminates in the act of understanding.[11]

Sensation produces nothing that could be likened to a concept, although it leaves behind itself a variety of effects, the most obvious of which is the lasting impression which we call image or memory. But sensation does not *consist in* the production of an impression capable of being activated later: it is an activity by itself and independent of what it leaves behind it. If, contrary to general opinion, there existed sensations unproductive of any image or memory, these would still be as genuine as

[10] Any action which *consists in* the production of an effect is transitive, whether its effect resides in an external subject or remains within the agent. In the latter case what is immanent is the effect rather than the action itself. The operations of vegetative life, precisely considered as vital, do not purely and simply consist in the production of effects: inasmuch as there is in them something qualitative which transcends the sheer production of an effect, they would not be adequately described as transitive actions terminating inside the substantial whole where they originate. It is worth noticing, however, that in St. Thomas and his great commentators immanent action is always exemplified by acts of cognition (to see, to understand, to know) or appetition (to will, to love), never by vegetative operations such as nutrition and growth.

[11] The relation between the act of understanding and the utterance of concepts is explained with incomparable lucidity by John of St. Thomas, *Cursus philosophicus*, *Phil. nat.*, iv. 11. 1 and 2.

any others, even though their function in animal and human life would be quite different. To be sure, it cannot be said that the sensation of a red spot is related to the image or memory of this spot as the act of building is related to the house. Again, what makes the difference is not whether the box of the effect is full or empty. It is the character and meaning of the finality relations involved in the actions. The act of building is altogether for the sake of the inhabitable house. Sensation, no matter how significant its traces may be, is not exhausted and is not intelligibly constituted by the production of traces. It has a nature of its own and a worth of its own as a qualitative accomplishment which is the fundamental actualization of animal life.

Inasmuch as it does not consist in the production of a change, the immanent act of sensing is an instance of motionless activity. No doubt, sensation is surrounded with, and entirely dependent upon, change: its organ is modified by the action of the stimuli, the sensorial environment is ceaselessly changing, and a forcible attempt at immobility impairs sensing. Yet, if only we bear in mind the characteristics of activities by way of motion, it is easy to understand that sensation, no matter how imperfectly, exists in a condition of rest.

To shape wood into a chair is absolutely nothing else than to bring about definite changes in a definite matter. The act of the carpenter, which coincides with the becoming of his work, is, by essence, a thing fluent and unfinished which belongs to the past as soon as it is completed, as soon as what was intended is obtained. When the chair is finished, the carpenter may start working toward another chair, or do something else, or be idle; the thing that he cannot do is to keep bringing about changes in a thing that is assumed to be completed. Or, to use the most simple example, it is impossible to carry a thing to a certain place when the thing is already in that place. Neither is it possible to discourse toward a conclusion when the conclusion is already established, nor to keep striving toward an object of desire when this object is present and actually enjoyed. But contemplation implies the actual grasp of truth, and joy the actual possession of the good, whereas it is possible to love both things present and things absent. Love exists both in movement and in rest; contemplation and joy are, by essence, above movement. Shaping, walking, learning, building are acts of imperfect subjects, i.e., acts of subjects which have not yet attained their ends. But suppose that we want to see what there is on the other side of a hill: when we have climbed up to the vantage point we may stay there and contemplate the scenery as leisurely as we please. The fact that we have been seeing this scenery for a while in no way excludes the possibility of looking at it for another while. But, having climbed up to the vantage point, we no longer can be climbing toward the same point. Such is the difference between move-

63   Y. R. Simon

ment and sensation. Unlike movement, sensation is an activity by way of rest. It is the first image of eternal life.[12]

In order to understand how autonomic passivity and immanent activity are related in sensation, let us now consider the character of presence which, as recalled, distinguishes so sharply the object of sensation from such objects as those of imagination and memory. A familiar example will help to clarify the meaning of this issue.

At night and in a silent place a friend is walking away. For a while we can hear the sound of his steps, but the time soon comes when we no longer know whether we are still hearing these sounds or only imagining and remembering them. Until he comes back, and perhaps throughout our life, we shall remember our listening to these steps, remember this last experience of a presence that nothing can replace. Again, we never knew exactly when presence and experience came to an end; it is true that a weak sensation and an image may be, on their borderline, empirically undistinguishable. Yet, there is a world of qualitative difference between them. It is also true that vivid images convey a feeling of presence. Dreams are sometimes cherished as the only things that can bring relief to the sufferings of prolonged separation. What they procure is a soothing illusion. The vivid image of dream may imitate successfully the intuitiveness of sensation. But, far from blurring the distinction between sensation and its imaginative likeness, acquaintance with illusion is of help in understanding that the object of sense experience is characterized by a unique sort of presence, by a presence unqualifiedly asserted.

The notion of presence admits of degrees, and an object may be said to be present in a variety of ways. Let us survey the main kinds of presence, beginning with the weakest, the most qualified. An object devoid of real existence, devoid of real possibility and afflicted with internal contradiction, may be said to be present to the mind, and, in this weakest of all kinds of presence, it may significantly contribute to the establishment of truth. To understand, for instance, that the "best possible world" is a contradictory fiction is a valuable step in the theory of evil. Next to such contradictions come the beings of reason whose constitution is in no way contradictory, even though it would be contradictory to represent them as capable of real existence. Such are the second intentions which make up the object of logic. There is nothing contradictory about the notions of subject, predicate and middle term; but attributing a real existence to the property of being a middle term would imply contradiction, for such

---

[12] Aristotle, *Met.* 9. 6. 1048b30. "For it is not true that at the same time a thing is walking and has walked, or is building and has built, or is coming to be and has come to be, or is being moved and has been moved, but what is being moved is different from what has been moved, and what is moving from what has moved. But it is the same thing that at the same time has seen and is seeing, or is thinking and has thought." Tr. by W. D. Ross, *The Basic Works of Aristotle* (New York: Random House, 1941).

properties accrue to things by reason of the second existence that they assume as objects of intelligent consideration. Next to the beings of reason come various conceptions and constructions whose possibility cannot be determinately negated although their existence cannot be established. Many can be found in the hypotheses of physical science. Then come the things—e.g., dinosaurs—whose real possibility is certain, although they are out of actual existence. Then come the things whose actual existence is known with certainty, but indirectly, i.e., through an inference or a testimony. But actual existence would not admit of indirect ascertainment; it could not be inferred or believed in, if it had not first been grasped directly. At the basis of all our cognition of things existent, possible or fictitious, there is an act which implies in essential manner the physical presence of its object.[13]

Considering, again, the example of the steps in the night, I understand very well what it means to say that we do not know exactly when sensation ceases and imagination alone remains active. These two may be empirically undistinguishable in the vicinity of their borderline; they nevertheless constitute types whose intelligible diversity is unmistakable. By saying that I do not know when sensation came to an end and imagination alone remained at work, I imply that, at an indeterminable moment, my relation to the sounds of the steps was no longer caused by the physical action of the sounding steps upon my sense organs. The most successful popularizer of psychology in the nineteenth century (Taine) attracted some attention with the paradox that perception is an hallucination which turns out to be true (*une hallucination vraie*). Clearly, hallucination and the complex called perception have much in common; in both of them an assertion of existence is involved, but in the case of perception alone the relation to existence is established by the physical action of a present object, which makes much difference. This action and this presence

---

[13] This constant tenet of Aristotelian doctrine is powerfully treated by John of St. Thomas in the discussion of the following problem: Is it in the power of God to cause sensation actually to exist when its object is absent? Suarez answers affirmatively: he does not see any reason why God could not maintain in the sensory faculty the form of an object which is no longer present; in such a case sensation would have become an abstractive cognition, but it would still be a genuine sensation. According to John of St. Thomas, sensation is essentially experiential, and it is contradictory to speak of a sensation relative to an absent object. The reason why the physical presence of its object pertains to the essence, the specific identity of sensation, is that the external senses are ultimate in the system of human faculties. Whether we inquire into the origin of our cognitions or carry out their analysis, the sensorial power is absolutely terminal, and there is nothing beyond it. Hence this disjunction: either sensation is essentially relative to things present, or the soul never reaches physically existent objects. But in the latter case the whole system of human cognition is devoid of certitude. (*Cursus philosophicus, Phil. nat.* iv. 6. 1; Ed. Reiser, vol. 3, 170 ff.) We recognize here the central intuition expressed in a variety of ways by empiricist philosophies, and thus we are led to understand that it is possible to preserve this intuition and to get the best out of it without the interpretations, negations and systematizations which define empiricism.

pertain essentially to sensation, and sensation is the core of perception. It is by reason of this action and presence that perception and hallucination are set in contrast as truth and illusion. But then the paradox of sensation described as a particular case of hallucination disappears into meaninglessness. Suppose that in a party comprising a number of reliable witnesses, one person declares that he hears a frightening noise—say, that of heavy balls rolling, or of chains being dragged, on the upper floor—when all others certify that silence is complete; suppose, further, that the fellow who claims to hear things not heard by anyone else presents a set of symptoms frequently associated with hallucinations. Let us ask what we imply as we oppose the reliable testimony of the normal persons to the utterances of the psychotic. True, it is not impossible that balls should roll or a chain be dragged on the upper floor about midnight; if such is the case, sensation occurs under the physical influence of these noise-making things. But the victim of hallucinations attributes to objects whose presence is not physical and unqualified (it is merely imagined) the same meaning, the same relation to existence and experience, as the normal person does to things physically present and in act of physical influence upon the organs of sense.

From all this it follows that sensation is an incomplete form of immanent action.[14] The immanent act of the sensorial power strictly coincides with the transitive action exercised by the stimuli and the objects upon the senses and their organs. It is one and the same act which is immanent on the part of the sense and transitive on the part of the thing that is sensed.[15] To interpret these as distinct acts would be to deprive the sensed object of the characteristics of physical presence and of physical activity which constitute the hard core of our experience. An immanent act of sensing which would not be at the same time a transitive action of the thing sensed would no longer be an experience; it would become the most suspicious of all abstractive processes. Abstraction is an operation validly exercised upon the data of antecedent experience, but if the immanent act of sensing did not coincide with the transitive action of a physically present thing, sensation would disappear into the fictitious entity of an abstraction exercised on no previous experimental data.

Let us now focus our inquiry on sensation considered as the *union* of a thing alive with some aspect of its environment. We have described a

---

[14] Aristotle, *On the Soul,* 2. 5. 416b33; 417b20; 11. 423b31; 12. 424a17; 3. 2. 425b26; *On Sense and Sensible Objects,* 2. 438b22; St. Thomas, *Sum. theol.* i. 27. 5. ". . . the act of sensation . . . cannot be reckoned as wholly removed from the sphere of external actions; for the act of sensation is perfected by the action of the sensible thing upon sense." Tr. by A. C. Pegis (New York: Random House, 1945).

[15] Aristotle, *On the Soul,* 3. 2. 425b26. "The activity of the sensible object and that of the percipient sense is one and the same activity." Tr. by J. A. Smith, *The Basic Works of Aristotle* (New York: Random House, 1941).

contrast between the passivity of the sense and the common ways of being passive, and another contrast between the act of sensing and the common ways of being active. These descriptions suggest that it is worth determining whether there is a corresponding contrast between the union of the sense with its object and the common ways in which a subject unites with a state or quality.

A more precise statement of this problem can be derived from the analogy of intelligence. So far as intellectual knowledge is concerned, it is a familiar fact that 'to be such and such' and 'to know a thing which is such and such' are immensely different conditions, which indeed may, but also may not, accompany each other. A man well acquainted with Spanish culture may be a Spaniard, but it is also possible to know Spanish culture without being, in any way, a part of the Spanish world. It is fitting for a Moslem to be learned in the dogmas of his religion, but it is possible to be a Moslem scholar without belonging to the Islamic faith. An expert in the things of the theatre may happen to be a dramatist or an actor, but he may just as well be a critic who never thought of writing a play or appearing on the stage. Without begging the question of the ultimate relation between to know and to be, it can be safely said that the diversity between knowing and the common ways of being ranks as a primary fact in the philosophy of knowledge.

The problem of *union* with which we are concerned now can be stated as follows: Bearing in mind the diversity which obviously holds between 'to be such and such' and 'to understand the meaning of being such and such,' in other words, the diversity of sheer existence and intellectual apprehension, we are wondering whether a corresponding diversity holds in the case of sensation. What distinguishes knowing from being is that whereas the known object retains its otherness and the knowing subject its identity, a subject which acquires a state or quality in the world of sheer existence becomes other than it was. An Englishman who becomes a Spanish scholar does not thereby lose any of the English ways, nor does he necessarily acquire any Spanish manners. In his scholarly progress, which is one of pure knowledge, he remains what he is, and the thing that he comes to know remains something else than what he is. There is union between the scholar and the object of his scholarship, but it is an altogether objective union. Quite different is the case of an Englishman who settles in a Spanish country, changes his language and undergoes assimilation to the Spanish environment. Here, a certain identity is replaced by another identity, and union with the thing which is such and such affects the subject in its subjectivity. What used to be an Englishman has become a Spaniard. This is a *subjective* union. Since it is the kind of union which characterizes the relation of form and matter, it is most precisely described as a matter-form union. What we want to know is whether sensation is a matter-form union or, like understanding, a union of the objective type. Greater precision can be obtained by bringing in the celebrated formulas of Averroes: in the matter-form union the things united merge into a whole, a compound, a third thing made of a matter and a form, but in the objective union the things united remain face to face and do not give birth to any third thing, and this is, in the words of Averroes, the reason why the objective union is the most intimate of all.[16] What we want to know is whether sensation, like understanding, leaves a subject and an object face to face and free from merger into any compound.

Let us consider first the sense of sight which, by its excellence at getting information and effecting precise discriminations, is closest to the understanding. Here, it is clear that the union between the sense and what is sensed is of the objective description. It would be extremely arbitrary to hold that to see a blue spot is to merge with the blue color into a new blue thing and that to perceive a multitude of red spots is to merge with those spots into a compound characterized by redness and multiplicity. Things may be deemed more obscure in the case of touch, which is, so to say, the opposite of sight in the system of the senses. The hand exposed to the heat of the fireplace becomes hot, and the hand which holds a golf ball is shaped by the pressure of the hard thing inside it. These are obvious instances of matter-form union, in strict coincidence with the alterations, the heteronomic passions described in the foregoing. But the relevant fact is that the matter-form union, though a voluminous and conspicuous concomitant of sensation, is not sensation itself. The hard ball causes the hollow of the hand, and this is a matter-form union; but the hand senses the round of the ball, and this is a union of the objective type. The bad thing with anesthesia, i.e., the suppression of sensation, is that it allows matter-form unions which may be detrimental—e.g., in the case of burning heat or crushing pressure—to go on unnoticed. Sensation, which begins where heteronomic passion ends, also begins (from a slightly different standpoint) where the union is no longer of the matter-form type: this holds as certainly in the case of touch and smell as in the case of hear-

---

[16] Averroes, *Major Commentary on Aristotle's On the Soul,* 3. 5. (The following translation is from the Latin text as established by F. Stuart Crawford [The Mediaeval Academy of America, Cambridge, Mass., 1953, 501–508], the Arabic original being lost.) "Thus, let us say that it is clear that man is not understanding in act except through the actual connection of the understood with him. It is also clear that matter and form unite with each other in such a way that what is made of them be one, and most of all the material intellect and the idea actually understood; for what is made of these is not a third thing other than them, as is the case with the other composites of matter and form." The expression "material intellect" stands for the power which Aristotle likens to matter and of which he says that it is "potentially all things." (*On the Soul,* 3. 5. 430 a 10); it is the understanding, as distinct from the power of abstraction and illumination called the active intellect. The word "idea" is taken here in its objective sense.

ing and sight. There is objectivity, union of the objective type, wherever there is sensation, although the relation of the sentient self to the physical self is widely different in the so-called lower senses—touch, taste, smell— from what it is in the so-called higher senses. Let it be said, in rough outline, that in the lower senses the physical self is, and in the upper senses is not, a part of the sensed object. When I rub my fingers on the edge of a board I feel both the pressure of the edge and the change brought about in my flesh by this pressure. The hand which firmly holds a golf ball senses the round of the ball indeed but also its own hollow. On the contrary, under the conditions that are best for distinct vision, one perceives colors and shapes without being aware of the changes brought about by light in the eye and the other parts of the visual organ. As I walk toward a beacon, I gradually become aware that something is going on in me, and I rub my eyes: from a great distance a beacon is merely an object of sight, from a short distance it is a cause of strongly felt contractions in the muscles of the eye. Touch, in all its variety, always involves proprio-ceptive sensations, whereas the sensations of sight and hearing are extero-ceptive.[17] For the present discussion, what is decisively important is that even in the proprio-ceptive sensation, i.e., in the sensation by which a thing alive is aware of its own physical self, a certain kind of objectivity is achieved. The physical self is the object of the proprio-ceptive sensation. Concealed as it is by the relation of the sentient self to the physical self, the objective union is as genuine here as anywhere else.

The questions asked in the introduction to this paper now have received an answer. Inasmuch as sensation is an autonomic passion, an immanent action and an objective union, it is a psychical, not a merely physical process. Its being an objective union further determines that it is a cognition rather than an affection. Finally, the physical presence and the

[17] These expressions are derived from the theory of reflexes worked out by Charles S. Sherrington, who divides the receptors of reflex actions into three fields: the extero-ceptive, made of the receptors stimulated from the outside, the intero-ceptive, made of receptors stimulated by bodies contained in the digestive track, and the proprio-ceptive, made of receptors adjusted to stimulations originating in the organism itself. "The deep tissues underlying the surface sheet are not provided with receptors of the same kinds as those of the surface, yet they are not devoid of receptors. . . . The receptors which lie in the depth of the organism are adapted for excitation consonantly with changes going on in the organism itself, particularly in its muscles and their accessory organs (tendons, joints, blood vessels, etc.). Since in this field the stimuli to the receptors are given by the organism itself, their field may be called the proprio-ceptive field." (*The Integrative Action of the Nervous System,* New Haven: Yale University Press, 1906, p. 130.) As Roland Dalbiez remarks (*Psychoanalytical Method and the Doctrine of Freud,* Tr. by T. F. Lindsay, London, New York, Toronto: Longmans, Green and Co., 1941, vol. 2, 18), "It is quite natural to model the division of sensations upon that of reflexes," and to speak of extero-ceptive, intero-ceptive and proprio-ceptive sensations. Philosophically, what matters is whether the stimulus and object of sensation does or does not belong to the physical self perceived as such, and the relevant division is bipartite, viz., into extero- and intero-ceptive sensations on the one hand, and proprio-ceptive sensations on the other.

transitivity which belong to the sense object demonstrate that sensation has a distinct nature as a cognition and cannot be reduced to any kind of thought or abstract representation.

It is in direct relation to the theory of sensation as objective union that the problem of how sensation is caused by external things is most fittingly brought in. Let us first recall what becomes of this problem in the Cartesian and dualistic framework which, for so many generations and under such a great diversity of circumstances, has exercised decisive control, whether outspokenly or silently, over psychological theories. A good statement of the case is found in the work of the psychologist Bourdon. Having written 126 pages on sensation from an experimental point of view, he found it necessary to write, by way of conclusion, four pages and a half on the "Philosophy of Sensation." These philosophic pages deserve never to be forgotten, for they contain these invaluable statements: "The emergence of sensation, as a consequence of stimulation, is unexplainable. If it is assumed that stimulation remains, as well as the stimulus itself, an essentially mechanical phenomenon, of the same nature for all senses, it is impossible, indeed, to understand how it can result in phenomena thoroughly different from each other and from movement, viz., smells, pressures, sounds, colors, etc., such as we sense them." [18] These are the words of an honest man. To be sure, mechanism, with its postulation of universal homogeneity, raises special difficulties whenever there is a question of accounting for any fact of qualitative diversity. But if, having discarded the postulations of mechanism (or, better, having confined them to the methodological role where they often proved so fruitful), we hold that the physical world comprises a real diversity of natures and of qualities, we still are confronted by an exceptionally difficult problem of causality. Briefly: assuming that we have in mind not the mechanistic world-picture of Descartes but one of Aristotelian type, to explain "the emergence of sensation as a result of stimulation" remains an arduous task. For no matter how qualitatively diverse smells, colors, pressures, etc. are held to be in the real world, physical qualities do not account directly for autonomic passions, immanent actions and unions of the objective type.

At this point, progress in the statement of the issue requires a comparison between sensation and abstract knowledge. Common language and diverse philosophies testify to our belief in the existence of entities whose primary function is not to *be,* but to *represent* something else than themselves. We use a variety of names to designate these entities: notions, representations, concepts, mental pictures, images, memories, ideas, etc. What is paradoxical about idealism, at least in its most classical forms, is

[18] B. Bourdon, *Nouveau Traité de Psychologie* par Georges Dumas (Paris: Alcan, 1932), vol. 2, 212.

that it causes the thing to disappear into the idea; yet, by common interpretation, the idea merely stands for the thing. To say that things reduce to their ideas is a paradox akin to the proposition that to be is nothing else than to be perceived. If such were the case, things, as Bertrand Russell puts it, would be possessed of "a jerky life," [19] and trains, in the words of G. E. Moore, would have no wheels except in stations.[20] At the center of the dialogue there is an ambiguity which, if properly managed, no longer causes confusion but effectively helps to manifest the relation between ideas and things and leaves little appeal to most idealistic philosophies.

The entities which we designate by such words as images, memories, ideas, etc. are two-sided. Their two-sidedness may be instrumental in producing endless illusion. What do we mean, for instance, when we speak of a memory? We may be designating a mode of the psyche, a psychological reality engaged in a context of psychological existence where it can be affected by such psychological occurrences as emotions, or by physiological accidents, such as brain injuries. Under the impact of a sudden and extreme sorrow, I may lose irretrievably the memory of an event: this has nothing to do with the reality of the event itself, which either has or has not taken place, regardless of what happens in the brain or the emotions of the witnesses. But "memory" may also designate the event that is remembered, as when I say that the destruction of my father's workshop by fire *is* the earliest of all my dated memories. The destruction of a workshop is not a psychological reality; it is the object represented by the psychological reality designated as a memory. True, we never hesitate to call memories events that no one, with the exception of the most radical among the idealists, ever thought of placing in the psyche. A big fire is said to *be* my first dated memory, and I like to describe as one of my happiest memories the meeting of a person who became a dear friend. Such is the double-sided character of memories, images, concepts, etc.[21] Inasmuch as these entities have a subjective side, they are modes of the psyche and pertain to psychology, but by their objective side they are one with their object. An objective concept, that is, a concept objectively understood, is an object of concept; it is that aspect of a thing which the mental reality, also called a concept, discloses and represents. If a physics teacher says, "Today, gentlemen, we are going to study the concept of energy," if a teacher of literature declares that he is going to work out the concept of classical tragedy, no one will suspect that these gentlemen have turned psychologists: clearly, they are using "concept" in the objective sense and what they intend to define is the object which is

[19] *A History of Western Philosophy* (New York: Simon and Shuster, 1945), p. 647.
[20] See Bertrand Russell, *Ibid.*, p. 657.
[21] Aristotle, *On Memory and Recollection,* 1. 450a25.

energy and the object which is classical tragedy. But if you are skillful at substituting the mental side of the concept for its objective side and vice versa at the appropriate moment, the proposition that thought never goes beyond its own concepts—understood, this time, in the subjective and psychological sense—assumes some degree of plausibility.[22]

The purpose of these remarks is to explain the great division of entities into things and ideas.[23] A thing may represent something else than itself; yet, what it does primarily is to exist, and representing is but, for a thing, a secondary and super-added function. In the words of an artist "a painting, prior to its being . . . any kind of anecdote, is essentially a plane surface covered by colors assembled in a certain order."[24] Before it exercises representation, a thing is a way of being; in this capacity, it enjoys an intelligibility of its own. But, for the idea, the function of representing is primary. An idea, considered psychologically, i.e., as distinct from the object itself, enjoys no intelligibility except in relation to the object that it stands for. The idea of energy makes no sense unless it is referred to energy, and the idea of classical tragedy is equally nonsensical if it is not referred to classical tragedy.

Within a great diversity of interpretations, most philosophers have asserted the existence of ideas in the intellect, where they are called ideas, notions, and concepts; in the imagination, where they are called images or representations; and in the memory, where they are called memories. Describing the development of mental life, from elementary sense impressions to the most abstract concepts and arrangements of concepts, is a job that has been done with brilliancy by several philosophical psychologists. Strikingly, quite a few of them take the sense impression for granted, and their skillful analyses begin with the evolution which leads from the data of sensation to images capable of entering into a multiplicity of combinations. *But how did the sense impression get there?* This is a question that many like to dodge. How is communication primarily established between the mind and physical nature? As soon as a content has been provided by sense experience, a plausible description of the mind's development, up to the loftiest ways of thought, can be worked out in a system which claims to be nothing but empiricism. Yet the sense impressions have to be taken for granted, the communication between

---

[22] See Bertrand Russell's discussion of Berkeleyan idealism in *The Problems of Philosophy* (New York: Henry Holt, 1912), pp. 62–63. ". . . there is a confusion engendered by the use of the word 'idea.' We think of an idea as essentially something *in* somebody's mind, and thus when we are told that a tree consists entirely of ideas, it is natural to suppose that, if so, the tree must be entirely in minds. But the notion of being 'in' the mind is ambiguous. We speak of bearing a person in mind, not meaning that the person is in our minds, but that a thought of him is in our minds."

[23] Cajetan on *Sum. theol.*, i. 55. 3.

[24] Maurice Denis, *Théories* (Paris: L. Rouart and J. Watelin, 1920), p. 1.

the mind and physical nature is left unexplained, and few are so frank as to say, like Bourdon, that it is unexplainable. Working toward an explanation of what is absolutely initial in mental development, working toward an intelligible interpretation of the first relationship between the mind and physical nature, is the most indispensable, as well as the most difficult part of the philosophy of sensation.

To the question, "How did sense impressions get there?" a typical answer was given by Epicurus and his school.[25] A simulacrum is a tiny duplicate of a big thing. Owing to its small dimensions, this duplicate is capable of subtleties that the big external thing never could accomplish by itself. The small images that things continually emit find their way through the pores of the skin and reach the group of distinguished atoms which is called the soul. Sense impressions are accounted for by the presence, inside the soul, of likenesses which substitute for the things external. Concerning the nature of these likenesses, the decisive question is whether they are ideas or things. The exposition of Lucretius and the historic role of Epicureanism make it impossible to doubt that the simulacra are things, not ideas. They are little things which marvelously resemble the big things. They belong to the family of paintings, pictures, portraits, photographs, miniatures. But then they cannot do anything that a thing is unable to do. The explanation of sensation by simulacra raises difficulties which can be summed up as follows: Does the presence of a thing inside a thing account for an autonomic passion? Does it account for an immanent action? Above all, does it account for an objective union? Clearly, the miniature of a red spot, if it is supposed to penetrate into the eye, the optic nerve and the brain, causes an alteration of the visual organ; but this is a heteronomic passion. The movement of this miniature is the transitive action of the environment upon the sentient body; it is not the immanent act of sensing. And the alteration of an organ results in a union of the matter-form type. Unwillingness to press these questions and readiness to ignore what is specific about such facts as autonomic passion, immanent action and objective union could serve to define the Epicurean brand of materialism. The decision not to bother about explaining these *uncommon* facts is contained in the all-embracing proposition that the soul, after all, is but a group of particularly smooth and quickly moving atoms.[26]

[25] Lucretius, *On Nature*, iv.

[26] The historic significance of the Epicurean theory is forcefully expressed by V. Jankélévitch, in his exposition and defense of Bergson's views on sensation. "Bergsonism ranks very highly 'the sense of the real' and truly supplies the philosophical vindication of realism. Bergson never tires of saying that 'pure' perception is faithful, that, if left to itself, it would place us in the midst of things, and that, *de jure*, it belongs to matter. The problem of its 'genuineness' does not even exist, it is a pseudo-problem raised by the subjectivistic relativism which first appears in Hobbes and is connected with what we would like to call the theory

Concerning the origin of sensation, Aristotelian interpretations sometimes were thought to be akin to those of the Epicureans, and the worst is
that the blame for such a shocking confusion cannot be put entirely on
misreading and prejudice. The Epicureans explain sensation by the reception of a likeness of the object which they call simulacrum, in Greek,
εἴδωλον. Aristotle and his school explain sensation by the reception of a
likeness of the object which they call εἶδος, in Latin, *species*. Between
the two Greek words the kinship is obvious; further, the Aristotelian
theory, whose development was arrested, at the very latest, in the 17th
century, remained surrounded by illusions which never allowed it to unfold itself with unmistakable clarity and consistency.

*Aristotelianism is the philosophy which places ideas not only in the in-
tellect, the memory and the imagination, but also in the external senses.*[27]

of the miniature. Just as thought, according to parallelism, is merely a transcription of
cerebral language, so cerebral motions would represent, as it were, in miniature, the simultaneous events which unfold in external reality. But how is the projection of this cerebral
miniature effected? On this point, opinions diverge and theories have become gradually more
complicated. Since the ancient theory of the simulacra, sensible emanations have undergone
more and more subtle deformations. For instance, in the system of 'critical idealism,' whatever has a character of externality is so effectively filtered by the *a priori* that the mind
gathers only 'phenomena.' Perception thus becomes a radical alteration as the macrocosm
is transformed into a 'brain phenomenon.' The nervous system, instead of remaining the
instrument, the organ, which connects us with the external world, becomes a screen which
insures our isolation from it. Perception lies, and science is only the well-organized system
of its lies. This is how cerebral idealism inevitably entails skepticism. At the root of subjectivism there is also the postulation that things external leave small size records of themselves in the brain, and that it is theoretically possible to find the things external in the brain,
complete indeed though highly condensed, by way of traces or 'engrams,' just as a photographer watches, in his finder, the miniature of the complete landscape. . . . To explain
how the macrocosm got into the brain, the theory of the miniature thus anticipates the
subjective elaboration and presupposes thought itself, although, by hypothesis, thought
should develop after the cerebral registering. . . ." *Bergson* (Paris: Alcan, 1931), pp. 133–
134. By courtesy of Presses Universitaires, Paris.

[27] Aristotelian inquiries into sensorial ideas (often designated by the expressions "sensible
intentional forms" or "sensible species") are centered about the well-known statement:
"Concerning each and every sense, it must be held that sense is that which is receptive of the
sensible forms without the matter, as wax receives the print of the signet ring without the
iron and the gold." *On the Soul,* 2. 12. 424a17. The comparison used is inevitably defective,
and what Aristotle really means is not easy to establish. As St. Thomas says (*On On the
Soul,* 2. les. 24, Ed. Pirotta, 551 ff), to receive the form without the matter seems to be
nothing else than what happens in any kind of passion. For, every agent acts in virtue of its
form, impresses in the patient a form similar to its own, and keeps its matter for itself.
What distinguishes reception by the sense from the common way of receiving, St. Thomas
goes on to say, is the special relation which obtains, in the case of sense, between the form
that is received and the subject that receives it: in an ordinary reception, the relation between the form received and the receiving subject is the same as the relation that obtains, in
the agent, between the same form and the agent's matter. Thus, together with the form
itself, an ordinary reception involves the communicating of a certain relation between form
and bearer, of a certain mode pertaining to the existence of the form in its subject [e.g.,
when a cold body placed near a warm body becomes itself warm, heat exists in the same
way in either body]. It is this *way of being* of the form in its subject which is not communicated by the action of the sensible upon the sense, for in the thing the sensible form

It is the philosophy which explains sensation by the daring theory that the first ideas are not generated in any part of the soul but in physical nature. It is the philosophy which bridges the gap between nature and mind by holding that some qualities of the natural world can assume, inside the senses, the capacity of ideas. Whereas the εἴδωλον of the Epicureans is a thing, a subtle one indeed and one capable of many tricks that ordinary things cannot do, the Aristotelian εἶδος is an idea and belongs to the distinct world of entities that images, memories, and concepts exemplify more clearly. One reason why modern expositions of the Aristotelian theory of sensation are generally unintelligible is that they use, to render the Greek εἶδος and the Latin *species,* words which suggest things rather than ideas. True, "idea" designates preferably intellectual representations, and still preferably representations conceived as the patterns of things to be brought into existence. Yet, our vernaculars allow the extension of the word "idea" to the whole set of the entities whose primary function is not to be but to represent. As soon as the division of entities into things and ideas is understood, the expression "sensorial idea" is no longer paradoxical. The εἶδος of Aristotle, the *species sensibilis* of the Schoolmen, is an idea which is to sense experience what an image is to an act of imagination, a memory to an act of remembrance, and an intellectual representation to an act of understanding. Let us think, again, of those systems of philosophic psychology where the most refined forms of human cognition are shown to derive from initial data that are sense impressions. Human knowledge purely and simply remains unexplained so long as there is no answer to the question, "How did sense impressions get there?" The Aristotelian answer is that just as remembering is made possible by two-sided realities that are called memories, so sensation is made possible by another instance of those two-sided realities whose primary function is not to be but to represent, and which are, in one way,

---

possesses a physical way of being, whereas in the sense it exists in an intentional and spiritual way [e.g., when the hand in contact with a warm body senses the heat, the difference between this and a sheer process of warming is that the heat does not bear the same relation to the sensorial power as it does to a warm body. The living hand exposed to a source of heat becomes hot indeed but it does not *just* become another hot body, and this makes all the difference between sense life and the privation of the same]. With his customary precision, Cajetan (*On On the Soul,* 2. 11., Ed. Coquelle (Rome: Apud Institutum Angelicum, 1939) vol. 2, sec. 262) remarks that the complement "without matter" can be related either to the adjective "receptive" or to the noun "forms"; the first interpretation, he says, is ambiguous, the second is not and should be preferred: what the sentence of Aristotle means is that the sense receives *immaterial forms;* in other words, forms are not material in the sense as they are in the thing.

A sensible form—say, a spot of color—existing in a subject *without* the form-to-matter relationship which characterizes its way of existing in the thing is what we mean by sensorial idea. It is the sensory quality itself in another way of being. An ample discussion of the reasons why ideas are needed in the sense and other cognitive powers is found in John of St. Thomas, *Cursus philosophicus, Phil. nat.,* iv. 6. 2., Ed. Reiser, vol. 3, 177 ff.

states of the psyche and in another way are the object that they stand for.

Indeed, Aristotelian texts on the subject of sensorial ideas are not unmistakably clear. The interpretation of "species" in terms of representative things can derive an illusory vindication from certain functions with which "species" were accidentally burdened, down to a recent past. Briefly: the experimental approach of the Aristotelians is macroscopic, and when things or physical influences are too small, or too numerous, to be perceived or at least imagined, it is readily inferred that the entities at work are not things but "species." The followers of Democritus and Epicurus, on the contrary, never feared that the things postulated by their systems might be too small in size or too large in number; this is one of the reasons why they are considered forerunners of modern science. But for St. Thomas Aquinas the fact that vultures are attracted from several miles by the smell of carrion proves that the "species" of smell are capable of travelling all by themselves without the help of any particles, for it seems unbelievable that carrion should emit particles to such distance in all directions without any noticeable decrease in size.[28] As already mentioned, St. Thomas also believes that there is no alteration—either on the part of the object or on the part of the organ—in sight sensations. Along the same line, John of St. Thomas says that when a sound is heard from the other side of a wall, the "species" alone go through the wall: sound waves, well known to medieval science,[29] would be stopped dead by such a hard obstacle.[30] These and other examples show that because of crudeness in observation, the "species" are entrusted with tasks which really belong to things. (Sound waves are things, no less certainly than particles.) Now, inasmuch as they are believed to exercise such functions the "species" are inevitably conceived, in some measure, after the pattern of things, and their meaning as ideas is somewhat blurred. But in our time the refined methods of scientific experience remove all temptation to burden sensorial ideas with duties pertaining to things. It was perhaps impossible to dissociate the Aristotelian notion of sensorial idea from counterfeits more or less reminiscent of Epicureanism so long as a microphysical approach did not do better justice to the power of things and physical influences.

Back to the example used at the beginning of this discussion, let it be said that when the hands placed near a heater get warm and feel the heat, this double effect calls for a double system of influence. Inasmuch as a thing which was cold becomes warm, there is production in it of a quality which is, itself, a kind of thing. But the autonomic passion of the sense, its immanent action, and its objective union with the sensed imply

[28] *On On the Soul*, 2. les. 20, Ed. Pirotta, 494.
[29] *Ibid.*, les. 16, Ed. Pirotta, 447.
[30] *Cursus philosophicus, Phil. nat.,* iv. 7. 3. Ed. Reiser, vol. 3, 217.

that the sensible quality is there not only in the state and capacity of thing but also in the state and capacity of idea. This double capacity of the sensible quality raises problems of causality to which philosophers have not given enough attention. Explaining how a hot body causes another body to become hot is hard enough; however, there is, beyond doubt, a proportion between this type of causal process and the way of being which pertains to the things of nature. Historic controversies abundantly evidence the difficulty of explaining how a physical thing sets another thing in motion, whether the motion be just local or belong to some other species of change. Yet the sheer fact that physical things, mutable things, exercise causality by way of motion is unquestioned, except in the most radical systems of occasionalism, which deny creatures all power of causation. But sensation is distinguished from common processes by features—autonomic passivity, immanent activity, and above all, objective unity—which imply that the sensible quality is produced in the sense according to ways at variance with those of motion. When a hand holds a hard ball tightly, the pressure of the ball, which is a case of causality by way of motion, accounts for the hollowness of the hand, but it does not explain that both the hollowness of the hand and the roundness of the ball unite *objectively* with the sense of touch. Few philosophers went deeply into this problem of causality. Among these few, some maintain that the things of nature, over and above causal ways proportionate to their own mode of being, enjoy a participation in the causal ways proper to spiritual substances. In the present state of the question, the most urgent task is to understand precisely why such a daring theory ever was held necessary.[31]

[31] The causal problem raised by the nonmaterial (objective, intentional) condition of sensory qualities in the sensorial power does not seem to have been treated by Aristotle. He who said that "the sense is that which is receptive of forms without matter" [i.e., of immaterial forms] did not say by what agency this condition of immateriality is produced. Averroes played a distinguished role in the history of this problem. See his *Major Commentary* on Aristotle's *On the Soul*, 2. sec. 60. (The text commented on is 5. 417b22.) "But one might say that it is not in the way in which they exist outside the soul that the sensibles move the sense; for they move the sense inasmuch as they are intentions, but in matter they are not intentions in act but in potency. It cannot be answered that this diversity results from a diversity of subjects, as if intentions came into existence because of the spiritual matter which is the sense, not because of an external mover. It is indeed better to hold that what causes diversity in matter is diversity on the part of the forms than to hold that the diversity of the forms is caused by diversity on the part of the matter. Accordingly, it is necessary to posit, in sensation, an external mover distinct from the sensible objects, as it was necessary in the case of the intellect. Thus, it is clear that if we hold that the diversity of the forms is the cause of the diversity of the matter, it is necessary that there be an external mover. But Aristotle did not speak of this in the case of the sense because here it [i.e., the need for an external mover capable of causing the determination of a cognitive power] is concealed, whereas it is obvious in the case of the intellect. But you, [reader], must give your attention to this subject, for it needs to be inquired into." This advice of Averroes was heeded by only a few philosophers. In several places St. Thomas says that the sensible object is a sufficient cause of the impression of sensible forms in the sensorial power, his design being to exclude the theory of an "active sense" patterned after

the active intellect of Aristotle. (See in particular *Quodlibet Questions*, 8. 3.) But in a well-known passage of *On the Power of God* (5. 8.) St. Thomas says that the ability of physical things to produce qualities in an immaterial state embodies a participation in the causal privileges of separate substances. "It must be known that bodies exercise two kinds of action. (a) One of them corresponds to the condition proper to bodies; it is action by way of motion. Indeed, to move and act under motion is the condition proper to bodies. (b) But bodies exercise another kind of action inasmuch as they are in contact with the order of the separate substances and enjoy some participation in the ways proper to these substances. It is a common fact that inferior natures enjoy some participation in what properly belongs to the superior nature; this is manifest in some animals which possess a faculty akin to prudence, although prudence properly belongs to men. This (b) is the action of bodies which is not aimed at the transmutation of matter, but at a certain diffusion of a likeness of the form in the medium, according to the likeness of the spiritual intention which from the thing is received in the sense or the intellect. This is how the sun illuminates the air and the color multiplies its *species* in the medium." This text is far from clear and it is hard to determine the bearing of the comparison used by St. Thomas. When he says that some animals participate in prudence, which properly belongs to rational beings, what he means is this: the typical animal behavior is instinctive and fixed, whereas the typical behavior of the rational being is a prudential one, always ready to change as a result of new experience. Now it is a fact that some animals take advantage of individual experience and modify their behavior accordingly; thereby they resemble man and can be said to participate in his privileges. The question that the present text does not seem to decide is whether, when St. Thomas speaks of the participation of bodies in the way of acting proper to separate substances, he speaks only of a resemblance between the lower and the higher—as a smart dog resembles a prudent man—or implies that the causal power of the higher is in some way at work in the production, by the lower, of effects that the lower, all by itself, would be unable to produce.

The causal problem with which we are concerned is discussed at some length by Cajetan (*On On the Soul*, Ed. Coquelle [Rome: Apud Institutum Angelicum, 1939], vol. 2, sec. 264–267). Referring to the above quoted text of Averroes, Cajetan first presents two theses: (a) there is a specific distinction between the sensible and its intentional form (*intentio*). To avoid misunderstanding, it should be noticed that a specific distinction can result either from a diversity of natures (this is how whiteness is specifically distinct from sweetness) or from a difference in *ways of being*. If two beings are specifically distinct by reason of a difference of natures, one of them cannot be produced by the other, for every agent produces something similar to itself. But if the specific distinction results from a difference in ways of being, one of two specifically distinct beings can be produced by the other. It is in the second way, not in the first, that color and its intentional form are distinct. (b) Intentional being is in a certain way spiritual, and accordingly it is nobler than physical being. Now, the less noble cannot produce the more noble, and this is why Averroes raises this problem: what is the cause of this spiritual state of the sensible forms? The error of Averroes, Cajetan says, is to hold that the cause of the intentional being of sensible forms is not the sensible object itself. This view is contrary to the teaching of Aristotle, who holds that color is visible *per se*, which implies that it has in itself the cause of its visibility. It is also contrary to truth, for experience shows that the visible object produces its intentional form in the mirror, and to deny this would be as arbitrary as to deny that fire burns: we would not be far from the error of the Mutākallimūn (*Loquentes*) who denied things any causal power of their own, an error that is strongly criticized by Averroes (*Com. on Met.*, 12. sec. 18). "In agreement with Aristotle, Albert the Great, and St. Thomas" (but his only reference is to the above quoted passage of *On the Power of God*), Cajetan says that the cause of the intentional being is the sensible object, not inasmuch as it is material, but inasmuch as its form participates in the properties of separate forms. Bodies and other natures have two kinds of traits, viz., those that are proper to them and those that they hold by participation. Some traits belong to bodies because they are bodies and other traits belong to bodies because they participate in the privileges of separate forms. This is manifested by activities: bodies act in two ways, viz., as moved, and without motion. To act as moved belongs properly to bodies; to act without being moved belongs to separate forms properly, and to

Let us consider *together* (a) the features which distinguish sensation from the common processes of nature—most of all, the character of *objective* union—and (b) the *experimentality,* the relation to a physically present and active object, which distinguishes sensation from other autonomic passions, immanent actions and objective unions. When the mind achieves an objective union with a thing absent, as in memory, the problem of causality does not concern directly the thing objectively united with the mind. In the recollection, say, of the destruction of a building by fire, the problem of causality is contained within the mind and its organs. The fire itself is not directly involved. The past sense impression is taken for granted. But building, fire, smoke, fire trucks and firemen are directly involved when the problem is to account for that which is antecedent to memory, viz., the sensations themselves. To sum up: when it is essential for an object to be physically present; and when its physical presence is procured by its transitive action, the means of objective union, i.e., the idea, must itself be produced by the physically present object. The "sense impression" cannot be taken for granted. The familiar ways of physical causation account for the alteration of an organ by stimuli, but the thing which acts as stimulus also plays the part of object: the problem is to determine by what ways physical things, in the exercise of their presence and of their transitive action, bring about *the means of objective unions which involve the physical presence of the things objectively united with the senses.*

The signification of these remarks will become clearer as we inquire into the nature of the sensorial environment and, concomitantly, into the validity of sense experience.

*

* *

Let us bear in mind, together with familiar reports on sensory illusions, the widespread belief that the testimony of the senses is thoroughly unreliable. This belief was often associated with a skeptical interpretation

---

bodies by participation. For example, the warm body exercises two kinds of activities, one by which it causes heat in physical being, the other by which it causes the intentional form of heat in the medium and in the sense. To sum up: the proximate efficient cause of the intentional being of the sensible form is the form of the object, but the primary principle by participation in which this causation takes place is a separate agent. The difficulty considered by Averroes does not lead to a proximate separate agent; all that is proved is that the sensible object, as material, is not a sufficient cause: it is a sufficient cause by reason of participation in a superior nature; owing to this participation, it is able to actualize its intentional form within some limits of materiality. "This I say because of the intelligible species which, by reason of their complete immateriality, require the operation of an active intellect."

The state of the question has not much improved since the time of Cajetan, except inasmuch as we are no longer tempted to burden intentional forms with subtle duties of physical character, or to attribute to the sun, or to the heavens, semi-spiritual faculties. The final advice of Averroes remains as timely as ever.

Y. R. Simon

of human knowledge; the Greek Skeptics contributed much to the literature on the errors of the senses. But, in a number of cases, the most significant of which is the philosophy of Descartes, a thoroughly negative critique of sense experience combined with rationalistic dogmatism. A basic implication of the *Cogito* is that the primary objects of thought are constituted by thought itself and its own modes. In other words, cognition, according to Descartes, is primarily intellectual self-consciousness. True, Descartes is not a complete idealist, and after having posited the consciousness of the intellectual self as primary, the problem is for him to go beyond the modes of thought and, through causal inference, to reach the universe of physical reality in the science of which he is greatly interested. But the fact that some modes of thought are illusory makes it necessary to work out a criterion for determining which ones are in genuine relation to external things and consequently convey knowledge of the world. Clarity and distinctness are the Cartesian characteristics of the dependable modes of thought. The idea of extension is clear and distinct, but the representations of colors and tastes are obscure and confused in the extreme. These cannot be traced to corresponding realities. The real world of Descartes is devoid of the qualities represented by the senses. The qualitative diversity of the sensorial environment is only a consciousness phenomenon which exerts great powers of deception when there is a question of building the science of nature. In historic association with the Galilean and Cartesian theories of natural science, it is rather commonly believed that the really strong objections to the truthfulness of the senses originate in modern science: in fact these objections express a philosophic theory as old as anything in the disputes of the philosophers; this is well established by the history of skepticism and mechanism.

In a celebrated passage of the treatise *On the Soul*,[32] objects of sensation are divided into those sensible by essence (the *per se* sensibles) and those which are sensible in a merely accidental fashion. As recalled at the beginning of this paper, sense perception embraces many things inaccessible to the senses, but constantly associated with essentially sensible objects in psychological complexes. The accidental objects of sense are (1) objects of intellectual apprehension, such as substances and relations, (2) significations, such as usefulness and harmfulness, which are grasped by instinct or animal intelligence, (3) objects imagined or remembered, and (4) the proper objects of other senses. The sense of sight certainly cannot apprehend moral qualities, substances, relations and intellectual communications, yet there is not necessarily any falsehood in such statements as, "I saw, on the scene of the disaster, a good-hearted man who was giving all possible help," "I see the first cousin of my brother-in-law," "I see a student of our best mathematician." The intelligible things (1) referred

[32] *On the Soul*, 2. 6. 418a7.

to, in these sentences, by the grammatical objects of the verb "to see," are parts of complexes whose core is an essentially sensible object. Likewise, in the reading of a clause where some letters are missing, imagined letters (3) merge in such organic fashion with letters actually seen that it is generally impossible, if the experience is short, to say with certainty what letters are present and which ones are missing. The work of Proust describes the living unity of the things sensed and the things remembered in privileged experiences which fill the soul with overwhelming joy, for the vivid apprehension of the past in a complex centered on a thing present conveys the feeling of a victory over the destructive power of time. Here, the sensible by accident comprises, among other things, an instinctive apprehension (2) of time, of destruction and of salvation. As an example of the fourth kind of association, let us just recall that in order to know if a fruit is sweet or sour it often suffices to look at it.

So far as the validity of sense experience is concerned, the case of the accidentally sensible objects is expressed by one simple law: the sensorial nature supplies no guaranty of truthfulness in the apprehension of objects that are related to the sense in a merely accidental way. A frightened lady hears heavy steps in the attic, and it turns out to be a rat: if we please to call this an illusion of sense, let us, at least, be aware that no defect of the sensorial nature is involved. Such species as man and rat are not objects of sensation except by accident, that is, by reason of their being associated with objects of sense experience. Steady success in the apprehension of the sensibles by accident is an effect of training, not a result of natural determination. All children learn to identify things, and skill in associating sense appearances with nonsensible significations (perceived both instinctively and intelligently) plays an important role in many crafts. Thus, the training of a physician comprises the association of nosological species with such sense appearances as complexion, murmurs, etc. The constitution of nonsensible objects into sensibles by accident is not effected by nature, except in initial and rudimentary fashion. It has to be completed by habit and intelligent skill. At best, it remains widely subject to error, for in many cases the possibility of imitation cannot be ruled out. With these simple considerations, a large portion of the traditional arguments concerning the deceptiveness of sensation disappear into irrelevance.

The essentially sensible objects are those which make an impression upon the sense and its organ. They comprise, first, all the sense qualities and, secondly, modes which pertain, in a variety of ways, to quantity. What acts upon sight is not unmodified color, but color determined by such modes as "movement, rest, number, shape, magnitude." [33] This is the list of Aristotle, which may not be exhaustive. Clearly, the sense of sight is acted upon by a spot of color of a certain shape, or by several spots each

[33] *On the Soul*, 2. 6. 418a18.

of which has a shape, and these spots are—in their relation to the sense—at rest or in motion, and they are large or small. Between the sense qualities themselves and their quantitative modifications the primary difference is that each kind of sense quality belongs exclusively to one sensorial power, whereas movement, number, etc., can be apprehended by more than one sense. To ascertain the number of marbles in a bag, I can choose among a variety of methods, viz., I may spread them on a table and use my eyes to count them, or pull them out of the bag one by one and count with my fingers, or drop them one after the other and use my ears. But sight is the only way to the sensation of colors, and hearing to that of sounds. The sense qualities are sensible not only in essential fashion, but also in the capacity of *proper* objects. Their quantitative modifications are common. This is of decisive significance for the problem of truthfulness. From the fact that movement, number, etc., are apprehended by more than one sense, we know that they do not pertain to the specific constitution, the distinct nature, the *identity* of the sensorial power. True, we have little understanding of sense qualities, and when we want to define the blue or the red we can do no better than have recourse to such mechanistic substitutes as wave lengths: then we obtain very precise definitions, but these do not express the quality in its qualitative way of being. Sense qualities cannot be defined except by direct appeal to experience, and this method yields only a low grade of intelligibility. But no matter how limited our ability to define color or sound and their varieties, it cannot be doubted that sight is essentially relative to color and hearing to sound. We would know more about hearing and sight if we knew more about sound and color. Let it be recalled that whereas some relations are *pure,* and consist in absolutely nothing else than relatedness—e.g., "greater than" is absolutely nothing else than a relation to what is smaller—other relations exist by way of identity with a thing which is not a pure relation, but may be a substance, a quality or some other sort of being. Senses, as well as the understanding and the will, the arts, the crafts and the sciences, are relations of the second type, mixed relations, things relative, things which by essence involve a relation to a certain term and are defined, if at all, in relation to this term. We are able to define medicine because we have a fairly clear idea of its effect and object, viz., the healing and the prevention of disease. We would not be so unhappy when there is a question of defining mathematics if we knew better what a mathematical object is, and our definition of sight would be possessed of clarity and precision if our notion of color were clear and precise.

Here is a particularly vexing aspect of the problem of sensation. All our experience ultimately rests upon a firm basis of natural determination which is nothing else than the relation of each sense to its proper object. But because our understanding of sense qualities remains obscure, the critique of sense experience and, in a way, the whole critique of human knowledge terminate in a system marked by obscurity. No wonder that mechanistic science exerts never-ending fascination; among many other feats, it performs the invaluable service of substituting for an obscure reference to ill-defined qualities—e.g., the red and the green—a reference to nonqualitative entities—e.g., wave lengths—which admit of precise and easily communicable definitions. But, when all the enlightenment procured by mechanistic methods is duly acknowledged, the philosophical problem of the sense qualities remains as inescapable as ever.

To sum up: an essential relation to a particular genus of quality—color, sound, etc.—pertains to the constitution of each particular sense. This relation is a matter of natural determinism. Here, in the relation of the sensorial power to its proper object, we find a natural guaranty of normality, of soundness, of regularity, of truthfulness.[34] This guaranty does not extend to the common sensibles. And by this the bulk of the literature about the deceptiveness of sense experience is disposed of. Two straight lines which are declared equal by precise measurement happen to look unequal. Why should they not? Even though magnitude modifies every spot of color, it does not pertain to the proper object of sight, and consequently the correct perception of relations in magnitude is not guarantied by the natural determinism which controls sight sensations. The correct perception of the common sensibles, as well as that of the accidentally sensible objects, demands a training and remains subject to deception.

Leaving aside all objects which do not concern a sensorial power in specific fashion, the truthfulness of sense (in relation to the proper sensibles) still raises great difficulties. We propose to survey these difficulties, beginning with the most external and ending with those which pertain most intimately to the nature of sensible qualities and of sense experience.

Cartesian doubt derives an appealing argument from the fact that, in dreams, vivid images are mistaken for sensations. Clearly, this error is not restricted to accidentally sensible objects and to common sensibles; colors and sounds that are not actually present are believed to be sensed. All that is established by this remark is that sensation can be deceitfully imitated, but the same holds for every natural process. The case can be likened to what happens in intellectual life when the kind of necessity involved in a habit of thought is mistaken for an objective and intelligible necessity.

[34] Aristotle sometimes declares, purely and simply, that the sense is truthful with regard to its proper object (On the Soul, 2. 6. 418a11; 3. 3. 427b11; 428a11; 6. 430b29; On Sense and Sensible Objects, 4. 442b8), but elsewhere he says that it admits only of a minimum of error (On the Soul, 3. 3. 428b18). This duality of expression is easily accounted for. In Aristotle's doctrine the unqualified assertion of truthfulness holds (a) as expression of an essential determination, unaffected by what happens accidentally, and (b) as expression of factual occurrence if the proper sensible is considered with the modes of its action upon the sense; the reference to infrequent error concerns factual occurrence in the distinctions, the judgments exercised by the sense.

This is a trivial accident to which no one is entirely immune. At all times, progress in science and philosophy has been hampered by the deceptive resemblance that habitual ways of thinking bear to intelligible connections. Those who use propaganda intensively, whether for profit or for the purposes of politics and war, know very well that the feeling of necessity which, in a process of genuine conviction, results from proof, may be produced at much lower cost and with greater efficacy by the sheer repetition of assertions which not only need not be true but can afford to be extremely improbable. It is worth remarking that the imitations of sense experience, whether normal, as in dream, or pathological, as in hallucination, are incomparably easier to correct than the imitations of rationality which constantly impede the progress of science and philosophy.

Consider, now, the difficulties that arise from particular conditions affecting the instruments of sensation, i.e., its organ and its medium. If I place my right hand in hot water and my left hand in cold water, and then place both hands in a tray containing lukewarm water, the same will appear warm to one hand and cold to the other. Think also of the patient with jaundice who finds a bitter taste in all food, and of the color blind, who cannot distinguish the green from the red. Peculiarities due to the state of the medium fall under the same system of difficulties. It happens that a man in good health, seen in a room lighted by a lamp with a green shade, looks diseased and ghastly. The healthy and the diseased are not perceptible to the senses, except by accident, but the greenish appearance of a healthy man under a light colored by a green shade concerns the relation of the sense to its proper object. Along the same line let us mention the disappointment of the housewife who displays at noon curtain material that she purchased the day before in an artificially lighted shop: she believed that this material was rather blue, and such was the color of her choice; but now she sees that it is rather green, and she does not like it.

All these examples suggest that sense experience can be falsified if certain conditions of neutrality are not realized both on the part of the organ and on that of the medium. The significant issue is whether such falsifications should be understood in a merely pragmatic way, or should be said also to bear meaning in relation to a truth independent of human purpose. In the first interpretation, the blue color of the curtain material under artificial light would be just as true as the green color under natural light; more exactly, the question, Which one is the true color of this material? would be meaningless except in relation to practice. The privilege of natural light would be due to practical and social circumstances. For one thing, curtain material is more often looked at under natural than under artificial light, and for another, there is a silent convention that when we communicate about colors and other sense qualities, we refer to conditions deserving to be called standard by reason of their frequency.

It seems that an answer can be derived from the similarity between the role of the medium and that of the organ in the distorted apprehension of sense qualities. In the case of the patient with jaundice, as well as in that of the color blind, whatever is unusual about sensation follows upon an abnormal condition of the sense organ. True, it is not only in terms of adjustment to the conditions of city traffic but also in terms of genuineness that the sensorial equipment of those who can distinguish a red from a green light is better than that of the color blind. Regarding the experiment of the lukewarm water, it is clear that to perceive temperature as genuinely as possible hands should not first be exposed to conditions widely different from a certain average whose limits are set by the normal temperature of the human body. No doubt, all such considerations manifest factors of relativity. *Inasmuch as these factors are involved, sense is not the power of the absolute:* this is one of the few propositions on which the philosophers are almost unanimously agreed.

Let us now try to determine where error lies in those "falsified" apprehensions of sense qualities. If a color-blind person asserts that there is no difference between what normal people call a red light and what they call a green light, his error resides in a judgment. This sort of error can be corrected, without improvement of vision, provided the color-blind person is willing to trust the majority of his fellow men and to concede that he is unable to perceive a difference that others hold obvious.

Supposing, now, that through dependence upon testimony or any other method, error has been removed from such intellectual operations as the judgment that there is or is not qualitative unity between two spots of color: In what way can it still be said that the sensations of the color blind are untruthful? Since truth and error are, primarily, properties of judgment, the question is whether instinct and sense are capable of judging. Indeed, there is such a thing as an instinctive distinction between the useful and the harmful. There is also such a thing as a sensorial distinction between diverse genera of quality, e.g., color and taste. The latter distinction is traced by Aristotle to a central power—the first of the internal senses.[35] Finally, a distinction between sense qualities of the same genus— e.g., red and green—is effected by the external sense itself. It is perfectly reasonable to speak of judgment in nonrational powers, external senses included, inasmuch as distinguishing natures from each other and to be from not to be is a judicative function.[36] Any act of distinguishing between objects is a sort of judgment. The external sense can be said to judge, for it distinguishes between a shape and another shape, a color and

[35] *On the Soul*, 3. 2. 426b11.

[36] On judgment in external senses, see Aristotle, *Topics*, 2. 4. 111a13; *Post. An.*, 2. 19. 99b35; *On the Soul*, 3. 2. 426b9; St. Thomas, *On Truth*, 1. 2; *Quodlibet Questions*, 8. 3; *Com. on On Sense and Sensible Objects*, les. 19 (Ed. Pirotta, 292); John of St. Thomas, *Cursus philosophicus, Phil. nat.* iv. 5. 2. Ed. Reiser, vol. 3, 140 ff.

another color. The failure of the sensorial judgment may constitute—as in the case of the color blind—an error of the sense in relation to its proper object. This remark leads to an important specification of the principle that the truthfulness of the senses, so long as the proper objects alone are involved, is guaranteed by nature. Here, as in any domain of mutable reality, essential determination does not exclude accidental failure. In actual experience, greater frequency distinguishes determinations that are essential. It is only in fewer cases that senses err concerning their proper objects—that is, fail to apprehend such distinctions as that of the red and the green.

Below the aspect of sensation which is fittingly called a judgment, all that remains is the apprehension of the sense quality *as engaged in its action upon the sense.* The dispositions of the medium and of the organ, which may cause error in sensorial judgment, are modes of this action; accordingly, there is no error or possibility of error in the relation of the sense to the sensible quality so considered. With regard to the sense qualities modified by the circumstances of their action, the senses are purely and simply indefectible. A bitter taste is actually present to the patient with jaundice, even though the food may be experienced as sweet when the organ of taste is in a normal condition, and the green material is genuinely experienced as blue under the circumstances produced by some particular lighting system.

The relation of the sensorial powers to their proper objects taken *with* the modes of their action constitutes the nucleus of all certainty in sense experience and, ultimately, of all certainty in human knowledge. Again, this indefectible truthfulness does not suffice to insure truthful judgment, i.e., successful distinction, even on the strictly sensorial level, when the power of the sense is impaired by an abnormal disposition of the organ or a particular state of the medium. No doubt, there is a constant possibility of accidental error in the judgment of the sense about its most proper object, and such error has to be corrected by various factors involving conditions more complex and elaborate than those of immediate experience. Thus, the color-blind know, from the almost unanimous testimony of their fellow men, that they cannot trust themselves with stop-and-go lights and that they should watch the behavior of drivers and pedestrians. The housewife comes to know, through trial and error, that she cannot safely distinguish the rather blue from the rather green under artificial light and that she should go shopping for curtains in the daytime. And a physician is supposed to know that the complexion of a patient cannot be a significant factor of diagnosis if the examination takes place in the bewildering aftermath of an electric storm.[37]

[37] Bertrand Russell, *The Problems of Philosophy* (New York: Henry Holt, 1912), p. 18. "Thus colour is not something which is inherent in the table, but something depending

The problem of truthfulness in sense experience ultimately concerns the nature of *that which is attained, in the capacity of proper object, by sensation.* Let it be assumed that all the conditions of genuineness are satisfied, that no cause of distortion is at work either in the organ or in the medium. The proposition that, under such circumstances, sense experience is true and sensorial judgments do not deceive us involves a difficulty of the first magnitude. Indeed, whatever truth pertains to sensation and to sensorial judgment is relative to the *way of being* constituted by sense quality *precisely considered as sensible:* this way of being remains to be defined.

We interpret the world as primarily made of things, and "thing" primarily signifies substance. It is not for no reason that the words meaning "substance" and those meaning "intelligible object" coincide or communicate in various ways. "Substance," "essence," "being," "whatness," "quiddity," "that which is," "concept (objectively understood)," sometimes can be used interchangeably; the same holds for the corresponding words of other languages, and first of all for the Greek of Aristotle. Yet, accidents also are ways of being; they have essences, whatnesses and concepts of their own, but because substance exists in a distinguished and primordial way, any term expressing a subject of existence or an object of understanding involves some sort of relation, no matter how indirect, to what is both the primary subject of existence and the primary object of understanding, viz., substance. The felicitous management of these manifold connections and distinctions makes up a large part of philosophical intelligence. Having understood that some relations are real, it is not so easy to resist the temptation of conceiving their reality after the pattern of substance, and, having understood that their way of being and of facing the intellect is widely different from the modes of substance, it is not so easy to resist the temptation of losing sight of their reality and letting them disappear into the universe of the beings of reason. Along the same line, let it be remarked that much of the historic trouble with the "faculties" of the soul originates in the danger of conceiving the intellect, the will, the sense ap-

---

upon the table and the spectator and the way the light falls on the table. When, in ordinary life, we speak of *the* colour of the table, we only mean the sort of colour which it will seem to have to a normal spectator from an ordinary point of view under usual conditions of light. But the other colours which appear under other conditions have just as good a right to be considered real; and therefore, to avoid favouritism, we are compelled to deny that, in itself, the table has any one particular colour."

By using the word "normal" in the case of the spectator, Russell commits himself to the view that, as far as the spectator is concerned, there is a distinguished case, viz., that of the normal spectator as against all the varieties of abnormal ones. We are suggesting that there is also a distinguished case, and not only in a practical sense, with regard to the medium. The existence of a "normal" medium does not impair the reality of unusual colors any more than the existence of a "normal" spectator. All "favouritism" disappears when we consider colors in their action on the organ of sight.

petite, etc., as so many substantial units: some fail to sense the danger, and produce monsters of shattering analysis; others speak as if such powers as the intellect and the will were not really distinct from each other. True, it is not so easy to understand that the intellect is really distinct from the will and that both are really distinct from the soul, without indulging in the fancy that the soul, the intellect, and the will are so many substantial units, unintelligibly held together. A basic treatment of these issues is found in Aristotle's *Categories*. The meaning of this book and its relation to logic and to metaphysics remain somewhat enigmatic; in spite of this, it turned out to be good pedagogy to use the study of the categories as an introduction to the philosophical sciences.

Thus, we want to know in what way a sense quality *is*, just as in other contexts we would ask in what way a relation or a faculty is said to *be*. Sense qualities are characterized by a way of being which not only is accidental (i.e., nonsubstantial) and vulnerable, but also involves ceaseless motion. Here, our eagerness for intelligence is badly held in check: for one thing, inasmuch as the proper objects of sensation are accidents, it is not in primary fashion that they bear the act of existing; it is but indirectly and dependently that they embody the notion of "that which is." Further, those things are subject to multiple interference. Thirdly and most importantly, their "to be" does not have a character of finished actuality but one of becoming and of stream-like instability. Granted that the physical world would remain closed to us if it were not for these unstable manifestations, it is no wonder that several schools of thought held it impossible to work out a science of such a world. Cratylus, who was so honest as to keep silent in order not to lie about things that had already changed, Plato, with his conversion to a separate universe of numbers and ideas, and the mechanistic philosophies of the Cartesian type all express the belief that the fluid "to be" of sense qualities neither can be an object of knowledge nor can constitute a way to knowledge. When Descartes declared that he did not accept in his physics any principles not accepted in mathematics, he perhaps suggested, much against his conscious and explicit determination, that he, also, gave up, as a definitely impossible task, the working out of a physical science. With reference to both Platonism and the scientific approach of modern times, the attempt at constructing a *physical* science appears as one of the most daring aspects of Aristotle's work. The Wolfian classification, in which cosmology and psychology become parts of metaphysics, removes the paradox of a genuinely *physical* philosophy—a paradox which will be successfully vindicated if, and only if, there turns out to be, within the changing diversity of appearances, ways that take us where we want to go, i.e., to a world of scientific intelligibility.

The problem is now to determine what relation there is between the sense qualities as sensed and the same qualities as understood. By describing their nonsubstantial character, their vulnerability and the fluidity of their "to be," we have brought forth some of their intelligible characteristics. Turning now to the same qualities as given in sense experience, the overwhelming fact is their concrete uniqueness. Under exceptional circumstances we allow ourselves to be intoxicated, for joy or for sadness, with the realization that the sensorial environment apprehended in this instant is at variance with all precedent and admits of no repetition. The poetic faculty comprises a readiness to stop at any time in the midst of a scenery which never was and never again will be such as it now is. But most of the time we pay no attention to that which is unique about the scenery. We are too busy and too intelligent. For these reasons, the best of our attention goes to the regularities observed in changing situations. Granted that this cedar tree has never been modified exactly as it is right now by its own state of growth, by the winds, by the sunshine and the clouds, and by the relations between its colors and the colors of the sky and of the surrounding trees, I still can safely recognize it. It is a somewhat blue and somewhat green thing, which ever since I began to take walks in this part of the forest has been describable as a thing somewhat blue and somewhat green. These colors convey a characteristic shape; I was never tempted to mistake this cedar for a tree of another kind or for another individual of the same species. (So far as we know, a dog identifies his master just as safely as I identify a cedar tree.)

It is true that sensorial aspects are never twice the same, and this is why our intelligent eagerness for things necessary and eternal is so badly frustrated by the immediate data of sense experience. These are ceaselessly moving indeed, yet their change is contained within limits. To speak of such limits is to declare that in the sensory order itself, and prior to any interpretation in terms of instinct, memory, or understanding, there exist resemblances, recurrences, kinships, regularities, uniformities. These are strongly expressed in the practical vision of the world, for the life of action, in all its phases, depends upon the identification of individuals, species and genera in the sensorial environment. Again, the busy man has little time for wondering about the strict uniqueness of the scenery offered, at any instant, to our senses. Action demands that attention be constantly centered on identities, whether generic, specific or individual. What the philosophers would like to know is whether these identities, whose consideration is of such obvious relevance in regard to action, also convey a meaning in terms of reality, intelligibility and truth. Unless they do, albeit in narrowly restricted ways, how would they retain their relevance for action? A definite system of sensible regularities signifies the presence of a thing called an edible mushroom, say a chanterelle; another system of sensible regularities is held to signify the presence of the deadly fly agaric. But how should such regularities be interpreted? Do the constant characteristics of the fly agaric merely constitute a warning that the mushroom lover must keep away?[38] Indeed, this warning, if faithfully heeded, works with perfect regularity, and the lover of mushrooms will have to die by some other cause than fly agaric poisoning. But why do such warnings work so regularly? The ambiguities of pragmatism help us to understand that whenever a system of sense appearances works, it also expresses, on the part of that which appears, a readiness to act in a definite way. The system of appearances by which the mushroom lover is warned to keep away from fly agaric, also and inseparably expresses the readiness of fly agaric to cause, if ingested by a human organism, definite effects terminating in death. At this point, we have already transcended the interpretation of things in terms of human utility. When William James declares that Aristotle used "methodically" the pragmatic method, all he can reasonably mean is that, in Aristotelian doctrine, the ways traced by action may lead to intelligible truth. Aristotle's views on the role of instinct and animal intelligence in the approach to the universal entirely warrants this interpretation.[39] No doubt, a set of sensorial regularities considered as a

[38] Descartes holds (*Principles of Philosophy*, 2. 3.) that we "ordinarily" know through the senses the utility or harmfulness of external bodies, but not their nature, "except, possibly, in rare and fortuitous fashion." Since sense impressions are not, for Descartes, likenesses of external things, it may be asked how they ever can tell us about their natures. The answer seems to be that a fortuitous resemblance cannot be ruled out: but it should occur exceptionally, if at all. The regular information given by senses about the practical significations of things raises a much more difficult problem: if sense impressions do not resemble bodies, except fortuitously, how can they supply *regular* information about the effects that their nature exerts upon ours? The great metaphysical myths of occasionalism and pre-established harmony will soon be needed to account for the dependability of the senses, with regard to utility and harmfulness, in a system which denies them all dependability with regard to the real state of affairs.

[39] There is, on this point, an illuminating contrast between Aristotle and Bergson. For Bergson, representations shaped in answer to the demands of action are inevitably at variance with the kind of absolute that the philosophic mind is striving to attain. Bergson has a pragmatic notion of the intellect inasmuch as he holds that all conceptual and demonstrative knowledge is essentially relative to the purposes of action. Yet, the philosophy of Bergson, considered as a whole and in its most central aspects, is the antithesis of pragmatism, for it is entirely animated by an aspiration toward disinterested and really contemplative knowledge. The meaning of this aspiration is made more unmistakable by the high valuation of intelligence in the philosophy of Bergson. It has been rightly said that the interpretation of Bergsonism as a philosophy adverse to thought is no more accurate than Aristophanes' story of Socrates busy measuring the jump of a flea. Anything in Bergson that sounds like disparagement of intellectual work expresses only the conviction that the ways of the intellect are irretrievably biased by the urge to satisfy human needs—which urge already causes bias on the level of sense perception. This pragmatic interpretation of the intellect raises two basic issues: for one thing, is it true that the intellect is altogether incapable of transcending the world of action? If the discussion of this question succeeds in vindicating the intellect's ability to achieve contemplation, the next issue is whether a practical approach to things, i.e., an approach controlled by human purposes, necessarily leads away from the disinterested apprehension of things such as they are. Indeed, the meaning of a concept and the truth of a proposition can be altogether practical. Such

warning may not fully coincide with the regularities in which the theoretical mind is interested; however, the practical meaningfulness of a warning, if it is constant, leads ultimately to signification and truth in terms of what is and what is not.

*

*   *

As a result of all the preceding inquiry, the decisive question is whether the senses ever achieve certain conformity to a real state of affairs. Again, the negative critique of sensation which is commonly associated with modern science actually is a very ancient thing. Concerning the problem of a natural science in Plato, Duhem writes:

. . . whereas sense perception grasps nothing else than indefinitely changing accidents, appearances which today are and tomorrow no longer will be, geometry deals with permanent and eternal objects, with realities; through the study of these immutable objects, it prepares our souls for the intuition which alone can contemplate essences and, in particular, the first of all essences, viz., the supreme Good. This Platonic doctrine is characterized by the distrust that it professes regarding the data of sense perception . . . there is no science worthy of this name except where the things known are immutable and eternal as it is the case with the truths of geometry and the ideas that intuition contemplates.[40]. . . If there is no science except of realities, and if every reality is necessarily immutable, there is no science except of things immutable; mathematics, i.e., the study of the invariable properties of numbers and figures, and theology, the intuitive contemplation of eternal ideas, were the only two sciences that a Platonist could acknowledge. In daring opposition to the most essential dogmas of Platonism, Aristotle defines a third science,

---

concepts and propositions may well be at variance with reality taken independently of human purposes. The Bergsonian critique has made us better aware that it is necessary to check our concepts and our propositions with regard to the possibility of their being so influenced by the purposes of human action as not to express nature in its independent intelligibility. There is such a thing as a distortion of theoretical intelligibility by practical concerns, but from this it does not follow that practical concerns always and necessarily lead the mind away from the disinterested apprehension of things. A practical approach, provided that it is intelligently interpreted, often prepares the way to genuinely theoretical understanding.

Buffon held that the division of living species into those useful and those harmful to man is by far the most convenient. If such a view had prevailed, no attempt would have been made at a scientific taxonomy, and botany would be but an aggregate of disciplines auxiliary to agriculture, pharmacy and gardening. The stand of Buffon recalls that the ambitions of the practical mind must be restrained if science is to exist. On the other hand, the history of the sciences in their relation to practical experience and technique shows that in countless cases the interpretation of a warning, i.e., of a practical signification, is what led to the apprehension of the independent intelligibility of things. The example of the fly agaric tells the whole story: those sensorial regularities, primarily interpreted as a warning, lead the mind to the understanding of a nature.

[40] *Le système du monde de Platon à Copernic* (Paris: Hermann, 1913), vol. 1, 130.

viz., physics.[41] . . . When the mathematician saves the appearances with the help of a theory, Plato believes that he lets something of the certainty that the geometrical method is capable of come down to these appearances; Aristotle, on the contrary, believes that a part of the truth directly grasped by the senses is carried up to the level of the theory.[42]

Duhem was himself an extremist in the interpretation of physics along the line of Simplicius' celebrated phrase, "saving the appearances. . . ." In fact, the epistemological reflections of our contemporaries give weight to three theories, each of which may have a part to play in the interpretation of what is going on under the name of natural science.

(1) According to Duhem, a physical theory is nothing else than a construct placed by the human mind underneath that which appears to the senses. From this construct, observable regularities can be deduced, but from the observable regularities it is not possible to deduce the construct. That a theory successfully "saves the appearances," does not give it an exclusive privilege. Another theory, not yet devised, might save the same appearances with equal or greater success. Physical theories satisfy the need for simplicity and consistency in the representation of nature; further, so long as they do save the appearances, they make prediction possible. But they do not in any way constitute an explanation of the real world. In close relation to the views of Duhem, Henri Poincaré declared:

And hence this affirmation: "the earth turns round," has no meaning, since it cannot be verified by experiment; since such an experiment not only cannot be realised or even dreamed of by the most daring Jules Verne, but cannot even be conceived of without contradiction; or, in other words, these two propositions, "the earth turns round," and, "it is more convenient to suppose that the earth turns round," have one and the same meaning. There is nothing more in one than in the other.[43]

(2) Even though the "saving the appearances" theory can be called positivistic inasmuch as it forbids science any ontological ambition, the most representative schools of positivism rather favor the view that science boils down to the expression of observable regularities. This was held as a dogma by Auguste Comte; for him, to explain a fact is nothing else than to connect it with a law, and a law is nothing else than a general fact. He was sharply opposed to hypotheses concerning the structure of matter, e.g., the kinetic theory of gases, in which he saw the work of a "vain curiosity" and a threat to the principles which were to insure the intellectual reorganization of Western society. True, Comte had the soul of a social

[41] *Ibid.*, 135.
[42] *Ibid.*, 140. See also Pierre Duhem, *The Aim and Structure of Physical Theory*, Tr. by Philip P. Wiener (Princeton: Princeton University Press, 1954).
[43] Henri Poincaré, *Science and Hypothesis*, Tr. by W. J. G. (New York: Dover Publications, 1952), p. 117.

reformer, rather than that of a scientist. Meyerson has shown, with a great wealth of evidence, that the factual development of science entirely failed to coincide with the blueprints drawn by the founder of positivism, and according to Georges Sorel science would have ended in bankruptcy if Comte had been taken seriously by physicists. Yet, the determination to deal only with facts, particular and general, reappears in such scientific minds as Ernst Mach and Hans Reichenbach. The latter writes:

What we mean by explaining an observed fact is incorporating that fact into a general law. We observe that as the day progresses a wind begins to blow from the sea to the land; we explain this fact by incorporating it into the general law that heated bodies expand and thus become lighter with respect to equal volumes. . . . We observe that living organisms need food in order to exist; we explain this fact by incorporating it into the general law of the conservation of energy. . . . The explanatory power of Newton's law derives from its generality. . . . Explanation is generalization.[44]

(3) Finally, some physicists of our time, the most outspoken of whom is Max Planck, do away with restrictions that have been conventional since the early days of positivism. They de-emphasize the contrast between science and philosophy, place an ontology inside science, and go so far as to say that the ultimate purpose of the physicist is "to know the thing in itself."[45]

Let us consider what stand each of these theories implies, or suggests, regarding the truthfulness of sensation. If science is concerned only with general facts, the problem becomes entirely meaningless, and this is, to be sure, one of the strongest objections that can be made to strict phenomenism—the philosophy that, by the convincing testimony of Meyerson, is never embodied in the actual products of scientific thought. Comparing now the views of Duhem with the ontological interpretation of Planck, it is clear that anything demanded by the former regarding the truth value of sense experience, would be also demanded, with much greater force, by

[44] *The Rise of Scientific Philosophy* (Berkeley and Los Angeles: Univ. of California Press, 1956), pp. 6, 7.
[45] "I have said that the first step which every specialized branch of science takes consists of a jump into the region of metaphysics. . . . Of course there is the positivist theory that man is the measure of all things. And that theory is irrefutable insofar as nobody can object on logical grounds to the action of a person who measures all things with a human rule, and resolves the whole of creation ultimately into a complex of sensory perceptions. But there is another measure also, which is more important for certain problems and which is independent of the particular method and nature of the measuring intellect. This measure is identical with the *thing* itself. Of course it is not an immediate datum of perception. But science sets out confidently on the endeavor finally to know the *thing* in itself, and even though we realize that this ideal goal can never be completely reached, still we struggle on towards it untiringly." Max Planck, *Where Is Science Going?* Tr. by James Murphy (New York: W. W. Norton and Co., 1932), p. 138 and p. 139. By courtesy of the publisher.

the latter. Thus, to ascertain the stand of science on the truthfulness of sense experience, the most effective method is to inquire into the implications of the saving the appearances theory. If *even* this theory implies indispensably the belief in some truthfulness on the part of sense experience, we shall know that the stand of science is not adequately expressed in the traditional formulas handed down by the followers of Democritus, Plato and Descartes and uncritically repeated by popularizers.

Thus, considering a deductive system which repudiates all claim to be an explanation of physical reality and restricts its ambition to the saving of the appearances, let it be remarked that such a system would not have *any* relation to physical nature if it were not postulated that the reading of measuring instruments admits of regularity and of some sort of certainty. It can be taken for granted that there is in modern science a constant and essential tendency to replace the consideration of qualities by that of measures which admit of ever-increasing precision and lend themselves to unmistakable communication. Behind each particular conclusion, there may be an impressive chain of mathematical reasonings, yet, ultimately, the deductive system is fed with data delivered by sensation and no more reliable than sensation itself. To use the simplest example: temperatures would not retain, in a deductive system, *any* physical meaning if it were not assumed that there is something dependable about the sensation of a white ground, a dark line and a silvery strip whose top does or does not coincide with the dark line. In the words of Duhem interpreting Plato, certainties of mathematical character come down to the world of sense experience, but even this participation in the privileges of a loftier order would not be possible if sense experience itself were not certain in some way. Mathematical necessity coming down upon data completely devoid of firmness could not result in a deductive system whereby appearances be saved. The derived certainties of which Duhem speaks call for a steady bearer, an unshakable receiver: they cannot be received into a vacuum; they cannot be applied to representations which in no way whatsoever achieve certain conformity to the real state of affairs; and they cannot be applied to dream images ready to disappear into other dream images without any objective law. Plato holds that the Cratylean stream does not lead to science: if no aspect of it admits of certain cognition, let us say, further, that this famous stream is not a thing to which certainties derived from mathematics can be applied. It is impossible to work out the physiology of a chimera, there is nothing scientific about the psychology of an undine, and the behavior of zombis cannot be incorporated into a deductive system possessed of physical ambition. Even if it is held, in Platonic fashion, that the science of number and of space does not in any way result from an abstraction, the very fact that this science is applied to sense data, and that this application works, shows that sensation in some way achieves conformity to some aspects of the real world. In all the critique of sense knowledge, the most decisive question is to determine what kind of conformity sensation achieves to what aspects of nature.

We have been insisting on the fluidity and relativity of all that pertains to sensory life. Inasmuch as the absolute involves necessity and eternity, it is clear to all that sense is not the faculty of the absolute. These views must be supplemented by the consideration that the senses possess, in their own way, a power of ultimate decision. A classical exercise, for beginners in philosophy, is to analyze a "scientific fact" into its components, a great many of which belong to theoretical constructs, and often to highly elaborate ones. Yet, all the interpretations and constructs involved in the constitution and expression of a scientific fact are, either directly or indirectly—perhaps most indirectly, but, to be sure, ultimately—centered about data of sense intuition. These data answer by yes or no questions which cannot be eluded without the deductive system losing all essential relation to physical reality. There is something absolute about the thing which, ultimately, depends upon the sense and its truthfulness. With due allowance for the voluminous parts played by interpretations and constructions, the analysis of scientific facts brings forth a core of existential decisiveness by reason of which the fact can be called *the experimental absolute*. In this existential decisiveness, we recognize the crucial *difference* brought forth at the beginning of this paper, the immense qualitative distance between sensing an object and imagining it (no matter how vividly) or understanding it (no matter how clearly and distinctly) or constructing it (no matter how elaborately). Without a minimum of strictly experimental determinations, a deductive system, if it is essentially designed to save physical appearances, utterly fails in its design, for it no longer is an approach to nature. Granted that Duhem's interpretation is right and that a properly physical science is impossible in Platonism, let it be said that both the science of nature and its Platonic substitute collapse if the experimental absolute is unqualifiedly negated.

Many difficulties encountered in the philosophic study of sensation seem to follow upon this basic paradox: a certain absolute, viz., the experimental absolute, the fact, the thing by reason of which we make the difference between to be and not to be, is primarily delivered to us in an act that relativity and fluidity characterize. By going more deeply into the contrasted meanings of the experimental absolute and of the flux in which it is attained, much could be learned about sensation, and also about human nature, for the definition of man implies, among other things, that it is in the flux of a relation to sense qualities that he achieves his first acquaintance with the absolute.

THE EXPERIENTIAL ELEMENT:

N. Goodman : SENSE AND CERTAINTY

C. I. Lewis : THE GIVEN ELEMENT IN EMPIRICAL KNOWLEDGE

PROFESSOR *Nelson Goodman of the University of Pennsylvania and Clarence Irving Lewis, Emeritus Professor of Harvard University, take up in complementary essays the difficult aspects of knowledge through experience of objects. The linguistic and the psychological passages—and barriers—are discussed in the treatment of the relation of sense and knowledge. These papers, and a third one by Hans Reichenbach, were presented at a symposium on "The Experiential Element in Knowledge" conducted by the Eastern Division of the American Philosophical Association, in December 1951, at Bryn Mawr College. Reprinted by permission from* THE PHILOSOPHICAL REVIEW, *LXI (1952), pp. 160–67; 168–75.*

• The argument for empirical certainties has two phases. The first is the effort to point out actual statements or kinds of statements that are plainly immune to doubt. The second is the effort to show, quite aside from the question just *what* statements are certain, that on theoretical grounds there must be *some* empirical certainties.

The popular hunting ground for empirical certainty is among statements confined to immediate phenomena. Statements concerning physical objects involve prediction in one way or another, and so may always turn out to be wrong. But, the argument runs, between the presentation of an element in experience and my simultaneous judgment that it is presented, there is no room for error or doubt. We may have trouble formulating these judgments correctly in language, but misuses of language or slips of tongue must not be confused with errors in judgment. If the judgment is immediate and confined to what is fully before me, it cannot be wrong. For how can I be mistaken at a given moment about the sheer content of my experience at that moment?

Despite the forthright appeal of this argument, the fact seems to be that my judgments at a moment about what I immediately apprehend at that moment are often wrong. That is to say, they are often withdrawn for good reason. This is sometimes denied on the ground that, since the momentary experience is instantly gone, the judgment is forever safe from further test. But the judgment I made a few moments ago that a reddish patch occupied the center of my visual field at that moment will be dropped if it conflicts with other judgments having a combined stronger claim to preservation. For example, if I also judged that the patch occupying the same region an instant later was blue, and also that the apparent color was constant over the brief period covering the two instants, I am going to have to drop one of the three judgments; and circumstances may point to the first as well as to either of the others. Indeed judgments concerning immediate phenomena may be rejected in favor of judgments concerning physical objects, as happens when I conclude that it could not have been a reddish patch after all since I was looking at a bluebird in sunlight with my eyes functioning normally. In either sort of case, I cannot reasonably plead a mere slip of the tongue; I am deciding that a judgment was wrong. If a statement may be withdrawn in the interest of compatibility and other statements, it is not certain in any ordinary sense; for certainty consists of immunity to such withdrawal.

Now someone may object that all I have shown is that a judgment concerning phenomena at a given moment may be doubted at some later moment, while what is being claimed is merely that such a judgment is certain *at* the moment in question. This seems to me a confusion. When we talk of certainty we are not—I take it—talking about a feeling of utter conviction; nor are we asking whether a judgment made at a given moment can be withdrawn at that same moment. We are talking of knowledge without possibility of error—or, in practice, of judgment immune to subsequent withdrawal for cause. I cannot be said to be certain about what occurs at a given moment, even at that moment, if I may justifiably change my mind about it at a later moment.

The advocate of empirical certainty, however, is not put off by a failure to find instances or by the problems encountered in arriving at an unexceptionable statement of his thesis. The difficulty of formulating the given must not, Mr. Lewis warns, lead us to suppose that there is no given; for if there were no given there would be no experience as we know it at all. No argument can erase the fact that experience and knowledge are not purely arbitrary, willful inventions. The sheer stubbornness of experience recognized by even the most thoroughgoing idealists is proof enough that there is *something there* in experience, some element not manufactured but given. This cannot be denied whatever may be the difficulties of articulating it.

But this all seems to me to point to, or at least to be compatible with, the conclusion that while something is given, nothing given is true; that while some things may be indubitable, nothing is certain. What we have been urged to grant amounts at most to this: materials for or particles of experience are given, sensory qualities or events or other elements are not created at will but presented, experience has some content even though our description of it may be artificial or wrong and even though the precise differentiation between what is given and what is not given may be virtually impossible. But to such content or materials or particles or elements, the terms "true," "false," and "certain" are quite inapplicable. These elements are simply there or not there. To grant that some are there is not to grant that anything is certain. Such elements may be indubitable in the vacuous sense that doubt is irrelevant to them, as it is to a desk; but they, like the desk, are equally devoid of certainty. They may be before us, but they are neither true nor false. For truth and falsity and certainty pertain to statements or judgments and not to mere particles or materials or elements. Thus, to deny that there are empirical certainties does not imply that experience is a pure fiction, that it is without content, or even that there is no given element.

Some of Mr. Lewis' arguments, however, are aimed directly at showing that there must be some indubitable judgments or statements, not merely that there is something presented. Unless some statements are certain, he argues, none is even probable. Mr. Reichenbach has disputed this argument on mathematical grounds, but perhaps Mr. Lewis intends only to make a somewhat less technical point. It plainly does us no good to know that a statement is probable with respect to certain premises unless we have some confidence in these premises. And we cannot just say that the premises themselves need merely be probable; for this means only that they in turn are probable with respect to other premises, and so on without end. Probability will be genuinely useful in judging the truth of sentences—the argument runs—only if the chain of probability relationships is somewhere moored to certainty. This is closely akin to the argument against a pure coherence theory of truth. Internal coherence is obviously a necessary but not a sufficient condition for the truth of a system; for we need also some means of choosing between equally tight systems that are incompatible with each other. There must be a tie to fact through, it is contended, some immediately certain statements. Otherwise compatibility with a system is not even a probable indication of the truth of any statement.

Now clearly we cannot suppose that statements derive their credibility from other statements without ever bringing this string of statements to earth. Credibility may be transmitted from one statement to another through deductive or probability connections; but credibility does not spring from these connections by spontaneous generation. Somewhere along the line some statements, whether atomic sense reports or the entire system or something in between, must have initial credibility. So far the argument is sound. To use the term "probability" for this initial credibility is to risk misunderstanding since probability, strictly speaking, is not initial at all but always relative to specified premises. Yet all that is indicated is credibility to some degree, not certainty. To say that some statements must be initially credible if any statement is ever to be credible at all is not to say that any statement is immune to withdrawal. For indeed, as remarked earlier, no matter how strong its initial claim to preservation may be, a statement will be dropped if its retention—along with consequent adjustments in the interest of coherence—results in a system that does not satisfy as well as possible the totality of claims presented by all relevant statements. In the "search for truth" we deal with the clamoring demands of conflicting statements by trying, so to speak, to realize the greatest happiness of the greatest number of them. These demands constitute a different factor from coherence, the wanted means of choosing between different systems, the missing link with fact; yet none is so strong that it may not be denied. That we have probable knowledge, then, implies no certainty but only initial credibility.

Still, I am not satisfied that we have as yet gone to the heart of the matter. Just why is it so important to decide whether or not there is some empirical certainty? Mr. Reichenbach says that Mr. Lewis' view is a vestige of rationalism; but unlike the rationalists, Mr. Lewis obviously is not seeking certainties in order to use them as axioms for a philosophical system. If he could once prove that there are some empirical certainties, I doubt if he would be much disposed to go catch one. Rather he is convinced that such certainties are somehow essential to knowledge as we possess it. And I suspect that both his specific arguments and my counter-arguments may leave him, as they leave me, with a feeling that the real issue has not yet been brought into relief. The underlying motivation for Mr. Lewis's whole argument is to be found, I think, in the problem of relating language to what it describes.

Consider the familiar problem faced by a common version of pragmatism. The meaning and truth of a statement are said to lie in its predictive consequences. These consequences are themselves statements; for from statements we can deduce, or even infer with probability, nothing but other statements. But, if the truth of these predictions depends in turn upon the truth of others derived from them, we are lost in an endless regress. The theory rests upon our being able, when a particular moment arrives, to decide with some degree of confidence whether a prediction made concerning that moment is or is not fulfilled. Accordingly, statements describing immediate experience are specifically exempted from the predictive criterion. But what, then, is to be said concerning them? What sort of relationship to experience makes such a statement true or credible? The connection between a statement and the very dissimilar experience it describes is not easy to grasp. Testimony to the rather mysterious character of the relation is found in the oblique way it is referred to in the literature. Mr. Quine wrote recently that a system of statements "impinges at its edges" upon experience; and he has been twitted for waxing so metaphorical. I suspect that the metaphorical term was chosen purposely to intimate that we have here an inadequately understood relationship. Again, Mr. Lewis, choosing simile rather than metaphor, merely likens the relationship to that between an outcry and the fearful apparition that evokes it.

What I am suggesting is that Mr. Lewis is actually more vitally concerned with the directness and immediacy and irreducibility of this relation between sensory experience and sentences describing it than with the certainty of these sentences. For, if this crucial relation seems inexplicable, perhaps—the thought runs—that is just because it is so fundamental and simple as to require no explanation. Learning a language may involve becoming acquainted with this elementary and irreducible relation, of which subsequent cases are instantly recognized. The claim that statements describing bare sense experience are certain then becomes an accidental by-product of the view that their truth is immediately and directly apprehended. And the real challenge that emerges is not to muster arguments showing that there are no empirical certainties, but to point a way of explaining the root relation between language and the nonlinguistic experience it describes.

Plainly we cannot look to resemblance for any help. The English statement "There is a blue patch" and its Chinese equivalent are very unlike, and both are even more unlike the blue patch itself. In no literal sense does language mirror experience. Yet this false start has something in its favor. The explanation in terms of resemblance is very good except for being so wrong. By that I mean that to explain the relation in question is to subsume it under or analyze it into more general relations. Such terms as "describes," "is true," "denotes," and "designates," require explanation because they are idiosyncratic to cases where the first element in question is linguistic. Only words and strings of words denote or are true. Our problem is to reduce these purely semantic predicates to predicates that have familiar instances in nonlinguistic experience.[1]

A clue to a better starting point than resemblance lies in the fact that a toot may warn of an oncoming train or that a ray of dawn foretells the approach of daylight. Here are nonverbal events standing as *signals* for others. In like fashion two sensory experiences or phenomena are often such that the earlier is a promise or warning or signal of the later. A feeling of warmth may signal the imminent appearance of a fiery red patch in the visual field; an evenly shaded patch may signal a certain tactual experience to come. Of course, the situation is seldom quite so simple. More often, an isolated presentation signals another only conditionally upon certain behavior; that is, the tactual experience ensues only if I reach out my hand in a certain way. But this can be accommodated without difficulty merely by recognizing that a presentation is itself usually a partial, incomplete signal that combines with other presentations (such as those of bodily movements) to constitute a signal for a subsequent experience. In other words, a signal is often comprised of more than one presentation; but this does not affect the important point that some nonlinguistic experiences function as signals.

If asked for a psychological account of signaling, we might say that the earlier experience arouses an expectation that is fulfilled, or a tension that is released, by the later one. But this and the various questions it inspires are not quite apposite to the present task. Our primary objective is not to explain this relation but to explain certain semantic predicates in terms of it. So long as we are satisfied that the relation clearly obtains in nonlinguistic experience, we can postpone consideration of its anatomy and genealogy.

If experiences comprised of such presentations as shaded patches can signal, there is no mystery about how an irregular black patch or a brief stretch of sound may function in the same way. And a statement-event[2] or other string of word-events, is simply some such patch or stretch. Just

---

[1] Thus our problem differs from that considered by Tarski in *Der Wahrheitsbegriff in den formalisierten Sprachen,* in which he defines truth in terms of the purely semantic notion of *satisfaction.*

[2] I use the term "statement-event" at times to emphasize that I think of a statement as an actual utterance or inscription-at-a-moment.

as a blue patch and some kineaesthetic presentations may signal the coming appearance of a red patch, so also does a statement-event—let us name it "F"—say in advance that there will be a red patch in the visual field at the time in question, t. Statements are merely more complicated, and hence often more specific, than some other signals. It is clear enough how a signaling system can be elaborated and refined, once even a few signaling relationships are available. Under some circumstances or other, almost anything can be made to serve as a signal for almost any subsequent experience. Differentiation between conditioned and unconditioned signaling is irrelevant to our present purpose.

It may be contended that statements signal by virtue of their meaning and that their signaling is thus essentially different from that of nonlinguistic elements. On the contrary, I should say rather that statements mean by virtue of their signaling; for "means," like "denotes," is one of the puzzling semantic predicates that constitute our problem. Yet this is not to say that a statement either means or denotes what it signals; the explanation of meaning or denoting in terms of signaling would have to be much more complex than that.

So far, however, only statements like F that are in the future tense have been provided for. What are we to do about statements in the present tense? Suppose the statement P "There is now a red patch in the visual field" occurs at the time t above in question. P does not *signal* the simultaneous occurrence of the red patch; for signaling is always forecasting. Nevertheless, we know that P is true if and only if F is true. Hence P is true just in case F is a genuine signal. Although P does not itself signal the occurrence of the red patch, the truth of P is explained in terms of the truth of the earlier statement F, which does signal this occurrence. Statements in the past tense can be handled in the same way as those in the present tense; and tenseless statements, depending on whether they occur before, during, or after the time they pertain to, in the same way as statements in, respectively, the future, present, and past tense. A key point of the present proposal lies in its radical departure from the usual attack, which rests the truth of all statements upon that of statements in the present tense and leaves us at a loss to deal with these. After all, a thoroughly predictive theory can be carried through only by basing all truth upon the truth of statement-events concerning later events.

What I have been saying is meant to apply just to rather simple statements, like those illustrated, about phenomena. The relation of other statements to these is not part of my present problem. But even with respect to the simple statements in question, a number of problems must be left untouched. For example, I cannot here discuss the means available for dealing with a statement, in the present tense, such that no correlative statement in the future tense ever happened to occur.

I expect to be told that what I offer is a fragment of a time-worn theory in a somewhat topsy-turvy version. But I make no claim to a complete or unprecedented or pretty theory. Nor am I at all complacent about pragmatic-predictive epistemology in general. What I have tried to do here is to suggest how, in terms of a pragmatism not entirely alien to Mr. Lewis' point of view, the connection between language and what it describes may be given a reasonable explanation. In that case, this relation need no longer be regarded as immediate, mystic, and inexplicable. And this, if I am correct, will remove the last and deepest motivation for the defense of empirical certainty.

THE GIVEN ELEMENT IN EMPIRICAL KNOWLEDGE

• Since I have already said in print how I would propose to deal with our present topic, and my colleagues on this program have made references to that view, let me here omit any attempted summary and try instead to emphasize those basic considerations which, as I see it, dictate this conception of an incorrigible datum-element underlying empirical beliefs which are justified.

Empirical knowledge—if there be any such thing—is distinguished by having as an essential factor or essential premise something disclosed in experience. That is a tautology. To express this tautological fact circumstantially and circumspectly can be a matter of some difficulty; but, if anyone should deny what we so attempt to state, he must impress us as philosophizing by the Russian method of the big lie, and argument with him might well be useless. It is this essential factor in knowledge which comes from experience which I would speak of as 'the given.'

But since experience and the functioning of it as the basis of empirical knowledge is something open to the inspection of all of us, each in his own case, how comes it that we tell such different tales about it? The account which I have offered has frequently met with dissent; and this dissent with respect to something which, if correctly stated, should be obvious gives me pause. If those who so find fault held a rationalistic theory, I might offer myself the excuse that they philosophize in the interest of an unsound major premise. But the greater number of my critics have been as firmly empiricistic in their professed convictions as myself. That is just what puzzles me most, because I seem to find only two alternatives for a plausible account of knowledge: either there must be some ground in experience, some factuality it directly affords, which plays an indispensable part in the validation of empirical beliefs, or what determines empirical truth is merely some logical relationship of a candidate-belief with other beliefs which have been accepted. And in the latter case any reason, apart from factualities afforded by experience, why these *antecedent* beliefs have been accepted remains obscure. Even passing that difficulty, this second alternative would seem to be merely a revival of the coherence theory of truth, whose defects have long been patent.

There undoubtedly is some logical relation of facts—or more than one —to which the name 'coherence' might aptly be given. And there is equally little doubt that such logical and systemic relationships are important for assuring credibility—once a sufficient number of antecedent and relevant facts have been otherwise determined. But no logical relationship, by itself, can ever be sufficient to establish the truth, or the credibility even, of any synthetic judgment. That is one point which logical studies of the last half century have made abundantly clear. Unless the beliefs so related, or some of them, have a warrant which no logical principle can assure, no logical relation of them to one another constitutes a scintilla of evidence that they are even probable.

Let us assume that the whole of the truth has even that strongest type of coherence illustrated by a system of geometry. The statements of the system (postulates and theorems together) are so related that, if we should be doubtful of any one of them, the other statements of the system would be sufficient to assure it with deductive certainty. But that relationship, as we know, is insufficient to determine any truth about the geometric properties of actual things. If Euclid is thus coherent, then so too are Riemann and Lobachevsky; though given any denotation of the geometric vocabulary, these three geometries are mutually incompatible systems. If the truth about our space is ever to be ascertained, something disclosed in experience must be the final arbiter. Since this is the case for geometric truths, which cohere by the strong relations of deductive logic, *a fortiori* it must be the case for empirical truth at large, for the determination of which we must so often rely upon induction, which affords a probability only, on the supposition that our premises are certain or that they have some antecedent probability on other grounds.

In brief, we have nothing but experience and logic to determine truth or credibility of any synthetic judgment. Rule out datum-facts afforded by experience, and you have nothing left but the logically certifiable. And logic will not do it.

Such argument by elimination is admittedly not final, and I would not rest upon that but would appeal additionally to the facts of life. However, I would ask my critics where they stand on this point. Have they repudiated a fundamental requirement of any empiricistic theory? Are they rationalists who think to extract from logical considerations alone some sufficient ground for empirical beliefs? Or are they really skeptics who dislike to acknowledge that fact in so many words? Or do they find some third alternative which I have overlooked?

One class of those who disagree have made their point of objection clear; it concerns my supposition that what is given in experience is incorrigible and indubitable. Empiricists generally are agreed that nonperceptual synthetic knowledge rests finally on knowledge which is perceptual and so find the root problem in the nature of perception. Practically all empiricists recognize that some items of perceptual cognition are less than indubitable; perception is subject to illusion and mistake. They differ among themselves as to whether all perceptions, or some only, are subject to doubt. Mr. Moore, for example, regards such convictions as "This is my hand" (under appropriate circumstances) as subject to no doubt. But many, perhaps most of us, can find differences of degree only in the valid assurance of perceptual judgments: we recognize that most of them have what may be called 'practical certainty' but think that none of them is theoretically and validly certain. Those of us who come to this conclusion are then confronted with the following question: Is there, either antecedent to and supporting the perceptual belief in objective fact, or in the perceptual experience itself, an element or factor which is the basis of the perceptual judgment but is not, like this judgment of objective fact, subject to theoretical doubt?

My own answer to this question is affirmative. When I perceive a door, I may be deceived by a cleverly painted pattern on the wall, but the presentation which greets my eye is an indubitable fact of my experience. My perpetual belief in a real door, having another side, is not an explicit inference but a belief suggested by association; nevertheless the *validity* of this interpretation is that and that only which could attach to it as an inductive inference from the given visual presentation. The given element is this incorrigible presentational element; the criticizable and dubitable element is the element of interpretation.

The arguments which have been offered in criticism of this view are literally too numerous to be mentioned here. Some of them have been of the casual variety which may be advanced without reference to any attempted full account of empirical knowledge. The objections of Goodman and Reichenbach, however, are not of that sort but are made in the interest of alternative views which are complex and worked out. Neither of them has had time to do more than suggest his alternative conceptions; and I shall have time only to suggest where, as it seems to me, some of the critical issues lie.

I hope I shall not give offense if I say that Reichenbach's view impresses me as being an unabridged probabilism; a modernized coherence theory with two immense advantages over the older one so named. First, he makes provision for observation-statements, though he insists that these should be in objective ('physical') language, and that they are both dubitable and corrigible. And second, he substitutes for the vague relation, historically called 'coherence,' meticulously described relations of probability-inference.

First, as to observation-statements: Let us suppose that I look over yonder and report that I see a horse. You (being epistemologists) may reply that you find my report ambiguous; that statements of the form "I see an X" are assertions of objective fact if and only if the constants substitutable for 'X' are understood to be confined to expressions denoting physical entities, but that statements of this form are in the protocol or expressive idiom if and only if the expressions substitutable for 'X' are understood to be designations of *appearances*. In the one case—you observe —I have made a dubitable assertion of an existent horse; in the other case, I have merely reported a specific given presentation which, whether dubitable or not, at least asserts no real horse as being present. This protocol statement, in its intended meaning—so I would claim—will be true just in case I am not lying or making some verbal mistake in the words I use. I am unable to see that Reichenbach's denial of this second and expressive idiom, is other than a dogmatism. (Even his 'phenomenal language' seems not to coincide with what I deem essential for any formulation of the given in experience.) I would, moreover, emphasize that the near absence of any restricted vocabulary or syntax for expressive statements is an unimportant matter for empirical knowledge itself: no one needs verbal formulation of his own present experience in order to be aware of it; and obviously, nobody else's protocols are indubitable to us. Protocol expression is as inessential to what it expresses as a cry of fear is to the fearful apparition which may cause it. It is for purposes of epistemological discussion that the notion of protocol statements is principally needed; though there are, of course, statements so intended, and the requisite idiom is one which finds exemplification in natural language.

Let us pass these points, however, and take it that the observer of the horse has formulated his observation in objective ('physical') language, and that what he reports is dubitable and only probable. Reichenbach himself refers to the difficulty which then arises (attributing the objection to Russell): a statement justified as probable must have a ground; if the ground is only probable, then there must be a ground of it, and so on. And to assess the probability of the original statement, its probability relative to its ground must be multiplied by the probability of this ground, which in turn must be multiplied by the probability of its own ground, and so on. Reichenbach denies that the regressive series of probability-values so arising must approach zero and the probability of the original statement be thus finally whittled down to nothing. That matter could be discussed for the rest of the afternoon or longer; it makes a difference whether one is talking about determined probabilities on known grounds, or merely what are called 'a priori probabilities.' However, even if we accept the correction which Reichenbach urges here, I disbelieve that it will save his point. For that, I think he must prove that, where any such regress of probability-values is involved, the progressively qualified fraction measuring the probability of the quaesitum will converge to some determinable value other than zero; and I question whether such proof can be given. Nor do I think that the difficulty can be removed by his 'argument from concatenation.' It is true that, by the rule of inverse probabilities, we may proceed in either direction, determining the probability of a 'consequence' from the probability of a 'ground,' or of a 'ground' from a 'consequence.' (But what I would emphasize is that, as Reichenbach mentions, you cannot take even the first step in either direction until you are prepared to assign numerical values to the 'antecedent probabilities' called for by the rule. These must literally be determined *before* use of the rule will determine the probability of anything. And, if the answer be given that these can be determined by another use of the rule, the rebuttal is obvious: in that case you must make that *other* use of it *before* you can make *this* one. An interminable progressus or regressus need not defeat theoretical purposes provided you are on the right end of it—the end from which its members are successively determinable. But in the kind of case here in point, one is always on the wrong end of any segment of the series, always required to determine something else first before one can determine what one wants to determine. The supposition that the probability of anything whatever always depends on something else which is only probable itself, is flatly incompatible with the justifiable assignment of any probability at all. Reichenbach suggests that the craving for some certainty here is a retained trace of rationalism; my countersuggestion would be that it is the attempt to retain a trace of empiricism.

Even more crudely put: the probabilistic conception strikes me as supposing that if enough probabilities can be got to lean against one another they can all be made to stand up. I suggest that, on the contrary, unless some of them can stand alone, they will all fall flat. If no nonanalytic statement is categorically assertable, without probability qualification, then I think the whole system of such could provide no better assurance of anything in it than that which attaches to the contents of a well-written novel. I see no hope for such a coherence theory which repudiates data of experience which are simply given—or no hope unless a postulate be added to the effect that *some* synthetic statements are probable a priori; the postulate, for example, that every perceptual belief has *some* probability just on account of being a perceptual belief.[3]

There is time only for very brief comment on one other point. Both

[3] This was suggested to me by Professor Paul Henle—though not as a supposition which he would adopt.

Goodman and Reichenbach would impose a requirement of consistency —or 'inductive consistency'—on protocols. This goes along with their supposition that what protocols report is dubitable and corrigible. Briefly and inadequately, there is no requirement of consistency which is relevant to protocols. A protocol is a report of given appearances, of experience as such. Looking out over this audience, I see in one place two heads on one neck. When I lift my own head a bit, I see only one head there. But that is no reason to alter my first protocol and deny this apparition of two heads. I do not, of course, believe the two apparent heads to be actual. It is at *that* point that the requirement of inductive consistency comes in. But the critique by which I avoid that conclusion as to objective fact is criticism of a suggested interpretation—of a perceptual *belief* —and not a criticism of what the protocol reports. What it further indicates is only the desirability of some objective explanation of this apparition. The careless observer's protocols, the insane man's direct experience, and the content of the dreamer's dream must not be corrected or eliminated in the interest of consistency; to do that would be simple falsification of facts of experience. The problem of empirical knowledge at large is the problem of an account of objective facts which will accord with the occurrence of the experiences reported in all truthful and verbally accurate protocols. That is one test of adequate empirical knowledge. And the capacity of the objective account to explain any puzzling and apparent incongruities of experience is a further such test. To call a given experience an illusion, or a dream, or a careless observation, is to indicate the kind of objective fact which will explain it—just as the laws of optics and the fact of my looking through the edge of my glasses explains my apparition of two heads. We must not forget that experience is all that is given to us for the purposes of empirical knowing and that such knowledge of objective facts as we achieve is simply that body of beliefs which represents our over-all interpretation of experience. If we could not be sure of our experience when we have it, we should be in poor position to determine any objective fact, or confirm the supposition of one, or assign any probability to one.

I regret not to make the further and detailed comments which Goodman's paper merits. Disbelieving that my conception of an indubitable given element in experience can be maintained, he suppresses further criticisms he might have, in the interest of a possible pragmatic reformulation of statements describing experience.

Putting it oversimply one may say that what he proposes is the interpretation of observation-statements in terms of the forward-looking import of what they lead us to expect. But that proposal is, I fear, a little more pragmatic than I dare to be. However plausibly such reformulation could be carried out, it would fail to satisfy me because of a conviction I have concerning the task of epistemological study; the conviction, namely, that a principal business of epistemology is with the *validity* of knowledge. And validity concerns the character of cognition as warranted or justified.

In order to be knowledge, empirical judgment must not only have predictive import of what will verify or confirm it; it must also be distinguished from a merely lucky or unlucky guess or hazard of belief by having some justifying ground. And in the nature of the case, what so justifies an empirical judgment cannot be something future to it and presently uninspectable but must lie in something antecedent to or compresent with it. Where it is perceptual cognition which is in question, the point is that the interpretation of experience—the perceptual belief—*is* significant of the future and verifiable, but, in order that this belief have *validity,* that which functions as the ground of it must be present and given.

That is precisely the point with which I am here principally concerned. It is on account of that point that I have felt it necessary to depart from or to supplement other pragmatic theories. And it is on account of that point that I could not accept Goodman's pragmatic proposal: by interpreting empirical findings in terms of what is future to them, it would invite confusion of the ground of knowledge which is there and given with what is not there but anticipated. It is also on that same account that I must disagree with various other current theories, put forward as empirical, which fail to recognize the datum-element of experience. In terms of such conceptions—so I think—no explanation of the validity of knowledge is forthcoming or even possible, and the holders of them can escape the skeptical conclusion only by failing to look where they are going.

I consider skepticism something worse than unsatisfactory; I consider it nonsense to hold or to imply that just any empirical judgment is as good as any other—because none is warranted. A theory which implies or allows that consequence is not an explanation of anything but merely an intellectual disaster.

BIBLIOGRAPHY FOR PART II

Adrian, E. D., *The Physical Background of Perception*, Oxford University Press, London, 1947.

Allers, R., "Remarks on Some Problems Concerning Sensation," *The Modern Schoolman*, XXII (1944-45), pp. 76-87; 155-67.

——, "The Cognitive Aspect of Sensations," *The Thomist*, IV (1942), pp. 589-648.

Aldrich, V. C., "What We See With," *The Journal of Philosophy*, XXXV (1938), pp. 253-63.

Barnes, W. H. F., "On Seeing and Hearing," *Contemporary British Philosophy*, 3rd series, ed. H. D. Lewis, The Macmillan Co., New York, 1956, pp. 63-81.

Bentley, A. F., "Sights-Seen as Materials of Knowledge," *The Journal of Philosophy*, XXXVI (1939), pp. 169-81.

Boas, G., "Learning from Experience," *The Journal of Philosophy*, XXXXIII (1946), pp. 466-71.

Bradley, F. H., "On our Knowledge of Immediate Experience," *Mind*, n.s., XVIII (1909), pp. 40-64.

Delvolvé, J., "Les paliers de la connaissance et la constitution spirituelle de l'homme," *Revue de Métaphysique et de Morale,* XXXVIII (1931), pp. 527–68.

Ducasse, C. J., "Introspection, Mental Acts, and Sensa," *Mind,* n.s., XXXXV (1936), pp. 181–92.

Fabro, C., "Knowledge and Perception in Aristotelic-Thomistic Psychology," *The New Scholasticism,* XII (1938), pp. 337–65.

Garnett, A. C., "A Naturalistic Interpretation of Mind," *The Journal of Philosophy,* XXXXV (1948), pp. 589–603.

Gibson, J. J., *The Perception of the Visual World,* Houghton-Mifflin Co., Boston, 1950.

Hammond, A. J., "On Sensation," *The Philosophical Review,* LIII (1944), pp. 260–85.

Hartnack, J., *Analysis of the Problem of Perception in British Empiricism,* E. Munksgaard, Copenhagen, 1950.

Hodgson, R., "The Consciousness of External Reality," *Mind,* X (1885), pp. 321–46.

Hutten, E. H., "Perception and Sense Knowledge," *The Journal of Philosophy,* XXXXIV (1947), pp. 85–97.

Joseph, H. W. B., "The Psychological Explanation of the Development of the Perception of External Objects," *Mind,* N.S., XIX (1910), pp. 305–21; 457–69.

Klubertanz, G. P., *"De Potentia* 5.8. Note on the Thomist Theory of Sensation," *The Modern Schoolman,* XXVI (1948–49), pp. 323–31.

——, "Internal Senses in the Process of Cognition," *The Modern Schoolman,* XVIII (1941–42), pp. 27–31.

——, "St. Thomas and the Knowledge of the Singular," *The New Scholasticism,* XXVI (1952), pp. 135–66.

Kneale, W., "Sensation and the Physical World," *The Philosophical Quarterly,* I (1950–51), pp. 109–26.

Krikorian, Y. H., "An Empirical Definition of Consciousness," *The Journal of Philosophy,* XXXV (1938), pp. 156–61.

Lemaire, J., *Notes complémentaires sur une théorie de la connaissance sensible,* Desclée, Burges, 1923.

Mach, E., *Analysis of Sensations,* Open Court Publishing Co., Chicago, 1915.

Mailloux, N., "The Problem of Perception," *The Thomist,* IV (1942), pp. 266–85.

Marc, A., "Problèmes de Psychologie: 1. De la sensation à l'image . . ," *Archives de Philosophie,* 1936, No. 12, pp. 371–94.

Marcotte, J. N., "Materiality and Knowledge," *The New Scholasticism,* XXI (1947), pp. 349–70.

Martin, O., "The Given and the Interpretative Elements in Perception," *The Journal of Philosophy,* XXXV (1938), pp. 337–45.

McNapsy, C. J., "Augustine on Sensation," *The Modern Schoolman,* XV, No. 1 (1937), pp. 6–9.

Moore, A., "Verifiability and Phenomenalism," *The Journal of Philosophy,* XXXXVII (1950), pp. 169–77.

Moore, T. V., "The Scholastic Theory of Perception," *The New Scholasticism,* VII (1933), pp. 222–38.

Oakeley, H. D., "Mind in Nature," *Philosophy,* XX (1945), pp. 30–39.

Patricia, Sister M., "Validity of Sense Perception," *Proceedings,* American Catholic Philosophical Association, XII (1938), pp. 121–34.

Péghaire, J. L., Simon, Y. R., "The Philosophical Study of Sensation," *The Modern Schoolman,* XXIII (1945–46), pp. 111–19.

Pieron, H., *The Sensations,* Yale University Press, New Haven, 1952.

Prall, D. W., "Knowledge as Aptness of the Body," *The Philosophical Review,* XXXXVII (1938), pp. 128–54.

Presson, V., "G. E. Moore's Theory of Sense-Data," *The Journal of Philosophy,* XXXXVIII (1951), pp. 34–42.

Prichard, H. A., *Knowledge and Perception,* Oxford University Press, New York, 1950.

Robson, J. W., "Going Beyond Experience," *The Journal of Philosophy,* XXXXIV (1947), pp. 197–205.

Ryan, E. J., *The Role of the "Sensus Communis" in the Psychology of St. Thomas,* The Messenger Press, Carthagena, Ohio, 1951.

Salzi, P., *La Sensation,* Alcan, Paris, 1934.

Sellars, R. W., "Sensations as Guides to Perceiving," *Mind,* N.S., LXVIII (1959), pp. 2–15.

Simon, Y. R., "Positions aristotéliciennes concernant le problème de l'activité du sens," *Revue de Philosophie,* n.s., IV (1933), pp. 229–58.

Strong, C. A., "On the Relation of Appearances to Real Things," *Mind,* n.s., XXXVII (1928), pp. 173–91.

———, *Why the Mind Has a Body,* The Macmillan Co., New York, 1903.

Swabey, W. C., "Do Material Things Exist," *The Journal of Philosophy,* XXXVIII (1941), pp. 655–65.

Tusquets, J., "Crítica de la Sensació," *Criterion,* IV (1928), Fasc. 15.

Walsh, F. A., "Phantasm and Phantasy," *The New Scholasticism,* IX (1935), pp. 116–33.

Yolton, J. W., "The Ontological Status of Sense-Data in Plato's Theory of Perception," *Review of Metaphysics,* III (1949–50), pp. 21–58.

Part III : INTELLECTUAL KNOWLEDGE

". . . In spite of the fact that the cognitive processes lie more fully open to our inspection than the world at large and what goes on in it, the epistemological questions fail to show progress toward any clearer and better assured determination of them than do the metaphysical ones. And this difficulty we find in arriving at any general consensus on matters which are as familiar and easily observable to any one of us as to any other may arouse suspicion that the questions themselves are not well put; that there is some lack of clarity as to what, if it could be determined, would constitute an acceptable answer to them; or even whether there is any answer which could be given and would prove final. Such examination of the questions themselves sends us back to a third kind of problem: "What does this issue mean? Is it perhaps meaningless?" Even this, as we are all aware, is not the end. Meanings are something entertained by individuals in the privacy of their own minds; but any conveying of them depends on language. Also, we largely think in words; and language, being mainly developed for practical rather than theoretical purposes, can betray a philosophic question or subvert an intended answer. Some penetration of the ambiguities and obscurities of language is called for, and perhaps some devisement of linguistic instruments having a higher order of precision. So we retreat once more; this time into syntax and semantics. And here, finally, we discover one further question still: "What is it that is meant by 'meaning'?". We encounter the complication that there is more than one sense of that which language can express and more than one dimension of the import of thought itself."

C. I. Lewis
"Realism or Phenomenalism?",
The Philosophical Review, vol. 64, 1955, pp. 233–4.

A. I. Melden : THOUGHT AND ITS OBJECTS

Pᴿᴏꜰᴇꜱꜱᴏʀ *A. I. Melden of the Department of Philosophy, University of Washington, suggests the difficulties encountered in the analysis of propositions and such terms as "thinking of" and "meaning" as intentional statements. The existent reality, the statement of knowledge of it, and the statement of "thinking of" or "meaning" involve the knower in complexities sketched out in this essay. Reprinted by permission from* ᴘʜɪʟᴏꜱᴏᴘʜʏ ᴏꜰ ꜱᴄɪᴇɴᴄᴇ, *vii* (1940), *pp. 434–41.*

• What are the objects of thought? To consider a familiar case, may we assert that the proposition "I am thinking of a unicorn" entails that there is some object which is being thought of? Theories of subsistent objects provide an affirmative answer and seem to be based on the consideration that we are thinking of something when we think of a unicorn. Otherwise, to paraphrase G. E. Moore's well known statement of the argument, we would be thinking of the same thing whether we thought of a unicorn or a griffen, namely, nothing. But, as G. E. Moore has shown, subsistence theories fail to distinguish between the logical and grammatical forms of such statements as "I am thinking of a unicorn" and "I am hunting a lion." [1] The latter is of the form $(\exists x) \cdot \phi x \cdot \psi x$; the former is not since it does not assert that the property of being a unicorn and the property of thought of by me both belong to something. But the problem that suggests itself is the nature of the contention that something is being thought of when, for example, we think of a unicorn. To begin with, is there no acceptable alternative to the various forms of the theory of subsistent objects according to which it would be correct to say that the proposition "I am thinking of a unicorn" entails the proposition "$(\exists x) \cdot x$ is being thought of?" And if saying that we are thinking of something, when we think of a unicorn, does not mean that there exists something that is being thought of, what is the force of the contention that we are thinking of something?

It is sometimes assumed that the verb "to think" which occurs in sentences of the grammatical form "I am thinking of x," always functions in the same way. In order to secure a more precise statement of our problem, let us examine this matter in the light of a suggestion once made by Miss L. S. Stebbing. Following G. E. Moore's discussion of the propositions "I am thinking of a unicorn" and "I am hunting a lion," Miss Stebbing contended that the reason why the first proposition does not assert that the property of being a unicorn and the property of being thought of by me both belong to something is the fact that *being thought of by me* is not a property at all.[2]

There is, however, a very broad sense of "property" according to which a property is that which may be asserted of an existent. While we think of unicorns as unreal, we think of the Golden Gate Bridge as real, and it would be correct to say of this existent that it is being thought of. It is true, however, that we cannot deduce that anything is real from the fact that we think of it as real. Did Miss Stebbing intend, therefore, that *being thought of by me* is not a property in the sense that it never follows from any proposition of the form "I am thinking of x" that x exists? Properties

[1] *Philosophical Studies*, "The Conception of Reality," esp. pp. 215–218.
[2] *A Modern Introduction to Logic*, p. 160.

are properties of real objects, and *being hunted by me* is a property, since if it is a property of anything, it is of necessity a property of something real.

Let us imagine the following situation: I enter a room in which a number of persons are speaking of the table in the next room. There is no such object, but they suppose that there is. I am unaware of their error and say, apropos of the familiar question, "I am thinking of the table in the next room." Suppose I then discover that there is no such object, would I not retract my statement? I couldn't possibly have been thinking of the table in the next room since there was no such object. Not that I was really thinking of something else and somehow confused it with what I took to be a table in the next room. By hypothesis no such error arose, and I simply took it for granted that there was the described object. I meant that there was the object in question, for the verb "to think" in the sentence I uttered not only expressed the fact that there was thinking of a certain kind going on, but it had in addition the force of an assertion to the effect that this thinking was about something real. Compare the uses of "thinking" in the following sentence: "I couldn't possibly have been thinking of the table in the next room because there was no such object; but I was thinking of something even though I was thinking of nothing real." It is this first use of "thinking" which is analogous to that of "hunting." We must not therefore generalize from the use of the verb in "I am thinking of a unicorn" to all grammatically similar cases.

The most important class of cases for our purposes have to do with the understanding of the meaning of substantival words or expressions. In so far as we think of or understand the meaning of such terms as "the table in the next room," "unicorn," "lion," etc., we are apparently neither thinking of any entities which could be designated by these terms as real or unreal, nor are we asserting that they exist. How these cases differ from or are related to such cases as thinking of a unicorn, the table in the next room, etc., I do not propose to examine, although there is, evidently, an important family resemblance. The question of intentionality with which this discussion is immediately concerned may then be stated as follows: Given any substantival word or expression which may significantly occur in sentences of the form "x exists" and "x does not exist," does it follow from the fact that we think of or understand the meaning of the term that there exists any object of which we may be said to think?

G. F. Stout in his essay "Real Being and Being for Thought" has challenged the view that there are no intentional objects for the following reason: "It seems to involve an absurdity to suppose that what I am thinking of has no being except the being thought of. For how can the being of anything be merely constituted by its being related to something else. Is it not a logical precondition of its being related to something else that it should have a distinct being of its own?" [3] And he goes on to add, "if the possible severance of what really is and what is thought is once admitted in some cases it must be admitted in all." And since we can transcend our thoughts, that is to say, since we can think of what is not merely a thought but of what is real, it will always follow from the fact that we think of anything that $(\exists x) \cdot x$ is being thought of. Stout's view, while primarily intended as an analysis of judgment, can be applied to the present issue as follows: When, for example, we think of what "unicorn" means, we think of something. This means that there exists something which stands to our minds in the relation that constitutes knowledge by description. Since there are no unicorns, this object cannot have all of the properties connoted by "unicorn." It will, however, be some object of which alternative descriptions, including the one involved in the connotation of "unicorn" are possible. The intentional object will thus be some object known to exist, i.e., of which we have descriptive knowledge, and which is a member of the class of entities which may be defined as those which can significantly occur as values of x in the function "x is a unicorn." If we know that there are animals, the intentional object will be *some* animal. Failing this knowledge it will be some physical object. If, when we think of what "lion" means, we know that there are lions, the intentional object will be some lion. The intentional object will therefore vary with our descriptive knowledge, for the relation in which the mind stands to what it is thinking of is the relation which constitutes such knowledge. Let us examine this view:

1. It is proper to say when we think of what "unicorn" means that we are thinking of something—a certain kind of animal. On the present view, since we know that there are animals, what we are thinking of is some real animal. But while we may have learned what a unicorn is by being shown some animal and by being given some account of the relevant similarities and differences, clearly we are not, in thinking of what "unicorn" means, thinking of any animal we have ever seen, or could see. Consider what is perhaps the most favorable case for the present view, namely, when what we are thinking of is real, e.g., a lion. Since we know there are lions, there will be, on this view, some lion or lions of which we are thinking. It may be true that when we think of a lion we happen to have some lion in mind, e.g., the lion we saw in the zoo. But suppose we have no particular lion in mind—we merely think of what "lion" means. While it is true that when we think of what "lion" means we are thinking of something which we happen to know exists, it is false that there is *any* lion which we have in mind at all. It won't do to say that the intentional object was an undetermined lion, which one we don't know; if the inten-

[3] Published in *Studies in Philosophy and Psychology*, p. 335.

tional object was *some* lion then it must be true to say of *some* real lion that it was being thought of. And the plain fact of the matter is that when we thought of what "lion" means we had *no* real lion in mind. It isn't that we don't know or are undecided about which lion we were thinking; it is simply false to say of *any* given lion that it was being thought of.

2. On the present view, if there are two persons who both think of the meaning of "lion," and who are such that one knows and the other does not know that there are lions, there will be different intentional objects. Since the intentional object is, in each case, what is being thought of, they will necessarily be thinking of different things. But we would say ordinarily that the presence of knowledge of the existence of lions in the one case and its absence in the other does not constitute a difference in what is being thought of, but only in the way in which something is being thought of. One person will think of a lion as something he knows is real, the other will not; in either case they will be thinking of the same thing. But on the present view there will be different intentional objects, and hence a difference in the meaning of "lion." For the person who knows that there are lions, the statement "I am thinking of what 'lion' means" will entail that there are lions, since thinking of what "lion" means will be the same thing as thinking of some object which is a lion and which is known to exist. Accordingly, for that person the statement "Lions are unreal" will be impossible, for if he attaches meaning to the word "lion" he will understand the word to mean a real object which he knows exists, and the statement "Lions are unreal" will be equivalent to the nonsensical statement, "Something which is a lion does not exist."

These objections hinge on the allegation that in all cases there is an intentional object which, properly speaking, is being thought of. And the point is that thinking of what "unicorn," "lion," etc., mean must be distinguished from knowing that these or similar entities exist. It may be that one of the ways in which we learn to use words is by being shown entities of the kind which these words signify or, failing this, entities having some of the characteristics connoted by these terms. And it is true that in some cases we associate some object known by us to exist with the meaning we attach to a given word. But we must not confuse either the knowledge of the entities by means of which we gain our understanding of words, or the associations that come into play, with the actual understanding we have.

Why then should intentionality theories seem plausible, even necessary? It is not enough to observe that such views arise from the misleading grammatical similarity of such statements as "I am hunting a unicorn" and "I am thinking of what 'unicorn' means." Grammatical similarities very often fail to deceive. It would be far more enlightening to say that the grammatical similarity merely contributes to a more fundamental mistake which consists in the supposition that thinking and meaning are objects capable of some generic description. For if thinking is an object it can only be the kind of object which relates us to something. Thought, it will be said, is no purely immanent activity; we think not of our thoughts but of that of which our thoughts are thoughts. Hence thinking and meaning come to be regarded as relations or relational properties, and it seems plausible to argue that even when we are thinking of something unreal there must none the less exist something of which we are thinking.

This supposition seems to be encouraged by a view regarding the nature of philosophical analysis, according to which analysis consists in the disclosure of the constituents of propositions. What is meant by a constituent is not easy to determine. What specifically are the constituents of the class of propositions we have been considering? Miss Stebbing, for example, argues that *being thought of* is not a constituent; but what the supposed constituents are, she nowhere says. Are constituents observable or introspectible? If they are, the proposition "I am thinking of what 'unicorn' means" will be merely about images, whether word or memory images, muscular tensions, physiological activities, etc. But naturalistic and behavioristic analyses of propositions about thought and meaning seem altogether hopeless. If a constituent is in some sense something about which a proposition is a proposition, then thinking does seem to be a constituent. And if it is in this sense a constituent the question still remains whether it is or is not a kind of object. Is the question whether *being thought of* is a constituent to be decided by determining whether *being thought of* is or is not an incomplete symbol in the sense in which, as Russell has shown, the expression "the King of France" is an incomplete symbol? The peculiar fact about propositions concerning thinking and meaning is that no such analysis seems possible; if we attempt to say what thinking and meaning are we are reduced to the unhappy expedient of either using synonyms or grammatical equivalents or resorting to sheer metaphor. And if this is the issue, whether *being thought of* is a constituent, then we seem to be obliged to accept some intentionality doctrine.

I do not now propose to discuss the more general question of philosophical analysis. The conclusion I wish to urge is that thinking and meaning are not entities in the sense that they are objects of which a generic description or analysis is possible.[4] We can say what "table" means

---

[4] It is linguistically correct to say that the proposition "I am thinking of what 'unicorn' means" is *about* thinking and we do speak about thought, characterizing the thought of this or that man as facile, ingenious, true, etc. But it is just as fallacious to infer from these proprieties that thinking is a kind of object as it would be to suppose that since "unicorn" means something that this something is an object of which "unicorn" is a name (or, as it would be to suppose that since the proposition about thinking is also about me that I am a kind of object, an unchanging ego). The present point is another instance of the familiar warning concerning grammatical considerations.

without employing synonyms or metaphors. No corresponding analysis seems possible in the case of thought and meaning. They are unique and *sui generis*. The view that there are intentional objects presupposes that they are objects and hence relations or relational properties. But this is wholly gratuitous. Do thought and meaning thereby become mysterious and elusive? They become such if we ask what meaning or thought *as such* are, for the very question involves the mistake of supposing that they are describable objects. Does thought have objects, or, more specifically, does thinking of what "unicorn" means consist in there being an object of thought? It does not if by this we mean that $(\exists x) \cdot x$ is being thought of. It does if by this we mean that something is thought of. But the sense in which something is thought of is ultimate and unanalyzable. What can be analyzed and described is what it is that is being thought of, i.e., the kind of entity which anything would be if it were a unicorn. But what cannot be analyzed or described is the kind of entity which understanding itself is, precisely because it is no kind of object at all.

J. Maritain : BEING

THE activity of the mind as it confronts Being and is penetrated by it is described by Professor Jacques Maritain who here notes the acts of the mind—apprehension, judgment, and intuition of being—in the framework of a study of existentialism. Reprinted by permission from EXISTENCE AND THE EXISTENT, tr. by L. Galantière and G. B. Phelan, Pantheon Books, Inc., New York, 1949, pp. 10–35.

• Thomas Aquinas, I have remarked in another essay,[1] reaches existence itself through the operation of the intellect itself. He has the most exactingly classical idea of science; he is scrupulously attentive to the slightest requirements and the most highly refined rules and measures of logic, of reason, and of the art of putting ideas together. What he knows is no picture-book, but is that very heaven and earth in which there are more things than are dreamt of in all the philosophies. It is that existent universe, set firmly upon primary facts, which we are required to discover, not deduce; that universe traversed by all the influxes productive of being which vivify it, unify it, cause it to push onward towards the unforeseeable future; that universe, also, which is wounded by all those deficiencies of being that constitute the reality of evil and in which we must see the price paid for the interaction of beings, the price paid for created liberty, capable of evading the influx of the First Being.

Veritas sequitur esse rerum is the first Thomist position of which, in the present connection, we must note the significance. Truth follows upon the existence of things, i.e. of those trans-objective subjects with which thought stands face to face. Truth is the adequation of the immanence in act of our thought with that which exists outside our thought. True knowledge consists in a spiritual super-existence by which, in a supreme vital act, I become the other as such, and which corresponds to the existence exercised or possessed by that other itself in the particular field of intelligibility which is its peculiar possession.

Thus knowledge is immersed in existence. Existence—the existence of material realities—is given us at first by sense; sense attains the object as existing; that is to say, in the real and existing influence by which it acts upon our sensorial organs. This is why the pattern of all true knowledge is the intuition of the thing that I see, and that sheds its light upon me.[2] Sense attains existence in act without itself knowing that it is existence. Sense delivers existence to the intellect; it gives the intellect an intelligible treasure which sense does not know to be intelligible, and which the intellect, for its part, knows and calls by its name, which is *being*.

The intellect, laying hold of the intelligibles, disengaging them by its own strength from sense experience, reaches, at the heart of its own inner vitality, those natures or essences which, by abstracting them, it has detached from their material existence at a given point in space and time. But to what end? Merely in order to contemplate the picture of the essences in its ideas? Certainly not! Rather in order to restore them to existence by the act in which intellection is completed and consummated, I mean the judgment pronounced in the words *ita est,* thus it is. When, for

[1] J. Maritain, *De Bergson à Thomas d'Aquin*, Paris, 1927, p. 308.
[2] Cf. Aristotle, *On the Heavens*, Bk. III; St. Thomas Aquinas, *De Veritate*, 12, 3, *ad* 2, and *ad* 3.

example, I say: 'In every Euclidean triangle the sum of the angles is equal to two right angles,' or, 'The earth revolves round the sun,' what I am really saying is that every Euclidean triangle *exists* in mathematical existence as possessing the property described; that the earth *exists* in physical existence as characterized by the movement described. The function of judgment is an existential function.[3]

SIMPLE APPREHENSION

Some explanation is necessary concerning, in the first place, the abstractive perception which is the first operation of the mind, and, in the second place, judgment. On the first point we shall remark that a kind of holy horror comes over the existentialist philosophers, whether Christian or atheist, in the presence of what they call the universe of objects—a horror which, while on the one hand it entails serious results, to wit, the formal rejection of the conditions of intelligibility of knowledge, is, on the other hand, futile in origin, born as it is of a really shabby misunderstanding that goes far back in time to the Cartesian theory of idea-pictures.[4] They imagine, or construe the object as a reified idea, as a bit of pure externality, passive and inert, an obstacle to the mind, something interposing itself between the mind and the world of existence, or real subjects. Consequently, they contend that only the actual experience of subjectivity could reach those subjects. They do not see that object and objectivity are the very life and salvation of the intellect. The object is the term of the first operation of the intellect (simple perception, or 'simple apprehension'); what is it therefore if not, under a given specific aspect determined and cut out by abstraction, the intelligible density of an existent subject, rendered transparent in act to the mind and identified with the mind's vital activity by and in the concept? Briefly, the object as present in the mind is the intelligible objectivization of a trans-objective subject. But this trans-objective subject is, in its concrete existence, inexhaustible; therefore it admits of being attained in an indefinite number of new objects of concept linked to the preceding ones. Besides they do not see that this universe of objects which they seek industriously to drive out of ex-

---

[3] J. Maritain, *De Bergson à Thomas d'Aquin*, pp. 309–311. When phenomenology elected gratuitously to recast concepts according to its method, the result, as concerns the existentialist phenomenologists, was to void the infinitive *to exist* of its natural content. As M. Michel Sora has rightly observed (*Du dialogue intérieur*, Paris, 1947, p. 30), *ex-sistere* does not mean 'to stand outside oneself' but 'to stand outside of one's causes,' or 'outside nothingness,' to emerge from the night of non-being, or from that of mere possibility, or that of potency.

[4] On the Cartesian theory of idea-pictures see J. Maritain, *Le songe de Descartes*, Paris, 1932, pp. 153 ff., Eng. trans., N. Y., 1944, pp. 168 ff. I have never identified the Cartesian idea with a *sensible* image, as M. Wahl believes. He seriously misunderstands my statement on this point. (Jean Wahl, *Tableau de la philosophie française*, Paris, 1947, p. 228.)

istence does not in fact claim to exist in itself; it exists only in the mind; what exists is subjects, or supposita, objectivization, indeed, in the mind in order to become known, but posited for themselves in the world of concrete and contingent existence where nature and adventure go hand in hand. I shall come back later to the importance in Thomist philosophy of this notion of subject or suppositum. From another and merely logical point of view I wish only to remark here that for this philosophy (following a distinction too often neglected) what a science tends to know is a determinate *subject* in its existential inexhaustibility, whereas the *object* of that science consists, in rigorous terms, in the conclusions to which the science leads.

The Marxists, for their part, are faithful to the notion of objects; but, biased as they are by an inverted Hegelianism and a dialectical idealism transmuted into a philosophy of the real, they actually neglect the universe of existence, or of subjects, and attribute an existence, that in reality is nothing but an extraposition of the Idea, to a universe of reified objects and of natures which are mere contingent aspects of the immanence of becoming. They thus leave themselves open to the accusation which the existentialists level against the idealistic myth of the object.

We may therefore dismiss them both to argue it out among themselves and conclude our first consideration by saying that what the intellect, in abstractive perception (which is the first phase and condition of all its activity), lays hold of is not those eternal things which it would contemplate in some fanciful separate and intelligible universe, or mirage of hypostasized grammatical forms, proceeding from the shoddy Platonism which positivists and nominalists, existentialists and Marxists, consider inseparable from the notion of essences or natures endowed with unchangeable, intelligible structures. The metaphysician knows that his task is to search for the ultimate foundation of the intelligibility of things as of every other quality or perfection of being. He finds it in the pure Act, and understands that in the final analysis there would be no human nature if the divine Intellect did not perceive its own Essence, and in that Essence the eternal idea of man, which is not an abstract and universal idea, as our ideas are, but a creative idea. What we perceive, however, is not this divine idea; it is not in this intelligible heaven that we grasp human nature. The intelligible heaven in which we grasp and manipulate essences and natures is within ourselves, it is the active immanence of our immaterial thought. In that path which the intellect cuts through reality and sense experience in order to obtain its sustenance, that is to say, in abstractive perception, what the intellect lays hold of is the natures or essences which are in existent things or subjects (but not in the state of universality or intelligibility in act), which themselves are not things, and which the intellect strips of existence by immaterialising them. These are what, from the very beginning, we call intelligibles, or objects of thought.

The second consideration, however, which concerns judgment, is what is chiefly important to us here. I said a moment ago that the function of judgment was an existential function, and that judgment restored the essences (the intelligibles, the objects of thought) to existence or to the world of subjects—to an existence that is either necessarily material, or merely ideal, or (at least possibly) immaterial, accordingly as we deal with physical, mathematical, or metaphysical knowledge. Here a central problem arises, the problem of the philosophical significance of judgment, and of that existence itself which, according to Thomists, it is its function to affirm.

Descartes holds that judgment is an operation of the will, not of the intellect, and that the existence which it affirms is merely the positing of the *ideatum,* in itself inaccessible, of which the *idea* is the portrait. For Kant, judgment itself possesses an ideal and nonexistential function; it effects the concept by subsuming an empirical matter under a category; and existence is a mere positing absolutely devoid of all intelligible value or content. In St. Thomas's view, in contrast to that of Descartes, judgment is not only an operation which takes place following simple apprehension and the formation of the concept; it is the completion, the consummation, the perfection, and the glory of the intellect and of intellection, just as the existence it affirms is the glory and perfection of being and of intelligibility.

As I wrote in *The Degrees of Knowledge,*[5] when I 'form a judgment,' I accomplish on my *noemata,* within my thought, an operation which has meaning only because it relates to the fashion in which they exist (at least possibly) outside my thought. The function proper to judgment thus consists in transposing the mind from the plane of simple essence, of the simple *object* presented to thought, to the plane of the *thing,* of the subject possessing existence (actually or possibly) and of which the predicate-object of thought and the subject-object of thought are intelligible aspects. In a different sense to Lask's,† we may say with him that every judgment supposes an 'intact harmony' (on the side of the thing) and a 'reconciliation after struggle' (effected by the judgment itself). The 'embrace,' preceding that 'state of severance' which it is the function of judgment to

---

[5] J. Maritain, *Les Degrés du Savoire,* 4th ed., Paris, 1946, pp. 188–90.

† EDITOR'S NOTE: Emil Lask (1875–1915). For a summation of Lask's philosophic contribution and for his bibliography, cf. José Ferrater Mora, *Diccionario de Filosofía,* cuarta edición, Editorial Sudamericana, Buenos Aires, 1958, pp. 782–3.

'vanquish,' is given in the thing, in the trans-objective subject. Judgment restores to the trans-objective subject its unity which simple apprehension (laying hold upon different objects of thought within that subject) had severed. This unity could not precede severance in the mind since the mind operates the other way round, dissolves the unity in order, subsequently, to reestablish it. In existence, outside the mind, this unity precedes severance (that is, is posited initially); and existence itself, inasmuch as it is something *had* (*exercita*), lies outside the order of simple representation or simple apprehension.

What does this mean? 'Judgment is not content with the representation or apprehension of existence. It affirms existence, it projects into it, as effected or effectible outside the mind, the objects of concept apprehended by the mind. In other words, when the intellect judges, it lives intentionally, by an act proper to itself, this same act of existing which the thing exercises or is able to exercise outside the mind.' [6] Existence thus affirmed and intentionally experienced by and in the mind is the consummation or completion, in the mind, of intelligibility in act. It corresponds to the act of existing exercised by things. And this act of existing is itself incomparably more than a mere positing without intelligible value of its own; it is act or energy *par excellence;* and as we know, the more act there is, the greater the intelligibility.

And yet existence is not an essence. It belongs to another order, an order which is other than the whole order of essences. It is therefore not an intelligible nor an object of thought in the sense given above to these words (which is synonymous with essence). What are we to conclude if not that existence goes beyond the object strictly so called, beyond the intelligible strictly so called, because it is an act exercised by a subject, whose eminent intelligibility, we may say super-intelligibility, objectizes itself in us in the very act of judgment? In this sense we could call it a trans-objective act. It is in a higher and analogical sense that it is an intelligible. 'The intelligibility with which judgment deals is more mysterious than that which notions or ideas convey to us; it is not expressed in a concept but in the very act of affirming or denying. It is the super-intelligibility, if I may put it so, of the act of existing itself, either possible or actually given. And it is on this super-intelligibility of existence that St. Thomas hangs the whole life of the intellect.' [7]

THE INTUITION OF BEING

This is why, at the root of metaphysical knowledge, St. Thomas places the intellectual intuition of that mysterious reality disguised under the

[6] *Les Degrés du savoir,* p. 191, note. Eng. trans., p. 119.
[7] J. Maritain, *De Bergson à Thomas d'Aquin,* p. 311.

most commonplace and commonly used word in the language, the word *to be;* a reality revealed to us as the uncircumscribable subject of a science which the gods begrudge us when we release, in the values that appertain to it, the act of existing which is exercised by the humblest thing—that victorious thrust by which it triumphs over nothingness.

A philosopher is not a philosopher if he is not a metaphysician. And it is the intuition of being—even when it is distorted by the error of a system, as in Plato or Spinoza—that makes the metaphysician. I mean the intuition of being in its pure and all-pervasive properties, in its typical and primordial intelligible density; the intuition of being *secundum quod est ens.*[8] Being, seen in this light, is neither the *vague* being of common sense, nor the *particularized* being of the sciences and of the philosophy of nature, nor the *de-realized* being of logic, nor the *pseudo*-being of dialectics mistaken for philosophy.[9] It is being disengaged for its own sake, in the values and resources appertaining to its own intelligibility and reality; which is to say, in that richness, that analogical and transcendental amplitude which is *inviscerated* in the imperfect and multiple unity of its concept and which allows it to cover the infinitude of its analogates and causes it to overflow or superabound in transcendental values and in dynamic values of propensity through which the idea of being transgresses itself.[10] It is being, attained or perceived at the summit of an abstractive intellection, of an eidetic or intensive visualization which owes its purity and power of illumination only to the fact that the intellect, one day, was stirred to its depths and trans-illuminated by the impact of the act of existing apprehended in things, and because it was quickened to the point of receiving this act, or hearkening to it, within itself, in the intelligible and super-intelligible integrity of the tone peculiar to it.

There are diverse ways and paths leading towards the attainment of this intuition. None is traced in advance, none is more legitimate than another —precisely because here there is no question of rational analysis or of an inductive or a deductive procedure, or of a syllogistic construction, but only of an intuition which is a primary fact. The senses, and what St. Thomas calls the 'judgment of sense,' the blind existential perception exercised by the senses, play here a primordial and indispensable part. But this is no more than a prerequisite; the eyes of him who was blind from birth must be opened; the touch of the spiritual virtues of the intellect must release into intelligible light this act of existing which sense attains without discovering it and touches without perceiving it. It matters little whether the intuition of being resembles the innate gift of an imperial in-

---

[8] St. Thomas, *In Metaph. Arist.*, IV, 1, (Cathala ed., pp. 530–533).

[9] Cf. J. Maritain, *Sept Leçons sur l'Etre*, Paris, n.d., pp. 35–50, Eng. trans., *A Preface to Metaphysics*, N. Y., 1939, pp. 33–42.

[10] Ibid., *Leçons* iii and iv, Eng. trans., pp. 43–89.

telligence serenely relying upon its limpid strength and upon the co-operation of a pure and delicate flesh, and of a vivid and perfectly balanced sensibility, as seems to have been the case for Thomas Aquinas; whether, alternatively, it spring unexpectedly like a kind of natural grace at the sight of a blade of grass or a windmill, or at the sudden perception of the reality of the self; whether it proceed from the implacability with which the being of things independent of ourselves becomes abruptly evident to us, suddenly casting our own being back upon its solitude and its frailty; whether I make my way towards it by inner experience of duration, or of anguish, or of certain moral realities which transcend the flow of time— these alternatives, I repeat, are of slight moment. What counts is to take the leap, to release, in one authentic intellectual intuition, the sense of being, the sense of the value of the implications that lie in the act of existing. What counts is to have seen that existence is not a simple empirical fact but a primitive datum for the mind itself, opening to the mind an infinitive supraobservable field—in a word, the primary and super-intelligible source of intelligibility.

It is not enough to teach philosophy, even Thomist philosophy, in order to possess this intuition. Let us call it a matter of luck, a boon, perhaps a kind of docility to the light. Without it man will always have an opining, precarious and sterile knowledge, however freighted with erudition it may be; a *knowledge about*. He will go round and round the flame without ever going through it. With it, even though he stray from the path, he will always go farther than he can advance by years of mere dialectical exercise, critical reflection, or conceptual dissection of phenomena; and he will have the added privilege of solitude and melancholy. If the poet can be called a seer, the philosopher is no less entitled to this name, though in his own way. He may at times be the victim of some bewilderment; but at other times he will know the joy of discovery; and for all of the knowledge he will have got out of books, for all of his knowledge of life, he will owe both bewilderment and joy to the fact that he remains enraptured with being.

THE CONCEPT OF EXISTENCE OR OF TO-EXIST (ESSE) AND THAT OF BEING
OR OF THAT-WHICH IS (ENS)

The foregoing reflections face us with a paradox which we must attempt to clear up. We said that the intelligible apprehended in our ideas was essence. But existence is not an essence; it is shut off from the whole order of essence. How then can it be the object of the intellect and its supreme object? How can we speak of the concept or the idea of existence? Ought we not to say rather that existence is not apprehended by the intellect, or apprehensible by it? that existence does not admit of conceptualization, is no more than a limit (set up on every side by reality) upon the philosophical chase after essences? that existence is an unknowable upon which metaphysics builds without itself attaining to it?

What has already been said gives a premonition of the answer. Essences are the object of the first operation of the intellect, or *simple apprehension*. It is *judgment* which the act of existing confronts. The intellect envelops itself and is self-contained, is wholly present in each of its operations; and in the initial upsurge of its activity out of the world of sense, in the first act of self-affirmation accomplished by expressing to itself any datum of experience, it apprehends and judges in the same instant. It forms its first idea (that of being) while uttering its first judgment (of existence), and utters its first judgment while forming its first idea. I say, therefore, that it thus lays hold of the treasure which properly belongs to judgment, in order to envelop it in simple apprehension itself; it visualizes that treasure in an initial and absolutely original idea, in a privileged idea which is not the result of the process of simple apprehension alone, but of the laying hold of that which the intellect affirms from the moment it judges, namely, the act of existing. It seizes upon the eminent intelligibility or the super-intelligibility which the act of judging deals with (that of existence), in order to make of it an object of thought.

Thus existence is made object; but, as I pointed out earlier, in a higher and analogical sense resulting from the objectizing of a trans-objective act and referring to trans-objective subjects that exercise or are able to exercise this act. Here a concept seizes upon that which is not an essence but is an intelligible in a higher and analogical sense, a super-intelligible delivered up to the mind in the very operation which it performs each time that it judges, and from the moment of its first judgment.

But this concept of existence, of *to-exist* (*esse*) is not and cannot be *cut off* from the absolutely primary concept of being (*ens,* that-which is, that-which exists, that whose act is to exist). This is so because the affirmation of existence, or the judgment, which provides the content of such a concept, is itself the 'composition' of a subject with existence, i.e., the affirmation that *something exists* (actually or possibly, simply or with such-and-such a predicate). It is the concept of being (that-which exists or is able to exist) which, in the order of ideative perception, corresponds adequately to this affirmation in the order of judgment. The concept of existence cannot be visualized completely apart, detached, isolated, separated from that of being, and it is in that concept of being and with that concept of being that it is at first conceived. Here we touch upon the original error that underlies all the modern existentialist philosophies. Ignorant of, or neglecting the warning of, the old scholastic wisdom, that 'the *act of existing* cannot be the object of a perfect abstraction,' these philosophies presuppose that existence can be isolated. They contend that existence alone is the nourishing soil of philosophy. They treat of existence without treating of being.[11] They call themselves philosophies of existence instead of calling themselves philosophies of being.

All this simply amounts to saying that the concept of existence cannot be detached from the concept of essence. Inseparable from each other, these two make up one and the same concept, simple although intrinsically varied; one and the same essentially analogous concept, that of being. This is the first of all concepts, because it springs in the mind at the first awakening of thought, at the first intelligible coming to grips with the experience of sense by transcending sense. All other concepts are variants or determinations of this primary one. At the instant when the finger points to that which the eye sees, at the instant when sense perceives, in its blind fashion, without intellection or mental word, that *this exists;* at that instant the intellect says (in a judgment), *this being is* or *exists* and at the same time (in a concept), *being.*[12] We have here a mutual involution of causes, a reciprocal priority of this concept and this judgment, each preceding the other in a different order. To say, 'this being is or exists,' the idea of being must be present. To have the idea of being, the act of existing must have been affirmed and grasped in a judgment. Generally speaking, simple apprehension precedes judgment in the later stages of the process of thinking; but here, at the first awakening of thought, each depends upon the other. The idea of being ('this being') precedes the judgment of existence in the order of material or subjective causality, and the judgment of existence precedes the idea of being in the order of formal causality. The more one ponders this issue, the more it appears that this is how the intellect conceptualizes existence and forms its idea of being—of the *vague* being known to common sense.

When, moving on to the queen-science, metaphysics, and to that higher intuition of which I spoke a while back, the intellect disengages being from the knowledge of the sensible in which it is immersed, in order to make it the object or rather the subject of metaphysics; when, in a word, it conceptualises the metaphysical intuition of being (seen now in the light of all the values proper to it, in its typical and primordial intelligible density), what the intellect releases into that same light[13] is, here again, first and foremost, the act of existing.

[11] Or rather (and this is no better) they claim, as Heidegger does, to propound a treatise on being when, starting from existence or rather from the existential spot of actuality, they only phenomenalize it.

[12] Of course, I am not speaking here of verbally formulated operations, nor even of operations explicitly thought. The essential thing is that they be there implicitly, *in actu exercito.* There are primitive languages which do not possess the word 'being.' But the idea of being is implicitly present in the mind of the primitive men who use those languages. The first idea formed by a child is not the idea of being; but the idea of being is implicit in the first idea which the child forms.

[13] At the moment when sense apprehends an existent sensible, the concept of being and

the judgment, 'this being exists,' which condition each other, arise simultaneously in the intellect, as I have pointed out above. In this first of all our concepts released for its own sake, the metaphysical intellect perceives being in its analogical amplitude and in its freedom with respect to empirical conditions. With this notion as point of departure—a notion whose fecundity is inexhaustible—metaphysics formulates the first divisions of being and the first principles. The principle of identity has a significance which is not only 'essential' or 'copulative' ('every being is what it is'), but also and primarily existential ('that which exists, exists'). Cf. *Sept Leçons sur l'Etre,* p. 105, Eng. trans., pp. 93–94.) When, by the 'reflection' which judgment has primed, the subject grasps itself as existent, and grasps the extra-mental existence of things, it merely renders reflexively explicit that which it already knew. The extra-mental existence of things was given to it from the very start in the intuition and concept of being. (I mean to say that this intuition presents being according to the very analogicity of this concept, so that being is grasped as existing, actually or possibly, contingently or necessarily; and that, in the particular analogate of being most immediately attained—the sensible existent, and, more generally speaking, things—this extra-mental existence is given as contingent and not as forming part of the notion of things.)

In other words, the following stages should be distinguished:

1. 'Judgment' (improperly so-called) of the external senses and the aestimative, such as it is found in animals, and bearing upon a sensible existence given to perception. This is, in the sphere of sense (with its treasure of intelligibility in potency, but in no wise in act), the 'blind' equivalent of what we express in saying, 'this exists.'

2. Formation—in one simultaneous awakening of the intellect and the judgment which mutually involve each other—of an *idea* ('this being' or simply 'this thing' in which the idea of being is implicitly present) and a *judgment* composing the object of thought in question with the act of existing (not with the *notion* of existence, but with the *act* of existing): 'this thing exists' or 'this being exists.'

In forming this judgment the intellect, on the one hand, knows the subject as singular (indirectly and by 'reflection upon phantasms'), and, on the other hand, affirms that this singular subject exercises the act of existing. In other words, the intellect itself exercises upon the notion of this subject an act (the act of affirming) by which it lives intentionally the existence of the thing. This affirmation has the same content as the 'judgment' of the aestimative and the external sense (but in this case that content is no longer 'blind' but openly revealed since it is raised to the state of intelligibility in act); and it is not by reflection upon phantasms that the intellect proffers the affirmation, but by and in this 'judgment' itself, and in this intuition of sense which it grasps by immaterializing it, in order to express it to itself. It thus reaches the *actus essendi* (in judging)—as it reaches essence (in conceiving)—*by the mediation of sensorial perception.*

3. Formation of the idea of existence.— From the point when, conjointly with the first judgment of existence, the idea of being ('that which exists or is able to exist') has thus emerged, the intellect grasps the *act* of existing affirmed in the first judgment of existence, in order to make of it an *object* of thought; it makes unto itself a concept or notion of existence (*existentia ut significata*).

4. Intuition of first principles, especially of the principle of identity ('that which exists, exists'; 'every being is what it is').

5. Only thereafter, by an *explicit* reflection upon its act, does the intellect become explicitly conscious of the existence of the thinking subject. It does not merely live the *cogito,* it expresses it. And by opposition:

6. It knows explicitly, as extra-mental, the being and the existence which in their extra-mental reality had already been given to it in fact at stages 2, 3, and 4.

This analysis concurs with that of Father Garrigou-Lagrange (De intelligentia naturali et de primo objecto ab ipsa cognito, in *Acta Pontif. Acad. Romanae S. Thoma Aq.,* Rome, 1940) in that it places the intuition of the principle of identity *before* the moment when the thinking subject becomes conscious of its own existence. It differs in placing the first judgment of existence (which conditions the formation of the idea of being and is conditioned by it) *before* the moment when the thinking subject becomes conscious of its own existence and even *before* the intuition of the principle of identity.

At that point, according to classical Thomist doctrine, it has reached the third degree of abstraction.[14] But it is clear from this how false it would be

[14] The doctrine expounded by St. Thomas in the commentary on the *De Trinitate* of Boethius (in *De Trin.,* q. 5, a. 3, c.; cf. the important note in which Father Geiger cites the article in question in its exact import and from the autographic manuscript: L. B. Geiger, *La Participation dans la philosophie de saint Thomas d'Aquin,* Paris, 1942, pp. 318–319) confirms the thesis that the metaphysical concept of being, as earlier the common sense concept formed by the intellect upon its first awakening, is an eidetic visualization of being apprehended in judgment, in the *secunda operatio intellectus, quae respicit ipsum esse rei.* This doctrine shows indeed that what properly pertains to the metaphysical concept of being is that it results from an abstraction (or a separation from matter) which takes place *secundum hanc secundam operationem intellectus.* ('Hac operatione intellectus vere abstrahere non potest, nisi ea quae sunt secundum rem separata.') If it can be separated from matter by the operation of the (negative) judgment, the reason is that it is related in its content to the act of existing which is signified by the (positive) judgment and which over-passes the line of material essences—the connatural object of simple apprehension.

In this article on the *De Trinitate* St. Thomas reserves the noun *abstractio* strictly understood for the operation by which the intellect considers and grasps separately an object of thought which in reality cannot exist without the other things which the intellect leaves outside its consideration. (Wherefore, 'ea quorum unum sine alio intelligitur sunt simul secundum rem.') When, accordingly, he distinguishes between the *abstractio* 'common to all the sciences' (first degree of intensive abstraction) and the *abstractio formae a materia sensibili* which is proper to mathematics (second degree of intensive abstraction) on the one hand, and, on the other hand, the *separatio* proper to metaphysics where, because it takes place *secundum illam operationem quae componit et dividit,* the intellect divides one thing from another *per hoc quod intelligit unum alii non inesse,* he means (as he teaches constantly, for example, in his commentary on the Metaphysics) that things which are the object of metaphysics *exist or are able to exist without matter,* are or are able to be separated from every material condition in the very existence they exercise outside the mind (*separatio secundum ipsum esse rei*). It is in a judgment declaring that being is *not* necessarily linked to matter nor to any of its conditions that the intellect abstracts being from all matter and makes for itself the metaphysical concept of being as being. If St. Thomas thus emphasizes the distinction between the *separatio* proper to metaphysics and the mere *abstractio* which belongs to the other sciences, the reason is that he seeks to show, against the Platonists, that transcendentals can exist apart from matter, but that universals and mathematicals cannot. 'Et quia quidam non intellexerunt differentiam duorum ultimorum (common abstraction and mathematical abstraction) a primo (metaphysical 'separation'), inciderunt in errorem, ut ponerent mathematica et universalia a sensibilibus separata, ut Pythagorici et Platonici.'

There is nothing more to be looked for in these texts, and they do not at all signify that the *separatio* in question ought to be substituted for the 'abstraction called analogical' (third degree of intensive abstraction). The fact that St. Thomas here employs the word *separatio* rather than the word *abstractio* (reserved for cases where the object separately grasped cannot exist separately) in no wise prevents this *separatio*—since it ends in an idea, and an idea the object signified by which is the farthest removed from matter—from being an abstraction in the general or rather proportional meaning of the word (but which is not produced in the line of simple apprehension of essences!). This 'separation' *is* the analogical abstraction of being.

In this very text St. Thomas, as a matter of fact, employs the word *abstrahere* with reference to the separation which takes place in judgment: 'Secundum hanc secundam operationem intellectus *abstrahere* non potest vere quod secundum rem conjunctum est, quia in *abstrahendo* significatur esse separatio secundum ipsum esse rei, sicut si *abstraho* hominem ab albedine dicendo: homo non est albus, significo separationem esse in re. . . . Hac igitur operatione intellectus vere *abstrahere* non potest, nisi ea quae sunt secundum rem separata, ut cum dicitur: homo non est asinus.'

Between the *triplex distinctio* of the commentary on the *De Trinitate* of Boethius and the

to place the degrees of abstraction upon the same line as if mathematics were merely more abstract and more general than physics and metaphysics more abstract and more general than mathematics. By no means! What is common to the three degrees of abstraction is only analogically common to them. Each corresponds to a typically and irreducibly different manner of confronting and grasping reality, to a 'hold' that is *sui generis* in the struggle of the intellect with things. The abstraction proper to metaphysics does not proceed from a 'simple apprehension' or an eidetic visualization of a universal more universal than the others. It proceeds from the eidetic visualization of a transcendental which permeates everything and whose intelligibility involves an irreducible proportionality or analogy—*a* is to its own *act of existing* (*esse*) as *b* is to its own *act of existing* (*esse*),—because this is precisely what judgment discovers, namely, the actuation of a being by the act of existing, grasped as extending beyond the limits and conditions of empirical existence, grasped, therefore, in the limitless amplitude of its intelligibility.

If metaphysics is established at the highest degree of abstraction, the reason is precisely that, unlike all the other sciences, in concerning itself with being as being, as a proper object of analysis and scientific disquisition, it concerns itself with the very act of existing. The object of metaphysics is being, or that whose act is to exist, considered in its quality as being, that is to say, according as it is not linked to the material conditions of empirical existence, according as it exercises or is able to exercise, without matter, the act of existing. In virtue of the type of abstraction which characterizes it, metaphysics considers realities which exist, or are able to exist, without matter. It abstracts from the material conditions of empirical existence, but it does not abstract from existence! Existence is the term as a function of which metaphysics knows everything that it does know; I say, real existence, either actual or possible, not existence as a singular datum of sense or of consciousness, but as disengaged from the singular by abstractive intuition; existence not reduced to this moment of existential actuality actually experienced (in which alone the existentialist phenomenologists are interested) but liberated in that intelligible amplitude which it possesses as the act of that which is and which affords a grasp on the necessary and universal certainties of a scientific knowledge properly so-called. Moreover, it is in things themselves that metaphysics finds its ob-

---

three degrees of abstraction of Cajetan and John of St. Thomas there is a difference of vocabulary, there is no difference of doctrine. The doctrine of the three degrees of abstraction has its basis in the Metaphysics of Aristotle, where it finds an equivalent formulation. Cf. St. Thomas, *In Metaph. Aristotelis*, Prooemium, VI, 1, Cathala ed., 1156–1165; XI, 7, Cathala ed., 2259–2264. On this doctrine of degrees of abstraction cf. my writings: *Les Degrés du Savoir*, pp. 71–76, 265–268, 414–432, Eng. Trans., pp. 44–47, 165–167, 257–268; *Sept Leçons sur l'Etre*, pp. 85–96; Eng. Trans., pp. 75–86. *Quatre Essais sur l'Esprit dans sa condition charnelle*, Paris, 1939, pp. 231–232, 237–238.

ject. It is the being of sensible and material things, the being of the world of experience, which is its immediately accessible field of investigation; [15] it is this which, before seeking its cause, it discerns and scrutinizes —not as sensible and material, but as being. Before rising to the level of spiritual existents, it is empirical existence, the existence of material things, that it holds in its grasp—though not as empirical and material, but as existence.

Thus, its being more universal than the other sciences is but a quasi-incidental consequence of the immateriality of its object and its vision. By the nature of metaphysical knowledge and by the very fact that its own peculiar insight (which consists in seeing that which, according to its proper intelligible constitutive characteristics, is free of matter) enables it to penetrate into things without being halted by material characteristics, metaphysics is concerned with that which is most profound in things concrete and individual—their being, discovered in its quality of being and in the act of existing which things exercise or are able to exercise. If it does not reach individuality, that is not because it cannot do so by reason of its own noetic structure. I should say that that is not its own fault; rather, it is the fault of matter, which is, in the individual, the root of non-being and unintelligibility. The proof of this is that when metaphysics passes from being to the cause of being, the supreme reality that it knows (wrapped, it is true, in the veils of analogy) is the supremely individual reality, the reality of the pure Act, the *Ipsum esse subsistens*. It is the only science that is able to reach the individual, I mean, the individual *par excellence*. The worst metaphysical heresy is that which regards being as the *genus generalissimum* and makes of it at one and the same time a univocal thing and a pure essence. Being is not a universal; its infinite amplitude, its super-universality, if the reader prefers, is that of an implicitly multiple object of thought which, analogically, permeates all things and descends, in its irreducible diversity, into the very heart of each: it is not merely that which they are, but is also their very act of existing.

There is a concept of existence. In this concept, existence is taken *ut significata*,[16] as signified to the mind after the fashion of an essence, although it is not an essence. But metaphysics does not treat of the concept of existence; no science stops at the concept; all sciences proceed through

---

[15] The *goal* of metaphysics is knowledge of the *cause* of being-common-to-the-ten-predicaments, but its *subject* is that *common being* itself: 'Quamvis autem subjectum hujus scientiae sit ens commune, dicitur tamen tota de his quae sunt separata a materia secundum *esse* et *rationem*. Quia secundum esse et rationem separari dicuntur, non solum illa quae nunquam in materia esse possunt, sicut Deus et intellectuales substantiae, sed etiam *illa quae possunt sine materia esse, sicut ens commune*. Hoc tamen non contingeret, si a materia secundum esse dependerent.' St. Thomas Aquinas, *In Metaph. Aristotelis*, Prooemium.

[16] Cf. Cajetan, *In Sum. theol.*, 1, 2, 1, *ad* 2; and my *Songe de Descartes*, pp. 192–198, Eng. trans., pp. 131–132.

it to reality.[17] It is not of the concept of existence, it is of existence itself that the science of being treats. And when it treats of existence (it always treats of it, at least in some fashion) the concept of which it makes use does not display to it an essence but, as Etienne Gilson puts it,[18] that which has for its essence not to be an essence. There is analogy, not univocity, between such a concept and the concepts of which the other sciences make use. They use their concepts in order to know the realities signified by those concepts; but those realities are essences. Metaphysics uses the concept of existence in order to know a reality which is not an essence, but is the very act of existing.

I have mentioned that the concept of existence cannot be detached from that of essence: existence is always the existence of something, of a capacity to exist. The very notion of *essentia* signifies a relation to *esse*, which is why we have good grounds for saying that existence is the primary source of intelligibility.[19] But, not being an essence or an intelligible, this primary source of intelligibility has to be a super-intelligible. When we say that being is *that which exists or is able to exist, that which exercises or is able to exercise existence,* a great mystery is contained in these few words. In the subject, *that which,* we possess an essence or an intelligible —in so far as it is this or that, in so far as it possesses a nature. In the verb *exists* we have the act of existing, or a super-intelligible. To say *that which exists* is to join an intelligible to a super-intelligible; it is to have before our eyes an intelligible engaged in and perfected by a super-intelligibility. Why should it be astonishing that at the summit of all beings, at the point where everything is carried to pure transcendent act, the intelligibility of essence should fuse in an absolute identity with the super-intelligibility of existence, both infinitely overflowing what is designated here below by their concepts, in the incomprehensible unity of *Him Who is?*

[17] Which holds also for faith: 'Actus credentis non terminatur ad enuntiabile, sed ad rem' holds also for science: 'Non enim formamus enuntiabilia nisi ut per ea de rebus cognitionem habeamus, sicut in scientia, ita et in fide.' St. Thomas, *Sum. theol.,* II–II, 1, 2, *ad* 2.
[18] Cf. Etienne Gilson, 'Limites existentielles de la philosophie,' in *L'Existence,* Paris, 1945, p. 80.
[19] Cf. above, p. 132.

Wm. P. Montague : THE PSYCHOLOGICAL GENESIS OF UNIVERSALS

Iɴ *the following essay, a chapter from the late Professor Wm. Pepperell Montague's* THE WAYS OF KNOWING, *an attempt is made to clear up the debate between rationalists and empiricists regarding the nature of abstractions. Professor Montague (1873–1953) cuts below the arguments of both by pointing out that the term "abstraction" is generally misused. He holds that the conceptual mode of existence of an object is not a separate mode, but is merely the mind turning its attention to one quality of the object, forgetting the others. The existence of concepts in the mind is thus a "crossing" of these various qualities of the object. Reprinted by permission from* THE WAYS OF KNOWING OR THE METHODS OF PHILOSOPHY, *George Allen & Unwin Ltd., London; The Macmillan Company, New York, 1948, pp. 69–78.*

• The two theories of method which we are now to consider are so closely related to one another that it will be profitable to discuss them together rather than in succession. Rationalism is the method of proving propositions by appealing to abstract and universal principles; empiricism is the opposite method of proving propositions by appealing to concrete and particular occurrences. The ordinary person makes use of both these methods as a matter of course. If we wanted to prove the proposition that the sum of the angles of a particular triangle were equal to two right angles, we could either measure the angles, and so prove it empirically, or on the other hand we could prove it deductively by appealing to the familiar theorem of geometry in which the truth of the proposition is made to follow from the general properties of triangles. But although we undoubtedly use both methods of proof, and although our experience undoubtedly reveals to us both facts and principles, both particulars and universals, yet the problem arises as to which is the more fundamental. The empiricist, with his preference for proving his beliefs by appeal to specific cases, naturally holds that particulars are fundamental and that universal and abstract concepts and universal and necessary judgments are derived from them; while the rationalist maintains the contrary. The problem before us is of course primarily methodological, i.e. a matter of evaluating these rival criteria of truth. But the nature of the contending schools and the historical development of their contentions combine to make it advisable to divide our discussion into two chapters. We shall in this chapter consider the relation of universals to the individual mind, discussing, first, the question of the origin of universal and abstract concepts and, secondly, the question of the origin and validation of universal and necessary judgments. In the next chapter we shall consider the relation of universals to the objective world, discussing, first, the question of the ontological status of universals and, secondly, the question of the extent to which the world is pervaded by universal law and rationalistic necessity.

THE ORIGIN OF UNIVERSAL CONCEPTS

The rationalist contends that our knowledge of universals is far superior to our knowledge of particular objects and in no sense derived from that knowledge.

The empiricist, on the other hand, holds that universal concepts, in so far as they can be admitted as genuinely present to the mind, are derived from the concrete particulars of experience and that their importance is secondary and instrumental.[1]

---

[1] This question of the origin of universals must not be confused with that other phase of the historic controversy as to innate ideas which concerns the genesis of imaginary objects. The imaginary objects which figure in dreams and day-dreams as well as in works of

By universals are meant such objects of thought as are signified by class-names—e.g. "horse," "man," "triangle"; and by abstract names—e.g. "humanity," "roundness," "redness." Now, although we speak of horses in general or as a class, and make assertions such as "all horses are animals" or "the horse is an animal," yet we have never seen "all horses" or "the horse," but only particular horses of a particular size and colour, existing at particular times and places. In the same way, although we talk about roundness in relation to squareness, and redness in relation to blueness, yet "roundness" and "redness" have never been experienced by themselves, but only as distinguishable aspects of round things and red things. Shall we then say that these general and abstract ideas are furnished by the mind and not derived from experience? Before surrendering the empirical position thus easily, let us consider what is actually given in the experience of a particular object, such as a horse. There is in the first place a complex of qualities, some of which are common to other animals of his species, and others of which are peculiar to this particular individual. Then besides these qualities there are the characters of position in a particular part of space and at a particular moment of time. Let us represent these various distinguishable elements of the perception of an individual horse as follows:

H = the qualities common to this horse and to others.
h = the qualities peculiar to this individual horse.
S = the property of being in space.
s = the particular space where the horse is seen or heard as distinguished from other places.
T = the property of being in time.
t = the particular time when the horse is seen or heard.

The entire experience-complex of a particular horse seen at a particular time and place may thus be symbolized as H, h, S, s, T, t. Every other experienced object could be analysed in a similar way into generic and specific qualities and into the generic and individual space and time characters. In short, the psychologically primary and ultimate experiential unit is always some specific complex of qualities possessing a specific date and a specific place, and anything more general than this is, from the psychological point of view, an abstraction. Now, it is probably true that we never can perceive or even concretely imagine any of these properties in isolation. We cannot picture a horse that appears at no time and no place, and we certainly cannot form a mental picture of a horse that is of no particular colour and no particular size. The imagined horse must have

literary art are most of them particulars like the real objects revealed in perception. They are derived from the latter through the mind's power to synthesize the elements of perception which have been retained in memory.

his particular colour and size, just as truly as the imagined triangle must have its individual size and form—scalene, isosceles, or equilateral.

This inability to *imagine* anything except particulars has led some thinkers to the notion that we could not conceive or think of anything but particulars, in spite of the self-evident fact that a general name, like triangle or horse, certainly does mean something and certainly does not mean a particular horse or a particular triangle. But though we may not be able to imagine one of the elements or aspects of a concrete object of experience apart from the other elements or aspects, we can attend to it more emphatically than to others, and in that way conceive it. In the case of the individual horse perceived at a given time and place which was symbolized as H, h, S, s, T, t, I can attend to, interest myself in, and talk about any of these elements in distinction from the others. The time at which the horse was seen, the place where he was, his qualities, generic and individual, may become in turn the exclusive object of my thoughts. If I attend to the part of the complex consisting of H, h, S, T, then I have formed the concept as an enduring *individual* whose existence is not bound up with the particular place and time at which I have perceived him. Such a concept as this is connoted by a proper name, like Bucephalus, Dobbin, Pegasus, etc. If I restrict my attention still further and consider only the elements, H, S, T, I shall have formed the concept of the *general class* of existent horses, which is connoted by the concrete common noun "horse." If, finally, I restrict my attention to the generic elements of the particular experience, apart from any occupancy of space or time—if in our chosen example I think simply of H—then I have formed the concept of the *abstract essence* "equinity" or "horseness." Thus we have (1) the percept, sense-datum, or event, H, h, S, s, T, t, which, as such, is never named because it never recurs; (2) the proper noun or singular term, H, h, S, T; (3) the common noun or "general term," H, S, T; and (4) the abstract noun H, each representing successive degrees of restriction in attention, with corresponding increases in the universality of the object attended to.

The process of restricting attention to parts of the manifold of essences embodied in a concrete object of perception can of course be carried out in various ways according to the direction of one's interest. Instead of directing our attention to the common equine qualities which this particular horse of our illustration shared with other horses, and which we symbolized by H, we could have selected the quality of being owned by Farmer Smith, and so have attained the class concept of "domestic animals that are the property of Smith," or the still simpler and broader class concept "property of Smith." Or again, we could have fastened our attention on the animal's colour and thus arrived at the class-concept "brown," or the still broader universal of "colour" or "coloured thing." The only limit to the process of successively higher generalizations in any direction is the simplicity or unanalysableness of the essences to which we attend. Mere "being" or "thinghood" is perhaps the simplest, as it is certainly the broadest, of our concepts. But besides this *summum genus* there are universals that are, as it were, off on the side, in a dimension of their own. Examples of such universals are "temporality," "spaciality," and "consciousness." We call them *sui generis,* because of the difficulty of analyzing them into further significant genera. We can, to be sure, class them under such genera as "ultimate concepts" or "philosophical abstractions"; but analyses of this kind are felt to be formal and in a sense accidental. For we are no longer attending to the intrinsic properties of the essence, but rather to its extrinsic relations to knowledge and language.

The real nature of the process of forming universals has been obscured by the fact that an important and perhaps even psychologically necessary motive for analyzing a perceptual object into its constituent essences is a previous experience of them in other contexts. Cognition of new concepts results from recognition of old percepts; and our selective attention is so unoriginal that it tends to pick out qualities that are already familiar. This unfortunate limitation in our psychological processes has generated the confused logic of nominalism according to which the class itself is thought of as constituting the universal, and "denotation" and "extension" are conceived as prior to "connotation" and "intension." As a matter of psychology this would be correct, but in logic the reverse is correct. In the psychological *order of knowing* the class of objects comes before the universal, as its *ratio cognoscendi.* But in the logical *order of being,* the universal is prior to its class of particulars, and constitutes their *ratio essendi.* The Frege-Russell definition of the number two as the class of all couples is a good example of the neo-nominalism of modern writers on logistic, and illustrates what I believe to be a mistaken tendency to treat denotation as prior to connotation. Psychologically, we should probably never arrive at the concept of *two* except for antecedent experiences of many perceptual couples. The varied material qualities of these concrete *twos* help our poor minds to discriminate their invariant formal quality of *twoness.* We can only reach the abstract universal by a bridge of concrete particulars. But when once we have reached it, we should realize that what is last in knowledge was first in nature and that no one of these existential couples could have been a *two* unless there had subsisted from all eternity a *two* for it to be. In this respect the relation of the universal to the particular is like the relation of my friend to the hearing of his words and the seeing of his face. These latter experiences constitute the *ratio cognoscendi.* They are the antecedent conditions of my knowing him. But he himself is their *ratio essendi,* and hence is logically and ontologically prior to them. Although only a layman as regards the new logic,

I dare say that many of its admitted awkwardnesses are due to the wanton nominalism of its procedure, and that many of its admitted achievements have come in spite of rather than because of its preference of an extensional to an intensional interpretation of universals.

When we come to induction, where not universal concepts but universal propositions are to be derived from perceptual experience, we shall see that the traditional treatment of the subject suffers from the same mistake that we have just been considering. Denotation has usually been regarded as prior to connotation, and the establishing of a universal proposition has been made to appear as a mysterious leap from the perceptual *some* of the premises to the conceptual *all* of the conclusion—an illegitimate synthesis in "extension" instead of a legitimate analysis in "intension."

It is customary to designate the process of restriction or concentration of attention by which the mind arrives at its knowledge of universals by the word "abstraction." We are told, for example, that "the universals of the intellect are derived by abstraction from the particulars of sense." The word "abstraction" is a natural name for the process in question, but it has proved disastrous to clear thinking because it has been often interpreted to mean the taking away of one of its qualities from the concrete experience. When the term is thus interpreted the question immediately arises as to the relation between the system of concepts and the system of percepts from which the concepts have been abstracted, or as it were *stolen*. It cannot be too much emphasized that the universal or concept is not another particular existing alongside of the particulars of experience. It is, rather, an attribute of the particular which is shared by other particulars. The process of forming abstract notions does not consist in the abstraction of anything from the object, but rather in the abstraction of our attention from the complex of properties that, as a complex, is peculiar to a single sense-datum and the concentration of it upon separate properties that are common to many sense-objects. Consequently the forming of concepts by abstraction does not in any way change the nature of the objects, but only the nature of our consciousness of such objects. It is a great advantage to be able to think of the qualities common to different objects without having always to take account of all the qualities possessed by each object. By object I mean here, of course, anything that can be perceived or conceived—not only concrete objects like horses, men, etc., but also relations and activities such as might pertain to them and from whose occurrence at particular times and places we can abstract our attention.

To each of the universals which, through being selected by our attention, becomes a concept, we attach a name which preserves it from being lost in the flux. These verbal symbols serve as counters by means of which we can compare with one another the particular percepts of our experience, however remotely separated they may be from one another in space or in time. Things, events, and relations, quantitative and qualitative, can, in virtue of their similarity or identity of kind, be grasped in a single act of thought, even though they have been experienced years apart. The mind thus groups into classes the particulars of experience and, by comparing these classes, forms concepts having still higher universality. Our concepts are, as James says, like the seven-league boots in the old fairy tale. By their aid the mind is enabled to travel with the swiftness of thought over the entire realm of its experiences. The mind of the brute, which appears to lack the faculty of forming concepts by fixation of attention, is submerged by each successive wave of experience. The human mind, on the other hand, through its power of discovering universals and preserving them in names, is set free from the bondage of the here and the now and, rising above the flux of experience, is able to survey at a single glance the past and the future, the near and the remote.

What then must we say as to the bearing of this theory of the nature and origin of universals upon the dispute between empiricist and rationalist?

The rationalist has usually defended the doctrine of innate ideas. Plato even went so far as to maintain that all knowledge was innate and that the only function of sensory experience was to awaken the mind to a realization and memory of the universal ideas with which it had been endowed prior to its existence in this life. Other less radical rationalists have held that the mind possessed as its native endowment only the more abstract and exalted universals, such as those dealt with in logic and mathematics. Empiricists on their side have sometimes denied altogether the possibility of genuinely universal ideas on the ground that they could not be pictured or imagined. We cannot form an image of a colour apart from an extent, or of a triangle that is neither scalene nor isosceles, or of a relation such as contrast or distance apart from some terms between which such a relation obtains. But the fact that we may not be able to *imagine* a universal does not mean that we cannot *conceive* or think of it. For as we have seen, to conceive a universal it is not necessary to take it out of its context and dangle it before the mind's eye. To form a general concept it is necessary only to fix the attention upon the quality or relation as it exists *in situ,* and to affix a name to that part of the complex which has been thus discriminated. Consequently, the objection to universals on the score that they cannot be imaged or pictured, we must regard as irrelevant.

When empiricists have not denied outright our possession of general concepts, they have conceived of the process by which they are formed as one in which given elements of experience which are regarded as particular and nothing but particular either get combined by association under one name or through a kind of alchemy become fused and transmuted into a composite image. Now with this position we must disagree, for if the given elements of experience were nothing but particulars, if each particular that we perceived were as separate from every other particular, as are the moments in which they occurred, then indeed it would be as impossible to derive from them universal concepts as to get gold out of lead. Both rationalists and empiricists commit the same error, for they regard the originally given elements in experience as particulars and nothing but particulars and as lacking anything that can be called universality. The rationalists, however, meet the difficulty that arises by attributing to the mind a mysterious power of supplying from its own inner nature the element of universality, while the empiricists, by an equally unwarranted procedure, explain away our universal notions altogether, or else vainly attempt to conceive a process by which what is not universal can combine to produce what is. Our comment on the situation is simply this: the fundamental assumption made in common by the two parties to the quarrel is wrong. Experience is indeed originally of particulars, that is, of objects that are presented at particular times and places. But each of these experienced objects has a universal nature which is as indefeasibly its *inclusive* property as is its unique position in space and time its *exclusive* property. In other words, the given elements of experience are complexes of universals, each complex being associated with a particular position in the space and time series. It is this latter factor of position which constitutes particularity and makes each individual numerically different from every other individual. To form the concept of a universal, it is, as we have already seen, not necessary for the mind to manufacture or create anything different from what is given, but only to abstract the attention from the particular position of the given complex and concentrate it upon some one or more of its qualitative or non-positional elements. *In short, a particular is nothing but a complex of universals endowed with a position in space and time.*

E. D. Simmons : THE THOMISTIC
DOCTRINE OF THE
THREE DEGREES OF
FORMAL
ABSTRACTION

Dr. *Edward D. Simmons of the Department of Philosophy, Marquette*
University, in this essay synthesizes the various and sometimes conflicting
positions of Thomistic philosophers on the different levels of abstraction
and modes of knowing them. Reprinted by permission from THE THOMIST,
XXII, 1 (1959), pp. 37–67.

• There is current controversy among Thomists as to the Thomistic authenticity of the doctrine of intellectual abstraction as presented by Cajetan and John of St. Thomas.[1] According to these traditional commentators there is, first of all, a twofold distinction between total abstraction (*abstractio totalis,* the abstraction of a logical whole from its subjective parts) and formal abstraction (*abstractio formalis,* the abstraction of an intelligible object from the matter which shrouds its intelligibility). There is, further, a threefold distinction between types of formal abstraction (each depending upon the distinct degree of matter from which the intelligible object is abstracted). Total abstraction is common to all the sciences, while each type of formal abstraction is proper to a distinct level of science as specificative of that level. Physical abstraction, the first degree of formal abstraction, is proper to natural science; mathematical abstraction, the second degree of formal abstraction, is proper to mathematics; and metaphysical abstraction, the third degree of formal abstraction, is proper to metaphysics.[2]

[1] It is not the purpose of this paper to trace the development of this controversy. However, it may be fitting, for purposes of orientation, to indicate some of the literature contributing to it. Principal among the earlier articles on it were these three: L.-M. Régis, O. P., "La philosophie de la nature. Quelques apories," *Etudes et Recherches,* Cahier I: Philosophie (1936), 127–156; L.-B. Geiger, O. P., "Abstraction et séparation d'après S. Thomas," *Revue des Sciences Philosophiques et Théologiques,* XXXI (1947), 3–40; J.-D. Robert, O. P., "La métaphysique, science distincte de toute autre discipline philosophique selon S. Thomas d'Aquin," *Divus Thomas,* L (1947), 206–222. These were followed shortly by two significant articles: M.-V. Leroy, O. P., "*Abstractio et separatio* d'après un texte controversé de Saint Thomas *(In Lib. Boeth. de Trin.,* V, 3 & 4)," *Revue Thomiste,* XLVIII (1948), 328–339; M.-D. Philippe, O. P., "Abstraction, addition, séparation dans la philosophie d'Aristote," *Revue Thomiste,* XLVIII (1948), 461–479. More recent articles on the subject include: F. G. Connolly, "Science vs. Philosophy," *The Modern Schoolman,* XXIX (1952), 197–209, and "Abstraction and Moderate Realism," *The New Scholasticism,* XXVII (1953), 72–90; V. Smith, "Abstraction and the Empiriological Method," *Proceedings of the American Catholic Philosophical Association,* XXVI (1952), 35–50; G. Van Riet, "La théorie thomiste de l'abstraction," *Revue Philosophique de Louvain,* L (1952), 353–393; P. Merlan, "Abstraction and Metaphysics in St. Thomas' *Summa,*" *Journal of the History of Ideas,* XIV (1953), 284–291; W. Kane, O. P., "Abstraction and the Distinction of the Sciences," *The Thomist,* XVII (1954), 43–68; E. Simmons, "In Defense of Total and Formal Abstraction," *The New Scholasticism,* XXIX (1955), 437–440; F. Cunningham, S. J., "A Theory on Abstraction in St. Thomas," *The Modern Schoolman,* XXXV (1958), 249–270. A highly significant brief treatment of the problem is found in J. Maritain, *Existence and the Existent,* trans. L., Galentière and G. B. Phelan (New York, 1948), pp. 28–30, note 14. Other notes are found in G. Klubertanz, S. J., *The Philosophy of Human Nature,* p. 400, note 19; F. Wilhelmsen, *Man's Knowledge of Reality* (Englewood Cliffs, N. J., 1956), pp. 194–195, note 3. Extended treatments are found in E. Simmons, *The Thomistic Doctrine of Intellectual Abstraction for the Three Levels of Science: Exposition and Defense* (University of Notre Dame doctoral dissertation, 1952, published by University Microfilms, Ann Arbor, Mich.); F. Wilson, S. J., *The Modes of Abstraction According to St. Thomas Aquinas* (Georgetown University doctoral dissertation, 1949, unpublished).

[2] Cajetan, *In De Ente et Essentia,* prooem., q. I (Laurent): ". . . *duplex* est *abstractio* per intellectum, scilicet qua formale abstrahitur a materiali, et qua totum universale abstrahitur a partibus sujectivis . . . primam voco abstractionem formalem, secundam vero voco abstractionem totalem, eo quia quod abstrahitur prima abstractione, est ut forma ejus, a quo

Many have questioned the Thomistic authenticity of this presentation on the basis of St. Thomas' own presentation of the doctrine in the third article of the fifth question of his *Commentary on the De Trinitate of Boethius*. In this highly significant and somewhat controversial article, St. Thomas begins by distinguishing between abstraction, generally taken, according to simple apprehension and according to negative judgment. He calls the first an abstraction, strictly taken, and the second a separation. He further distinguishes between abstractions, strictly taken, which are abstractions of a whole (*abstractio totius*) and those which are abstractions of a form (*abstractio formae*). He then assigns the abstraction of a whole to natural science, the abstraction of a form to mathematics, and separation to metaphysics.[3] On the basis of this article it would seem perhaps that for St. Thomas the distinction between total and formal abstraction is in fact the distinction between physical and mathematical abstraction and not, as the Commentators teach, a distinc-

---

abstrahitur. Quod vero abstrahitur secunda abstractione, est ut totum universale respectu ejus a quo abstrahitur . . . penes diversos modos abstractionis formalis scientiae speculativae diversificantur. . . . Abstractio autem totalis communis est omni scientiae. . . ." Cajetan treats particularly of the division of the sciences into natural science, mathematics, and metaphysics according to the *three* degrees of formal abstraction in *In Summa Theol.*, I, 1, 3 (Leonine) (cf. *infra*, note 15). John of St. Thomas treats of both the general distinctions and the division of the sciences into the three branches in *Curs. Phil.*, I, *Ars Log.*, II, q. 27, a. 1 (Reiser).

[3] *In Boeth. de Trin.*, V, 3, c. (Decker): ". . . duplex est operatio intellectus. Una, quae dicitur 'intelligentia indivisibilium,' qua cognoscit de unoquoque, quid est. Alia vero, qua componit et dividit, scilicet enuntiationem affirmativam vel negativam formando. . . . Hac ergo operatione intellectus vere abstrahere non potest nisi ea quae sunt secundum rem separata. . . . Sed secundum primam operationem potest abstrahere ea quae secundum rem separata non sunt, non tamen omnia, sed aliqua. . . . Si vero unum ab altero non dependeat secundum id quod constituit rationem naturae, tunc unum potest ab altero abstrahi per intellectum ut sine eo intelligatur, non solum si sint separata secundum rem . . . sed etiam si secundum rem coniuncta sint. . . . Sic ergo intellectus distinguit unum ab altero aliter et aliter secundum diversas operationes; quia secundum operationem, qua componit et dividit, distinguit unum ab alio per hoc quod intelligit unum alii non inesse. In operatione vero qua intelligit, quid est unumquodque, distinguit unum ab alio, dum intelligit, quid est hoc, nihil intelligendo de alio, neque quod sit cum eo, neque quod sit ab eo separatum. Unde ista distinctio non proprie habet nomen separationis, sed prima tantum. Haec autem distinctio recte dicitur abstractio. . . . Et ita sunt duae abstractiones intellectus. Una quae respondet unioni formae et materiae vel accidentis et subiecti, et haec est abstractio formae a materia sensibili. Alia quae respondet unioni totius et partis, et huic respondet abstractio universalis a particulari, quae est abstractio totius, in qua consideratur absolute natura aliqua secundum suam rationem essentialem, ab omnibus partibus, quae non sunt partes speciei, sed sunt partes accidentales. . . . Sic ergo in operatione intellectus triplex distinctio invenitur. Una secundum operationem intellectus componentis et dividentis, quae separatio dicitur proprie; et haec competit scientiae divinae sive metaphysicae. Alia secundum operationem, qua formantur quidditates rerum, quae est abstractio formae a materia sensibili; et haec competit mathematicae. Tertia secundum eandem operationem quae est abstractio universalis a particulari; et haec competit etiam physicae *et est communis omnibus scientiis*." (cf. *infra*, note 23, for a discussion of the final phrase in this text and the question of the community of *abstractio totius* in reference to each of the levels of speculative science.)

tion between an abstraction common to all the sciences and that general type of abstraction which in its specific manifestations respectively specifies each level of science. It seems also that for St. Thomas there are not three types of abstraction specifying respectively the three levels of science, but only two abstractions of this kind, plus separation. And it would seem, finally, that there are not three, nor even two, formal abstractions, but only one, namely, the abstraction proper to mathematics.

Must we then scrap, in the interests of Thomistic authenticity, the traditional distinction of the Commentators between total and formal abstraction on the one hand and between the three degrees of formal abstraction on the other? I suggest that we need not do this. It seems to me that whatever disparity there is between the Commentators and St. Thomas on this point is more terminological than doctrinal. In a previous paper I have attempted to show as much in reference to the first distinction made by the Commentators, i.e., the distinction between *abstractio totalis* (as common to all the sciences) and *abstractio formalis* (as specificative in its three degrees of the three levels of science).[4] This distinction is simply not the distinction that St. Thomas has in mind when he distinguishes between *abstractio totius,* as belonging to natural science, and *abstractio formae,* as belonging to mathematics. In fact, it is not a distinction explicitly made by St. Thomas, but it is a distinction legitimately called for by the Thomistic notion of human science. Human science, strictly taken, is a knowledge of the real effected in the demonstrative syllogism. In order that the real be scientifically grasped, therefore, it must be yielded to the intellect as intelligible—able to be known—and as communicable—able to take on the logical interrelationships of superiority and inferiority through which syllogism "works." Formal abstraction, the abstraction of the intelligible object from the matter which shrouds its intelligibility, yields the object as intelligible; and total abstraction, the abstraction of the logical whole from its subjective parts, yields the object as communicable. Accordingly, both total and formal abstraction are demanded by the Thomistic notion of human science, and this, though St. Thomas himself never explicitly makes the distinction and never names these types of abstraction, makes this distinction, explicitly given to us by Cajetan and John of St. Thomas, authentically a Thomistic distinction.

There remains to be considered the second of the traditional distinctions, i.e., the distinction between the three degrees of formal abstraction as respectively specifying the three levels of science. Can the Commentators legitimately speak of the first degree of formal abstraction as specifying natural science, the second degree of formal abstraction as specifying

---

[4] Cf., *supra,* note 1, "In Defense of Total and Formal Abstraction."

mathematics, and the third degree of formal abstraction as specifying metaphysics when St. Thomas, in the *Commentary on the De Trinitate, V, 3*, speaks rather of a total abstraction (*abstractio totius*) as belonging to natural science, a formal abstraction (*abstractio formae*) as belonging to mathematics, and a separation (*separatio* as distinct from *abstractio*) as belonging to metaphysics? The burden of this paper will be to show that they can, that the traditional doctrine of the three degrees of formal abstraction is completely consonant with the doctrine of *abstractio totius, abstractio formae*, and *separatio* as proposed by St. Thomas in the *De Trinitate*.

Inasmuch as the original difficulty seems to be of terminological genesis, we will first examine the problem from this point of view in order to show that the carefully chosen expressions of the *De Trinitate* in no way rule out the presentation of the Commentators. Then we shall turn from the terminological issue to the more important doctrinal issue in an attempt to show that the doctrine of the three degrees of formal abstraction, *rightly understood*, faithfully represents the mind of St. Thomas in reference to the specification of the speculative sciences.

THE TERMINOLOGICAL ISSUE

The terminological differences between the presentation of Cajetan and John of St. Thomas on the one hand and St. Thomas in the *Commentary on the De Trinitate, V, 3*, on the other are clearly apparent. That they seem to pose a problem cannot be denied. The Commentators teach that there are three degrees of formal abstraction (*abstractiones*). And St. Thomas teaches, in this article, that there are three types of intellectual distinctions (*distinctiones*), only two of which are in the strict sense abstractions (*abstractio totius* and *abstractio formae*). St. Thomas teaches that what corresponds to Cajetan's third degree of formal abstraction is not an abstraction in the strict sense but a separation (*separatio*). Because St. Thomas carefully speaks of three distinctions rather than three abstractions and because he explicitly distinguishes between two abstractions and separation, it would seem perhaps that the traditional presentation of the doctrine in terms of the three types of abstraction cannot be accepted as authentically Thomistic.

However, if we accept the fact that the precise terminology of the *De Trinitate* repudiates the teaching of Cajetan and John of St. Thomas, we must as well admit that it repudiates the teaching of St. Thomas himself in many other passages. For St. Thomas does not bind himself to the strict terminology of the controversial article every time he speaks on the subject of intellectual abstraction. There are numerous passages in which he shows little regard for the precision of expression stressed in the controversial article. These passages fit into several types, including passages in which "abstraction" is used in reference to all three scientific levels, those in which "separation" is used in reference to all three scientific levels, and those in which "abstraction" and "separation" are interchanged indiscriminately. We shall take note of several of these passages in what follows.

Perhaps the most obvious passage in which St. Thomas uses "abstraction" for all three scientific levels is found in the *Summa Theologiae*, I, q. 85, a. 1, ad 2. Here, in answer to an objection made concerning the abstraction especially proportioned to natural science, we find St. Thomas comparing this abstraction with its mathematical and metaphysical counterparts.

The intellect therefore abstracts (*abstrahit*) the species of a natural thing from the individual sensible matter, but not from common sensible matter. . . . Mathematical species, however, can be abstracted (*abstrahi*) by the intellect not only from individual sensible matter, but also from common sensible matter; not however from common intelligible matter, but only from individual intelligible matter. . . . But certain things can be abstracted (*abstrahi*) even from common intelligible matter, such as *being, unity, potency, act,* and the like, which even can exist without matter, as is evident in the case of immaterial substances.[5]

If St. Thomas had intended in the *De Trinitate,* a work earlier than the *Summa,* to eliminate the possibility meaningfully to speak of abstraction in reference to each of the levels of science he would certainly not have expressed himself as he did in this passage of the *Summa.*

Another passage, typical of the context in which we find it, in which St. Thomas speaks of abstraction in reference to each genus of science and not exclusively to the first and second is found at the very beginning of the *Commentary on the Physics.*

Therefore, it must be known, since every science is in the intellect, that something is intelligible in act insofar as it is abstracted (*abstrahitur*) from matter; thus, insofar as things are diversely related to matter, they pertain to diverse sciences.[6]

[5] *Summa Theol.,* I, 85, 1, ad 2 (Leonine): "Intellectus igitur abstrahit speciem rei naturalis a materia sensibili individuali, non autem a materia sensibili communi. . . . Species autem mathematicae possunt abstrahi per intellectum a materia sensibili non solum individuali, sed etiam communi; non tamen a materia intelligibili communi, sed solum individuali. . . . Quaedam vero sunt quae possunt abstrahi etiam a materia intelligibili communi, sicut ens, unum, potentia et actus, et alia huiusmodi, quae etiam esse possunt absque omni materia, ut patet in substantiis immaterialibus."

[6] *In I Phys.,* 1, n. 1 (Pirotta): "Sciendum est igitur quod, cum omnis scientia sit in intellectu, per hoc autem aliquid fit intelligibile in actu, quod aliqualiter abstrahitur a materia; secundum quod aliqua diversimode se habent ad materiam, ad diversas scientias pertinent."

In this passage St. Thomas speaks of abstraction *generally* in reference to each level of speculative science, just as in the passage previously quoted he speaks of abstraction *particularly* in reference to natural science, mathematics, and metaphysics. Certainly there is no indication in either passage that "abstraction" is used improperly in reference to metaphysics; rather there is positive indication of the propriety of this usage in a Thomistic exposition.

A good example of the second type of passage is found at the beginning of the *Commentary on the De Sensu et Sensato*. Here St. Thomas clearly reveals his willingness to speak of separation in reference to each level of science. In this passage he uses "separation" explicitly for metaphysics and mathematics and implicitly for natural science.

And since the habits of any potency are distinguished in kind according to a difference in that which is formally the object of that potency, it is necessary that the habits of science, by which the intellect is perfected, be distinguished according to a difference in separation (*separationis*) from matter. Therefore, the Philosopher in the sixth book of the *Metaphysics* distinguishes the genera of the sciences according to the diverse modes of their separation (*separationis*) from matter. For those things which are separated (*separata*) from matter insofar as they exist and insofar as they are known pertain to *metaphysics;* those which are separated (*separata*) insofar as they are known but not insofar as they exist pertain to *mathematics;* and those which in their very meaning include sensible matter pertain to *natural science.*[7]

Not only does St. Thomas on occasion speak of abstraction in connection with each of the three genera of speculative science, and on other occasions of separation with this same general application, but sometimes he speaks indiscriminately of abstraction and separation within the same passage. We find an example of this type of passage in the preface to the *Commentary on the Metaphysics* where St. Thomas uses a form of *"separare"* in reference to each of the levels of science along with a similar usage of a form of *"abstrahere."*

Those things are indeed separated (*separata*) from matter to the greatest degree, 'which not only abstract (*abstrahunt*) from individual matter as the natural forms received in the universal about which natural science is concerned,' but from all sensible matter; not only insofar as they are known, as is

---

[7] *In De Sensu et Sensato,* 1, n. 1 (Spiazzi): "Et quia habitus alicuius potentiae distinguuntur specie secundum differentiam eius quod est per se obiectum potentiae, necesse est quod habitus scientiarum, quibus intellectus perficitur, etiam distinguuntur secundum differentiam separationis a materia; et ideo Philosophus in sexto *Metaphysicorum* distinguit genera scientiarum secundum diversum modum separationis a materia. Nam ea, quae sunt separata a materia secundum esse et rationem, pertinent *ad metaphysicum;* quae autem sunt separata secundum rationem et non secundum esse, pertinent *ad mathematicum,* quae autem in sui ratione concernunt materiam sensibilem, pertinent *ad naturam."*

the case with mathematical objects, but also insofar as they exist, as is the case with God and the angels.[8]

As a matter of fact we find this same indiscriminate use of "abstraction" and "separation" in the very article which has most of all occasioned the attack upon the traditional interpretation of St. Thomas by the Commentators. Early in the controversial article in the *De Trinitate*, St. Thomas speaks indiscriminately of abstraction and separation, precisely distinguishing between the use of "abstraction" and "separation" only afterwards.

And since the truth of the intellect consists in a correspondence to reality, it is evident that according to the second operation the intellect cannot truly abstract (*abstrahere*) what is conjoined in reality, because in abstracting (*abstrahendo*) thusly there would be an existential separation (*separationem*) signified, as when I abstract (*abstraho*) man from white by saying 'the man is not white' I signify a separation (*separationem*) in the real. . . . By this operation the intellect can truly abstract (*abstrahere*) only those things which are separated (*separata*) in the real, as when I say 'the man is not an ass.'[9]

Thus St. Thomas himself, not only elsewhere but even in the controversial article itself, indicates a willingness not to restrict himself to the strict terminology which limits "abstraction" to natural science and mathematics and "separation" to metaphysics. In the light of this we must surely admit that we cannot question the Thomistic authenticity of the doctrine of the Commentators *simply* because they speak of three degrees of abstraction without distinguishing terminologically between abstraction and separation.

The apparent terminological difficulty can be resolved in terms of a simple distinction between strict terminology on the one hand and general terminology on the other. Speaking generally we can legitimately use the terms "abstraction" and "separation" interchangeably, as St. Thomas usually does. But because of a radical difference between the first two types of abstraction or separation, speaking generally, and the third we should be prepared to distinguish in the strict sense between them. St. Thomas does this in the *De Trinitate* by speaking of the first two as abstractions, strictly speaking, and the third as separation, strictly speaking.

[8] *In Met.*, prooem. (Cathala-Spiazzi): "Ea vero sunt maxime a materia separata, quae non tantum a signata materia abstrahunt, 'sicut formae naturales in universali acceptae, de quibus tractat scientia naturalis,' sed omnino a materia sensibili. Et non solum secundum rationem, sicut mathematica, sed etiam secundum esse, sicut Deus et intelligentiae."

[9] *In Boeth. de Trin.*, V, 3, c.: "Et quia veritas intellectus est ex hoc quod conformatur rei, patet quod secundum hanc secundam operationem intellectus non potest vere abstrahere quod secundum rem coniunctum est, quia in abstrahendo significaretur esse separatio secundum ipsum esse rei, sicut si abstraho hominem ab albedine dicendo: homo non est albus, significo esse separationem in re. . . . Hac operatione intellectus vere abstrahere non potest nisi ea quae sunt secundum rem separata, ut cum dicitur: homo non est asinus."

There is no doubt that St. Thomas is making an especially strict distinction in the controversial article. To emphasize this he repeatedly uses the term *proprie* when he speaks of separation as distinct from abstraction. The reason for the strict distinction is clearly the fact that he is here bent upon showing that it was precisely a failure on the part of the Platonists to make this distinction which led them into the error of positing the *real existence* of abstract forms and universals.[10] Whenever St. Thomas sees fit pointedly to speak of the difference between abstraction by way of simple and absolute consideration and abstraction by way of composition and division he does so in a similar context.[11] He speaks in each of these instances with his mind on the error of the Platonists, an error best exposed in terms of a strict distinction between types of abstraction generally taken, or, as he expresses it in the *De Trinitate,* between abstraction strictly taken and separation strictly taken. There is nothing more than this to look for in this refinement of doctrine and language. Certainly, the fact that St. Thomas himself, whenever he is not aiming directly at the Platonists, is content to employ the general terminology, which is that employed by Cajetan and John of St. Thomas, should be guarantee enough that there is no conflict necessarily in evidence just because the Commentators do not choose to employ the strict terminology used in the controversial article in the *Commentary on the De Trinitate.*

THE DOCTRINAL ISSUE

It seems evident that we cannot rule out the interpretation of the Commentators on intellectual abstraction as lacking Thomistic authenticity simply because they do not use the terminology of the controversial article in the *De Trinitate,* nor even because their terminology seems contrary to that here used by St. Thomas. Otherwise we should rule out much of what St. Thomas teaches elsewhere as being inauthentic for the same reason; for, as we have seen, St. Thomas, even in his latest work, the *Summa Theologiae,* chooses on occasion to speak, like the Commentators after him, of three types of abstraction analogously alike in that each is proper to a distinct level of speculative science.

But admitting that the presentation of the Commentators cannot be thrown out simply on the basis of some terminological differences, should

[10] *Ibid.*: "Et quia quidam non intellexerunt differentiam duarum ultimarum (namely, *abstractio totius* and *abstractio formae*) a prima (namely, *separatio*), inciderunt in errorem, ut ponerent mathematica et universalia asensibilibus separata, ut Phythagorici et Platonici."
[11] Cf., *Summa Theol.,* I, 85, 1, ad 1: here, it is interesting to note, St. Thomas makes this distinction precisely in reference to the error of Plato *without,* however, using the terms "abstraction" and "separation" but speaking rather of a twofold abstraction (". . . dicendum quod abstrahere contingit dupliciter. Uno modo, per modum compositionis et divisionis. . . . Alio modo, per modum simplicis et absolutae considerationis. . . .")

we not still discard the teaching of the three degrees of formal abstraction as being *doctrinally* at odds with that of St. Thomas? Let us see.

Cajetan and John of St. Thomas teach that the speculative sciences are diversified according to differences in their formal objects, and that these objects differ precisely as objects to the extent to which they abstract differently from matter. Mobile being is the formal object of one branch of speculative science, natural science, as abstracting from individual matter. Quantified being is the formal object of a second branch of speculative science, mathematics, as abstracting from individual and sensible matter. And being as such is the formal object of the third branch of speculative science, metaphysics, as abstracting from all matter. These three abstractions from matter are known respectively as physical abstraction, mathematical abstraction, and metaphysical abstraction; and they are, as yielding the *formal* objects specificative of the types of speculative science, the three degrees of formal abstraction.[12]

The Commentators expose this doctrine very carefully with the use of several illuminating distinctions. To begin with, of course, they distinguish sharply between the material object and the formal object. The material object is simply the thing known. The formal object is the thing known, precisely insofar as it is an object of speculation. They then distinguish a twofold aspect (*ratio*) within the formal object itself. The first of these is that formality or formal perfection in virtue of which the object is rendered scientifically knowable. This formality is defined as the "character (*ratio*) of the object known which immediately terminates the act of a given scientific habit." It is the scientifically characteristic aspect of the object "from which flows the properties of the subject of this science, and which is, in fact, the middle term of the primary demonstration of this science."[13] It is precisely that in the object known, in virtue of which it is scientifically knowable. The second aspect (*ratio*) of the formal object is its degree of freedom from matter. This is the "mode of immateriality belonging to the formal object as object, that is, the mode of abstraction and definition proper to it."[14] Sciences are distinguished on the basis of differences in formal objects. Formal objects are formally objects precisely insofar as they involve that intelligible characteristic or formality in virtue of which they are formal objects. And this formality is

[12] Cf. especially Cajetan's exposition in *In Summa Theol.*, I, 1, 3. John of St. Thomas treats the same matter in *Curs. Phil.*, I, *Ars Logica*, II, q. 27, a. 1.

[13] Cajetan, *loc. cit.*: Cajetan here points out that there is a "duplex ratio obiecti in scientia" and that the first of these is the "ratio formalis obiecti ut res" or the "ratio formalis quae," which is the "ratio rei obiectae quae primo terminat actum illius habitus, et ex qua fluunt passiones illius subiecti, et quae est medium in prima demonstratione."

[14] *Ibid.*: Cajetan teaches that the second aspect of the formal object is the "ratio formalis obiecti ut obiectum" or the "ratio formalis sub qua," which is "immaterialitas talis, seu talis modus abstrahendi et definiendi."

precisely a formality making the object object insofar as it involves a distinctive abstraction from matter and a characteristic mode of defining. Because there are three abstractions from matter and corresponding modes of defining (1. abstraction from individual matter and definition with sensible matter, 2. abstraction from individual and sensible matter and definition with intelligible matter, and 3. abstraction from all matter and definition with no matter), there are three types of speculative science. These three abstractions from matter, respectively specificative of the three types of speculative science, are the three degrees of formal abstraction.[15] They are three *degrees* because each abstracts differently, the one more intensely than the other, from matter. They are degrees of *formal* abstraction because each determines a distinct *formality* in virtue of which being is precisely an object of scientific speculation. This then, in brief, is the doctrine of the three degrees of formal abstraction as presented by the traditional Commentators.

Nor does this presentation differ essentially from that of St. Thomas himself. If we examine only some of his most significant texts in this regard we see that he teaches explicitly that the distinction between the three genera of speculative science (natural science, mathematics, and metaphysics) rests ultimately on the degree of abstraction from matter and mode of defining proper to each. And this, as we have indicated, is precisely the position held by the Commentators in their presentation of the doctrine of the three degrees of formal abstraction.

In the first article of the fifth question in his *Commentary on the De Trinitate of Boethius*,[16] St. Thomas discusses the division of speculative

---

[15] *Ibid.*: Cajetan points out that for the physical, mathematical and metaphysical habits of science the *ratio formalis quae* is respectively *mobilitas, quantitas,* and *entitas;* the *obiectum materiale* in each case is *ens;* the *obiectum formale quod* is respectively *ens sub ratione mobilitatis, ens sub ratione quantitatis,* and *ens sub ratione entitatis;* and the *ratio formalis sub qua* in each case is respectively *modus abstrahendi et definiendi cum materia sensibili non tamen hoc, cum materia intelligili tantum,* and *sine omni materia.* Cf. John of St. Thomas, *op. cit.*, 820b 22–40: "Est autem triplex materia a qua potest fieri abstractio, . . . scilicet *singularis,* quae reddit rem individuam et singularem; *sensibilis,* quae reddit illam accidentibus sensibilibus subiectam, saltem in communi; *intelligibilis,* quae est substantia, et subiacet quantitati etiam aliis accidentibus. Et ex abstractione seu carentia diversa huius materiae sumitur triplex genus scientiarum: Physica, quae abstrahit solum a materia singulari et tractat de sensibili; mathematica, quae etiam a materia sensibili et tractat de quantitati; metaphysica, quae etiam a intelligibili et tractat de substantia seu ente."

[16] *In Boeth. de Trin.*, V, 1, c: "Speculativarum vero scientiarum materiam oportet esse res quae a nostro opere non fiunt. . . . Et secundum harum rerum distinctionem oportet scientias speculativas distingui. Sciendum tamen quod, quando habitus vel potentiae penes obiecta distinguuntur, non distinguuntur penes quaslibet differentias obiectorum, sed penes illas quae sunt per se obiectorum in quantum sunt obiecta. . . . Et ideo oportet scientias speculativas dividi per differentias speculabilium, in quantum speculabilia sunt. . . . Sic ergo speculabili, quod est obiectum scientiae speculativae, per se competit separatio a materia et motu vel applicatio ad ea. Et ideo secundum ordinem remotionis a materia et motu scientiae speculativae distinguuntur. Quaedam ergo speculabilium sunt, quae dependent a materia secundum esse, quia non nisi in materia esse possunt. Et haec

science into three parts, namely, natural science, mathematics, and meta-physics. He begins by pointing out that a habit is distinguished by its object; however, not by any object whatsoever, i.e., the object materially taken, but only by an object precisely insofar as it is properly an object of this habit, i.e., the object formally taken. Next he points out that that kind of habit which is a speculative science must be distinguished by an object precisely insofar as it is an object of speculation, i.e., precisely insofar as it is speculatively intelligible. Finally, St. Thomas points out that the speculative intelligiblity of an object is determined by its separation or remotion from matter and motion. Thereupon, he concludes, in terms not unlike those of the Commentators later, that the speculative sciences are distinguished into three on the basis of the degree of remotion, which is the same as abstraction, from matter and motion evidenced in the mode of defining proper to each. This is to teach the same doctrine later taught by the Commentators that there are three degrees of objective independence from matter which determine three distinct formalities respectively constituting objects specificative of the three types of speculative science, natural science, mathematics, and metaphysics.

Perhaps the most clear-cut and concentrated formulation by St. Thomas of the doctrine later taught by the Commentators is found at the very beginning of the *Commentary on the De Sensu et Sensato.*

. . . just as things are separable from matter so also are they related to the intellect. For each thing is intelligible to the degree to which it is separable from matter. Thus those things which are by nature separated from matter are in themselves intelligible in act; but those which are abstracted by us from material conditions become intelligible in act through the light of our agent intellect. And since the habits of any potency are distinguished in kind according to a difference in that which is formally the object of that potency, it is necessary that the habits of science, by which the intellect is perfected, be distinguished according to a difference in separation from matter. Therefore, the Philosopher in the sixth book of the *Metaphysics* distinguishes the genera of the sciences according to the diverse modes of their separation from matter. For those things which are separated from matter insofar as they exist and insofar as they are known pertain to *metaphysics;* those which are separated insofar as

distiguuntur, quia quaedam dependent a materia secundum esse et intellectum, sicut illa, in quorum diffinitione ponitur materia sensibilis; unde sine materia sensibili intelligi non possunt, ut in diffinitione hominis oportet accipere carnem et ossa. Et de his est physica sive scientia naturalis. Quaedam vero sunt, quae quamvis dependeant a materia secundum esse, non tamen secundum intellectum, quia in eorum diffinitionibus non ponitur materia sensibilis, sicut linea et numerus. Et de his est mathematica. Quaedam vero speculabilia sunt, quae non dependent a materia secundum esse, quia sine materia esse possunt, sive numquam sint in materia, sicut Deus et angelus, sive in quibusdam sint in materia et in quibusdam non, ut substantia, qualitas, ens, potentia, actus, unum et multa et huiusmodi. De quibus omnibus est theologia, id est scientia divina . . . quae alio nomine dicitur metaphysica."

they are known but not insofar as they exist pertain to *mathematics;* and those which in their very meaning include sensible matter pertain to *natural science.*[17]

In this passage from the *De Sensu et Sensato* St. Thomas teaches that the sciences are divided into three genera according to "diverse modes of separation from matter" (*secundum diversum modum separationis a materia*). In the previous passage from the *De Trinitate* he divides the sciences into three genera on the basis of "the different orders of remotion from matter and motion" (*secundum ordinem remotionis a materia et motu*). Cajetan later divides the sciences into three, according to "diverse modes of formal abstraction" (*penes diversos modos abstractionis formalis*). Since formal abstraction is for Cajetan the abstraction of that which is formal in respect to the intellect from the matter which shrouds its intelligibility (*scilicet qua formale abstrahitur a materiali*), it seems clear that Cajetan is expressing the same doctrine as that expressed by St. Thomas, and, as a matter of fact, in language not so radically different from that of St. Thomas after all.

In the opening lesson of the sixth book of the *Commentary on the Metaphysics*[18] St. Thomas treats at length the question of the diversification of the speculative sciences and once again concludes that this de-

[17] *In De Sensu et Sensato,* 1, n. 1: ". . . sicut separabiles sunt res a materia, sic et quae circa intellectum sunt. Unumquodque enim intantum est intelligibile, inquantum est a materia separabile. Unde ea quae sunt secundum naturam a materia separata, sunt secundum seipsa intelligibilia actu: quae vero a nobis a materialibus conditionibus sunt abstracta, fiunt intelligibilia actu per lumen nostri intellectus agentis. Et quia habitus alicuius potentiae distinguuntur specie secundum differentiam eius quod est per se obiectum potentiae, necesse est quod habitus scientiarum, quibus intellectus perficitur, etiam distinguantur secundum differentiam separationis a materia; et ideo Philosophus in sexto *Metaphysicorum* distinguit genera scientiarum secundum diversum modum separationis a materia. Nam ea, quae sunt separata a materia secundum esse et rationem, pertinent *ad metaphysicam,* quae autem sunt separata secundum rationem et non secundum esse, pertinent ad *mathematicam;* quae autem in sui ratione concernunt materiam sensibilem, pertinent *ad naturalem."*

[18] *In VI Met.,* 1, nn. 1155–1165: ". . . Cum enim definitio sit medium demonstrationis, et per consequens principium sciendi, oportet quod ad diversum modum definiendi, sequatur diversitas in scientiis speculativis. . . . Et ex hoc palam est quis est modus inquirendi quidditatem rerum naturalium, et definiendi in scientia naturali, quia scilicet cum materia sensibili. . . . In hoc ergo differt mathematica a physica, quia physica considerat ea quorum definitiones sunt cum materia sensibili. Et ideo considerat non separata, inquantum sunt non separata. Mathematica vero considerat ea, quorum definitiones sunt sine materia sensibili. Et ideo, esti sunt non separata ea quae considerat, tamen considerat ea inquantum sunt separata . . . si est aliquid immobile secundum esse, et per consequens sempiternum et separabile a materia secundum esse, palam est, quod eius consideratio est theoricae scientiae. . . . Et tamen consideratio talis entis non est physica. Nam physica considerat de quibusdam entibus, scilicet de mobilibus. Et similiter consideratio huius entis non est mathematica; quia mathematica non considerat separabilia secundum esse, sed secundum rationem, ut dictum est. Sed oportet quod consideratio huius entis sit alterius scientiae prioris ambabus praedictis, scilicet physica et mathematica. . . . Advertendum est autem, quod licet ad considerationem primae philosophiae pertineant ea sunt separata secundum esse et rationem a materia et motu, non tamen solum ea; sed etiam de sensibilibus, inquantum sunt entia. . . ."

pends ultimately upon the diversification in the modes of separation or abstraction from matter proper to the various scientific subjects. He begins by arguing, as he does elsewhere, that sciences are differentiated in terms of formal differences in their principles. But the most significant principle of scientific argumentation is the middle term of demonstration. And the middle term of demonstration is the definition of the subject of scientific inquiry. Accordingly, any formal diversity in speculative sciences will follow from a formal diversity in the mode of defining found in each. From St. Thomas' discussion and in his examples, it is clear that he considers differences in definitions to be formal in respect to the differentiation of the sciences when these differences reflect distinctly diverse relationsips to matter. Because these diverse relationships to matter are generically three, he concludes that there are three genera of speculative science, namely, natural science, which defines with sensible matter a subject which can exist only in matter; mathematics, which defines without sensible matter a subject which can exist only in matter; and metaphysics, which defines without any matter a subject which can, but need not, exist without any matter. In other words, these three sciences are, in the final analysis, distinct from one another precisely insofar as the object formal to each is related in a radically different way to matter, i.e., insofar as each is differently separated from or abstracted from matter. This is to teach, in equivalent terms, the same doctrine held by the Commentators when they teach that speculative science is divided into natural science, mathematics, and metaphysics on the basis of the three degrees of formal abstraction.

In an equally significant passage in his *Commentary on the Posterior Analytics* [19] St. Thomas argues in a similar fashion for a principle of diversification for the sciences which reduces itself to that of the degrees of

[19] *In I. Post. Anal.*, 41, nn. 361–371 (Spiazzi): . . . Scientia dicitur una, ex hoc quod est unius generis subiecti. . . . Est autem considerandum circa primum, quod cum rationem unitatis scientiae acceperit ex unitate generis subiecti, rationem diversitatis scientiarum non accepit ex diversitati subiecti, sed ex diversitate principiorum. Dicit enim quod una scientia est altera ab alia, quarum principa sunt diversa; ita quod nec ambarum scientiarum principia procedent ex aliquibus principiis prioribus, nec principia unius scientiae procedent ex principiis alterius scientiae. Ad huius ergo evidentiam sciendum est, quod materialis diversitas obiecti non diversificat habitum, sed solum formalis. Cum ergo scibile sit proprium obiectum scientiae, non diversificabuntur scientiae secundum diversitatem materialem scibilium, sed secundum diversitatem eorum formalem. . . . Patet ergo quod ad diversificandum scientias sufficit diversitas principiorum, quam comitatur diversitas generis scibilis. Ad hoc autem quod sit una scientia simpliciter utrumque requiritur et unitas subiecti et unitas principiorum. . . . Nec tamen intelligendum est quod sufficit ad unitatem scientiae unitas principiorum primorum simpliciter, sed unitas principiorum primorum in aliquo genere scibili. Distinguuntur autem genera scibilium secundum diversum modum cognoscendi. Sicut alio modo cognoscantur ea quae definiuntur cum materia, et ea quae definiuntur sine materia. . . . Et sic patet quod unitas generis scibilis in quantum est scibile, ex quo accipiebatur unitas scientiae, et unitas principiorum, secundum quae accipiebatur scientiae diversitas, sibi mutuo correspondent. . . ."

formal abstraction. Here St. Thomas notes, with Aristotle, that the diversification of the sciences depends on the diversification of the principles whereby they proceed. Thus one science is distinct from another whenever the principles from which it proceeds do not themselves depend on the same prior principles upon which depend the principles of the other and when the principles of the one do not depend upon the principles of the other. This is true whether we speak of the complex principles of science or the incomplex principles, though St. Thomas is here speaking of the incomplex principle of demonstration, namely, the middle term. Thus the diversification of the sciences rests on a diversity in middle terms. This is to say that the sciences are distinguished on the basis of a distinction in the degree of abstraction from matter proper to a given science. For the middle term in a demonstration is a probative principle precisely inasmuch as it is the definition of the subject of the demonstration expressing the cause of the property to be proven of the subject in the conclusion of the demonstration. Hence, middle terms will be distinguished as principles of science according to differences in them as far as mode of defining is concerned. And, since the mode of defining of an object depends upon its degree of abstraction from matter we must conclude that St. Thomas here once again teaches that the speculative sciences are distinguished according to the degrees of abstraction from matter. That this is his point seems evident when he indicates, by way of illustration, that the distinction between natural science and mathematics rests ultimately on the diverse mode of defining proper to each, the one with sensible matter and the other without sensible matter.

St. Thomas, following Aristotle, begins his discussion in this lesson by distinguishing between the principle of the unity of science and the principle of the diversity of the sciences. Yet, ultimately, these two are the same, as St. Thomas indicates later on in the lesson. The unity of a science rests on the unity of its generic subject. But the subject of demonstration is properly subject only insofar as it is speculatively intelligible. And it is speculatively intelligible only insofar as it is free from matter, the principle of non-intelligibility. Thus, scientific subjects are one only insofar as they identically abstract from matter, this being revealed in their identical mode of defining. Accordingly, the unity of a science within itself, as well as the distinction of a science from other sciences, is ultimately dependent upon the same specifying principle, namely, the degree of abstraction from matter proper to the science. Thus we find St. Thomas teaching, both in reference to the unity and the diversity of the sciences, the doctrine presented later by the traditional Commentators as the doctrine of the three degrees of formal abstraction.

These several texts of St. Thomas, to which others could be added,[20] in-

[20] Notably, *Summa Theol.*, I, 85, 1, ad 2; *In I Phys.* 1, nn. 1 & 2; and *In Met.*, prooem.

dicate the *general* agreement between the doctrine of St. Thomas on the specification of the sciences and that of the traditional Commentators expressed in terms of the three degrees of abstraction.[21] There remains, however, the task of *particularly* reconciling St. Thomas' *abstractio totius* with the first degree of formal abstraction, his *abstractio formae* with the second degree of formal abstraction, and his *separatio* with the third degree of formal abstraction.

I. Abstractio Totius

At first glance it would seem impossible to find Cajetan's notion of formal abstraction realized in St. Thomas' *abstractio totius*. The latter

[21] I have indicated above that the Commentators discuss the division of the sciences in terms of five notions, namely, 1. the scientific habit itself, 2. its material object, 3. its formal object, 4. the *ratio formalis quae* of this formal object, and 5. the *ratio formalis sub qua* of the formal object. St. Thomas expresses himself in terms of these same notions. It might be worthwhile here in support of my thesis to note the exact terminology of St. Thomas and his traditional Commentators as they express themselves in reference to these notions. J. Maritain has on several occasions ably defended the traditional interpretation of the Commentators and in doing so has happily introduced into modern Thomistic language his own illuminating terminology for these five notions. Because of the aptness of his expressions I shall include his with those of St. Thomas and the Commentators. The expressions shall be numbered for each man according to the numbering already indicated above in this note.

St. Thomas
1. Habitus scientiae. (used extensively throughout his works)
2. Obiectum materiale, id quod materialiter cognoscitur (*Summa Theol.*, II–II, 1, 1, c.)
3. Subiectum scientiae, vel genus scibile. (*In I Post. Anal.*, 41, *passim*).
4. Ratio cognoscibilis. (*Summa Theol.*, I, 1, 1, ad 2).
5. Remotio a materia et motu seu modus separationis a materia, et diversus modus definiendi. (*In Boeth. de Trin.*, V, 1, c.; *In De Sensu et Sensato*, 1, n. 1; *In VI Met.*, 1, n. 1156).
    (These are not the only expressions used for these notions by St. Thomas, but they are typical.)

Cajetan (Cf. *In Summa Theol.*, I, 1, 3; *In Post. Anal.*, XXII; *In De Ente et Essentia*, prooem, q. 1).
1. Habitus vel potentia.
2. Obiectum materiale seu res.
3. Obiectum vel subiectum formale quod.
4. Ratio formalis obiecti ut res seu ratio formalis quae.
5. Ratio formalis obiectum seu ratio formalis sub qua (modus abstrahendi et definiendi respectu materiae).

John of St. Thomas (Cf. *Curs. Phil.*, I, *Ars. Log.* II, q. 1, a. 3; q. 27, a. 1).
1. Ratio formalis sub qua ex parte habitus.
2. Obiectum materiale.
3. Obiectum quod seu ipsum totum quod constat ex obiecto materiali et formalitate.
4. Ratio formalis quae ex parte obiecti.
5. Ratio formalis sub qua ex parte obiecti (diversa abstractio a materia et diversus modus definiendi).

Maritain (Cf. *La Philosophie de la Nature*, pp. 118–127, in English trans., pp. 125–135).
1. Scientific habitus, or subjective light in the effective order.
2. Material object.
3. Formal object, i.e., *sphère d'intelligibilité fondamentale*.
4. Inspect under which object presents itself to intellect, i.e., *appel d'intelligibilité*.
5. Mode of eidetic visualization and defining demanded by the object, or objective light.

is literally a type of total abstraction, and Cajetan himself sharply distinguishes between total abstraction on the one hand and formal abstraction on the other. However, the confusion here is basically one of terminology. In a very general sense both Cajetan's *abstractio totalis* and St. Thomas' *abstractio totius* are abstractions-of-a-whole, but without being identified as abstractions of the *same* whole. In fact, both Cajetan's first degree of formal abstraction and St. Thomas' *abstractio totius* are both also generally abstractions-of-a-form, and, in fact, are identified as being abstractions of the same form.

Cajetan's *abstractio totalis* is the mental separation of a logical whole from its subjective parts, the *abstractum* to be considered precisely as being more general than that from which it has been abstracted (*est ut totum universale respectu ejus, a quo abstrahitur*). The whole-part composition on which this abstraction depends is the composition of logical whole with subjective parts.[22]

St. Thomas' *abstractio totius* is the mental separation of the specific essence of the physical thing from the individuating characteristics which shroud its intelligibility, the *abstractum* to be considered precisely insofar as it involves an intelligible content determined by that point of intelligibility distinctive of the natural sciences (*in qua consideratur absolute natura aliqua secundum suam rationem essentialem*). The whole-part composition on which this abstraction depends is the composition of essential whole with non-essential parts.[23]

Inasmuch as each is an abstraction of a whole from its parts each is legitimately called an abstraction-of-a-whole or a total abstraction, but

[22] Cf., *supra*, note 2.

[23] Cf. *supra*, note 3; also *Summa Theol.*, I, 40, 3, c; *Comp. Theol.*, 62. A clarification in my exposition of St. Thomas is necessary at this point. The notion of *abstractio totius* as expressed by St. Thomas involves an *abstractum* which is an essential whole abstracted from its non-essential parts. This notion is broad enough to apply analogically to the abstractions proper respectively to natural science, mathematics, and metaphysics so long as essential whole is understood to mean formal ratio or intelligible object and non-essential parts are understood to mean material parts or non-intelligible matter. Understood in this broad sense *abtractio totius* can be identified with the *abstractio formalis* of the Commentators. St. Thomas certainly allows that *abstractio totius* be taken in this broad sense, for he says it can be understood as belonging to all the sciences because of the fact that each science disregards what is accidental to its object and regards only what is essential (". . . *est communis omnibus scientiis, quia in omni scientia praetermittitur quod per accidens est, et accipitur quod per se est*"). However, the notion of *abstractio totius* as expressed by St. Thomas is most clearly realized in the abstraction proper to the natural sciences. St. Thomas says that by way of *abstractio totius* some nature abstracted as a whole is considered absolutely in respect to its essential ratio ("*abstractio totius, in qua consideratur absolute natura aliqua secundum suam rationem essentialem*"). Understood strictly this would cut *abstractio totius* off from mathematics, where the abstraction is not of a whole but a part, and from metaphysics, where the abstraction or separation reveals its object not simply from the point of view of essential perfection but formally from the point of view of the act of existing. *Abstractio totius* is taken throughout this paper in the strict sense in which it is understood primarily as belonging to the natural sciences.

insofar as the whole is a formally different one in each case the abstractions in question are diverse. This is true despite the fact that each might be exemplified in apparently the same example. The abstraction of *man* from *this man* and from *that man* is an example both of Cajetan's *abstractio totalis* and St. Thomas' *abstractio totius*. However, though materially identical the example is formally diverse in each case. It happens, on the physical level at least, that the matter which individuates an essence is materially identical with the matter which shrouds the intelligibility of that essence. This is not formal identity, for it is not precisely insofar as a thing is singular or individual that it is non-intelligible, or else an individual angel would thereby be non-intelligible because it is singular. The principle of individuation and the principle of non-intelligibility are formally diverse principles. Yet in the physical thing they do coincide, so that matter which individuates the physical essence is also that matter which makes it as concretized in matter to be non-intelligible. Thus it is that the mental separation of *man* from *this man* and *that man* is an example both of Cajetan's *abstractio totalis* and of St. Thomas' *abstractio totius*. Yet these abstractions remain formally distinct from one another, *abstractio totalis* being the abstraction of a logical whole from its subjective parts, and *abstractio totius* being the abstraction of the essential whole (of the physical thing) from its non-essential parts.[24]

St. Thomas' *abstractio totius* is, therefore, the abstraction of a whole from its parts without being identical with total abstraction, which is also an abstraction of a whole from its parts. But this does not explain the reason why *abstractio totius* can be considered legitimately a type of formal abstraction.

Cajetan's formal abstraction, in contradistinction to his total abstraction, is the mental separation of an intelligible form, i.e., a knowable object of thought from the matter which shrouds its intelligibility. And St. Thomas' *abstractio totius* is the mental separation of the essential whole from the individuating characteristics which are its non-essential parts. As such it is precisely an abstraction of an intelligible object from the matter which shrouds its intelligibility and, hence, is a valid instance of Cajetan's formal abstraction.

St. Thomas is careful to point out on occasion that *abstractio totius* yields a whole and not a form. But he means this in a qualified sense. *Abstractio totius* frees for scientific investigation not just substantial form, but rather substantial form in its transcendental relationship to prime matter. It yields a form-matter composite rather than just form alone. Thus from this point of view it is an *abstractio totius* and not an *abstractio formae*. Yet the *abstractum* of this abstraction, the *totum* composed

---

[24] For a more complete treatment of this important point, cf. Simmons, *op. cit.*

of substantial form and prime matter, can be considered itself as a form in reference to the matter which individuates it. In fact, St. Thomas frequently makes this point explicit, insisting that the essential whole is related as form to the individual, despite the fact that it is already itself composed through a form-matter relationship.[25] Thus, there should be no difficulty in seeing why physical abstraction, on occasion labeled *abstractio totius,* because it is an abstraction of an essential *whole* from its non-essential parts, might also on another occasion be labeled a type of *abstractio formalis* because it is an abstraction of a *form* or intelligible object from matter.[26]

Thus understood, Cajetan's first degree of formal abstraction, yielding an object of thought abstracted from individual sensible matter and distinctive of the natural sciences, is identical with St. Thomas' *abstractio totius,* yielding, as St. Thomas teaches, an intelligible object mentally freed from individual sensible matter and involving thereby that degree of intelligibility distinctive of the natural sciences.

II. Abstractio Formae

The purpose of this paper is to establish the legitimacy of speaking authentically as a Thomist of three types of formal abstraction proper, respectively, to natural science, mathematics, and metaphysics. I have already tried to make the point that it is certainly Thomistic to speak of St. Thomas' *abstractio totius* as a type of formal abstraction. I will attempt shortly to establish the same point in reference to St. Thomas' *separatio.* In the meantime it may seem pointless to spend time on mathematical abstraction, for this is a type of abstraction most obviously considered a formal abstraction by St. Thomas, who calls it significantly *abstractio formae.* Nevertheless it might be worthwhile to indicate briefly the reason why St. Thomas might be moved to speak of this as an *abstractio formae* even though he does not use this terminology in reference to the other abstractions-of-a-form.

The fact is that even though *abstractio totius* and *separatio* are legitimately thought of as formal abstractions, *abstractio formae* is the formal abstraction *par excellence.* In its original derivation the philosophically technical term, "form," in Thomistic terminology has reference to the

---

[25] *In II Phys.,* 5, n. 179: "Natura igitur speciei constituta ex forma et materia communi, se habet ut formalis respectu individui quod participat talem naturem. . ." Cf. also, *Summa Theol.,* I, 85, 1, c. and *Cont. Gent.,* IV, 81.

[26] From the point of view of its intelligible content the object of natural science corresponds to what is called the *"forma totius"*; cf. *In VII Met.,* 9, n. 1467: "Forma partis dicitur secundum quod perficit materiam, et facit eam esse in actu: Forma autem totius, secundum quod totum compositum per eam in specie collocatur." The abstraction which yields the object for natural science can be spoken of either as an *abstractio formae* (i.e., *abstractio* FORMAE *totius*) or as an *abstractio totius* (i.e., *abstractio formae* TOTIUS).

specifying principle of motion or change, that is, to that active principle in the *quidditative* order which combines with matter to give us the mobile composite. Thus "form," in its strictest sense, connotes a *part* of a whole in the *quidditative* order. The formal *ratio* abstracted in physical abstraction is not a part in the *quidditative* order but rather a whole. And the formal *ratio* abstracted in metaphysical abstraction is not limited to the *quidditative* order but is principally of the existential order. Yet the formal *ratio* abstracted in mathematical abstraction, though it is not the substantial form which combines with prime matter to yield the mobile substance, is a *part* in that it is formally an accidental determination of a substance and is a part in the *quidditative* order. Hence mathematical abstraction can be considered more strictly an abstraction of a form than can either physical or metaphysical abstraction.[27]

Mathematical abstraction differs radically from the other two. Physical abstraction yields an object of thought (mobile being) inclusive of sensible matter—and mobile being exists extramentally in sensible matter. Metaphysical abstraction yields an object (being as such) in separation from all matter—and being *is* able to be realized in strictly immaterial substances. But mathematical abstraction yields an object (quantified being) in abstraction from sensible matter even though quantified being can extramentally exist only in sensible things.[28] The only existence that the mathematical entity has precisely in its characteristic as a *mathematical* entity, i.e., in separation from sensible matter, is in the mind of the mathematician. Accordingly, mathematical judgments must be verified in the mind of the mathematician and not in the extramental real as is the situation in the other sciences.[29] Thus the total rationale of the mathematical object is that of a form. It is a real essence but not a real nature. It involves no inner principle of activity and has no potentiality to become something other than it is. It is wholly and totally its own formal actuality, an actuality explicable only in terms of formal causality.[30] Accordingly, the mathematical object though originally abstracted from concrete sensible things (and, hence, real) is in a special sense a form enjoying a

---

[27] Cf. *In Boeth. de Trin.*, V, 3, c. and ad 2.

[28] *In I Phys.*, 1, n. 2: ". . . curvum vero, licet esse non possit nisi in materia sensibili, tamen in eius definitione materia sensibilis non cadit; et talia sunt omnia mathematica, ut numeri, magnitudines et figurae"; also *In VI Met.*, 1, nn. 1161 & 1162 (cf. *supra*, note 18); *In Boeth. de Trin.*, V, 1, c. (cf. *supra*, note 16).

[29] *In Boeth. de Trin.*, VI, 2, c.: "Sed quia secundum rationem diffinitivam non abstrahunt a qualibet materia, sed solum a sensibili et remotis sensibilibus condicionibus remanet aliquid imaginabile, ideo in talibus oportet quod iudicium sumatur secundum id quod imaginatio demonstrat. Huiusmodi autem sunt mathematica. Et ideo in mathematicis oportet cognitionem secundum iudicium terminari ad imaginationem, non ad sensum, quia iudicium mathematicum superat apprehensionem sensus."

[30] *In I Phys.*, 1, n. 5: "Nam mathematica non demonstrat nisi per causam formalem. . . ."

purely formal existence. Thus mathematical abstraction is, in this sense, the *formal* abstraction *par excellence*.

III. Separatio

In my attempt to resolve the doctrine of the traditional Commentators into the authentic doctrine of St. Thomas, I have tried so far to show that the *abstractio totius* of the natural sciences is a type of formal abstraction not to be confused with the total abstraction common to all the sciences, and that the *abstractio formae* proper to mathematics is not necessarily the only type of formal abstraction, though it is, in a certain sense, the formal abstraction *par excellence*. There remains to be discussed the case of *separatio*.

To some Thomists *separatio* seems so radically different from both *abstractio totius* and *abstractio formae* as to preclude any possibility of considering it as one of three types of formal abstraction. Nonetheless, there is community enough, albeit tenuously analogical, to establish the classification. *Separatio,* like *abstractio totius* and *abstractio formae,* is a mental separation of an intelligible object from the matter which shrouds its intelligibility. And this object, precisely in this abstraction separated from all matter, is so constituted intelligibly as to specify the science of metaphysics, just as the respectively radically different *abstracta* of *abstractio totius* and *abstractio formae* in turn specify natural science and mathematics. Admittedly there are great differences between the first two types of formal abstraction and this third, yet each is analogously an abstraction and a formal abstraction.

Abstraction, as St. Thomas says, can take place in two ways. First of all, there is the mental separation of one feature of reality from another though these features of reality do not, because they cannot, exist apart from one another. This abstraction is legitimately effected in an act of simple apprehension so long as what is conceptualized separately is ontologically prior to that from which it has been mentally separated. Secondly, there is the mental separation of one thing from another when this one thing does, or at least can, exist apart from the other. This abstraction involves a negative judgment enunciating this existential independence of the *abstractum* from that from which it has been abstracted. Each is generally an abstraction or mental separation, but the former is less radically a separation, involving only objective and not existential separation, than the latter, involving even existential separation, and is, when the intention is to stress this difference, spoken of strictly as an abstraction while the latter is spoken of as a separation.[31] The analogical notion of abstraction,

---

[31] *In Boeth. de Trin.,* V, 3, c. (cf. *supra,* note 3).

generally taken, is that of a mental separation of one thing from another. This mental separation can be considered psychologically, when we speak of the act of mentally separating, and/or objectively, when we speak of the ontological, sometimes even existential, independence of one thing from another; the latter, of course, is the measure of the former.[32]

Formal abstraction is the mental separation of an object, precisely as intelligible, from the matter which shrouds its intelligibility. Insofar as there are different degrees of matter from which objects can be freed by abstraction there are different degrees of formal abstraction yielding objects knowable on different levels of intelligibility. Since it is the intelligibility of an object which constitutes it precisely an object, and since the speculative sciences are specified precisely by objects insofar as they are objects, it follows that the different degrees of formal abstraction specify respectively the different branches of speculative science.

Separatio, according to St. Thomas, is the mental separation of being from all matter, a mental separation revealing being not only as ontologically prior to all matter—as is mobile being to individual matter and quantified being to sensible matter—but even as existentially independent of, i.e., able to exist without, matter.[33] This mental separation yields an object of thought, namely, being as such, intelligible to the highest degree and constitutive of a distinct science, metaphysics.[34] As a mental separation yielding the formal object of a distinct science, *separatio* is, like *abstractio totius* and *abstractio formae,* truly a type of formal abstraction. This is not to ignore at all the basic differences between *separatio* and the other two formal abstractions which, we should remember, are as between themselves radically disparate in nature. *Separatio* involves the second type of abstraction, generally taken, namely negative judgment. The object whose intelligibility is revealed in *separatio* is knowable on an entirely unique level. This object is, moreover, only analogically realized in its instances, being paradoxically a whole which actually includes its inferiors and not, as with the univocal whole, only potentially including its inferiors.[35] Yet despite these differences *separatio* is still proportionally like *abstractio totius* and *abstractio formae,* since each *in its own way* yields an object distinctively free from the restrictions of matter and ac-

[32] The two ways of viewing the modes of abstraction as specificative of the sciences are in no way opposed to one another such that an interpretation from one point of view must needs be at odds with an interpretation from the other. Rather, since the real as known is the form of the intellect knowing, they are but complementary views of the same thing. It has been pointed out that the Commentators chose the objective point of view and St. Thomas, in the controversial article at least, the psychological (cf. Kane, *op. cit.*). This need not at all call into question the Thomistic authenticity of the interpretation of the Commentators as some have suggested (cf. Regis, *op cit.*).

[33] Cf. especially, *In Boeth. de Trin.,* V, 3, c.

[34] Cf. especially, *In VI Met.,* 1, nn. 1162–1165.

[35] Cf. especially, *De Ver.,* I, 1, c.

cordingly proportioned to a given level of scientific investigation. The difficulties involved in accepting the abstraction proper to metaphysics as one of the three degrees of formal abstraction disintegrate in the face of a proper understanding of the traditional doctrine on the three degrees. These are not, as they are sometimes popularly misconceived to be, three *univocal* steps in progressively stripping away outer layers of reality to reveal in turn different inner layers. Nothing could be further from the truth. Rather they are three radically different mental separations of distinctly different intelligible objects from distinctly different degrees of matter. The three degrees of abstraction are only analogically like one another, meaning of course, that they are basically diverse in kind and only proportionally the same. Yet there is this *proportional* sameness, and this is sufficient to establish the legitimacy of speaking of the three degrees of formal abstraction as determining respectively the three branches of speculative science.

SUMMARY

The purpose of this paper has been to show that neither the terminology nor the doctrine of the traditional Commentators is at odds with the teaching of St. Thomas as far as the question of the specification of the speculative sciences is concerned.[36] I have tried to show, as far as the terminological issue is concerned, that St. Thomas himself in some texts has chosen to speak of three different abstractions as proper respectively to natural science, mathematics, and metaphysics despite the fact that in other texts he speaks rather of two abstractions and a separation. Further I have tried to show, in respect to the doctrinal issue, that the general teaching of St. Thomas on the specification of the sciences corresponds to the interpretation of the Commentators even though St. Thomas does not speak, as do the Commentators, explicitly of three degrees of formal abstraction. Both St. Thomas and the Commentators teach that the specification of a science depends on its distinctive degree of abstraction or remotion from matter, and that there are three generically different branches of science corresponding to the three different ways in which an object can be free from

[36] The fact that the Commentators do not emphasize the difference in the strict sense between abstraction according to absolute consideration (*abstractio proprie*) and abstraction according to negative judgment (*separatio*) is no doubt a weakness in their presentation of the Thomistic doctrine of abstraction. For this refinement of terminology and doctrine in St. Thomas underscores a point of major importance especially in respect to the nature of metaphysical science. However, this is by no means to say that this lack of emphasis on an important point suffices to vitiate the entire interpretation of St. Thomas by the traditional Commentators. It does, in a sense, leave the exposition of the Commentators incomplete. Nevertheless, their exposition remains generally faithful to the teaching of St. Thomas and in fact represents an admirably clear and pedagogically useful expression of the general doctrine of St. Thomas on the diversification of the sciences.

the restrictions of matter. Lastly, I have tried to show in particular the doctrinal identity of St. Thomas' *abstractio totius, abstractio formae,* and *separatio* respectively with the first (physical), second (mathematical), and third (metaphysical) degrees of formal abstraction *rightly understood.* To illustrate this last point—and, in fact, as a summary of the whole paper—I would like to suggest the following schema as an illustration of the terminological and doctrinal community between St. Thomas and his traditional Commentators on the question of intellectual abstraction.

Abstraction in general, i. e., mental separation of one thing from another

Abstraction in strict sense (according to simple apprehension- *abstractio proprie*)

Separation in strict sense (according to negative judgment- *separatio proprie*)

Mental separation of any whole from its parts (*abstractio totius* taken generally)

Mental separation of intelligible form or ratio from matter (*abstractio formalis*)

Mental separation of logical whole from subjective parts (*abstractio totalis*)

Mental separation of essential whole from individual matter (*abstractio totius*)

Mental separation of form of quantity from sensible matter (*abstractio formae*)

Mental separation of ratio of being from all matter (*separatio*)

Common to all the sciences

Proper to natural science

Proper to mathematics

Proper to meta-physics

B. L. Whorf : AN AMERICAN INDIAN
MODEL OF
THE UNIVERSE

Bᴇɴᴊᴀᴍɪɴ *Lee Whorf (1897–1941) was by training a chemical engineer, by passionate avocation—reinforced with the disciplines of field research and prolonged study—a linguistic scholar. The result of this avocation was the formulation—helped by the influence of Prof. Edward Sapir (1884–1939), Yale anthropologist and authority on American Indian languages—of the Whorfian Hypothesis, a statement and development, upon empirical grounds, of the interrelationships of thought and language. In the present essay, Whorf has indicated how linguistic considerations influence the whole cosmology of man in a particular culture; how the frame of reference for grasping experience is modified, and how the conceptual structure is thus ordered, by the language shared in the culture. The meaning of "truth" and the formation of categories are thus complex and culturally defined. Reprinted by permission from the* ɪɴᴛᴇʀɴᴀ-ᴛɪᴏɴᴀʟ ᴊᴏᴜʀɴᴀʟ ᴏғ ᴀᴍᴇʀɪᴄᴀɴ ʟɪɴɢᴜɪsᴛɪᴄs *(Indiana University), XVI no. 2 (1950), pp. 67–72.*

• I find it gratuitous to assume that a Hopi who knows only the Hopi language and the cultural ideas of his own society has the same notions, often supposed to be intuitions, of time and space that we have and that are generally assumed to be universal. In particular, he has no general notion or intuition of *time* as a smooth flowing continuum in which everything in the universe proceeds at an equal rate, out of a future, through a present, into a past; or, in which, to reverse the picture, the observer is being carried in the stream of duration continuously away from a past and into a future.[1]

After long and careful study and analysis the Hopi language is seen to contain no words, grammatical forms, constructions or expressions that refer directly to what we call *time,* or to past, present, or future, or to enduring or lasting, or to motion as kinematic rather than dynamic (i.e. as a continuous translation in space and time rather than as an exhibition of dynamic effort in a certain process) or that even refer to space in such a way as to exclude that element of extension or existence that we call TIME, and so by implication leave a residue that could be referred to as TIME. Hence, the Hopi language contains no reference to TIME, either explicit or implicit.

At the same time, the Hopi language is capable of accounting for and describing correctly, in a pragmatic or operational sense, all observable phenomena of the universe. Hence, I find it gratuitous to assume that Hopi thinking contains any such notion as the supposed intuitively felt flowing of *time,* or that the intuition of a Hopi gives him this as one of its data. Just as it is possible to have any number of geometries other than the Euclidean which give an equally perfect account of space configurations, so it is possible to have descriptions of the universe, all equally valid, that do not contain our familiar contrasts of time and space. The relativity viewpoint of modern physics is one such view, conceived in mathematical

[1] This article was left among the papers of Benjamin L. Whorf when he died in 1941, and was turned over by Mrs. Whorf to George L. Trager with partially completed materials and linguistic notes. In editing the paper here published, E. A. Kennard and G. L. Trager have made no substantial changes from Whorf's draft.

Previous publications of Whorf's relevant to this article are: "Gestalt Technique of Stem Composition in Shawnee," Appendix to Part IV of C. F. Voegelin, Shawnee Stems and the Jacob P. Dunn Miami Dictionary, Prehistory Research Series, No. 9, pp. 390–406 (Indiana Historical Society, 1940); "The Hopi Language, Toreva Dialect," in *Linguistic Structures of Native America*, pp. 158–183 (Viking Fund Publications in Anthropology, No. 6, 1946); "The Punctual and Segmentative Aspects of Verbs in Hopi," *Lg.* 12. 127–31 (1936); "Some Verbal Categories of Hopi," *Lg.* 14. 275–286 (1938); "Science and Linguistics," *Technology Review*, Vol. 42, No. 6 (1940); "Linguistics as An Exact Science," *Technology Review*, Vol. 43, No. 2 (1940); "Languages and Logic," *Technology Review*, Vol. 43, No. 6 (1941); "The Relation of Habitual Thought and Behavior to Language" in *Language, Culture and Personality*, pp. 75–93 (Menasha, Wis., 1941). The four articles immediately preceding have been reprinted by the Foreign Service Institute, Department of State: *Four Articles on Metalinguistics* (1949).

terms, and the Hopi *weltanschauung* is another and quite different one, nonmathematical and linguistic.

Thus, the Hopi language and culture conceals a *metaphysics,* such as our so-called naive view of space and time does, or as the relativity theory does, yet a different metaphysics than either. In order to describe the structure of the universe according to the Hopi, it is necessary to attempt—insofar as it is possible—to make explicit this metaphysics, properly describable only in the Hopi language, by means of an approximation expressed in our own language, somewhat inadequately it is true, yet by availing ourselves of such concepts as we have worked up into relative consonance with the system underlying the Hopi view of the universe.

In this Hopi view, time disappears and space is altered, so that it is no longer the homogeneous and instantaneous timeless space of our supposed intuition or of classical Newtonian mechanics. At the same time, new concepts and abstractions flow into the picture, taking up the task of describing the universe without reference to such time or space—abstractions for which our language lacks adequate terms. These abstractions, by approximations of which we attempt to reconstruct for ourselves the metaphysics of the Hopi, will undoubtedly appear to us as psychological or even mystical in character. They are ideas which we are accustomed to consider as part and parcel either of so-called animistic or vitalistic beliefs, or of those transcendental unifications of experience and intuitions of things unseen that are felt by the consciousness of the mystic, or which are given out in mystical and/or so-called occult systems of thought. These abstractions are definitely given either explicitly in words—psychological or metaphysical terms—in the Hopi language, or, even more, are implicit in the very structure and grammar of that language, as well as being observable in Hopi culture and behavior. They are not, so far as I can consciously avoid it, projections of other systems upon the Hopi language and culture made by me in my attempt at an objective analysis. Yet, if *mystical* be perchance a term of abuse in the eyes of a modern Western scientist, it must be emphasized that these underlying abstractions and postulates of the Hopian metaphysics are, from a detached viewpoint, equally (or to the Hopi, more) justified pragmatically and experientially, as compared to the flowing time and static space of our own metaphysics, which are *au fond* equally mystical. The Hopi postulates equally account for all phenomena and their interrelations and lend themselves even better to the integration of Hopi culture in all its phases.

The metaphysics underlying our own language, thinking, and modern culture (I speak not of the recent and quite different relativity metaphysics of modern science) imposes upon the universe two grand *cosmic forms,* space and time; static three-dimensional infinite space, and kinetic one-dimensional uniformly and perpetually flowing time—two utterly separate and unconnected aspects of reality (according to this familiar way of thinking). The flowing realm of time is, in turn, the subject of a threefold division: past, present, and future.

The Hopi metaphysics also has its cosmic forms comparable to these in scale and scope. What are they? It imposes upon the universe two grand cosmic forms, which as a first approximation in terminology we may call *manifested* and *manifesting* (or, *unmanifest*) or, again, *objective* and *subjective*. The objective or manifested comprises all that is or has been accessible to the senses, the historical physical universe, in fact, with no attempt to distinguish between present and past, but excluding everything that we call future. The subjective or manifesting comprises all that we call future, *but not merely this;* it includes equally and indistinguishably all that we call mental—everything that appears or exists in the mind, or, as the Hopi would prefer to say, in the *heart,* not only the heart of man, but the heart of animals, plants, and things, and behind and within all the forms and appearances of nature in the heart of nature, and by an implication and extension which has been felt by more than one anthropologist, yet would hardly ever be spoken of by a Hopi himself, so charged is the idea with religious and magical awesomeness, in the very heart of the Cosmos, itself.[2] The subjective realm (subjective from our viewpoint, but intensely real and quivering with life, power, and potency to the Hopi) embraces not only our FUTURE, much of which the Hopi regards as more or less predestined in essence if not in exact form, but also all mentality, intellection, and emotion, the essence and typical form of which is the striving of purposeful desire, intelligent in character, toward manifestation—a manifestation which is much resisted and delayed, but in some form or other is inevitable. It is the realm of expectancy, of desire and purpose, of vitalizing life, of efficient causes, of thought thinking itself out from an inner realm (the Hopian *heart*) into manifestation. It is in a dynamic state, yet not a state of motion—it is not advancing towards us out of a future, but *already with us* in vital and mental form, and its dynamism is at work in the field of eventuating or manifesting, i.e. evolving without motion from the subjective by degrees to a result which is the objective. In translating into English the Hopi will say that these entities in process of causation *will come* or that they—the Hopi—*will come to* them, but in their own language there are no verbs corresponding to our *come* and *go* that mean simple and abstract motion, our purely kinematic concept. The words in this case translated *come* refer to the process of eventuating without calling it motion—they are *eventuates to here* (pew'i) or *eventuates from it* (angqö) or *arrived* (pitu, pl. öki) which refers only to

---

[2] This idea is sometimes alluded to as the spirit of the Breath (hikwsu) and as the Mighty Something (ʔaʔne himu) although these terms may have lower and less cosmic, though always awesome connotations.

the terminal manifestation, the actual arrival at a given point, not to any motion preceding it.

This realm of the subjective or of the process of manifestation, as distinguished from the objective, the result of this universal process, includes also—on its border but still pertaining to its own realm—an aspect of existence that we include in our present time. It is that which is beginning to emerge into manifestation; that is, something which is beginning to be done, like going to sleep or starting to write, but is not yet in full operation. This can be, and usually is, referred to by the same verb form (the *expective* form in my terminology of Hopi grammar) that refers to our future, or to wishing, wanting, intending, etc. Thus, this nearer edge of the subjective cuts across and includes a part of our present time, viz. the moment of inception, but most of our present belongs in the Hopi scheme to the objective realm and so is indistinguishable from our past. There is also a verb form, the *inceptive* which refers to this *edge* of emergent manifestation in the reverse way—as belonging to the objective, as the edge at which objectivity is attained; this is used to indicate beginning or starting, and in most cases there is no difference apparent in the translation from the similar use of the expective. But at certain crucial points significant and fundamental differences appear. The inceptive, referring to the objective and result side and not like the expective to the subjective and causal side, implies the ending of the work of causation in the same breath that it states the beginning of manifestation. If the verb has a suffix which answers somewhat to our passive, but really means that causation impinges upon a subject to effect a certain result—i.e. *the food is being eaten,* then addition of the inceptive suffix in such a way as to refer to the basic action produces a meaning of causal cessation. The basic action is in the inceptive state; hence whatever causation is behind it is ceasing, and so the causation explicitly referred to by the causal suffix is such as *we* would call past time, and the verb includes this and the incepting and the decausating of the final state (a state of partial or total eatenness) in one statement. The translation is 'it stops getting eaten.' Without knowing the underlying Hopian metaphysics, it would be impossible to understand how the same suffix may denote starting or stopping.

If we were to approximate our metaphysical terminology more closely to Hopian terms, we should probably speak of the subjective realm as the realm of *hope* or *hoping*. Every language contains terms that have come to attain cosmic scope of reference, that crystallize in themselves the basic postulates of an unformulated philosophy, in which is couched the thought of a people, a culture, a civilization, even of an era. Such are our words 'reality, substance, matter, cause,' and as we have seen 'space, time, past, present, future.' Such a term in Hopi is the word most often translated 'hope'—*tunátya*—'it is in the action of hoping, it hopes, it is hoped for, it thinks or is thought of with hope,' etc. Most metaphysical words in Hopi are verbs, not nouns as in European languages. The verb *tunátya* contains in its idea of hope something of our words 'thought,' 'desire,' and 'cause,' which sometimes must be used to translate it. The word is really a term which crystallizes the Hopi philosophy of the universe in respect to its grand dualism of objective and subjective; it is the Hopi term for *subjective*. It refers to the state of the subjective, unmanifest, vital and causal aspect of the Cosmos, and the fermenting activity toward fruition and manifestation with which it seethes—an action of hoping; i.e. mental-causal activity, which is forever pressing upon and into the manifested realm. As anyone acquainted with Hopi society knows, the Hopi see this burgeoning activity in the growing of plants, the forming of clouds and their condensation in rain, the careful planning out of the communal activities of agriculture and architecture, and in all human hoping, wishing, striving, and taking thought; and as most especially concentrated in prayer, the constant hopeful praying of the Hopi community, assisted by their exoteric communal ceremonies and their secret, esoteric rituals in the underground kivas—prayer which conducts the pressure of the collective Hopi thought and will out of the subjective into the objective. The inceptive form of *tunátya*, which is *tunátyava*, does not mean 'begins to hope,' but rather 'comes true, being hoped for.' Why it must logically have this meaning will be clear from what has already been said. The inceptive denotes the first appearance of the objective, but the basic meaning of *tunátya* is subjective activity or force; the inceptive is then the terminus of such activity. It might then be said that *tunátya* 'coming true' is the Hopi term for objective, as contrasted with subjective, the two terms being simply two different inflectional nuances of the same verbal root, as the two cosmic forms are the two aspects of one reality.

As far as space is concerned, the subjective is a mental realm, a realm of no space in the objective sense, but it seems to be symbolically related to the vertical dimension and its poles the zenith and the underground, as well as to the 'heart' of things, which corresponds to our word 'inner' in the metaphorical sense. Corresponding to each point in the objective world is such a vertical and vitally *inner* axis which is what we call the wellspring of the future. But to the Hopi there is no temporal future; there is nothing in the subjective state corresponding to the sequences and successions conjoined with distances and changing physical configurations that we find in the objective state. From each subjective axis, which may be thought of as more or less vertical and like the growth-axis of a plant, extends the objective realm in every physical direction, though these directions are typified more especially by the horizontal plane and its four cardinal points. The objective is the great cosmic form of extension; it takes in all the strictly extensional aspects of existence, and it includes all intervals and distances, all seriations and number. Its *distance* includes what we call time in the sense of the temporal relation between events which have already happened. The Hopi conceive time and motion in the objective realm in a purely operational sense—a matter of the complexity and magnitude of operations connecting events—so that the element of time is not separated from whatever element of space enters into the operations. Two events in the past occurred a long *time* apart (the Hopi language has no word quite equivalent to our *time*) when many periodic physical motions have occurred between them in such a way as to traverse much distance or accumulate magnitude of physical display in other ways. The Hopi metaphysics does not raise the question whether the things in a distant village exist at the same present moment as those in one's own village, for it is frankly pragmatic on this score and says that any *events* in the distant village can be compared to any events in one's own village only by an interval of magnitude that has both time and space forms in it. Events at a distance from the observer can only be known objectively when they are *past* (i.e. posited in the objective) and the more distant, the more *past* (the more worked upon from the subjective side). Hopi, with its preference for verbs, as compared to our own liking for nouns, perpetually turns our propositions about things into propositions about events. What happens at a distant village, if actual (objective) and not a conjecture (subjective), can be known *here* only later. If it does not happen *at this place* it does not happen *at this time;* it happens at *that* place and at *that* time. But the *here* happening and the *there* happening are in the objective, corresponding in general to our past, but the *there* happening is the more objectively distant, meaning, from our standpoint, that it is further away in the past just as it is further away from us in space than the *here* happening.

As the objective realm displaying its characteristic attribute of extension stretches away from the observer toward that unfathomable remoteness which is both far away in space and long past in time, there comes a point where extension in detail ceases to be knowable and is lost in the vast distance and where the subjective, creeping behind the scenes as it were, merges into the objective, so that at this inconceivable distance from the observer—from all observers—there is an all-encircling end and beginning of things where it might be said that existence, itself, swallows up the objective and the subjective. The border land of this realm is as much subjective as objective. It is the abysm of antiquity, the time and place told about in the myths, which is known only subjectively or mentally—the Hopi realize and even express in their grammar that the things told in myths or stories do not have the same kind of reality or validity as things of the present day, the things of practical concern. As for the far distances of the sky and stars, what is known and said about them is suppositious, inferential—hence, in a way, subjective—reached more through the inner vertical axis and the pole of the zenith than through the objective distances and the objective processes of vision and locomotion. So the dim past of myths is that corresponding distance on earth (rather than in the heavens) which is reached subjectively as myth through the vertical axis of reality via the pole of the nadir; hence it is placed *below* the present surface of the earth, though this does not mean that the nadir—land of the origin myths—is a hole or cavern as we should understand it. It is *Palátkwapi* 'At the Red Mountains,' a land like our present earth, but to which our earth bears the relation of a distant sky—and similarly the sky of our earth is penetrated by the heroes of tales, who find another earth-like realm above it.

It may now be seen how the Hopi do not need to use terms that refer to space or time as such. Such terms in our language are recast into expressions of extension, operation, and cyclic process provided they refer to the solid objective realm. They are recast into expressions of subjectivity if they refer to the subjective realm—the future, the psychicmental, the mythical period, and the invisibly distant and conjectural generally. Thus, the Hopi language gets along perfectly without tenses for its verbs.

BIBLIOGRAPHY FOR PART III

Aaron, R. I., "Our Knowledge of Universals," *Proceedings, British Academy*, London, XXXI (1945), pp. 17–42.

——, *The Theory of Universals*, The Clarendon Press, Oxford, 1952.

Adams, E. M., "Primary and Secondary Qualities," *The Journal of Philosophy*, XXXXV (1948), pp. 435–42.

Adler, M. J., "The Hierarchy of Essences," *Review of Metaphysics*, VI (1952–53), pp. 3–30.

Alexander, S., "On Relations; and in Particular the Cognitive Relation," *Mind*, n.s., XXI (1912), pp. 305–28.

Allan, D. M., "Are Ideas Physical," *The Journal of Philosophy*, XXXIX (1942), pp. 645–54.

Allers, R., "The Intellectual Cognition of Particulars," *The Thomist*, III (1941), pp. 95–163.

——, "St. Augustine's Doctrine on Illumination," *Franciscan Studies*, XII (1952), pp. 27–46.

Aubron, P., "L'union du sujet et de l'objet dans la connaissance chez Aristote, d'après le commentaire de Cajetan," *Archives de Philosophie*, I, cahier 1 (1923), pp. 25–31.

Bart, P. J., "Reflections on Perception," *The New Scholasticism*, III (1929), pp. 19–23.

Barbotin, E., *La théorie aristotélicienne de l'intellect d'après Théophraste,* Vrin, Paris, 1954.

Baylis, C. A., "Universals, Communicable Knowledge and Metaphysics," *The Journal of Philosophy,* XXXXVIII (1951), pp. 636–44.

Berndtson, A., "Notes on Universals," *The Modern Schoolman,* XXVIII (1950–51), pp. 41–53.

Bertocci, P. A., "The Nature of Cognition," *Review of Metaphysics,* VIII (1954), pp. 49–60.

Black, M., "Linguistic Relativity: The Views of Benjamin Lee Whorf," *The Philosophical Review,* LXVIII (1959), pp. 228–38.

Boehner, P., *"Notitia Intuitiva* of Non Existents According to Peter Aureoli, O.F.M. (1322)," *Fransciscan Studies,* VIII (1948), pp. 388–416.

Brueggeman, E., "Reflection on Reflection," *The Modern Schoolman,* XII (1935), pp. 35–8.

Caussimon, J., "L'intuition métaphysique de l'existence chez Saint Thomas et dans l'existentialisme contemporain," *Revue de Métaphysique et de Morale,* LV (1950), pp. 392–407.

Chapman, H. M., "Reflection on the Reflective Standpoint," *The Return to Reason,* ed. J. Wild, Henry Regnery Co., Chicago, 1953, pp. 11–22.

Davies, W. G., "The Veracity of Consciousness," *Mind,* II (1877), pp. 64–74.

Dewey, J., "Reality and the Criterion for the Truth of Ideas," *Mind,* n.s., XV (1906), pp. 317–42.

Drake, D., "That Elusive Doctrine of Essence," *The Philosophical Review,* XXXVII (1928), pp. 53–71.

Farrell, B. A., "Intentionality and the Theory of Signs," *Philosophy and Phenomenological Research,* XV (1955), pp. 500–11.

Gassert, R. G., "The Meaning of *Cogitatio* in St. Augustine," *The Modern Schoolman,* XXV (1947–48), pp. 238–45.

Geach, P., *Mental Acts,* The Humanities Press, New York, 1957.

Halpin, A. J., "The Location of Qualitative Essence: I. Aristotle and Aquinas, II. Locke and Meyerson," *The New Scholasticism,* X (1936), pp. 145–66; 226–44.

Haserot, F. S., "Spinoza and the Status of Universals," *The Philosophical Review,* LIX (1950), pp. 469–92.

Heiser, B., "The *Primum Cognitum* According to Duns Scotus," *Franciscan Studies,* n.s., II (1942), pp. 193–216.

Kremer, R., "Sur la notion de réalisme épistémologique," *Philosophia Perennis,* Regensburg, Habbell, II (1930), pp. 733–41.

Kristeller, P. O., *Review of* P. Merlan, *From Platonism to Neo Platonism* (Martinus Nijhoff, The Hague, 1953), *Journal of the History of Ideas,* XIX (1958), pp. 129–33.

Krzesinski, A. J., "The Immanency and Transcendency of Our Knowledge," *Proceedings,* XIth International Congress of Philosophy, vol. II: Epistemology, North-Holland Publishing Co., Amsterdam, pp. 163–69.

Lauer, R. Z., "St. Albert and the Theory of Abstraction," *The Thomist,* XVII (1954), pp. 69–83.

Lee, O. H., "On the Knowledge of Individuals," *Review of Metaphysics,* II (1948), pp. 3–12.

Leighton, J. A., "The Objects of Knowledge," *The Philosophical Review,* XVI (1907), pp. 577–87.

——, "The Final Ground of Knowledge," *The Philosophical Review,* XVII (1908), pp. 383–99.

Maquart, F. X., "L'universel," *Revue de Philosophie,* n.s., I (1930), pp. 91–112.

Marcotte, J. N., "Materiality and Knowledge," *The New Scholasticism,* XXI (1947), pp. 349–70.

Maréchal, J., "Le dynamisme intellectuel dans la connaissance objective," *Revue Néo-scolastique de Philosophie,* XXVIII (1927), pp. 137–65.

Maritain, J., "On Human Knowledge," *Thought,* XXIV (1949), pp. 225–43.

——, "L'intelligence d'après M. Maurice Blondel," *Revue de Philosophie,* XXX (1923), pp. 333–64; 484–511.

——, *Réflexions sur l'intelligence et sur sa vie propre,* 3ème éd., Desclée de Brouwer, Paris, 1930.

——, "La vie propre de l'intelligence et l'erreur idéaliste," *Revue Thomiste,* n.s., VII (1924), pp. 268–313.

Markus, R., "Substance, Cause and Cognition in Thomist Thought," *The New Scholasticism,* XXI (1947), pp. 438–48.

McAndrew, P. J., "The Theory of Divine Illumination in St. Bonaventure," *The New Scholasticism,* VI (1932), pp. 32–50.

Merlan, P., "Abstraction and Metaphysics in St. Thomas' *Summa,*" *Journal of the History of Ideas,* XIV (1953), pp. 284–91.

Murray, J., "The Platonic Doctrine of Ideas," *Studies,* XXXX (1951), pp. 311–22.

Noël, L., "L'intelligible," *Revue Néo-scolastique de Philosophie,* XXXI (1930), pp. 396–402.

Pears, D., "Universals," *The Philosophical Quarterly,* I (1950–51), pp. 218–27.

Peifer, J. F., *The Concept in Thomism,* Bookman Associates, New York, 1952.

Prall, D. W., "Essences and Universals," *The Journal of Philosophy,* XXII (1925), pp. 264–72.

Price, K. B., "Hume's Analysis of Generality," *The Philosophical Review,* LIX (1950), pp. 58–76.

Quesnell, Q., "Participated Understanding: The Three Acts of the Mind," *The Modern Schoolman,* XXXI (1954), pp. 281–88.

Rosan, L. J., "The External World and the Self," *Review of Metaphysics,* VI (1953), pp. 539–50.

Sams, H. W., "Reflection," *The Philosophical Review,* LII (1943), pp. 400–08.

Sing-Nan, Fen, "On Being and Being Known," *The Journal of Philosophy,* XXXXVIII (1951), pp. 381–88.

Sisson, E. O., "Things, Images, Ideas," *The Journal of Philosophy,* XXXXV (1948), pp. 405–11.

Smith, G., "The Concept in St. Thomas," *The Modern Schoolman,* XV (1938), pp. 52–6.

Thomas, I., "Objects and Things," *Dominican Studies,* III (1950), pp. 317–30.

Thro, L., "A Note on 'Notes on Universals'," *The Modern Schoolman,* XXVIII (1950–51), pp. 53–8.

Walsh, F. A., "A Recent Study of the Universal," *The New Scholasticism,* IV (1930), pp. 37–45.

Whitehead, A. N., "Causal Components," *An Enquiry Concerning the Principles of Natural Knowledge,* The University Press, Cambridge, 1919, pp. 182–89.

———, "Perception," *An Enquiry Concerning the Principles of Natural Knowledge,* The University Press, Cambridge, 1919, pp. 8–15.

———, "Objects and Subjects," *The Philosophical Review,* XXXXI (1932), pp. 130–46.

Wood, L., "Concepts and Objects," *The Philosophical Review,* XXXXV (1936), pp. 370–81.

Part IV : THE HUMAN JUDGMENT
AND ITS TYPES

"The existence of a multitude of knowledges which present themselves as true and yet opposed to each other—such is the epistemological problem at its roots, a fact immanent and conscious, of which every man who reflects can be aware. This fact, moreover, is the starting point of many other questions or problems of an epistemological nature, all of which we can sum up in the following manner: (1) are the knowledges that present themselves as true, really true? (2) if they are true, how is this multitude of truths to be explained? (3) if they are multiple, how is their multiplicity to be reduced to unity? Such are the three great epistemological problems which have posed themselves since the start of philosophic speculation. Their solution is the proper subject matter of epistemology as I conceive it."

L. M. Régis, O.P.
"St. Thomas and Epistemology," Aquinas Lecture,
Marquette University Press, Milwaukee, 1946

H. B. Veatch : PROPOSITION AND KNOWLEDGE

Pᴿᴼꜰᴇꜱꜱᴏʀ *Henry B. Veatch of Indiana University explores the relations of propositions and existing beings in various modes, and indicates the failure of concepts to achieve the status of knowledge. Reprinted by permission from* ɪɴᴛᴇɴᴛɪᴏɴᴀʟ ʟᴏɢɪᴄ, *Yale University Press, New Haven, 1952, pp. 154–69.*

Propositions and the intention of existence

• Considered as intentions and instruments of knowledge, concepts are at once indispensable and insufficient. As to their indispensability, it is precisely the apprehension of essences, of what things are, that is effected through concepts.

Nevertheless, although correct, such a characterization of the function and work of concepts is apt to mislead. Taking the suggestion in one sense, one might say that if through concepts and merely through concepts it were possible to arrive at a knowledge of what things are, we might seem to have arrived already at the goal of knowledge, rather than to be merely at the beginning. Yet just to have a set of concepts—"brown," "justice," "meson," "taller than," etc.—is not to have knowledge in anything like a full and complete sense. True, each such concept may well be the intention of an essence, of the "what" of certain real beings. Still, the apprehension of these "whats" in concepts does not as such constitute an apprehension of the *fact* that these *are* the "whats" of real things. That this is brown, or that the meson was discovered by a Japanese physicist, or that the practice of religion is an exercise of the virtue of justice—such, obviously, is not the kind of knowledge that is conveyed simply in concepts and in nothing else. Instead, such knowledge can only come in propositions, which, unlike mere concepts, are susceptible of truth or falsity, and hence capable of disclosing not mere natures or essences but also that things *are* of such and such natures.

Accordingly, concepts being thus insufficient, and it being necessary to resort to propositions as a further instrumentality for the attainment of knowledge, let us inquire further concerning these propositions. For instance, just what is it that one is able to intend through propositions that one cannot intend through concepts alone? And how are propositions, through their peculiar nature and structure, adapted to perform this intentional function which is characteristically their own?

Addressing myself to these questions, I may begin by remarking once more that while concepts do acquaint us with what things are, they seem always to stop short of disclosing the fact that these "whats" are indeed the "whats" of real existing beings, the very "whats" that things actually *are*. In other words, it is the intention of essences *in their very existence* and as actually existing that concepts would seem not to suffice for. Moreover, since it is only insofar as intentions are directed toward things as they really are, that they can be said to be true or false, it is understandable why only propositions and not concepts should be susceptible of truth or falsity.

Nevertheless, one must be careful not to misunderstand this suggestion that it is essences as they exist and in their existence that are intended in propositions. *Existent* essences are intended in our concepts. Indeed, this is why the abstraction of concepts of essences from the concrete experience of real existing things was held to be so important.

However, the point here would seem to be that although the concepts which we arrive at by abstraction are concepts of existent essences, it is not in and through concepts as such that we recognize these essences as actually being or existing. Indeed, the situation with respect to concepts is not unlike that in regard to sensory experience, concerning which a remark of Gilson's may be recalled to the effect that the senses bear a message which they themselves are unable to read. So likewise, while the concept of "man," for example, may have been abstracted from our experience of actual existing human beings, and may thus be the concept of what certain things *are*, still from considering just the concept "man" alone, it is impossible to tell whether there are any human beings actually existing or not. Indeed, this is precisely the import of the fact that a concept is a product of abstraction: it abstracts the essence from its condition of actual existence.

This is not to say, of course, that we cannot have a concept of existence. It is possible intellectually to turn even existence into a kind of essence, and so to conceive it after the manner of our concepts of man, brown, meson, and whatnot. Yet so to have an abstract concept of existence is not to have a concept of any thing actually existing. In fact, it is not even to have a concept of existence itself actually existing, and this for two reasons.

In the first place, existence is not properly an essence which can be regarded as coming to be or to exist. Rather the concept of existence is supposed to be the concept of that "esse" or being which essences come to have. Hence it is a serious distortion to treat of existence as if it were itself just another essence which comes to have such existence or being. For "esse" or the act of existing being the act of some essence—of something which can be or is able to be—one cannot legitimately turn the concept of precisely that act into the concept of a potency for that act.

Quite apart from these considerations there is still another reason why an abstract or general concept of existence is in nowise a concept of any act itself of existing. Even if existence were an ordinary essence, and as such were a "what" that is or a something that either is or can be, still there is a real distinction between the "what" and the "is" in any "what" that is. Essence and existence, in short, are really distinct from one another, so that that which is or comes to be is always to be distinguished from its being. Indeed, the most telling evidence for this is the simple fact that with respect to any concept of an essence, it is always pertinent to ask whether there is such a thing or not. In other words, the concept of triangle does not indicate whether there are triangles or not; nor the concept of brown, whether anything actually is brown or not, etc. Consequently, even if the concept of existence could be treated as another essence, there would still be the question as to whether it existed actually or not.

In short, the fact that I *am*, or that you *are*, or that anything is, for that matter, always seems to be outside the concept of me or of you or of anything else. The concept of what I am is not as such indicative of the fact that I am. Even to conceive of me as actually existing, i.e., of the actual existence of a certain individual human being, still leaves open the question of whether such a conceived existence is in fact true—whether in fact I really am or not. In this sense, indeed, one can be said to conceive, say, of Xanadu, and one can even conceive of the existence of Xanadu. Yet there is still the question as to whether this Xanadu † which one has conceived of as existing—i.e., whose existence one has entertained conceptually or in thought—exists really and in fact.

The structure of the proposition: existence propositions and subject-predicate propositions

If we say that the very act of existing, or esse, of a thing can never be grasped in a concept of that thing but has to be apprehended in a proposition, the next question that arises is as to just what the structure of the proposition is and as to just how it is adapted to its function of apprehending existence. Immediately in answer to such a question, it might occur to one that since the problem is that of apprehending the existence of an essence, this could be solved by the use simply of a concept of that essence together with the judgment that it is or exists. Thus while the mere concepts of justice, brown, meson, etc., do not tell us whether there are such entities or not, certainly judgments such as "Justice exists," or "There is such a thing as a meson," or "The color 'brown' is real," etc., are unequivocal in this respect: they assert the actual being or existence of such entities and as such may be considered true or false.

Unfortunately, the conclusion to which such considerations would seem to point is likely to prove quite as embarrassing as it is plausible. While a propositional form of the type "X is" or "X exists" would seem altogether adapted to the function of intending the existence of an essence, at the

† EDITOR'S NOTE: See Samuel Taylor Coleridge's poem *Kubla Khan*; for a study of the role of the imagination in the construction of poetic statements, cf. J. L. Lowes, *The Roads to Xanadu*, Houghton Mifflin, Boston, 1930.

same time it is not the form that has always been regarded as standard in the Aristotelian tradition. On the Aristotelian view, a proposition is held to be made up of two terms and not just one, it being necessary in a proposition always to predicate one concept of another. Does this mean that I am on the horns of a dilemma? Must I either summarily discard the traditional subject-predicate form of the proposition as not being consonant with what I have been insisting is the proper nature and function of the proposition; or must I discard my whole account of the proposition as not being rightly compatible with the recognized S-P form of all propositions?

Of course, one might try the expedient of simply transforming what might be called "existence propositions" of the type of "X is" or "X exists" into propositions of the more familiar S-P type. That is to say, one might try to make of "existence" an ordinary predicate and say "X is existent" or "X is real," thereby preserving the characteristic subject-predicate structure. But unhappily, no sooner does one do this than one finds that "existence" simply will not behave as an ordinary predicate. Indeed, when cast in the role of predicate concepts, terms such as "existent" or "real" turn out to be either purely redundant or else not properly concepts at all.

As to their redundancy, one might argue that they add nothing to what is already expressed in the copula "is." Suppose one considers that the copula, as a form of the verb "to be," serves not merely to connect subject with predicate but also to point up the peculiar and distinctive nature of the proposition itself, in contrast to mere concepts. That is to say, on such a view the copula would signify no less than the very "to be" or existence of the conceived essences. Clearly, interpreting the copula in this light, one would have to admit that predicates like "existent" or "real" would have nothing to contribute in the proposition over and above what had already been signified by the copula.

On the other hand, if one does take the copula as a mere connective between two concepts, then presumably the predicate concepts "existent" or "real" would have to signify the very act of existence, the very esse, of the subject concept. And yet as I sought to point out in the preceding section, this is not a function which any mere concept is capable of performing. Indeed, even the concept of existence itself does not signify that anything actually exists in fact. Accordingly, to suppose that predicates such as "existent" or "real" do signify this much is to suppose that they are certainly more than mere concepts.

Existence simply is not and cannot be a predicate of the usual sort. But then there would seem to be no way in which what I have called existence propositions could be properly rendered as subject-predicate propositions; and if not, the afore-mentioned dilemma would appear inescapable.

Nevertheless, before submitting to this dilemma of having to admit either that the S-P form is not the proper form for propositions or that the function of the proposition is not properly the intention of existence, we might do well to consider first just why, in an intentional logic, the S-P form should be considered the proper propositional form. It may be that when we clearly understand the reason for this, we shall see also that such a form is by no means ill-adapted to the intention of the existence of essences.

To begin with, it may be noted that from the point of view of an intentional logic the relational structure of an S-P proposition is to be regarded as but a further development of the relational structure of the concept. As I tried to show, a concept involves the abstraction of a nature or essence from the individuals in which it either does or can exist. Nevertheless, since such a nature or essence does not really exist apart from its individuals, it having been only intellectually separated from them, the very fact that a concept is, as we say, abstract means that it at the same time is a relation of identity between what has thus been intellectually abstracted and the individuals from which such abstraction has thus been artificially made.

However, such a relation of identity between abstracted essence and individuals still leaves something wanting. If we are to understand the essence as it really is, we must actually reidentify it with the individuals, in which and only in which it can be and exist really, and from which it has been separated out intellectually and by the mind. It is precisely this reidentifying of an abstracted essence with the individuals from which it has been intellectually held apart that is effected in a proposition.

Indeed, being but a relation of identity, any concept of an essence is said to be *predicable* of the individuals in its extension. To predicate a concept of something is simply to identify it actually with some or all of the individuals from which it has been abstracted and to which it has remained related by a relation of identity. What else is the significance of saying, "This *is* brown," or "Men *are* mortal," or "Socrates *was* a great teacher"? Here, surely, there is no question of asserting that Socrates was a member of the class of great teachers or that men are included in the class of mortals or that "this" is an argument of the function "——is brown." Rather in such propositions one recognizes no less than the unity in being or in *esse* of those intellectually distinguishable elements or aspects that have been separated in thought and held over against one another in a relation of identity.

In other words, for a concept to be but a relation of identity means that a concept is predicable as such; and actually to predicate it means actually to identify it with one or more of the individuals to which it thus stands in a relation of identity. Thus the identification of predicate with subject in a proposition is but a development of the relation of identity in a concept. Moreover, just as intentionality is served by a relation of identity in the case of the concept, so also it is served by the identification of predicate with subject in a proposition: that is to say, it is by such identity and only thereby that we come to know, or cognitively intend, *what* a thing *is*.

The relation of identity as the proper instrument for intending existence

Just as we have been able to see that the subject-predicate structure of the proposition is in nowise arbitrary but rather is the indispensable and inescapable development of that intentional relation of identity present in the concept, so also we should be able to see how this same subject-predicate structure, far from being ill-adapted to the intention of existence, is precisely fitted for this function.

Suppose we ask ourselves just *where* it is that the abstracted essences or intelligible aspects of things are to be found in actual union with the things from which they have been abstracted in thought. The answer is: "In the concrete individual wholes existing in reality." That is to say, it is only in existent individuals that essences are or can be, just as it is only from such existent individuals that essences are abstracted.

Indeed, strictly speaking, an essence is not that which is or exists. Rather it is a constitutive principle *through* which that which is exists and exists as this or that, i.e., as having such and such a nature. For that matter, it is even misleading to say that a nature or essence is a "what" that is; rather it is always a what *something* is. Moreover, the reason for this is that essence and existence, although really distinct (i.e., the one is never reducible to the other), are still never themselves subsistent entities; rather they are that through which a subsistent entity comes to be. That is to say, they *constitute*, but are not themselves, the real subsistent individuals of the natural world.

Accordingly, if we are to intend or recognize these "whats" or essences as they actually are and in their very acts of being, we must recognize them as being *in* subsistent individuals, or better, as being the essences of such individuals. This is precisely what the subject-predicate proposition serves to do: it intends natures or essences in the very individuals in which they are or exist—thus "This is brown," "That is a meson," "This object is taller than that," etc.

In other words, since essences do not exist just as such, but only in subsistent individuals or supposits, one can begin to see why the relation of identity between subject and predicate in an ordinary S-P proposition is, after all, an intention of existence. It is in the actual identifying of an abstracted essence with the individual or individuals in which it exists that one comes to intend such an essence in its very esse or act of existing.

Likewise, from what has been said, one can also begin to see more clearly how, with respect to the intention of existence, this relation of identity in an S-P proposition goes beyond the relation of identity of the mere concept. While it is true that the concept "brown," for instance, is a relation of identity to the individual browns, still as I have insisted so often the concept just as such, i.e., as a concept, does not indicate whether there are any such individuals that are brown or not. On the other hand, the propositions, "This is brown" or "That is brown," are quite unequivocal on this score: they do intend existence.

If one presses further and wants to know why the relation of identity in the concept does not intend existence, whereas that in the proposition does, I could make the following suggestions. In the concept the universal is both separated from its instances and stands over against them, so to speak, in a relation of identity. On the other hand, in the proposition this artificially induced condition of an essence, whereby it is both separated from and yet related to the individuals in which it exists, is, so to speak, overcome, and the abstracted essence is recognized as actually *being* in the relevant individual or individuals.

In other words, it is the very abstractness of the concept which makes it nonexistential, just as in contrast it is the synthesizing function of the proposition which reintegrates the abstracted essence into the concrete individuals in which that essence *is* and can only *be*. This is not to say, of course, that the concept is not related to the items in its extension; on the contrary, it simply is such a relation. And yet such a relation being only the work of reason—no essence being really separated from its individuals or really related to them by identity—it is only insofar as in the proposition we go beyond this relation of identity between universal and particular and actually identify the one with the other in an existent individual or individuals that we become properly cognizant of that real unity in being or in *esse* which the preceding operation of conceptual analysis and abstraction had tended to dissolve.

The functions of existence propositions and of subject-predicate propositions compared

Granting the correctness of the argument so far, we would seem to have reached the following conclusion: all propositions have an existential intention—not just existence propositions but subject-predicate propositions as well. Yet this conclusion still leaves us with the problem of determining just why such intention of existence should be mediated through propositions of quite different types. That existence propositions and subject-predicate propositions are of different types would seem to be a consequence of my earlier observations. Thus a subject-predicate proposition necessarily involves at least two concepts, these concepts signifying either different essences or at least different intelligible aspects of the same essence. On the other hand, the act of existing not being a proper object of a concept, it is impossible for existence to function as an ordinary predicate. In consequence, existence propositions are not reducible to the two-term subject-predicate form.

Accordingly, if these two propositions are of different types, and if logical forms or types are nothing but intentions, it would seem that the difference in form between these two types of proposition must be indicative of a difference in intention. In fact, I should like to suggest that such a difference in intention involves no less than a difference in the kinds of knowledge that one seeks to attain through the enunciation of these two different types of proposition. To bring out what I mean by this suggested difference in kinds of knowledge, I suggest that the subject-predicate proposition represents an answer to a different kind of question from that to which the existence proposition answers. Put succinctly these questions are, on the one hand, questions as to *what* something is and, on the other hand, questions as to *whether* something is.

Moreover, these two questions as to *what* and *whether* represent very different cognitive concerns and arise from very different cognitive situations. Given that initial cognitive situation of the human being—a situation which I have already alluded to and described as being that in which the human individual is presented with a world of real existing things through his senses—the proper cognitive question would seem to be "What?" That is to say, in such a situation we want to know what the things are that are presented to us as being and existing. Derivatively, and following the doctrine of the categories, we may want to know how large these beings are, or where they are, or what they are doing, or what is happening to them, or in what relation they stand to other beings, etc.

To every such question the proper answer will have to be formulated in a subject-predicate proposition, i.e., a proposition that tells what a given thing is, or, derivatively, where it is, or how large it is, etc. In other words, in such a context there can be no question of whether a thing is, the fact of its existence being simply given in sense in the first place; rather one's cognitive concern is directed wholly toward trying to understand *what* such a given being is.

On the other hand, the existence of many things is not and sometimes cannot be given to us directly in sense. Accordingly, we may inquire concerning them as to *whether* they are or not; and to such a question the proper answer will quite naturally be in the form of an existence proposition. Moreover, in explanation of how such a cognitive situation arises, we need but point out that in contrast to the representations of the external senses proper, all other images, as well as all concepts, are representations only of what might be. That is to say, a mere consideration of what is thus intended in such images and concepts does not indicate whether these objects of intention actually exist in *rerum natura* or not.

To consider just concepts for the moment it is true, as we have seen, that concepts are abstracted from sense experience. Moreover, such abstract concepts are nothing but relations of identity to the individuals from which a given nature or essence has been abstracted and in which that nature or essence can alone exist. Nevertheless, once the nature or essence is thus abstracted and in consequence is made to stand in a relation of identity to the items in its extension, it is impossible to tell from the concept alone whether or not such individuals are actually existing here and now, or, for that matter, whether or not they ever have existed or ever will exist. As a result, questions as to whether there ever were dinosaurs, or whether there is such a thing as hydrogen, or whether irrational numbers are real, etc., become meaningful questions. And being meaningful questions, the existence propositions which are the proper answers to them become likewise meaningful: for example, "Dinosaurs did once exist," "There is such a thing as hydrogen," "Irrational numbers do not exist," etc.

In short, the differing intentions of subject-predicate propositions and existence propositions may perhaps be briefly characterized in this way: in subject-predicate propositions one recognizes the existence (in some sense or other) of the object of one's intentions as being given, and one goes on to declare *what* this object is; on the other hand, in existence propositions one begins simply with an intention of an essence as signifying possible objects, and one goes on to declare *whether* such possible objects actually are. That is to say, in the one case, the existent being given, one proceeds to determine what it might possibly be; in the other case, starting from a possible "what," one proceeds to determine whether there is any existent answering to it.

Of course, given the analogy of being, as well as the logical device of designation for getting at beings in these different senses, one can use subject-predicate propositions, not only to determine the "whats" of actual existents in *rerum natura,* but also to determine the "whats" of mere possibles, or of mere beings of reason, or of mere logical entities. And likewise the assertion that something is may mean that it is only in the sense of a being of reason or of a second intention, etc. These are further complications that I must treat of in a subsequent section when I undertake a full discussion of the so-called designation of terms or concepts.

THE COMPOSITION OF BEING AS DETERMINING THE COMPOSITION OF TERMS IN A PROPOSITION

The need for futher intentional flexibility and complexity in propositional forms

So far my discussion of the proposition has concerned itself only in the most general way with what it is that is intended by a proposition. My conclusion has been that the proposition intends not just essences but essences in their very acts of existing.

Nevertheless, as I have already had occasion to note in my efforts to distinguish subject-predicate propositions from existence propositions, the existence of essences is not quite the simple matter one might suppose. On the contrary, the very fact that it is an essence that exists means that the resultant existent being is not simple but composite—i.e., a composite of essence (what can be or is able to be) and *esse* (the act of existing). Furthermore, as I also intimated in the foregoing section, an essence would not ordinarily seem to exist just as such; rather it nearly always exists as the essence of something, i.e., of an individual that is or exists. Thus here again is a type of composition right within the unity of any existent being or entity.

Besides, as we shall see, there are the further compositions of matter and form and of substance and accident, all of which are indicative of the fact that the intention of any actually existing being must always be the intention of that which is not ontologically simple but complex. Accordingly, the form and structure of propositions, it would seem, would have to be adapted not merely to the intention of existence but also to the intention of existents in their very composition.

Indeed, if we place ourselves in that original and fundamental cognitive situation of the human being—the situation in which, presented through our senses with actual existent beings, we thereupon seek to understand what these beings are—it would seem inescapable that our progressive understanding should be formulated in subject-predicate propositions: "This (S) is so and so (P)." The P, in other words, signifies the "what" of the S, i.e., what it is. Would it not seem at least *prima facie* plausible that the compositeness of the S-P propositional structure must answer to a like compositeness in the being intended by such a structure? Thus, to say that S is P certainly involves a distinction between S and P; otherwise, subject and predicate would be wholly indistinguishable and the propositional structure would simply collapse.

Nevertheless, distinctions may be of either of two kinds, real distinctions or distinctions merely of reason. Thus a real distinction obviously is a distinction between two entities that are distinct really and in fact. On the other hand, as I have already had occasion to remark in passing in connection with abstraction, the human intellect is often able to separate in thought what is really together in fact. Accordingly, when S and P are distinguished in a proposition, are the objects of these intentions likewise really distinct, or is there involved here only a distinction of reason?

Unhappily the answer to these questions must be a little complicated. To be sure, one thing is quite certain and that is that if S is P, then S and P cannot possibly be really distinct as two things are distinct one from another, for then it could not possibly be affirmed that S is P. Thus John

Jones is not Tom Smith, nor is this paper in front of me the bookshelf over against the wall, nor is a human being his weight, nor a color an activity, nor a finite essence its existence, nor this place some other place, etc. In short, nothing is what it is not, or other than itself. Rather everything is just what it is; it is itself. Accordingly, it is not surprising that, as we saw in the preceding section, the relation between S and P in an affirmative proposition can only be a relation of identity.

But then if nothing may be or be affirmed to be other than itself, how can we possibly say that S is P? Are we not rather constrained simply to the assertion S is S? Would not such, indeed, seem to be the ultimate import of the principle that the relation between the two terms of a proposition is simply one of identity?

Yet any such conclusion is clearly untenable. Indeed, for purposes of knowledge we can no more confine ourselves to assertions of the form S is S than we can permit ourselves assertions to the effect that S is not S or is other than itself. To be sure, there is nothing wrong with a proposition of the form S is S; rather it is simply inadequate for purposes of knowledge. Indeed, the very possibility of our asserting S is S is an excellent illustration of how the intellect can make a distinction even where there is no difference—i.e., can set up a distinction of reason, for which there is no basis or foundation in reality.

Apparently we are faced with a paradox: subject and predicate must surely be distinct by some other distinction than a mere distinction of reason (such as the mere distinction of S from S); yet at the same time there must be some sort of relation of identity between subject and predicate, if we are to say that S is P. Nevertheless, to resolve this paradox, one need only recognize that while the distinction between subject and predicate is but a distinction of reason, it is not a distinction of reason comparable to that between S and S, but rather one that is founded on a real distinction or real composition in what is intended by the proposition.

For instance, to say that David Hume was a Scotsman, or that he was a human being, or that he was acquainted with Adam Smith—all these predications certainly involve relations of identity since they signify or represent what Hume *was,* not what he *was not.* Also, the very separation of the predicate from the subject in the proposition (a separation that is presupposed by the very relation of identity) is only a distinction of reason. Surely, in fact and in reality, Hume was not separated from his nationality or from his human nature or even from his acquaintance with Adam Smith. Rather it is only we who intellectually and in thought separate out and abstract the qualities and characteristics of things from the things in which they exist and from whose being their own is indistinguishable.

Indeed, the whole structure of the proposition, involving as it does the distinguishing of what is really one and the reidentification of what was never in fact two, is nothing but the work of reason, i.e., nothing but an *ens rationis*. At the same time, just as it is clear that both the distinction and the identity of the two terms in the proposition are products of reason, still one would never maintain that the notion of David Hume and the notion of human nature, to say nothing of the notions of Scottish nationality or of an acquaintance of Adam Smith, involve no difference in meaning. On the contrary, they all clearly mean different things. Indeed, insofar as the general concept of "being acquainted with" signifies a certain kind of relation that human beings stand in with respect to one another, one cannot even say that Hume was such a relation, for a relation is clearly a different thing from Hume. For that matter, one cannot even say that Hume was human nature or that he was the quality of being Scotch.

In other words, what these last considerations indicate is that the being of things is somehow composite, and that the subject and predicate concepts of a given proposition would seem to point up or bring into focus different phases or parts in such a composition. For instance, different categories represented different modes of being. In consequence, no one of them simply is any of the others: a substance not a quality, nor a quantity an activity, etc. Hence David Hume cannot properly be said to be the relation of "acquainted with." To be sure, a substance can have accidents and the accidents can only be in a substance. Yet for all that, their mode of being is different in that the being of an accident is only in a substance, whereas the being of a substance is in itself.

Nor is the composite character of finite being manifested only in the composition of substance and accident. For instance, if one accepts the Aristotelian theory of matter and form, these last two would be component parts of any physical substance; and to illustrate, a living being on such a view is usually regarded as having both a physical body and a *psyche* or animating principle. Accordingly, when it comes to predication, it is not infrequently the case that the logical distinction of P from S reflects the real distinction of material and formal parts within a composite substance. Of such an animate being, one can say it is alive or that it is corporeal. Moreover, not only does each of these predicates signify something different from the other, but also each has a different significance from its subject. The notion of being corporeal is different from the notion of an animate being, and the difference consists precisely in the fact that the former calls our attention to what is but a component part of a whole, while the latter signifies the whole as such.

Likewise, the so-called quantitative or integral parts of a substance often provide the foundation for predications made of that substance taken as subject. Thus, David Hume might be said to be two-legged, or to be possessed of various bodily organs such as heart, lungs, etc.

Even a thing's very essence is in some sense or another distinct from it. That is why the assertion, "David Hume is human," is quite different from the assertion, "David Hume is David Hume." As to just how the essence of a thing is different from the thing itself, or from the *supposit,* is a difficult metaphysical question. Nevertheless, that there is a real difference here is evidenced by the very fact that to predicate an essence of its supposit is not at all like predicating S of S. Hence the distinction of the predicate from the subject in such a case must certainly have its basis or foundation in a real distinction in things.

Granting that the distinction of predicate from subject would seem to be *founded* on a real distinction in being, we must not forget that at the same time it *is itself* only a distinction of reason; the subject and predicate that are *distinguished* in the proposition are also *identified* in the same proposition; S is said *to be* P. The explanation of this seemingly paradoxical situation is that while in our subject and predicate concepts we do take note of really different parts or aspects of a composite being, we at the same time, and in these same concepts, *connote* the whole of which these parts are parts.

To take one of the more trivial of our examples, it is obviously impossible to say that David Hume is his two legs; on the other hand, it is entirely possible to say that he is two-legged. In other words, the principle would seem to be that with respect to the quantitative parts of a whole, one cannot simply predicate one or more such parts of the whole, for a whole is not simply one of its parts or even any number of them short of the total number. Hence, no relation of identity can be established between them. Yet one can predicate "two-legged" of Hume for the reason that while such a predicate does signify certain integral parts of the human body, it signifies them in such a way as to connote the whole of which they are parts. In short, a whole cannot be set in a relation of complete identity to one of its parts; and yet it can be so related to itself, even though in relating it to itself one may be considering it with reference to certain of its parts.

Moreover, the same principle will apply in all the other examples of composition that we considered. As regards the composition of substance and accident, one cannot say that Hume is the relation of being acquainted with Adam Smith, any more than one can say that a leaf is greenness or that a certain plot of ground is triangularity; rather one has to say that Hume was acquainted with Adam Smith, or that a plot of ground is triangular. The point, in other words, is that one cannot say that a substance is an accident just as such, because it is not; it is a substance. On the other hand, one can predicate an accident of a substance, provided that one's concept of the accident connotes the whole of which it is a part.

Likewise with respect to the so-called hylomorphic parts: David Hume is not just a soul or psyche, nor is he even just a body; but he is alive and he is corporeal. As for the composition of essence with supposit, here again one cannot say that Hume is humanity, although one can say that he is human. That is to say, a whole cannot be totally identified with any one of its parts but only with itself. Consequently, if a predicate signifies one of the hylomorphic parts just as such, or the essence just as such, then it cannot be predicated of the whole which is more than one of these parts or more than just the essence. Nevertheless, if one's concept signifies such a part and at the same time connotes the whole of which it is a part, then predication is possible.

Here then we have the explanation of the seeming paradox of predication, according to which S and P would seem not to have the same meaning and yet to be identified with each other, or according to which S and P are said to be distinguished from each other only by a distinction of reason, and yet such a mere distinction of reason is said to have a basis in reality.

G. B. Phelan : VERUM SEQUITUR
ESSE RERUM

D R. *Gerald B. Phelan, who directed for many years Toronto's Institute of Mediaeval Studies and later directed a similar Institute at Notre Dame, where he was also Chairman of the Department of Philosophy, is now Professor of Philosophy at St. Michael's College, Toronto. In this essay he investigates the interpenetration of the epistemological and metaphysical problem in the relational concept of "truth." Reprinted by permission from* MEDIAEVAL STUDIES, *I (1939), pp. 11–22.*

• The question discussed in this paper belongs to that realm of thought in which problems of ontology overlap problems of knowledge. A recent French author [1] has called this common ground, appropriately, I think, *l'ontologie du connaître*—the ontology of knowing. It is plain that a discussion of truth inevitably involves problems of knowledge, since it is concerned with the instrument of knowing truth, the judgment. It is not less clear that, to deal with such problems, one must enter into the realm of metaphysics; for, *truth* is a transcendental attribute of being and *judgment* is an affirmation of being, declaring that, that which is connoted by the subject *is* that which is connoted by the predicate. Consequently, we are obliged to deal with this problem metaphysically or else to refrain from dealing with it at all.

THE PROBLEM OF TRUTH

Truth is essentially a relation.[2] Nothing created is, strictly speaking, true in itself.[3] It is true only by relation to something else.[4] Even in our conception of uncreated truth we introduce a mental relation between uncreated Intelligence and uncreated Being—two aspects of the Divine Essence which philosophers may distinguish in their concepts but which are really identical in Being.[5] The true, then, is that which is, or being, affected with a relation.[6] What is, is in itself being, a thing and one; for everything which is, *is*, is *what* it is, and is *one* thing. It possesses all these attributes in itself and without relation to anything else.[7] Nothing, however, can be said to be true except in relation to some being for whom it is true.[8] Here, it is imperative to note that truth, though it be a relation, is not

[1] YVES SIMON, *L'ontologie du connaître*, Paris, 1934.
[2] Veri enim ratio consistit in adaequatione rei et intellectus. (De Verit. I, 3, c).
[3] Res autem non dicitur vera nisi secundum quod est intellectui adaequata. (De Verit. I, 2, c).
[4] Res dicitur vera per ordinem ad intellectum. (De Verit. I, 3, c).
[5] Scientia Deo attributa significat aliquid quod in Deo est, et similiter vita, essentia et cetera huiusmodi; nec differunt quantum ad rem significatam sed solum quantum ad modum intelligendi; eadem enim res penitus in Deo est essentia, vita et quidquid huiusmodi de ipso dicitur; sed intellectus noster diversas conceptiones habet intelligens in eo vitam, scientiam, et huiusmodi. (De Verit. II, 1, c).
[6] Convenientiam vero entis ad intellectum exprimit hoc nomen *verum*. (De Verit. I, 1, c).
[7] Cfr. De Verit. I, 1, c. One cannot say, indeed, that whatever is has all these attributes *from* itself or *through* itself or *by* itself, but simply *in* itself. From the point of view of the *origin* of its being and unity, what *is* may or may not be related to something else. If the being in question be a contingent being, it is causally related to the necessary Being and dependent upon the Necessary Being for its origin; if, on the other hand, the being in question is the Necessary Being Itself, then it is not causally related nor dependent for its origin upon another being. However, these considerations belong to the realm of efficient causality and concern the question of *how* or *why* a thing exists, not *what* a thing is. Every being is *what* it is *in itself* although it may BE (i.e., exist) *through, by,* or *from* another.
[8] . . . secundum convenientiam unius entis ad aliud; et hoc quidem non potest esse nisi accipiatur aliquid quod natum est convenire cum omni ente. Hoc autem est anima quae quodammodo est omnia. (De Verit. I, 1, c).

relative. No relation on earth is relative: things are relative by relations. If, then, it is correct to say that nothing can be true except in relation to some being for whom it is true, it is by no means implied that a thing can be true for one and not true for another. It simply means that when a thing is related in a certain manner to another, then it is true; and it cannot properly be said to be true unless it is so related. In relation to God, all things are true, for God metes out to them their truth, or if you will, by creating them, puts them in that relation to Himself by which they can be said to be true.[9] In relation to things, the mind of men may or may not be true, for man does not give things their truth because he does not give them being; he does not put them in relation to his mind, he puts his mind in relation to them; he subjects himself to things in order that they may give him something of what they have received from God and mete out to him their being, which they have received from God, and so make his mind true in relation to them.[10] Thus the things of nature are situated between two minds—the mind of God and the mind of man—and may be said to be true in virtue of their relation to both. True, because they fulfil in themselves the order created by the mind of God; true, because they can give to the mind of man a just appreciation of what they are.[11]

Truth, then, is a relation. We may now proceed to ask: what is the nature of this relation? What are the terms of this relation? How are these terms related to each other? On what is the relation founded? What effect does this relation produce? What, in short, is truth?

DEFINITION OF TRUTH

The sceptical Roman Governor who asked the question, "What is truth?" of the King who was accused before him, did not wait for an answer. He never realized what a sublime answer might have come from Him who was the Truth Incarnate. But had he only known what a great Athenian teacher had replied to that same question some three and a half centuries before, Pilate would have had food enough for thought. Aris-

[9] In rebus creatis invenitur veritas in rebus et in intellectu . . . in rebus autem secundum quod imitantur intellectum divinum, qui est earum mensura. (De Verit. I, 8, c).

[10] Res existens extra animam per formam suam imitatur artem divini intellectus, et per eamdem nata est facere de se veram apprehensionem in intellectu humano. (De Verit. I, 8, c) . . . natae sunt facere veram apprehensionem in intellectu humano qui per res mensuratur. (ibid.)

[11] Res ergo naturalis inter duos intellectus constituta secundum adaequationem ad utrumque vera dicitur: secundum adaequationem ad intellectum divinum dicitur vera in quantum implet hoc ad quod est ordinata per intellectum divinum. . . . Secundum autem adaequationem ad intellectum humanum dicitur res vera in quantum nata est de se formare veram aestimationem. (De Verit. I, 2, c). Intellectus divinus est mensurans non mensuratus; res autem naturalis est mensurans et mensurata; sed intellectus noster est mensuratus non mensurans quidem res naturales sed artificiales tantum. (ibid.)

totle could not give an answer comparable in depth and meaning with that which Christ had given—"I am the Way, the Truth, and the Life"— but his answer is simple, clear, exact, and deep:—"To say of what is, that it is, and of what is not, that it is not, is true." [12] Here we have the relation we are in search of, the relation between what is said and what is. Later on, that relation will be explicitly stated in a definition which has become classical, but whose author is not known. For centuries it was believed and repeated that Isaac the Jew, Honain ben Ishak, an historian of Bagdad, who died in 876 A.D., was the author of the famous definition of truth—*Veritas est adaequatio rei et intellectus*—"Truth is the correspondence of the thing and the understanding"—but recent investigation has failed to reveal it in the writings of that Jewish compiler.[13†] Wherever it may have come from, that definition of truth has achieved triumphal success in the history of philosophy. Let us analyze it and try to see why it should have been so universally accepted.

First of all, since truth is essentially a relation, as we have seen, there must be two terms involved: nothing is related to itself.[14] Aristotle placed the terms of the relation of truth in *what is said* and *what is:* the Pseudo-Isaac's definition places the relation between *the thing* and *the understanding.* The divergence in these statements is only apparent. *What is said,* may be said verbally (orally) or mentally and after all, words as uttered are but signs of the understanding. *What is said,* therefore, means primarily what is said in the mind and secondarily only what is said in words.[15] The terms of the relation of truth then are *what is* or *the thing* and *what is said* or *the understanding.*

We may therefore proceed to investigate what relations may exist between things and the understanding. In things there is a twofold element, each, *suo modo,* making the thing to be what it is. Everything which is, *is* (exists) and it is *what* it is. There is thus in things that whereby they *are* and that whereby they are *what* they are.[16] Should it be possible to establish a relation solely between that whereby a thing is *what* it is and the understanding, knowledge of the thing would result,[17] but it would not be

---

[12] ARISTOTLE, *Metaph.* Bk. IV, cap. 7, 1011^{b}25.

[13] Cfr. J. T. MUCKLE, Isaac Israeli's Definition of Truth, in *Archives d'histoire doctrinale et littéraire du moyen âge,* Paris, J. Vrin (1933), Vol. VIII, pp. 1–8. †[EDITORS' NOTE: For a recent confirmation of Prof. Phelan's notation about the mistaken attribution, and an application of it in the case of, among others, Aquinas, cf. A. Altmann and S. M. Stern, *Isaac Israeli,* Scripta Judaica I, Clarendon Press, Oxford, 1958, pp. 58–9.]

[14] Idem autem non adaequatur sibi ipsi, sed aequalitas diversorum est. (De Verit. I, 3, c).

[15] Voces autem eodem modo recipiunt veritatis praedicationem sicut intellectus quos significant. (De Verit. I, 3, c).

[16] In omni creato essentia differt a suo esse. (Sum. Theol. I, 54, 3, c). Cuiuslibet creaturae esse est aliud ab ejus quidditate. (De Verit. X, 12, ad 1).

[17] Ex hoc quod cognoscens habet similitudinem rei cognitae, dicitur habere veram cognitionem. (In VI Metaph. lib. 4, Cathala ed. n. 1234).

complete because, the understanding, not yet put into relation with that whereby what is, *is* (i.e. exists), would have no knowledge of the likeness of what is known to what is in nature; it would not yet have taken cognizance of the fact that what it knows *exists* in a manner other than being understood.[18] To complete that knowledge a further relation must be established,[19] this time, reaching beyond that by which the thing is *what* it is to that whereby it *is* (exists).[20] That relation will then be set up by the act whereby the understanding affirms or denies that what *is* (exists) in the mode of existence proper to thought, is identical with what *is* in the mode of existence proper to things—in other words what *is understood* (exists as understood) *is real* (exists as a real being)—or again, in more technical language, the essence which has intentional existence in thought has physical (actual or possible) existence in reality.[21]

If the affirmation, or denial, is in accord with the facts, then it is true; if it is an affirmation contrary to the facts, then it is false. But, you may ask, how can it be ascertained whether the affirmation or denial is or is not in accord with the facts? Obviously, only by reducing it to the facts, by bringing it down to face the facts, by confronting it with the facts.[22] In other words, either corroborating that affirmation or refuting it, by the only means at man's disposal of getting in direct and immediate contact with the actually existent finite real, the fact, viz. sense experience.[23] If, however, the affirmation or denial is not an affirmation or denial of actual (factual) existence, but of possible existence or of the necessary implications of either actual or possible existence, then the reduction or confronting must be made between the affirmation or denial and the first principles of being and knowledge—the principles of identity, non-contradiction, sufficient reason, excluded middle and so forth.[24] For these are simply statements of what things *must* be in order *to be* at all and are immediately apprehended as such as soon as being is revealed to the intelligence, through the medium of sense perception.[25] If as a result of this con-

[18] Sum. Theol. I, 16, c.

[19] Sum. Theol. II–II, 173, 2, c.

[20] Cfr. Jacques Maritain, *Les degrés du savoir*. Paris, 1932, p. 175, note 1.

[21] In VI Metaph. lib. 4, Cathala ed. nn. 1230–1237.

[22] Judicium non dependet tantum a receptione speciei sed ex hoc quod ea de quibus judicatur, examinantur ad aliquod principium cognitionis sicut de conclusionibus judicamus eas in principia resolvendo. Sed quia primum principium nostrae cognitionis est sensus oportet ad sensum quodammodo resolvere omnia de quibus judicamus. (De Verit. XII, 3, ad 2).

[23] Sensus sunt extremi sicut intellectus principiorum. (*ibid.*)

[24] Sicut in demonstrabilibus oportet fieri reductionem in aliqua principia per se nota, ita investigando quid est unumquodque. (De Verit. I, 1, c). Sicut enim a veritate intellectus divini effluunt in intellectum angelicum species rerum innatae secundum quas omnia cognoscit, ita a veritate intellectus divini exemplariter procedit in intellectum nostrum veritas primorum principiorum secundum quam de omnibus judicamus. (De Verit. I, 4, ad 5).

[25] Omnis nostra cognitio originaliter consistit in notitia primorum principiorum indemonstrabilium. Horum autem cognitio in nobis a sensu oritur. (De Verit. X, 6, Praeterea).

frontation it is seen that the affirmation or denial is in harmony with these principles, the affirmation or denial is thus verified: if it is found to disagree with those principles, then the affirmation or denial is shown to be false. Hence, St. Thomas says that sense experience and first principles are not only the starting point of knowledge but the ultimate tests of the truth of judgments.[26] Suppose I should say, "this paper is blue"; I make a judgment in regard to a fact. The judgment I make is an act which puts together two essences or quiddities (*paper* and *blue*) and gives the composite (blue paper) an existence in my mind which, by the same act of judgment, I affirm to correspond to the existence which those two essences or quiddities exercise in this thing existing in the realm of extramental reality. To test the truth of that judgment (in the language of St. Thomas, to resolve that judgment, to reduce it to the facts), I must throw it into experience and see if the testimony of my senses corroborates my judgment, if, in a word, *this paper* and *blue* actually exist in the unity of the thing as I have made them exist in the union of my two concepts. In thus confronting my judgment with the facts, I find that *this paper* and *blue* do not exist together and that I am not justified in putting them together in my mind; because I would then be saying of what is not, that it is. My judgment, this paper is blue, is therefore seen to be false by the evidence of the senses.

Suppose, however, I say "angels are mortal." I have put two essences (*angel* and *mortality*) together and, affirming one of the other, I have given them existence in a single composite in my mind, affirming that they exist in reality (actually or possibly) in that unity. How can I test the validity of such a judgment? I cannot confront my judgment with the testimony of the senses for I cannot see or feel an *angel,* nor can I see or feel *mortal.* I proceed to study the essence of an angel, to analyze *what* (not *whether*) an angel is until I finally succeed in deducing from the very nature of an angel the necessity of its immortality. Then I can say that an angel cannot be an angel and still be mortal. Consequently, since a thing cannot be and not be at the same time, an angel cannot be what an angel cannot be, namely mortal, and still be an angel. Immortality is essentially wrapped up in the nature of an angel and consequently my judgment is shown to be false on the evidence of the first principles of knowledge. If the phrase, *Critique of Knowledge,* has any valid significance it can only apply to this procedure whose roots are in the study of what knowledge is in itself and with reference to what is not knowledge, but reality.

We may now trace the problem back to those Epistemological roots and investigate first what it means to set up a relation between the understanding and that whereby a thing is *what* it is, and how that relation may

[26] Dicit (Aristotle) quod sensus sunt extremi sicut intellectus principiorum; extrema appellamus illa in quae fit resolutio judicantis. (De Verit. XII, 3, ad 2).

be brought to completion by the establishment of a further relation between the understanding and that whereby a thing *is*.[27]

When the problem of knowledge is posited in the terms so familiar to philosophy since the seventeenth century—"How can the mind pass from knowledge to reality?"—it becomes an insoluble problem. Insoluble, not because it is too difficult to solve, but because it is a pseudo-question—a question which has no meaning and no answer. We are familiar with the story of the king who asked his wise men to explain why the weight of a pail of water with a fish in it was less than the weight of the water plus the weight of the fish. When the wise men had given him a great many reasons why it *had* to be so, the king suggested that they weigh the pail of water and the fish apart and then weigh the pail of water with the fish in it. The result showed, of course, that the sages had given learned and elaborate explanations of a fact which was not a fact. The king's question was a pseudo-question; it had no meaning and therefore no answer. It is the same for the question asked by those philosophers who have lost touch with the traditional principles of the metaphysics of knowing. If we weigh the words, as the king weighed the fish, the absurdity of the question becomes obvious. "How does the mind reach reality from knowledge?" supposes that what is first known is knowledge and from a knowledge of knowledge the mind passes to a knowledge of things. But how can the mind know knowledge unless there be knowledge to know and how can there be knowledge if the mind does not first know? To know knowledge presupposes that there first is something known which is not knowledge but is the cause or occasion or at least the antecedent of knowledge; this being known, then the knowledge itself may be known. But the mind cannot know knowledge before it knows something which is not knowledge any more than, in taking two steps, a man can take the second step first. It is necessary first to know; then, secondly, the knowledge thus acquired may be known.[28]

To attempt, therefore, to pass from knowledge to reality is futile and meaningless. The problem is badly stated in the familiar formula of modern epistemology. If we want an answer to the problem of knowledge we must first learn how to ask the question. A number of contemporary Thomists have written luminously on the way to ask the question and the way to answer it. The writings of Tonquedec, Noël, Simon, Gilson, Mari-

[27] Verum sequitur esse rerum. (De Verit. I, 1, 3rd. sed contra). Judicium est completivum cognitionis (Sum. Theol. II–II, 173, 2, c). Veritas fundatur in esse rei magis quam in quidditate. (I Sent. d. 19, q. 5, a. 1).
[28] Nullus autem percipit se intelligere nisi ex hoc quod aliquid intelligit; quia prius est intelligere aliquid quam intelligere se intelligere. (De Verit. X, 8, c).

tain, and others deal fully with this problem. Leaving aside further discussion of the point I shall state the situation as follows: it is not a question of the objectification of thought but the objectification of thing. In other words, the question is: How does a thing become an object? How does what *is* in physical existence (a thing), become existent in intentional existence (an object)?

Modern thinking has become so saturated with idealism that our very words are freighted with idealistic meaning. Thus, the terms "thing" and "object" have become almost synonymous. We speak quite casually about the *objects* around us (this table, these chairs, those trees) when we mean the *things* around us. We do not feel that it makes much difference whether we call them *things* or *objects*. Of course it is obvious that if things cannot *be,* apart from *being thought,* there can be no difference between a thing and an object. It becomes impossible to distinguish between them if we begin by imagining that knowledge projects itself into reality. Then, indeed, the only things that are, are the objects to which knowledge gives being. This is, of course, true for Divine Knowledge but not for human knowledge. So, if an object is what an object ought to be— a thing inasmuch as it is known or loved—then there is a considerable difference between things and objects. All things are objects in relation to God Who knows and loves all things but there are multitudes of things which are not objects for us because we do not know them, and not knowing them do not love them. So, when things become known they become objects, they are *objectified*. We shall not enquire now how things become objects; that would carry us too far afield. The works to which I have referred, particularly those of Maritain and Simon, furnish plenty of discussion on this point. I simply state the problem and pass on to discuss some points in the Thomistic theory of knowledge which elucidate the problem of truth.

INTENTIONAL BEING

To know is to be or to become what the thing known is in itself.[29] Beings which are capable of knowing differ from beings which are not capable of knowing in that the former, by their very nature, are apt to possess the essences of things other than themselves, as well as their own essences, while the latter can possess no essence but their own.[30] Knowledge is obviously impossible unless the known *is* known, i.e., exists in thought,

[29] Cognitio est secundum quod cognitum est in cognoscente (Sum. Theol. I, 16, 1, c). Dicitur animam esse quodammodo omnia, quia nata est omnia cognoscere (De Verit. II, 2, c).
[30] Cognoscentia a non cognoscentibus in hoc distinguuntur quia non cognoscentia nihil habent nisi formam suam tantum sed cognoscens natum est habere formam etiam rei alterius. (Sum. Theol. I, 14, 1, c).

in the mind which knows it, inside the knower, so to speak.[31] One must, however, beware of interpreting those expressions in a spatial sense. To exist in thought or to *be* outside of thought does not mean being in or outside the mind, spatially, as my watch may now be in my pocket and now outside of it. The expressions "in the mind" and "outside the mind" are purely metaphorical, and the surest way to succeed in misunderstanding the question of knowledge is to allow the spatial imagination to intrude where it does not belong.[32] These expressions simply mean that the thing known exists in one manner or mode of existence as *a thing* and in another manner or mode of existence as *known*.[33] *What* exists in each of these modes is identical[34]—the mode of existence of that thing alone differs when it is regarded as a thing in itself and as a known thing.[35]

I hasten to add a word of warning lest the term "thing in itself" arouse Kantian associations. For Kant the "thing-in-itself" was some inscrutable entity beyond the reach of reason which only an indefensible dogmatism or an act of faith or an irrational experience could lead one to accept. It has nothing to do with the *thing in itself* of which I am speaking. The thing in itself of which I am speaking is an essence exercising an act of existence in the world of reality—actual or possible—as contrasted with that same essence exercising an act of existence in the world of knowledge. The real world is the world of the possible as well as the world of the actual. Possibles are really possible. The correlatives are not *real* and *possible* but *real* and *logical* (or mental). However, this is not the place to go more fully into that question.

An essence, as such, does not imply existence.[36] Hence it is indifferent to various modes of existence and may exist only in the mode of being which it has in the Divine Mind or only in this mode and in the mode of existence it has in itself, or it may exist in both of these modes and in the mode of existence it has in our knowledge.[37] *The essence* which exists in each of those modes of existence is absolutely identical; the mode of ex-

---

[31] Cognitio non fit nisi secundum quod cognitum est in cognoscente. (I Sent. 38, 1, 2, c).

[32] Cfr. Jacques Maritain, *Les degrés du savoir*, Paris, 1932, p. 164 f.

[33] In qualibet cognitione potest considerari duplex modus: scilicet modus rei cognitae et modus cognoscentis. . . . Unumquodque est in aliquo secundum modum ipsius. (I Sent. 38, 1, 2, c).

[34] Nec etiam apud nos desinit esse propria natura in re quae intelligitur, ex hoc quod verbum nostri intellectus ex ipsa re intellecta habet ut intelligibiliter eamdem naturam numero contineat. (Cont. Gent. IV, 14).

[35] Species intelligibilis est similitudo ipsius essentiae rei et est quodammodo ipsa quidditas et natura rei secundum esse intelligibile non secundum esse naturale prout est in rebus. (Quodlib. VIII, a. 4).

[36] Omnis essentia vel quidditas intelligi potest sine hoc quod aliquid intelligatur de esse suo facto; possum enim intelligere quid est homo vel phoenix, et tamen ignorare an esse habeant in rerum natura. (*De Ente et Essentia* Cap. IV (Ed. Roland Gosselin, Cap. V; Ed. Mandonnet, Opuscula Omnia, I, p. 157).

[37] Omnes creaturae sunt in mente divina sicut arca in mente artificis . . . Ergo omnium rerum ideae sunt in Deo. (De Verit. III, 1, 7th sed contra). Est in eo idea etiam eorum quae nec fuerunt, nec erunt, nec sunt. (*Ibid.* III, 6, sed contra).

istence which it exercises alone is different.[38] We are here face to face with the most radical of metaphysical doctrines in the philosophy of St. Thomas—the doctrine of analogy—according to which the same, identical essence may exercise various acts of existence and thus *be* in several different ways each of which is absolutely different from the others and only in a qualified (proportional) sense the same. The *object* is analogically the same as *the thing:* it is the thing as it is objectified, i.e. made an object of knowledge.

Thus when the mind knows the thing, what is in the mind is identical with what is in the thing.[39] Regarded from the point of view of the mind, knowledge is an act of a very special kind, an immanent act, a vital act, affecting the subject after the fashion of a quality;[40] regarded from the point of view of the thing known, knowledge is an act of the thing communicating its essence to the mind and so affecting it qualitatively. Regarded formally in itself, knowledge is a reality whose whole and sole reality consists in carrying the thing to the mind and the mind to the thing. Its being is *intentional, tendential.* In virtue of this immaterial, relational act of existence the thing exists in the mind in a mode of existence distinct and different from the mode of its physical existence, and the mind is or becomes the thing in a mode of existence different from its own proper mode.[41] The thing *is* in the mind *intentionally;* the mind *is* or becomes the thing intentionally. Thus the thing actually known and the mind actually knowing it are identical.[42] Until there is an affirmation of this identity, however, there is no comparison set up; therefore, strictly speaking, no truth but only the principle from which truth may issue.[43] Where there is identity there can be no comparison.[44] So, a concept (which brings the essences of things within the mind but does not reach to the existence which they exercise) does not yet contain truth.[45] A com-

---

[38] Strictly speaking the essence does not exist but *by* the essence *something* exists "Non oportet quaerere quomodo ipsa essentia aliquo sit, sed quomodo aliquid alterum sit per essentiam," (De Verit. XXI, 4, ad 4). Thus, the essences of things in the mind of God, which are identical with the Divine Essence, are the ideas whereby *God* is *exemplariter et causaliter* all things; the essence of things in the things themselves is that whereby *they* are *realiter* what they are; the essences of things in the created mind are the forms whereby the *knowing subject* is or becomes the things known *intentionaliter.*

[39] Intellectum in actu est intellectus in actu. (Sum. Theol. I, 85, 2, c).

[40] The question of the qualitative character of immanent activity is treated at length by John of St. Thomas *Philosophia Naturalis*, III, q. 6, a. 4, and q. 11, a. 1. Cfr. Yves Simon, *L'ontologie du connaître,* Paris, 1934, p. 97 ff.

[41] Cfr. Jacques Maritain, *Les degrés du savoir*, pp. 217 ff.

[42] Cognoscens et cognitum sunt magis unum quam materia et forma. (Cajetan, *In Sum. Theol.* I, 14, 1. Leonine ed. of St. Thomas IV, p. 167).

[43] Idem non adaequatur sibi ipsi sed aequalitas diversorum est. (De Verit. I, 3).

[44] Quamvis formatio quidditatis sit prima operatio intellectus, tamen per eam non habet intellectus aliquid aliud proprium quod possit rei adaequari: et ideo non est ibi proprie veritas. (De Verit. I, 3, ad 1).

[45] Indivisibilium intelligentia in illis est in quibus non est verum et falsum. (De Verit. I, 3, 2nd sed contra).

parison must be made between the act of existence which things have in the mind and the act of existence which they have in nature. Thence comes a pronouncement, a judgment, stating that the self-same essence which exists in the mind in one mode of existence, exists also, in another mode of existence, in nature.[46]

THE JUDGMENT

No thing at once reveals itself to the intelligence in the fulness of its intelligibility [47] for the intellect by abstracting the form of the thing does not reach to the singular.[48] The abstracted forms (e.g. something, a living

[46] Compositioni et divisioni intellectus respondit quidem aliquid ex parte rei; tamen non eodem modo se habet in re, sicut, in intellectu. (Sum. Theol. I, 85, V ad 1). Cfr. *De Veritate* I, 3, c.

[47] Intellectus humanus non statim in prima apprehensione capit perfectam rei cognitionem. (Sum. Theol. I, 85, 5, c).

[48] Differt autem inter intellectum humanum et divinum; quia humanus non cognoscit directe singulare, divinus autem sic; quia cognitio fit per similitudinem cogniti in cognoscente; et haec est in intellectu nostro per abstractionem a conditionibus individuantibus et a materia, ideo . . . non cognoscit directe nisi universale. (Quodl. 12, q. 8).

The judgment is, in a measure, a compensation for the weakness of our intellectual intuition. Our minds cannot grasp the real in its totality, so we are obliged to work towards a reconstruction of the world of nature within our minds by reintegrating the different aspects of the thing which we have apprehended separately in the unity of physical existence. For, knowledge of what *is* comes to us piece-meal. Now we see this aspect, now that. Each separate aspect (M. Maritain would have us call them "inspects") comes to us distinct from the rest. We must gather them up—assemble them as the manufacturers of automobiles might say—and restore them to their unity in the thing by asserting that all these aspects which have come to us separately and which, by our judgment, we have combined together in the unity of mental existence, actually exist unseparated within the thing, which is the object of our knowledge, in the unity of its act of physical existence. This is, alas! a long, tedious and laborious task, for, in the last analysis it is nothing less than the whole business of acquiring knowledge. At once analytic and synthetic—in a word, discursive—its trials and its labours are without number; it is a task fraught with many difficulties, disappointments, subject to many errors and mistakes; fresh starts must constantly be made and failures must leave us still undaunted; courage and patience must combine with confidence and perseverance, else we shall labour in vain.

Because the objects of our knowledge are themselves very complex; because our intellectual insight is too weak to penetrate the real in its full, rich content (for, are we not in the lowest range of the hierarchy of intelligent beings?); because we cannot understand anything but the very simplest objects without a multiplicity of concepts, errors inevitably arise. Our effort to put things together in judgments is much like trying to solve a jig-saw puzzle. The danger of error is always immanent. So many parts look alike when they are not alike; we are constantly putting the wrong parts together and we have to watch attentively each step we take; sometimes we do not detect our mistakes until we have finished the picture and find that we still have some pieces left over. We must go back again over our work and check each decision again and again. Similarly in our efforts to acquire true knowledge we must frequently retrace our steps and check our progress. This is a true critique of reason, one quite different from that which Kant proposed.

Only when the mind is in the presence of the most simple things, things which possess no complexity whatsoever, can it grasp its object with absolute certainty and without danger of error. In the apprehension of appropriate intelligible forms the intelligence is infallible and

thing, a man, a white man, a tall white man, etc.) are separately abstracted and must be reintegrated to give to the understanding a fuller
and fuller likeness to the thing. The reintegration of these forms in the
unity of the object is the work of judgment.[49] The judgment thus essentially consists in affirming the existence (in the unity of real existence) of

---

it cannot go astray. But as soon as it begins to combine and divide in judgments the danger
of error arises. Judgments must be constantly checked by apprehensions for the judgment is
an instrument of knowledge in the service of simple apprehension and must therefore be
controlled by it.

The basic reason for this imperfect and, I dare say unsatisfactory, condition at the very
heart of our highest and noblest knowledge, knowledge completed in the judgment, is one
that is inherent in knowledge itself, God's knowledge and the knowledge of the blessed in
heaven alone excepted; it is that knowledge does not give possession of the thing known in
all the fulness of its being. Being—the real (actual or possible) existence of the thing known
—is indeed asserted, affirmed, recognized, corroborated by the judgment, and the mind is
thus carried by knowledge to the object in its actual existence, yet the thing thus known is
not grasped, held, embraced, possessed in its own proper, physical existence but in its essence
existing in a conceptual mode of being. Intellectual knowledge, although it be knowledge of
what is, *ad extra,* in the world of real existence, is knowledge of its object as it exists in
intentional existence, *prout est intra.* That which is known is identical with that which is,
but its mode of existence in knowledge is not identical with its mode of existence in the
physical world. Even sensation does not fully compensate for this imperfection for, although
it puts us in immediate contact with the real existing in its own proper existence, it reveals
only phenomenological aspects of the thing. In this life, the intellect knows what *is* only by
means of concepts. Moreover, in spite of the fact that the concept is a *medium quo* (and
therefore does not interpose itself between the mind and the thing as an object known but
simply and solely leads the mind to the thing) it is nevertheless always vicarious in respect
to the thing in itself and mediatory in respect to the knowledge of it. John of St. Thomas
points out that a pure *medium quo* or formal sign does not make our knowledge mediate
mediatione objecti cogniti but *mediatione formae informantis.* For this reason our knowledge
is not a knowledge of concepts but of things by means of concepts.

In knowledge, then, the knowing subject possesses the essence, form, or whatness of the
thing known and is perfected, i.e. given a greater amplitude of being, by that acquisition,
but by knowledge the knowing subject does not grasp the object in its proper physical existence. Could the subject reach still further and grasp the thing in its own proper existence,
the perfective power of reality with respect to the rational subject would be more complete,
for it would then give perfection both through its essence and through its existence. It is this
further fulfilment of the perfective power of reality which is effected by the good.

Truth, we have repeated again and again, is a relation, a correspondence. It is such, however, that it cannot strictly be said to exist in things but rather in the mind. Good, too, is a
relation but it is in things. Things are true in a mind but they are good in themselves; for
truth results from the essence being known while good is in the very being (*esse*) of what is.
Knowledge, we have said, is not complete until the mind *sees* the identity of the essence
existing in two different modes and thus achieves truth, i.e. recognizes that *what* it possesses
in knowledge is identical with *what* is held in physical existence by the thing itself. The
fulness of knowledge is therefore only achieved when the mind reaches out to the *esse* of its
object as a physical being. But knowledge cannot grasp that *esse* in itself, it can only see that
what has that *esse* is the same essence which has *esse* in thought. Through the good, however,
we are put in touch with beings as they exist in their own proper *esse.*

[49] (Intellectus humanus) primo apprehendit aliquid de ipsa (re) puta quidditatem ipsius
rei, quae est primum, et proprium objectum intellectus; deinde intelligit proprietates, et ac-
cidentia, et habitudines circumstantes rei essentiam et secundum hoc necesse habet unum
apprehensum alii componere, vel dividere et ex una compositione, vel divisione ad aliam
procedere. (Sum. Theol. I, 85, 5, c).

a thing in which two concepts united by the mind (in a unity of intentional existence) are actually or possibly realized. This is the composition and division effected by the judgment. Thus does the judgment reach out to being (existence) and affirm that certain essences actually or possibly exist. It is here that the relation of truth or correspondence enters in. Truth is in the mind—in the act of combining and dividing—in the judgment.[50] To judge is to combine or to divide, to put together or to set apart, to affirm or to deny that two forms or essences which have been separately abstracted and which, therefore, up to the time or moment of judgment, have existed as two separate concepts in the mind, must be put together or set apart, as the case may be. It is true to speak of the judgment as the act of combining or dividing concepts only when one bears in mind that the term *concept* in this context means the *objective concept,* i.e. the thing or essence which is known and which, therefore, exercises, and in as much as it does exercise, an act of existence in the intentional mode of being.[51] Truth is in the judgment when the act of judging puts together what should be put together and (or) sets apart what should be set apart. The judgment is erroneous, false, when it puts together what should be set apart and (or) sets apart what should be put together. So to judge truly is to say of what is, that it is and of what is not, that it is not. Here,

[50] Cfr. De Verit. I, 3, c; Sum. Theol. I, 16, 2.

[51] Through knowledge as completed in the judgment, the intellect attains the object both in its essence and in its existence. But, the object has a twofold existence modally distinct, one in the order of its individual reality (*esse naturale*), the other in the order of its universal intelligibility (*esse intentionale*). The judgment pronounces that the thing which exists in the intentional mode is identical with the thing which exists in the physical mode, or, if you will, that the thing is in itself as the intellect judges it to be. Of course the judgment is made in the mind, by the mind, and it does not exist in the thing itself. It is an affirmation (*synthesis*) or a denial (*diaeresis*) made within the mind, by the mind, in which it is asserted (or denied) that what is combined (or separated) by the mind exists (or does not exist) outside the mind, in the unity of one physical act of existence. The possibility of thus performing by the mind and within the mind an act which has validity in the realm of physical existence outside the mind, *in rerum natura,* is rooted in the nature of the concept. It is through the concept that the object exists in the intelligence, or more precisely, the concept is that by which the mind *becomes,* in its way, what the thing *is,* in its way. Of its very essence, the concept is relational; its whole reality is comprised in the referential tendency by which it carries the mind to its object and the object to the mind, making the known and the knower identical in the act of knowing. In other words the concept is a pure formal sign (a *quo,* not a *quod*). The act of judgment does not combine two concepts, for they are not things (*res quae*) *which* are susceptible of being combined, but simply *by which* (*quibus*) things are in the mind, and may be combined by the mind. Whether or not the combination which the mind makes is a valid combination, that is, whether it corresponds to the way in which things exist in themselves outside the mind, cannot be decided by the intellect which judges them to be so, for the intellect does not possess them in their physical existence but must be tested by reference to the experience of the senses, wherein direct contact is had with the world of physical existents. The appeal to sense experience is direct and immediate when it is a question of a judgment bearing on actual existence; it is indirect and mediate when the judgment asserts possible existence, the direct and immediate appeal being to the intellectual intuition of the first principles of being.

then, is where we find truth: in the act of equating what is in knowledge with what is in nature; or, in more technical terms, in the affirmation of the identity of the essence existing intentionally in the intellect, with the essence existing physically in the thing. Thus to judge is to affirm the unity, in the nature of things, of two essences which, having been separately presented to the mind in two concepts, are united by the act of judgment affirming their coexistence in the same object. When these two forms or essences coexist (actually or possibly) in the same object then the judgment is true; when they do not so coexist, the judgment is not true. Truth, therefore,—the equation of what is in knowledge with what is in nature —is found in the judgment and in the judgment only.

When what is in nature becomes present in knowledge by simple apprehension, truth is there *in actu primo,* in principle; but to effect the equation or correspondence between what is in nature with what is in knowledge, an act is necessary to carry knowledge to its term and so reach truth *in actu secundo.* When the concepts 7 and 5 are presented to the mind and juxtaposed in the concept $7 + 5$, the sum, 12, is there *in actu primo* but it is only when the judgment $7 + 5 = 12$ is made that the sum twelve is present *in actu secundo.* The concept $7 + 5$ is in itself neither true nor false. The judgment $7 + 5 = 12$ is true. But $7 + 5$ has in itself that whereby I can proceed to equate it with 12. It has truth *in actu primo,* is the principle from which arises the truth *in actu secundo,* the term of the judgment. The act of equating, judging, must intervene before I can say, "It is true," or "It is false." [52]

This act of judging is something which the intellect possesses but which is not in the thing. Corresponding to this act of judgment, there is in the thing an act whereby an essence exists (actually or possibly) so that the judgment consists in making the following equation:

$$\frac{\textit{Form in intellect}}{\textit{Intentional being}} :: \frac{\textit{Form in thing}}{\textit{Physical being}}$$

To put this into words: the judgment is an act whereby the intelligence affirms the actual or possible real existence of a thing in which, what the mind unites in *esse intentionali* are one in *esse physicum:* thus, the same thing is affirmed to be, or to have being, in two modes of existence—one in mind (*intentionale*), one in nature (*physicum*)—proportionately (according to proportionality) to the respective modes of its existence and in conformity with the conditions of its modes of existence. The correspondence, therefore, or the conformity affirmed by the judgment is not an

[52] By simple apprehension a relation is established between the essence or form of the thing known and the mind knowing: in the judgment this relation is completed, going beyond the *essence* to the *existence* of the thing. (Prima operatio respicit quidditatem rei; secunda respicit esse ipsius. I. Sent. D. XIX. q. 5, a. 1, ad 7). Thus, knowledge in simple apprehension is knowledge *in actu primo,* knowledge in judgment is knowledge *in actu secundo.*

identity in mode of existence but an identity in the analogical act of being. The thing known exercises an act of existence in the world of reality and at the same time in virtue of the judgment exercises an act of existence in the world of thought. What is known is identical in each of these two realms and, by the act of judgment, the mind affirms that identity, or if you will, gives existence in the order of thought to what exists in the order of nature by uniting in thought what is one in nature but what has come to the mind under two separate aspects, in two distinct concepts. "Man is mortal" does not mean that the concept man is the concept mortal, but that the same thing presents itself to the intelligence by the concept man and by the concept mortal and that thing, presented to the mind by these two concepts, is identical with itself in the mode of existence it exercises in the real world and in the mode of existence given to it by the judgment in the world of knowledge. Thus, if the thing is, or has being, in nature as the judgment says it is, or gives it being in thought, then truth is had, for then there exists an equation, a conformity, a correspondence, between the being which the thing has in the world of reality and the being which it receives in the world of knowledge—*adaequatio rei et intellectus*. Up to the moment when the mind makes the judgment there is no comparison between what is in the mind and what is in nature. In the act of knowledge the object and knowledge of the object are simply identical and no comparison is possible. It is only when the mind pronounces that the act of existence which the object exercises in the thing known and the act of existence which it exercises in knowledge are analogically the same—i.e. that it is the same essence existing in two diverse modes of being—that a comparison arises, that an *adaequatio* is present, that what is, *is said* to be.

Thus the judgment *completes* knowledge.[53] The act of judgment springs

[53] Although the object known (the thing existing in the cognitional or intentional mode) is identical with the physical thing itself existing in its own proper being, the identity of the object known and the existing thing is not necessarily complete or total in all respects. For example, in the judgment expressed in the proposition "Man is mortal" the being which corresponds to the concept *man* is identical with the being which corresponds to the concept mortal. But the identity is not absolute. Humanity and mortality are not identical. For, besides men, there are other things which are mortal; and, moreover, man is not only mortal but also rational, two-legged and, it has been said, laughable (*risibilis*). If the *whole being* of the thing which exists in its own proper existence were objectified in the concept (i.e. made an object of knowledge), then the identity of the thing itself and the concept of the thing would be complete and entire. But, the things which exist in the world of physical reality do not reveal their whole being (all that they are) all at once to the intelligence. Human knowledge is abstractive and all knowledge, save that of God alone, is partial. To comprehend the whole being of even the meanest thing on earth requires an infinite intelligence. Recall what Tennyson said about the flower in the crannied wall,

> Little flower, but if I could understand
> What you are, root and all, and all in all,
> I should know what God and man is.

And is it not in the same sense that Maritain says, "Comme si en ouvrant un brin d'herbe on en faisait sortir un oiseau plus grand que le monde"? Because God is all things by His very

from the mind itself. It is not, as Kant would have it, the imposition of a form upon a matter. The union of matter and form gives rise to a third thing which is neither the matter nor the form. It is the union of these two metaphysical elements which presides over production. But knowledge is not a *production* (although in our knowledge a concept is produced as a means whereby knowledge is had) but a *mode of being*. Nothing new is produced or made but the subject knowing perfects itself by becoming what other things are. Judgment, therefore, is a spontaneous, vital act originating in the intelligence and perfecting the intelligence, an immanent act, producing nothing outside the agent, but giving existence in the intelligence to what hitherto existed only in the nature of things (and, of course, in the mind of God). Through it the intelligence *lives* what it knows. Through it the intelligence becomes in an immanent fashion what is in the real world of nature. The forms of things other than itself are vitally assimilated by the intelligence, and the intelligence, living those assimilated forms, bestows upon them its own life and so raises them to the level of itself. The things of earth thus elevated to the life of the intelligence receive a new and vital existence analogous to their existence in the mind of God. In the divine mind essences live the very life of God, and from His mind they issue into their own existence. By our knowledge the things of creation are rescued from their inanimate existence and made to live again in our minds, that, living there they may be made to praise their Maker.

They have issued from the mind of God by the act of creation, and by knowledge they come into our minds to receive, through the judgment, our confirmation of the creative act whereby they were made to be. There is thus an analogy between the act of creation and the act of judgment. When we judge we affirm, declare, assert, and our judgments are, grammatically speaking, expressed in the indicative mood; when God judges He does not merely affirm that a thing is such and such but by that affirmation makes it to be such and such if it were not such before. His judgments are in the imperative mood—*Fiat!* not *Est.*

I might say, "This paper is pink" when really it is white. And I should err. But should God say, "This paper is pink" it would then be pink even

---

essence He knows all things and His knowledge is exhaustive of being. But the human mind can only take the forms (the *rationes*) of the things of nature revealed to the intelligence in the light of the active intellect, and by a vital, immanent act of judgment, by combining and separating them, give to them (or refuse to them) a composite existence within the mind by affirming (or denying) that what is one is likewise the other. We, poor human creatures, can do no more than this by our minds. By our best sort of knowledge, knowledge completed in judgment, we can only give to the essences of things existence within the mind and then, by comparing our work with the things which God has made (when the judgment affirms actual existence) or with the order of truth which He has established in the very being of things (when the judgment affirms possible existence), test the work of our minds and discover thereby whether we have judged truly or falsely.

though up to that moment it had been white; it would become pink—for the judgment of God cannot err, and when He says a thing is so, it is so, even though in order to be so it must come into existence or change from what it was before. This is what is meant by saying that God's judgment is a *fiat!* not an *est*. If God were to judge that this paper is white, His judgment would be no less a *fiat!* because it is white only because He constantly gives to it the very being whereby it is, is white, is smooth—in a word, is all that it is. Thus God's act is to give being—*dare esse;* His judgment is *est* only because it is *fiat!* Our judgments support, confirm, affirm, that gift. When God says "Let it be so!" we say "So it is." Judgment is in a sense our corroboration of creation. Yet it is a humble act because it is God's work which we acknowledge. To withhold our affirmation of the work of His hands would be pride. To give it is to rescue inanimate things from their lifeless condition and make them live again in our mind and there praise the God Who made them. *Caeli ennarrant gloriam Dei*—only when the heavens are known and through our knowledge give to God the glory which is at once the spontaneous uprush to the realm of act of our deepest potentialities and a hymn of praise and adoration to God.

F. H. Heinemann : ARE THERE ONLY TWO KINDS OF TRUTH?

D R. *F. H. Heinemann of Oxford, after sketching the development of the theory of two truths and two kinds of knowledge, here proposes the difficulties inherent in limiting knowledge to empirical and rational and offers a consideration of the interdependence and the variety of forms in the realms of meaning. Reprinted by permission from* PHILOSOPHY AND PHENOMENOLOGICAL RESEARCH, *xvi* (1956), *pp. 367–79.*

• In traditional Western Philosophy it has been generally assumed that there are only two kinds of knowledge and of truth; namely matter-of-fact knowledge and knowledge of the relations of ideas (Hume); and *vérités de fait* and *vérités de raison* (Leibniz). Neither Hume nor Leibniz, however, invented this distinction. It has its roots in Greek philosophy, and may be traced back to Parmenides, Plato, and Aristotle. All three of them decided in favor of rational knowledge of eternal unchanging being, and therefore for eternal truths. "Knowledge" of the changing phenomenal world was rejected by Parmenides, and reluctantly acknowledged by Plato, not as knowledge proper, but as belief (*doxa*),[1] which could either be commonsense belief in the reality of visible and tangible objects (*pistis*) or an opinion taking appearances at their face value (*eikasia*). Only Aristotle, deeply interested in biology and political science, defended and established the value of empirical knowledge. But even with him the distinction between the two kinds of knowledge remained dependent on the ontological difference of the two worlds, the world of unchanging objects and the world of change. In the modern era, however, the distinction became chiefly epistemological, and as such one of the fundamental assumptions of modern philosophy from Descartes to the present time.

Descartes[2] begins with a semi-ontological distinction of "knowledge of things and their affections" and "knowledge of truths." The first kind of knowledge refers to existence and forms the basis of metaphysics, the second to truths which are nothing outside our mind and which, by implication, concern merely possibility and necessity (e.g., in mathematics). Hobbes replaced Descartes' "knowledge of things" by "knowledge of sense" or "knowledge of fact," and his "knowledge of truth" by "knowledge of the truth of propositions" or by "knowledge of the consequence of one affirmation to another." In doing so he anticipated Leibniz' distinction. He said: "There be two kinds of knowledge, whereof the one is nothing else but sense . . . and remembrance; the other is called science or knowledge of the truth of propositions, and how things are called, and is derived from understanding." At the same time he stressed the importance of experience as the basis of both kinds of knowledge. "Both of these sorts are but experience; the former being the experience of the effects of things that work upon us from *without;* and the latter experience

---

[1] Cf. F. M. Cornford, *The Republic of Plato,* Oxford, 1944, p. 176: "*Doxa* and its cognates denote our apprehension of anything that "seems": (1) what seems to exist, sensible appearances, phenomena; (2) what seems true, opinions, belief, whether true or false; (3) what seems right, legal and deliberative decisions, and the many conventional notions of morality, which vary from place to place and from time to time."

[2] Cf. for the following my paper, "Truths of Reason and Truths of Fact," *The Philosophical Review,* Vol. LVII, No. 5 (1948), pp. 458 ff.

men have from the proper use of *names* in language." [3] In other words, he anticipated the Logical Positivists by giving a linguistic interpretation of rational knowledge. Locke substituted for Hobbes' distinction of empirical and deductive knowledge, that of experimental knowledge, which leads only to probability in the natural sciences, and that of universal knowledge, "which lies only in our own thoughts and consists barely in the contemplation of our own abstract ideas," i.e., in the perception of the agreement or disagreement between our ideas, and which therefore, e.g., in mathematics, is certain and necessary (Essay, IV, 6, 13 & 7). Berkeley is closer to Hobbes in his semantical interpretation of rational knowledge, which consists according to him in the correct manipulation of substitute signs according to specific rules, but he tries to refute Hobbes' materialism by a phenomenalist interpretation of material object statements. Leibniz, in all probability, accepted his distinction from Hobbes, introduced the terms *vérités de raison* and *vérités de fait,* and fixed their logical difference; "The truths of reason are necessary and their opposite is impossible, the truths of fact are contingent and their opposite is possible." He defined the truths of reason as analytic and added that *sub specie Dei* the truths of fact are also analytic though their analysis implies an infinite series of steps. Hume accepted Leibniz' distinction together with his modal characterization of it, but he rejected Leibniz' over-estimation of rational knowledge and also the analytic character of empirical propositions. He transformed the distinction fundamentally by translating it into the Hobbes-Locke language as "knowledge of the relations of ideas" and "matter-of-fact knowledge." At the same time, he substituted skepticism for Leibniz' dogmatism and formulated the famous question: "What are the foundations of empirical knowledge?" Kant accepted Hume's thesis that empirical propositions are synthetic, introduced the distinction of analytic and synthetic judgments, repeated Leibniz' distinction as that of *a priori* and *a posteriori* knowledge, but rejected Leibniz' claim that all *a priori* propositions are analytic, and maintained that all mathematical propositions are synthetic *a priori*. J. S. Mill formulated the extreme antithesis to Leibniz, namely that logical or mathematical axioms are merely generalizations from experience, that all deduction is induction, and that there are in the last instance nothing but matter-of-fact statements. Even now Hume and Leibniz carry the day. A. J. Ayer's celebrated and most successful book *Language, Truth and Logic* takes Hume's distinction as its starting point. In the first edition he claimed that *a priori* propositions are merely linguistic (they "simply record our determination to use symbols in a certain fashion"); and that matter-of-fact propositions are hypotheses, which can be probable but never certain. In

[3] *Human Nature,* Ch. 4 (ed. Molesworth, Vol. IV, p. 22).

the second edition he still, with Wittgenstein, regards *a priori* propositions as tautologies, but adds that they are true solely in virtue of the
meaning of their constituent symbols. The same fundamental distinction
reappears in C. I. Lewis' reply to Ayer in his monumental *Analysis of
Knowledge and Valuation* as that between Analytic Truth and Empirical
Knowledge. Lewis regards analytic truth as determined by meaning
alone, i.e., by intensional meaning, which is either *linguistic meaning* (referring to relationships between symbols), or *sense meaning* (referring to
the meaning of a symbol). Empirical knowledge, on the other hand, is
justified, warranted, rational belief in what is probable and demands
therefore verification as well as justification. These short remarks may suffice to show that the belief in two fundamentally different kinds of knowledge and truth, each of which is looked at as representing a single well-
defined type, has in fact dominated Modern Philosophy from Descartes to
the present time.

The following table may be useful for illustrating the fundamental
scheme and its variations:

Descartes

Knowledge of things (*res*) and their affections.	Knowledge of truths or eternal truths.
Metaphysics: knowledge of reality, i.e., of the existence of the Self, of God, and of material objects.	Mathematics: knowledge of possibility and necessity.
Axioms. *Cogito, ergo sum.* Dogma concerning clearness and distinctness.	Rules. Rule of clearness and distinctness, etc.

Hobbes

Knowledge of fact, or of sense.	Knowledge of the truth of propositions, and how things are called; knowledge of the consequence of one affirmation to another.
Based on experience, i.e., sense and memory.	Based on experience, i.e., on the use of names and reasoning.
History, natural and civil.	Philosophy, generally speaking; logic, mathematics and theoretical science.

Locke

Experimental Knowledge.	General Knowledge.
Basis: experience, i.e., perception of ideas.	Basis: experience, i.e., perception of the signification of signs, and perception of the agreement and disagreement of ideas, or intuition.
Probability.	Certainty.
Natural Science.	Mathematics. Ethics.

Berkeley

Knowledge of particulars. Basis: ideas of sense. Phenomenalist interpretation of physics.	Universal Knowledge. Basis: substitute signs. Semantic interpretation of mathematics.

Leibniz

Vérités de fait. Basis: (factual) perception; (logical) principle of sufficient reason. Empirical sciences; history.	*Vérités de raison.* Basis: reason; law of contradiction. Logic, Mathematics, Metaphysics, Morals, and Theology.
Contingent. Analytic (but infinite steps). Depend on God's will.	Necessary. Analytic (finite analysis). Independent of God's will, whereas in Descartes' case both depend on God's will.

Hume

Matter-of-fact knowledge. Physics, history. Basis: experience, i.e., impressions of sensation. (Law of causality?). Contingent. Not analytic, but (synthetic). Belief. Assurance, assent. Proof: confirmation by experience. Foundations?	Knowledge of the relations of ideas. Algebra, arithmetic, and geometry (in *Enquiry,* but not in *Treatise*). Basis: law of contraction (logical) ideas (empirical). Necessary. Analytic. Knowledge. Certainty. Demonstration. Foundations?

Kant

Mundus sensibilis. Empirical knowledge, based on 'intuition' and understanding. *A posteriori.* Contingent. *Wahrnehmungsurteile.* *Erfahrungsurteile.* The most general laws of nature are based on reason and are necessary, the special laws are contingent.	*Mundus intelligibilis.* Rational knowledge, based on understanding and reason. *A priori.* Necessary and of strictly universal validity. Analytic judgments *a priori* based on law of contradiction. Synthetic judgments *a priori* based on the highest principle of synthetic judgments. This restricts them to possible experience. All mathematical propositions are synthetic *a priori*.

F.H.Heinemann

Mill

Inductive Knowledge.	Deductive Knowledge.

Basis: observation and experiment.

Basis: experience, induction, and language.

Generalizations from experience, based on the assumption of the uniformity of nature and on four methods of induction.

The Theorems of geometry are necessary truths only in the sense of necessarily following from hypotheses. The axioms of geometry are experimental truths.

Lewis

Empirical Knowledge.
Arises as inference from empirically given data.

Analytic truth.
All *a priori* truth is analytic.
Basis: (empirical) the compatibility or incompatibility of sense-recognizable factors and the inclusion of one in another or its exclusion by another; (logical) a relation of classification.

This table, which could easily be enlarged, will, I hope, illustrate theme and variations of the problem under discussion.

On the basis of these historical facts the following questions arise: (1) Do we have to accept this distinction as the foundation of a Theory of Knowledge? (2) Are the traditional distinctions, especially those of Hobbes, Leibniz, Hume, and Kant satisfactory? For if they are, there is no need for further inquiry. (3) Are there really, as all these theories with varied emphasis maintain, only two different kinds of knowledge? In other words, is this distinction exhaustive? (4) Are those right who claim the complete difference of the two kinds (like Descartes, Hobbes, Locke, Berkeley, and Hume), or those who stress their final identity (Leibniz and Mill)? Or have both the overstressing of the difference and its attempted elimination more hampered than helped the solution of the problem? (5) Are the two kinds of knowledge not in fact interdependent, i.e., have meaning merely in their interrelation, although they may be treated in relative isolation? (6) Are they not perhaps merely two stages in a series of different kinds of knowledge? Do not certain facts impel us to abandon the dichotomy? (7) And do not, moreover, the two terms themselves refer to two families embracing many members? (8) Has the distinction perhaps merely "directive" value by directing our attention to different attitudes? But has it not to be reformulated even in this case? (9) Where do we find a clue for the solution of these problems?

In the limited space at my disposal I cannot discuss all these problems; I can only pick out the most important points. Most of the above distinctions suffer from what I should like to call the *monomorphic fallacy,* i.e., from the assumption either that there is only *one* kind of truth, or that there is only *one* kind of rational knowledge and *one* kind of empirical knowledge. This fallacy dominates Leibniz' thought and tempts him to define *veritas* as *praedicatum inesse subjecto*. The result of his analysis depends on this definition and its ambiguity, namely upon the two meanings of *inesse,* one of which is logical, the other ontological. Logically *inesse* means 'inclusion' or *involutio,* and is almost identical with implication, and this implication is thought of as based on the relation of identity, or part-identity, and on the principle of the substitution of similars. For instance, the analytic proposition, "All grey horses are grey," is true because the term "grey horse" includes the term "grey," or because of the part-identity of subject and predicate. Ontologically, however, *inesse* means "inherence of attributes or qualities in a substance." "Substance" is the ontological correlate to the grammatical or logical subject, a substance being a subject which remains identical in time. Leibniz conceives of substance as the sum total (*Inbegriff*) of its qualities, actual and possible; as an independent being that is in no way determined from outside and whose whole development is spontaneous. In a substance all its past, present and future attributes are implied. Therefore all propositions concerning it are analytic, provided there is an intellect able to analyze them. This second meaning of *inesse* or "inclusion" (*Inbegriffensein*) is based on the following fictitious assumptions: (1) that persons and things can exist in complete isolation; (2) that they are completely and necessarily determined from within; and (3) that there is no such thing as chance either within or without. These assumptions are not only unverifiable, they contradict our experience. For this very reason Leibniz had to introduce a new, again unverifiable hypothesis: namely, that contingent propositions are analytic from the point of view of God's infinite intellect. Because of his monomorphic definition of truth he had to conclude that necessary as well as contingent propositions are analytic. This result is so surprising that Bertrand Russell, in the first edition of his *Critical Exposition of the Philosophy of Leibniz,* attributed the thesis to him that contingent propositions are synthetic. The same monomorphic fallacy led Leibniz to assume that there is only one kind of rational and one kind of empirical knowledge. He said: "The truths of reason are necessary and their opposite is impossible, the truths of fact are contingent and their opposite is possible." Is this definition correct? That the truths of reason are necessary and that their opposite is impossible is not true in an absolute sense. It is merely correct with reference to a specific system; e.g., within Euclidean geometry the proposition that the sum of the angles of a triangle is equal to two right angles is true, and the contradictory proposition is false; but to say without qualification, that "its opposite is impossible," is not correct because it is possible and even true in non-Euclidean geometry. In other words, the necessity of mathematical theorems is hypothetical; they are true *if* certain axioms are accepted, but they do not necessarily remain true if the set of axioms is changed. Here then is a certain contingency introduced by the free choice of the set of axioms; and the possibility of alternative systems of geometry makes it possible that certain geometrical theorems may be called 'contingent' in Leibniz' language, because their opposite is possible, albeit in another system of geometry. In other words, the assumption that all mathematical propositions are absolutely necessary is a monomorphic over-simplification of the issues involved. In the sphere of Leibniz' truths of reason the modal distinctions play a much greater role than he assumed.

But is it true that "the truths of fact are contingent and that their opposite is possible?" Was Hume justified in accepting this proposition at its face value as the basis of his theory of knowledge? Nobody will deny that empirical propositions are not 'necessary' as based on, and derivable from, the law of contradiction. But is the expression, "Their opposite is possible" not ambiguous? Possible in which sense? "Logically possible," i.e., "it could be thought, or as Hume would say, it could be imagined" or "actually possible, i.e., it could happen?" Or, in other words, is the term 'contingent' not merely relational, being meaningful only in relation to a specific set of axioms? It must be noted that Leibniz' notion of contingency is formulated with reference to the law of contradiction as a logical as well as an ontological principle. But what if this assumption should prove incorrect? To take Hume's example. "The sun will rise to-morrow." This proposition may be contingent with reference to the laws of logic; i.e., its opposite may be thinkable. But does it remain contingent if referred to another set of axioms, e.g., to those of physics or astronomy? In this case the proposition, "the sun will rise to-morrow," acquires a degree of probability which approaches certainty, and the opposite, "the sun will not rise to-morrow," is physically and astronomically so improbable that it approaches the mode of impossibility. It is not false to say that matter-of-fact statements are contingent, but it is again an oversimplification; it is false if taken in an absolute sense, and needs a qualification as to the specific set of axioms with reference to which they are contingent. *The terms 'necessary' and 'contingent' are not absolute, but relative. A decision whether a proposition is necessary or contingent can only be reached with reference to a specific system.*

Every empirical proposition should be judged on its own merits and its degree of certainty determined accordingly. The monomorphic fallacy which restricts empirical propositions to one type only should be opposed in whatever form. It is likewise impossible to restrict empirical propositions to probable statements, or to 'hypotheses which can be probable, but never certain.' (A. J. Ayer). "There are three apple-trees in my garden." Is this statement merely a hypothesis about which I can never be certain? Is there, generally speaking, a complete break between probability and uncertainty? Are there not degrees of probability such that probability may approach certainty? If I go into my garden and verify my statement, does it make sense to say: "There are probably three apple-trees in my garden"? There is of course always the possibility that for some reason or other one or more of these trees may have been destroyed; and if I were pedantic I ought to say: "There were three trees in my garden, and if nothing unforseen has happened, they are still there." But in spite of this, specific empirical propositions have a justified claim to be regarded as certain.

The monomorphic fallacy refers, therefore, to the concepts of 'knowledge' and 'truth' underlying the whole scheme; and empiricists are just as liable to it as rationalists. This is confirmed by Mill's attempt to reduce deduction to induction, an attempt which does not seem to need further refutation seeing that even empiricists reject it. The fallacy refers, in the second place, to the two types of 'rational' and 'empirical knowledge' as such; and here again rationalists and empiricists are likewise sinners. Kant's thesis that all mathematical propositions are synthetic *a priori* is just as untenable as the fashionable antithesis that all mathematical propositions are analytic. If C. I. Lewis identifies analytic and *a priori* and speaks of "Analytic Truth," the question cannot be avoided: "Is this identification perhaps again based on the monomorphic fallacy?"

So far our considerations have been chiefly historical and critical. But that alone is not satisfactory. We feel that there is something of importance in this distinction and we want to know what is alive and what is dead in it. There seem to be three clues for the solution of these problems, one logical, one epistemological, and one semantical. Leibniz' distinction is based on the difference of two modalities, namely 'necessary' and 'contingent,' as a definite and complete disjunction, the necessary being understood as that whose contrary implies a contradiction (*qui est verus et unicus character impossibilitatis*); it is therefore defined as the 'possible' in opposition to the 'impossible,' and the contingent as the 'actual' (Dasein) or 'the best possibilities' (*Actualia nihil sunt, quam possibilium (omnibus comparatis) optima*) [4] whose contrary is (logically) possible, although not compossible, and does therefore not exist. The logic of modalities must therefore contain the first, and perhaps most important clue for the solution of these problems. But logic is not enough, and it may be that Leibniz erred in confining possibility to logical possibility. (*Possibilia sunt, quae non implicant contradictionem.*) [5] Epistemologically, the problem is intimately connected with the problem of universals; Locke, in dis-

---

[4] Leibnizens Mathematische Schriften ed. Gerhardt, III, p. 574.
[5] Math., III, 574.

tinguishing universal and particular truths, and all those who stress the fundamental difference of the two kinds of knowledge, make it clear that the alleged isolation of the universal and of the particular is at the root of the assumption of two fundamentally different sorts of knowledge and truth. A re-interpretation of the relation 'universal-particular' must therefore throw new light on our problem. If it could be shown that the universal and the particular are interdependent and that they can only be artificially isolated, this hypothesis of the interdependence of the universal and the particular would be of primary importance for the solution of the problem. It is quite true, that everything that exists is particular, but it is merely a half-truth. In fact, nothing exists which is *merely* particular and which does not belong at the same time to a specific class. Even the exceptional cases, and Kierkegaard's *Ausnahmen,* cannot escape this rule. This fact makes it probable that the two realms of knowledge are not interdependent of each other, and that at least in certain cases the propositions of the one species are correlative to those of the other, just as the different kinds of geometry are correlative to different kinds of physics. In other words, there may be a third possibility, besides either complete difference or identity, namely interdependence. The third clue arises from our critique of the monomorphic fallacy and is provided by the hypothesis of the polymorphic character of the realm of meaning and of truth, i.e., by the assumption that the meaning of meaning and the meaning of truth are not monistic, not dualistic, but polymorphic. There are many meanings of the terms "truth" and "fact."

There is general agreement as to the *modal* character of terms like 'necessary' and 'contingent,' but no agreement at all about the meaning and function of modality. This is an astonishing fact seeing that the logical analysis of modalities is of great importance for the solution of central philosophical and scientific problems, such as that of causality or of 'necessary connection' (Hume). Once again Aristotle, who introduced the term and who discussed four modes, the necessary, the possible, the contingent, and the impossible, forgot to define it; and the definition given by his commentator Ammonius, namely: "Mode (τόπος) is a word signifying how the predicate belongs to the subject" is so vague that Buridanus added that a qualification which is to make a proposition modal must attach to the copula and not to the subject or predicate. Aristotle moreover spoke of "potential being," "actual being," etc. Therefore the question arises: "Are these modes modes of being, of thought, or of linguistic expression?"

Kant gave this remarkable answer: "The modality of judgments is a quite peculiar function. Its distinguishing characteristic is that it contributes nothing to the content of the judgment, but concerns only the value of the copula in relation to thought in general. It indicates the manner in which something is affirmed or denied in a judgment. Problematic judgments are those in which affirmation or negation is taken as merely possible (optional); whereas in assertoric judgments it is viewed as real (true) and in apodeictic judgments as necessary." (*Cr. P.R.,* B 100; *Logic,* 30.) On this point Kant is right. *The modalities are modes of affirmation and negation. They indicate the manner in which something is affirmed or denied.*

It must be remembered that affirmation and negation are relations establishing a first-degree order among the elements of our mind.[6] They indicate a most primitive division of the objects of our thought according to which certain elements either belong, or do not belong, to a specific class. The modalities represent qualifications of affirmation and negation referring (1) subjectively, to the manner in which we affirm and deny, i.e., (a) to the mood in which we perform these acts and (b) to the degree of certainty with which we are able to express our propositions and (2) objectively, to the manner in which the object in question either belongs (as a possible, probable, real, or necessary member), or does not belong, to a specific class. *Modalities represent a second-degree order of affirmation and nagation.* Wherever we are able to make a straightforward decision, we establish a first-degree order: "X belongs to the class M." But wherever this simple order is not evident, we say that it is possible (impossible), probable (improbable), contingent (non-contingent), or necessary (non-necessary) that "X belongs to the class M." That the modalities repeat the order of affirmation and negation on a higher level comes out in all the theories of modality.

Aristotle	Kant	Carnap
possible—impossible	possible—impossible	necessary—non-necessary
necessary—contingent	existent—non-existent	possible—impossible
	necessary—contingent	contingent—non-contingent

This would remain so, if we were to add more modes, like 'probable, improbable.'

Up to this point, I think, I am in agreement with the so-called 'Logic of Modalities.' Professor R. Feys, for instance, says: "Nous saississions ainsi la modalité sous son aspect plus formel, comme modifiant l'affirmation et la négation sous leur forme la plus simple."[7] Also the following questions, which have to be asked, seem to me to be in accordance with this type of logic, namely: (1) In how many modes can I affirm or deny? (2) Are these modes finite or infinite, or perhaps indefinite, and (3) If they are indefinite, can they nevertheless be reduced to a finite number of

[6] "The Meaning of Negation," *Proc. Ar. Soc.,* 1943–44, pp. 127 ff.
[7] "Les Logiques Nouvelles des Modalités, *Rev. Néo-Scolatique,* XXXXI, p. 249.

modes and be interpreted as their variations? It seems to me to be a merit of the logic of modalities to have formulated implicitly these questions. But the assumption made in this type of logic, that truth and falsehood are modalities, is debatable. Are they really 'modes'? I should not think so. *True and false refer to the correct manner of affirming and denying; and there are specific rules for every case of correct affirmation and negation in the modes of possibility, probability, contingency, and necessity.* True and false represent a third-order of affirmation and negation, which refers to propositions and allows a decision as to which propositions are to be accepted in a specific system. In fact, even the multi-valued logics cannot get rid of this function of true and false. It is well known that, on the other hand, the multi-valued logics define modality as *toute qualification d'une proposition quant à sa validité* (Feys, *Loc. cit.*), and the modes as truth-values, and the "logics of modalities" as logics which accept more modes or truth-values than the two, true and false. I do not deny the possibility of this hypothesis, but the name 'logic of modalities' seems to be a misnomer, and has rightly been replaced by the term 'multi-valued logic.' But there seems a genuine problem of a logic of modalities to remain, which is not identical with the problem of multi-valued logics.

The problem of multi-valued logics has to be left outside the scope of this paper. But there may be one lesson to be learned from it. It is perhaps not out of place to call the type of theory of knowledge which we have discussed and which is based on the dichotomy of necessary and contingent, a two-valued theory of knowledge. The problem before us would then be that of the transition to multi-valued systems of epistemology. But it must be kept in mind that this problem is, in the first instance, qualitative and not quantitative. Nevertheless, here also a mathematical analysis is of fundamental importance. The theory of probability has established that modal distinctions are not absolute, that probability statements may tend, on the one hand, towards certainty and, on the other, towards impossibility. We have further to learn from the mathematicians [8] that some modes are simple and others complex, or that there are species and kinds to be distinguished among the modes, or that in every possible system of modality there are a limited number of fundamental modes which may be combined in derivative modes. In our context it is of importance that "reality" e.g., comprises the species "necessarily real" and "contingently real." This implies that matter-of-fact statements are not necessarily restricted to the "contingently real," as is usually assumed, but may refer also to the "necessarily real." We have, moreover, learned to distinguish between "contingency" (something is, but need not be, i.e., it may not be) and "potentiality" (something is not, but need not not be, i.e., it may

[8] Cf. Walter Bröcker, "Das Modalitätenproblem," *Zeitschrift für Philosophische Forschung*, Vol. I, pp. 35 ff, to whom I owe the following definitions.

be), and the complex mode "chance" (*Zufälligkeit*) (something which is either contingent or potential).

Thence it follows that empirical knowledge may refer (1) to reality, (2) to the "necessarily real," (3) to the "contingently real," (4) to the "potential," and (5) to "chance" in the just defined sense. On this broad basis the problem of empirical knowledge has to be reformulated, and we are no longer allowed to restrict empirical knowledge to 'belief in what is probable'; insofar as it is belief, it may be belief in what is either real, or contingent, or potential, or probable; and insofar as it attains the degree of certainty, it may be either knowledge of reality or of the "necessarily real."

On the other hand, *a priori* knowledge can no longer be restricted to "necessity"; it refers to "potentiality" and to probability as well. In short, the two realms of knowledge are not monomorphic, but polymorphic.

There is, I am afraid, no room left for a discussion of the two other clues, the interdependence of the universal and the particular, and the polymorphic structure of the realm of meaning. I can merely summarize my results as follows: (1) The distinction between two kinds of knowledge is of great heuristic value, because it draws attention to the fundamental difference between the formal knowledge of logic and mathematics, on the one hand, and the material knowledge of daily life and of the empirical sciences, on the other. We should therefore retain it as a basis of discussion. (2) We cannot, however, accept it uncritically as a foundation of a Theory of Knowledge, because as it stands it does not represent a real exhaustive dichotomy. It suffers from oversimplification and has thereby hampered our seeing the problems in their full complexity. (3) Rationalism and empiricism are both based on a faulty isolation of the universal and the particular, and on an overvaluation of either the one or the other. In fact, however, neither particulars nor universals exist in isolation. They, and therefore empirical knowledge and rational knowledge, logic and experience, mathematics and physics, are interdependent. This factual interdependence explains why it is possible to apply mathematical theories, e.g., systems of geometry which are creations of pure thought, to physics. For the same reason, truths of reason and matter-of-fact truths cannot be completely isolated from each other, but neither the reduction of Leibniz nor that of Mill is possible. (4) The interrelation between universals and particulars is polymorphic. The universal can prevail, as in mathematics, where sometimes the relation to the particular may be completely neglected; or the particular can dominate, as for instance in history, where some historians allegedly restrict themselves to a description of the past as it was. (5) We therefore reach the conclusion that a *polymorphic* interpretation of meaning, knowledge, and truth has to be substituted for their traditional *monomorphic* interpretation. There are different kinds of meaning. It is completely futile to reduce them to one kind, and to search for a general criterion of meaningfulness; all attempts to find it have broken down, simply because it does not exist. The celebrated principle of verifiability has gone the way of all flesh. (6) Consequently, the *two-valued* theory of knowledge, according to which there are only two classes of meaningful propositions (in Hume's and Ayer's sense) has to be replaced by a *multi-valued* theory of knowledge, which acknowledges the possibility of an indefinite number of classes of meaningful propositions. If we have the courage to jump over the wall of our prejudices, the realm of unlimited possibilities lies before us. *Cujusvis est errare; nullius nisi insipientis in errore perseverare.*[9]

[9] Some theses of this paper were first sketched in "Vérités de Raison et Vérités de Fait," *Proc. Xth International Congress of Philosophy,* Amsterdam, 1949. The history of the problem is more elaborated in "Truths of Reason and Truths of Fact," *The Philosophical Review,* Sept. 1948.

F. Kaufmann : THREE MEANINGS
OF "TRUTH"

T HE *late Dr. Felix Kaufmann considers the notion of "truth" with respect to rational and factual inquiries and offers problematic observations about the relationships of deductive logic and empirical knowledge. Reprinted by permission from* THE JOURNAL OF PHILOSOPHY, *XLV, no. 13 (1948), pp. 337–50.*

- The three meanings of "truth" to be discussed are:

(1) Truth as a nontemporal property of propositions.
(2) Truth as warranted assertability.
(3) Truth as an ideal of ultimate pervasive coherence in a total experience.

I shall make the point that the first meaning applies only to logical truth, i.e., to analytical propositions, whereas the second meaning is related to the process of validation of synthetic propositions. The discussion of the third meaning will be brief. I shall suggest that it be reinterpreted as a regulative principle for the establishment of rules of procedure (standards of validation).

The view to be outlined implies the rejection of a general notion of truth which comprises rational (necessary) truth and factual (contingent) truth. The conception of truth and falsity as nontemporal properties of propositions—synthetic as well as analytic propositions—is firmly embedded in philosophical tradition, and it also seems to be in tune with the common use of the two words. However, we are confronted with a serious difficulty as soon as we apply this notion to empirical inquiry, which is generally held to be a search for factual truth. This difficulty is raised by the question: How can we ever know that we have found a factual truth? The question becomes more pointed by contrasting the results of empirical inquiry with the results obtained by pure reasoning, e.g., in a mathematical proof. A rigorous mathematical proof establishes indubitable knowledge of rational truth; but knowledge obtained by empirical inquiry is not supposed to represent indubitable factual truth. The reversibility of every result obtained at a given stage of scientific inquiry is regarded as essential for scientific method.

These considerations were conducive to the view that knowledge of factual truth must be interpreted as imperfect (or probable) knowledge, as an approximation to factual truth rather than as its attainment. It was intimated that we can not obtain absolutely certain (perfect) knowledge, because we are incapable of gathering all relevant data, but that we can gradually approach certainty by gathering more and more relevant data.

But this interpretation is open to a stricture similar to the one it seeks to meet. How can we know—it may be asked—that continued scientific inquiry will lead us ever more closely toward perfect knowledge of factual truth, if every result obtained at any stage of inquiry is liable to be reversed in the course of subsequent inquiry? It does not seem to make sense to regard both a proposition *asserting* a certain state of affairs and a proposition *denying* this state of affairs, as approximations to the self-same factual truth. The view that a scientific result represents a probability of having attained the truth can be attacked on similar grounds. As soon as we assign a procedurally significant meaning to the word "probability," as used in this context, we find that such a meaning is unrelated to a notion of factual truth conceived as a nontemporal property of synthetic propositions.

Thus it would seem that this notion has no place at all in the logic of science and that we must not refer to it in the definition of any methodological term such as "scientific method," "empirical knowledge," "confirmation," "evidence," etc.

But this conclusion is open to the objection that we could not account for the applicability of the principles of deductive logic to empirical science unless we presupposed a general concept of nontemporal truth which comprises factual truth as well as logical truth. The conjoined principles of contradiction and excluded middle—it may be argued—assign to every proposition, whether synthetic or analytic, one, and only one, of the two truth-values "true" and "false"; and these principles are essential for the procedure of empirical science. Hence (it is concluded) we do imply in the meaning of "scientific inquiry" the notions of truth and falsity as nontemporal properties of synthetic propositions. Thus we seem to be confronted with the alternative: either we cling to the notion of nontemporal factual truth, and we have to admit that the standards of validation in empirical science can not be regarded as criteria of factual truth—so that factual truth becomes a transcendent notion—or we insist upon these standards being criteria of truth, and we have to grant that the principles of contradiction and excluded middle, which (purportedly) imply the notion of nontemporal truth, do not hold for factual truth.

It is the principle of excluded middle rather than the principle of contradiction which is supposed by contemporary philosophers to be primarily affected. Bertrand Russell, for instance, in his *Inquiry into Meaning and Truth* [1] points out that we can not escape from this dilemma. He resolves—rather hesitatingly—to stick to the principle of excluded middle and to pay the price of allowing for a notion of transcendent truth. I shall quote the sentences in which he lays down this resolution:

Although the above discussion has been so far very inconclusive, I find myself believing, at the end of it, that truth and knowledge are different, and that a proposition may be true although no method exists of discovering that it is so. In that case we may accept the law of excluded middle. We shall define "truth" by reference to events (I am speaking of non-logical truth), and "knowledge" by relation to "percepts." Thus "truth" will be a wider conception than "knowledge." It would be a practically useless conception, but for the fact that knowledge has very vague boundaries. When we embark upon an investigation, we assume that the propositions concerning which we are inquiring are either true

[1] New York, 1940.

or false; we may find evidence, or we may not. Before the spectroscope, it would have seemed impossible ever to ascertain the chemical constitution of the stars; but it would have been a mistake to maintain that they neither do nor do not contain the elements we know. At present, we do not know whether there is life elsewhere in the universe, but we are right to feel sure that there either is or is not. Thus we need "truth" as well as "knowledge," because the boundaries of knowledge are uncertain, and because, without the law of excluded middle, we could not ask the questions that give rise to discoveries.[2]

In examining Russell's argument we find that it does not penetrate to the core of the issue because it fails to distinguish between "technical impossibility" and "logical impossibility." The crucial question in an analysis of the meaning of "factual truth" and its relation to "empirical knowledge" is whether we ought to introduce a notion of factual truth which is logically independent of standards of validation. It does not matter whether verification in terms of these standards is technically possible at a given stage of inquiry. Russell suggests that before the invention of the spectroscope, it would have seemed impossible ever to ascertain the chemical constitution of stars; but the establishment of standards of verification for propositions concerning the chemical structure of bodies did not have to wait for Kirchhoff's and Bunsen's invention of the spectroscope. Such propositions could be verified by test-tube experiments. The technical impossibility of performing such experiments on the fixed stars is irrelevant for the logic of science.

Rudolf Carnap, in his first contribution to the Symposium on Probability,[3] agrees with Russell in rejecting the substitution of "verified" for "true," and in declaring that this substitution is incompatible with the principle of excluded middle.[4] But he differs from Russell in maintaining that this position does not involve the admission of a concept of transcendent (metaphysical) truth. Carnap makes the point that it is not required for the meaningfulness of a notion of factual truth that we should be able to attain truth, to acquire perfect factual knowledge. This, he grants, is impossible since every scientific result may have to be reversed; but he holds that imperfect knowledge—confirmation of truth to a certain degree—which is actually achieved by scientific inquiry, suffices for rendering the notion of nontemporal truth empirically significant. But I do not think that he has actually established his point. The notion of nontemporal factual truth is, according to his own admission, not internally related to confirmation; it can therefore not be vindicated by connecting it with confirmation. But I shall not develop this stricture here.[5]

[2] Pp. 360 f.
[3] Philosophy and Phenomenological Research, Vol. V (1945), pp. 513–532.
[4] P. 530.
[5] I have done this briefly in two papers in the "Symposium on Probability" and, in more detail, in another paper to be published in Philosophy and Phenomenological Research.

I shall rather try to refute the view that the applicability in empirical science of the principle of excluded middle, or of any other principle of deductive logic, depends upon the adoption of a notion of nontemporal factual truth; or, in other words, upon a general concept of truth which comprises both logical and factual truth.

In embarking upon this task we have to emphasize, first of all, that reference to the general concept of truth is not required in pure deductive logic, understood as a formal theory of internal relations among propositions and terms. But we need not dwell upon this point; for it is at present almost universally acknowledged that these relations are fully covered by intensional logic, which is not supposed to include the general notion of truth. Moreover, it is recognized that a proposition is logically true *qua* being analytical, and that a proposition is logically false *qua* being a contradiction; so that it is possible to replace the words "logically true proposition" by "analytical proposition" (or "tautology"), and "logically false proposition" by "contradiction."

However, the introduction of a general notion of truth is usually supposed to be required in describing the application of deductive logic in empirical science. This view was recently restated by Carnap in his attempt to vindicate the significance of the notion of nontemporal factual truth for the logic of science.[6] Having stressed that the concept of truth is not used in his definitions of range, L-implication and degree of confirmation, i.e., of those concepts which he regards as basic for deductive and inductive logic, respectively, he continues: "On the other hand, there are important relations between deductive concepts and the concept of truth. Thus, for instance, from the statement 'i L-implies j' . . . we can infer 'if i is true, then j is true.' . . . Note that the latter statement is merely a consequence of the former; it does by no means say the same."[7]

The reason why the two statements do not say the same is obviously that the latter contains a term which is not contained in the former, viz., the term "true." Accordingly it might be suggested that the relation between the two propositions is similar to the one between, say, "All men are mortal" and "All men who are vegetarians are mortal." There is, however, a decisive difference between the two cases. In deducing "All men who are vegetarians are mortal" from "All men are mortal," we presuppose that "vegetarian" has a definite meaning; otherwise there could not be any proposition containing a term "vegetarian." Similarly we have to presuppose in the case under consideration a definite meaning of "truth"; but the legitimacy of this presupposition is just the point at issue.

The following argument might be offered in an attempt to establish

[6] In his third Symposium paper "Rejoinder to Mr. Kaufmann's Reply," *ibid.*, Vol. VI (1946), pp. 609–611.

[7] P. 611.

this point. In testing a proposition, e.g., a proposed law, we assume tentatively the truth of the proposition, and derive from it, and other propositions which are supposed to be true, logical consequences which can be checked by observation. The description of this procedure—it may then be declared—includes reference to an operationally significant meaning of truth. This can, indeed, be readily admitted; but "truth" understood in this sense must not be interpreted as a nontemporal property of propositions. The words "true proposition" as used in this context may be replaced by "verified proposition" or (as I prefer to say) by "accepted proposition." By performing this substitution we make it clear that the argument does not establish the point it seeks to establish. But this result should not lead us to the rash conclusion that we can always replace the words "true synthetic proposition" by "accepted (verified) synthetic proposition."

Such a substitution can not be performed in the principle of excluded middle. First of all it is readily seen that we can not replace the sentence "Every proposition is either true or false" by the sentence "Every proposition is either accepted or unaccepted at a given time." The latter sentence obviously fails to convey the intended meaning of the term "false." If we replace "true proposition" by "accepted proposition," then we must not replace "false proposition" by "unaccepted proposition," but rather by "proposition the negation of which is accepted." When we do this, we obtain the statement: For every proposition p, either p or *non p* is accepted at any definite stage of scientific inquiry. It goes without saying that this statement is untenable, and that it does not represent an application of the principle of excluded middle to empirical science.

We have already intimated what the application of this principle in empirical science is taken to mean: it postulates the verifiability or falsifiability of every given proposition. Recent discussions concerning the bearing of Heisenberg's principle of indeterminacy upon the principle of excluded middle have brought this point into sharp focus. But in granting this we find ourselves confronted with the question: Do we actually dispose of truth and falsity understood as nontemporal properties of synthetic propositions by introducing the words "verifiable" and "falsifiable" for "true" and "false" respectively?

In examining Russell's view I have made the point that the terms "verifiability" and "falsifiability" as understood in the logic of science must not be taken to imply technical possibility of verification or falsification. But this very statement might seem to lead us back to the notions of nontemporal factual truth and falsity. How—it might be asked—can we know that every proposition is either verifiable or falsifiable, unless verifiability and falsifiability are properties of all propositions, unless they are implied in the meaning of the term "proposition"? But provided this is the case, why should we replace the time-honored words "true" and "false" by "verifiable" and "falsifiable" respectively?

A preliminary answer to the second question can be derived from the preceding argument, which stressed the point that the standards of validation provide for the reversibility of every result obtained in empirical science. It follows that verifiability and falsifiability can not be identified with, or even traced back to nontemporal truth and falsity respectively. But the first question requires some further analysis.

The view that standards of validation are implicitly referred to in every genuine (synthetic) proposition was presented in slightly different formulations by Peirce, Bridgman, and Wittgenstein, and unreservedly endorsed by logical positivists till the early 'thirties. Later on, logical positivists were led to various modifications of this tenet, primarily by reflections upon the nature of scientific laws. Ludwig Wittgenstein had emphasized that laws can not be verified and declared that they should, therefore, not be regarded as genuine propositions. They are, he intimated, rather suggestions for the formation of propositions. But Carnap and other members of the group became eventually dissatisfied with this formulation which didn't square with the general use of the term "proposition." Karl Popper, in his *Logik der Forschung*,[8]† tried to dispose of the predicament by pointing out that only falsifiability should be regarded as a standard of meaningfulness, as a criterion for discerning (*Abgrenzungskriterium*) between genuine sentences and the pseudo-sentences of metaphysics. Carnap—apparently influenced by Keynes's notion of degrees of rational belief and by Reichenbach's interpretation of probability—suggested that the requirement of verifiability should be replaced by the requirement of confirmability in different degrees. But it does not seem to me that either of these modifications of the tenet that propositional meaning implies verifiability is apt to dispose of the crucial objections which may be raised against this view.

It will suffice for our argument to mention but one of these strictures. We do not suppose that the propositional meanings with which we are concerned in deductive logic are affected by any changes in the adopted standards of validation that may take place in the process of empirical inquiry. Yet this would have to be the case if the meaning of the term "proposition," as understood in deductive logic, did imply reference to standards of validation. But when we acknowledge the cogency of this stricture we have still to answer the question, how the standards of validation are related to propositions.

It will be convenient though not essential for the following argument to introduce at this juncture the word "assertion." I shall make the point

---

[8] Vienna, 1935. †[EDITOR'S NOTE: Now available in English, *The Logic of Scientific Discovery*, translated by Dr. Popper (with 150 pages new), Basic Books, Inc., New York, 1959.]

that reference to standards of validation is not implied in the meaning of "synthetic proposition," whereas such reference is, indeed, implied in the meaning of "assertion." In developing this argument I shall define the methodological terms which have been used so far.

That we should discern between proposition and assertion has recently been emphasized by C. I. Lewis,[9] who credits H. M. Sheffer with having drawn his attention to this point. "A proposition," Lewis points out, "is a term capable of signifying a state of affairs. To define a proposition as an expression which is true or false, is correct enough but inauspicious, because it easily leads to identification of the proposition with the statement or assertion of it; whereas the element of assertion in a statement is extraneous to the proposition asserted. The proposition is something assert*able;* the *content* of the assertion; and this same content, signifying the same state of affairs, can also be questioned, denied, or merely supposed, and can be entertained in other moods as well."

In applying this distinction to the logic of science we have to realize that the process of validation is not related to propositions as such, but to the *acceptance* of propositions. We may conceive of a synthetic proposition as a presentation of a possible state of affairs; to accept the proposition is to assume that the proposed state of affairs is real. (This formulation is big with problems; but these problems do not directly concern us here.)

A sharp distinction, at each stage of inquiry, between propositions which are accepted, and propositions which are not accepted at this stage, must be postulated by the logic of science. This is readily seen if we consider that only accepted propositions—in other words, propositions which belong to the body of knowledge—are eligible for the function of grounds in empirical inquiry. This postulation is of course an idealization; but idealizations are as essential for the logic of science as they are for deductive logic. They are presupposed in *scientific criticism.* In judging whether a scientific argument is correct, we must be able to decide unambiguously whether the reasons advanced in its support are scientifically established; whether they are propositions which have been accepted in conformity with the adopted standards of validation.

To adopt standards of validation is to establish conditions for the acceptance of propositions and for the reversal of their acceptance. "Verification" and "falsification," as well as "verifiability" and "falsifiability," are to be defined in terms of these standards (rules). We mean by *"verification of a proposition"* the demonstration of its acceptability in terms of given rules. A proposition is called *"verifiable in principle"* within a given system of rules if conditions for its acceptance are established

[9] *An Analysis of Knowledge and Valuation,* La Salle, Ill., 1946, pp. 48 f.

within the system. A proposition is called *"actually verifiable"* at a given stage of inquiry if the conditions for its acceptance are fulfilled at this stage of inquiry. By *falsification* of a proposition *p* we mean the verification of *non p* and, accordingly, by *falsifiability* of *p,* the verifiability of *non p*.

We are now prepared to define the term *"assertion."* The assertion of a proposition *p* is taken to mean either (*a*) *p* is at present actually verifiable, or (*b*) *p* would become actually verifiable, if future inquiry were directed towards this goal. We may call assertions of the first type *"definite assertions"* and those of the second type *"indefinite assertions."* It is not required for our argument to stress the difference between these two types of assertion. The point that matters here is that "assertion"—in contradistinction to "proposition"—is defined in terms of standards of validation. We *warrant* the assertion of *p* by verifying *p,* that is, by demonstrating the acceptability of *p*.

The preceding definitions will be of avail in a reinterpretation of the principles of contradiction and excluded middle, understood as principles of empirical procedure. Bearing in mind that "falsification of a proposition *p*" has been defined as verification of *non p,* we see that the postulate of verifiability in principle of *every* proposition and the postulate of falsifiability in principle of *every* proposition are logically equivalent. They amount to but one postulate. The clear understanding of this postulate has been balked by its identification with the principle of excluded middle in deductive logic.

Similar considerations hold for the principle of contradiction. The two principles, as understood in deductive logic, are simply explications of the meaning of "negation." They do not establish any norms for the process of validation, whereas the corresponding principles in empirical science are, indeed, supposed to establish such norms. We shall therefore distinguish between the principles of contradiction and excluded middle in deductive logic and their *procedural correlates* in empirical science. What we mean by the procedural correlate of the principle of contradiction is the demand that the simultaneous presence of two logically incompatible propositions in the body of accepted propositions be ruled out. This demand imposes restrictions upon systems of standards of scientific validation. The demand is fulfilled if and only if the system of rules contains the following provisions:

(1) Simultaneous acceptance of contrary or contradictory propositions must be precluded.

(2) Simultaneously with the acceptance of a proposition *p* all propositions contradicting *p* must be eliminated from the body of accepted propositions.

It is seen that the procedural correlate of the principle of contradiction does not imply the conception of truth and falsity as nontemporal properties of synthetic propositions.

This holds likewise for the procedural correlate of the principle of excluded middle, which demands that the rules of procedure allow for *verifiability in principle* of every proposition. It is equivalent with the postulate of universal assertability. Empirical inquiry is exclusively concerned with assertable propositions, *qua* assertable; but deductive logic deals with propositions as such, irrespective of their assertability. It follows that we must clearly distinguish between meaningfulness and assertability. "Meaningfulness" is implied in "assertability"; but the converse relation does not hold. This remark applies to propositions the assertability of which is excluded by Heisenberg's principle.

Further light may be shed on the procedural correlate of the principle of excluded middle by comparing it with the postulate that every scientific result must be reversible; in other words, that the standards of validation must establish conditions for the elimination of every previously accepted proposition from the body of accepted propositions—from the corpus of knowledge at a given time. This postulate, which I have called the *principle of permanent control,* is a counterpart to the procedural correlate of the principle of excluded middle. The conjoint two principles stipulate that the status of every proposition at any given stage of scientific inquiry must be reversible.

We have reached the conclusion that the abandonment of the notions of factual truth and falsity conceived as nontemporal properties of propositions does not affect the principle of excluded middle, nor any other principle of deductive logic. This result vindicates the view that there is no place for these notions in the logic of science. Hence we must not refer to them in defining any term in the logic of science. Such terms as "scientific method," "problem," "solution," "evidence," "explanation" are rather to be defined in terms of standards of validation.

The terms "problem" and "solution" may serve as examples. We may introduce distinctions between "question" and "problem," on the one hand, and between "answer" and "solution" on the other, which correspond to the distinction between "proposition" and "assertion."

Let us suppose that the following three propositions have been offered as answers to the question: In what year was Aristotle born?

(*a*) Aristotle was born in the year 384 B.C.
(*b*) Aristotle was born in the year 338 B.C.
(*c*) Aristotle was born at Stagira.

No empirical investigation is required for the rejection of (*c*) as an answer to the given question; we can reject it *a limine* because it is not to the point. What we need for its rejection is only a comparative analysis of meanings. The propositions (*a*) and (*b*), however, do represent answers to our question, but neither of these answers may be regarded as the solution of the underlying scientific problem, unless it is verified, i.e., unless we demonstrate its acceptability in terms of given standards of validation. If we define "problem" as "demand for a *true* answer to a given question" and "solution" as "presentation of a *true* answer"—whereby truth is conceived as a nontemporal property of propositions—then we can never be able to vindicate the claim that an empirical problem has been solved. But scientific inquiry is, indeed, supposed to make possible the vindication of such claims. It is thus seen that definitions of "problem" and "solution" in terms of "nontemporal factual truth" are not in conformity with the use of these terms in inquiry.

I shall now briefly discuss the bearing of this conclusion upon the issue of the relation between deductive and inductive logic. Logicians who presuppose a general concept of truth, which covers both logical truth and factual truth, are apt to regard induction as an approximation to truth (as probable inference), and to interpret deductive logic as the limiting case in which truth (or certainty) is attained. But this interpretation is untenable. The conclusion reached by inductive inference from p_1 to p_2 is quite different from the conclusion obtained by the corresponding process of deduction. By deducing the synthetic proposition p_2 from the synthetic proposition p_1, we demonstrate that p_2 is logically implied in p_1. If we then introduce the term "acceptance," we can draw the conclusion that acceptance of p_1 includes acceptance of p_2. The reference to acceptance is here, as it were, a *secondary* matter. In an inductive inference, however, we are *primarily* concerned with the acceptance of propositions. We establish by an inductive inference from p_1 to p_2 that p_2—which is supposed not to be logically implied in p_1—may be accepted, if p_1 belongs to the body of accepted propositions. Here we have implicit reference to standards of validation, since "acceptability" is defined in terms of these standards (rules). When the rules are made explicit, it is seen that inductive inference demonstrates what it establishes. Inductive inference is subsumption under rules. It is therefore misleading to contrast inductive inference as nondemonstrative, with demonstrative deductive inference.

A misplaced analogy between the syntactical rules of deductive inference and the procedural rules of inductive inference suggests the demand for an ultimate justification of the rules of induction corresponding to the intuitive distinction between valid moods and invalid moods of the syllogism; David Hume has convincingly shown that this demand is ill-considered and unfulfillable.

But to discard this quest for *ultimate* justification of the rules of induction is not to deny that a genuine problem is raised by the demand for their justification; the problem, namely, of clarifying the standards by which we judge the appropriateness of rules of induction. To state that "success" in applying the rules is the standard is little more than another way of posing the problem; for we are now confronted with the question: what are the criteria of success? A tentative answer to this question is ready at hand. The conclusions which we obtain by inferences in conformity with the rules must be confirmed by observational tests. But this answer does not lead us very far either; for the meaning of "testing" points back to an intricate system of rules. This is readily understood as soon as we dispose of the erroneous view that a test is a confrontation of a proposition with data of immediate experience. Once this has been done, it becomes apparent that we have to refer to theoretical goals of inquiry, such as systematic unity and simplicity of knowledge, in defining "success" or "progress" in science.

The procedural significance of the third conception of truth which we listed above, viz., the conception of truth as an ideal of ultimate pervasive coherence, derives from the synthesis of the theoretical goals of scientific inquiry which it implies. But we should not conceive of these goals as preestablished infinitely remote signposts toward which inquiry moves, but rather as a set of interrelated regulative principles for the formation of rules of procedure. Rules of scientific procedure are vindicated, if their application leads to scientific progress, as defined in terms of these regulative principles. In the opposite case, the rules have to be altered. The question whether at a particular stage of inquiry a particular rule ought to be altered, refers implicitly to standards for the alteration of rules. These I have called rules of the second order. (Standards for changes of rules of the second order are then called "rules of the third order," and so on.) We might say that the ideal of ultimate pervasive coherence is embodied in the standards for the alteration of rules of procedure.

It thus turns out that we must clearly distinguish between three meanings of "truth," which are related to three different types of judgment in the logic of science, viz.:

(a) judgments concerning internal relations among propositions.
(b) judgments concerning the acceptability of propositions in terms of *given* standards of validation.
(c) judgments concerning principles for the establishment of standards of validation.

In dealing with internal relations among synthetic propositions we are not concerned at all with their validity.

We are passing to another type of logical analysis—namely, to the logic of science (methodology)—when we embark upon a clarification of empirical procedure, and here we must be constantly on our guard against confounding the two types of analysis by interpreting the process of validation in terms of a notion of truth which is supposed to apply to analytical propositions and synthetic propositions alike. This confusion is partly due to the conception of scientific inquiry as a means to a pre-established end, which can be characterized without reference to standards of validation. This conception underlies the usual interpretation of the "belief in truth." But every thorough attempt to determine the nature of this belief, without introducing the idea of an infinite mind, is bound to lead to the conclusion that standards of validation must be referred to in characterizing it.

Peirce's famous declaration of the "faith of the logician" is most revealing in this respect. I shall quote the familiar lines in "How to Make Our Ideas Clear." [10]

. . . all the followers of science are animated by a cheerful hope that the processes of investigation, if only pushed far enough, will give one certain solution to each question to which they apply it. One man may investigate the velocity of light by studying the transits of Venus and the aberration of the stars; another by the oppositions of Mars and the eclipses of Jupiter's satellites; a third by the method of Fizeau; a fourth by that of Foucault; a fifth by the motions of the curves of Lissajoux; a sixth, a seventh, an eighth, and a ninth, may follow the different methods of comparing the measures of statical and dynamical electricity. They may at first obtain different results, but, as each perfects his method and his processes, the results are found to move steadily together toward a destined centre. So with all scientific research. Different minds may set out with the most antagonistic views, but the progress of investigation carries them by a force outside of themselves to one and the same conclusion. This activity of thought by which we are carried, not where we wish, but to a fore-ordained goal, is like the operation of destiny. No modification of the point of view taken, no selection of other facts for study, no natural bent of mind even, can enable a man to escape the predestinate opinion. This great hope is embodied in the conception of truth and reality. The opinion which is fated to be ultimately agreed to by all who investigate, is what we mean by the truth, and the object represented in this opinion is the real. That is the way I would explain reality.

These impressive statements should be apt to eradicate the erroneous view that the interpretation of factual truth in terms of scientific method —i.e., in terms of standards of validation—amounts to an expression of disbelief in truth. Reflections upon the foundations of a *particular* belief are, indeed, frequently indicative of, or conducive to, pertinent doubts. But the belief in truth is not a particular belief, and the analysis of the meaning of this belief is not an analysis of the foundation of a particular belief.

[10] CP 5, 388–410.

The very quest for a foundation of beliefs implies the belief in truth, as conceived by Peirce. But it does not seem to me that we add something significant to an expression of this belief by stating that it has a foundation in the things; for this statement does not contribute in any way to a corroboration of the belief in truth, nor does it help us in establishing standards of truth.

The same stricture applies to correspondence theories of truth of any type. The preceding analysis has advanced some arguments in support of this stricture, but the correspondence theories raise other problems which lie beyond the scope of logical analysis in a strict sense.

Logical analysis is analysis on a specific level of reflection. Objective meanings are presupposed as given (constituted) on this level; they are data for the analysis to be performed. But philosophical reflection need not stop at this level; it may attempt to clarify the constitution of objective meanings, i.e., the presupposed identity of content of an indefinite number of psychic acts. It may even be suggested that the recognition of different levels of philosophical reflection is a prerequisite for an adequate analysis on each level.

The issue of the relation between meanings and standards of validation is a case in point. We do not establish, we rather presuppose, the meaning of "blue," in declaring that the proposition "there is a blue spot at place P at time T" may be verified by protocol statements reporting about blue-perceptions. But if we ask: "What is meant by 'blue'?" we are looking forward to an answer which relates this meaning to specific acts of perception. The expression "ostensive definition" is rather unfortunate; still it may be apt to provide a first clue to the understanding of questions of this kind. Such questions have been thoroughly treated in Husserl's phenomenology and particularly in his posthumously published book *Erfahrung und Urteil*.

E. Cassirer : THE GOAL AND METHODS OF THEORETICAL PHYSICS

U NIVERSITIES *in Germany, Sweden, and the United States were the fortunate centers in which Ernst Cassirer (1874–1945) contemplated the "problem of knowledge" that is the root of philosophic speculation in the modern world. In such works as the first three volumes of* DAS ER-KENNTNISPROBLEM IN DER PHILOSOPHIE UND WISSENSHAFT DER NEUEREN ZEIT *(1906–20),* PHILOSOPHIE DER SYMBOLISCHEN FORMEN *(1923–29),* AN ESSAY ON MAN *(1945), and the fourth volume of* DAS ERKENNTNISPROBLEM *(composed in 1940, and published in English as* THE PROBLEM OF KNOWLEDGE: PHILOSOPHY, SCIENCE, AND HISTORY SINCE HEGEL, *translated by W. H. Woglom and C. W. Hendel, with a preface by C. W. Hendel, Yale University Press, New Haven, 1950), from which the present essay is taken, Cassirer drew upon profound understanding of treatises in the exact sciences as well as linguistics, history, and philosophy in order to give a synoptic view of the conceptualization of the world as the mind encounters it. This essay indicates the ways in which the advances in theoretical physics have inspired and directed speculation in the area of epistemology. Reprinted by permission of Yale University Press from* THE PROBLEM OF KNOWLEDGE, *pp. 81–117.*

• No single realm of learning is so closely related to the general problem of knowledge, and none has exerted such a strong and lasting effect upon its historical development, as mathematical physics. Between theoretical physics and epistemology there is not only constant reciprocation and uninterrupted collaboration, but there seems to be a sort of spiritual community. In our discussion of the problem of knowledge we have been able to follow this association step by step from its inception at the very dawn of modern scientific thought and to see how it has become increasingly closer throughout the centuries. From the Renaissance on nearly all the great natural scientists have endeavored to maintain it.

Galileo was more than creator of the science of dynamics and a leader in the conflict over the Copernican world view. He never would have been able to erect the new physics and astronomy had he not been guided by a new definition of what scientific knowledge can and should be. It was his philosophical conception of truth that opened the way to his establishment of physics and the reform of cosmology.[1]

Kepler, too, had been the first to formulate exact laws of nature in his theory of planetary motion, and he was also a pioneer in purely methodological respects, having proposed in his published vindication of Tycho Brahe the first really precise definition of the meaning and function of scientific hypotheses.[2]

And Newton, also, included in his great work a special section in which he sought to bring the concept formation of physics under certain rules and to determine its object and limits. He reflected not only on the goal of natural science but on its methods as well, and the rules of reasoning in philosophy go side by side with the mathematical principles as a necessary and integral part of his system.[3]

Thus philosophy is tied up with all the efforts of research and it also brings them into unity. It attempts to represent them systematically and then critically to justify them. Kant's *Critique of Pure Reason* grew out of this ambition. It aimed to seal the covenant, as it were, that had existed between philosophy and mathematics ever since the Renaissance. This was not to be regarded merely as historical fact; it should be understood and explained as something necessary and inescapable.

This tendency was faithfully preserved, strengthened, and deepened by nineteenth-century science, though of course there were many, and prominent, investigators who were not only out of sympathy with it but actually saw serious danger in it. They wanted to restrict empirical science to

[1] See E. Cassirer, "Galilei," *Das Erkenntnisproblem* (Berlin, B. Cassirer, 1922), I, Zweites Buch, Kap. ii, 377 ff., and "Wahrheitsbegriff und Wahrheitsproblem bei Galilei," *Scientia,* LXII (1937), 121 ff., 185 ff.

[2] "Kepler," *op. cit.*

[3] Newton, Introduction, *Philosophiae naturalis principia mathematica,* Book III.

facts and thought it could most surely be done by avoiding all subtle epistemological reflection and speculation. But although this naïve realism
recommended itself to natural scientists as the only suitable way for them
to think, still it never succeeded in keeping them within the proposed limits. On the contrary, every advance into the world of new facts was accompanied by problems that appeared to be soluble only on the ground
of a theoretical analysis of knowledge, and it became increasingly clear
that this analysis was no mere supplementary task to be passed along to
philosophy after the conclusions of research had been reached. The questions to be answered had not been imposed upon natural science from
without but had arisen from within during the course of its own investigations. Empirical science itself would have to take them firmly and resolutely in hand if it meant to master them.

This is what actually happened and to an unprecedented degree. From
the middle of the nineteenth century onward the demand for reflective
criticism in the natural sciences was urged with ever mounting emphasis.
Works of an epistemological character occupy a significant place in
Helmholtz' writing,[4] and he himself maintained that critical examination
of the sources of knowledge is one of those philosophical tasks that no
generation can evade with impunity. Heinrich Hertz proved himself at
once a physicist and a disciple of Helmholtz by prefacing his book on the
principles of mechanics with a general discussion of the characteristic and
distinctive nature of scientific knowledge.

The necessity for such considerations had already been recognized
then in respect to the cosmology of classical physics, but it was felt far
more when this world view was unsettled by the crisis regarding funda-
mentals brought about through the general theory of relativity and the
development of the quantum theory. Then problems arose that had
never before been encountered, at least in the domain of natural science.
Heisenberg declared that the latest advances in atomic physics shatter all
belief "in the objective course of events in space and time, independent of
any observation," and said that physics will never return to this conviction in its original form, though it had been the heart of classical theory.

This poses a question that the great investigators of the seventeenth
and eighteenth centuries, Galileo and Kepler, Huyghens and Newton,
d'Alembert and Lagrange, not only had never raised but probably would
have regarded as inadmissible or impossible. Nevertheless it is evident
that physics, though it raises such a question, has in no way renounced
the idea of objective reality, nor has it succumbed to any sort of radical
skepticism. But just as little should there be any blurring of the line that

[4] See the collection of Helmholtz' articles on the theory of knowledge. *Hermann v.
Helmholtz Schriften zur Erkenntnistheorie*, hrsg. und erläutert von P. Hertz und M. Schlick
(Berlin, J. Springer, 1921).

separates the theory of knowledge from natural science. The "modern theories," Heisenberg expressly stated,

have not originated from revolutionary ideas brought into the exact sciences from without, so to speak; rather they are naturally forced upon science as it attempts to carry out logically the program of classical physics. . . . It is manifest that experimental investigation is always the necessary pre-condition of theoretical knowledge, and that significant progress is made only under pressure from the results of experiment, never through speculation. . . . The change that has come to pass in the foundations of exact science has been necessitated by experimental investigation." [5]

Limitation of space does not permit us here to follow in detail the course of these researches. Elsewhere [6] I have attempted to describe how they affected the establishment and systematization of the general theory of knowledge; hence I shall not return to the question here but merely select one definite problem that concerns not so much the content as the form of modern physics. For even in the conception of its form, too, a deep-seated change is encountered in the second half of the nineteenth century and the opening years of the twentieth. Now not only does the picture of nature show new features, but the view of what a natural science can and should be and the problems and aims it must set itself undergoes more and more radical transformation. In no earlier period do we meet such extensive argument over the very conception of physics, and in none is the debate so acrimonious. Even classical physics did not have this conception ready at hand; on the contrary, one of its first tasks had been to create the concept and then to defend it in constant battle with the Aristotelian-scholastic view. But this conflict was waged on a compact and united front in the conviction that reason and experience would be able to penetrate the nature of reality and progressively reveal it. The *ontological* significance of the physical theories was never seriously challenged, however widely these differed from each other in content.

In the nineteenth century, however, there came a sudden change. The realism of natural science was supplanted by a phenomenalism that disputed not only the possible existence of a solution but even the meaning of the problems that had been set up by physical thought. When Mach or Planck, Bolzmann or Ostwald, Poincaré or Duhem are asked what a physical theory is and what it can accomplish, we receive not only different but contradictory answers, and it is clear that we are witnessing more

[5] W. Heisenberg, *Wandlungen in den Grundlagen der Naturwissenschaft* (6. Aufl. Leipzig, S. Hirzel, 1945).
[6] For classical physics see *Substanzbegriff und Funktionsbegriff* (Berlin, B. Cassirer, 1910); for the special and general theory of relativity, *Zur Einstein'schen Relativitätstheorie* (same publisher, 1921); for the quantum theory, *Determinismus und Indeterminismus in der modernen Physik,* "Göteborgs Högskolas Årsskrift," XLII (1936), No. 3.

than a change in the purpose and intent of investigation. This new orientation in physics has slowly and steadily been brought to completion. Its logical consequences have been much less noted and emphasized than the concomitant revolution in the content of scientific ideas, in the concepts of space, time, and matter, and in the formulation of the law of causality.

Yet from the standpoint simply of the theory of knowledge the former development is hardly less consequential and pervasive than the latter, for it is always highly significant when a science, instead of directly and resolutely seeking its object, suddenly deserts this "natural" attitude for another; when it feels compelled to inquire into the nature of its object and into its own concept, and into the very possibility of the science itself. At such turning points in research it is clear that reflection gains a wholly different status and must be conceded a much more important role in the upbuilding of science than during more naïve periods. Indeed, the earlier ingenuous attitude had been lost beyond recall when this period of development came to a close; no great investigator any longer tries to evade the questions that here press upon him or to refer them to the court of "philosophical thinking." Everyone has to decide them independently, and his general conclusions almost always bear the stamp of his own scientific principles as well as that of his concrete research.

In the eighteenth century and until the middle of the nineteenth there was no serious doubt but that the ideal of knowledge to which physics was pledged once for all was the ideal of Newtonian science. Its fundamental concepts, which had been exposed to such grave doubts when they were first introduced, had not only lost more and more of their paradoxical character but were regarded as essential to any accurate understanding of nature, and there was a universal and prevailing effort to transfer to all other fields the type of thinking that Newton had made so influential in mechanics. At first it had seemed as if natural phenomena promised to conform to this expectation the more fully and exactly they were understood. They appeared to arrange themselves without difficulty in the general scheme set up by Newton in his theory of gravitation. Yet internal friction was never lacking throughout this development. In the field of thermodynamics the explanations connected with the second law of the theory of heat and with the idea of entropy led more and more constantly to the view of the distinction between reversible and irreversible processes as a basic feature in all natural events which cannot possibly be eliminated. Planck said, in his Leyden Lecture of 1908,[7] that this distinction, with better right than any other, could be made a pre-eminent basis for the classification of all physical phenomena and might eventually play the chief role in any cosmology of the physics of the future. Likewise

[7] M. Planck, "Die Einheit des physikalischen Weltbildes," *Wege zur physikalischen Erkenntnis* (2. Aufl. Leipzig, S. Hirzel, 1934), S. 7 ff.

in the development of the theory of electricity, the Faraday-Maxwell field concept, which was steadily proving itself a true and indispensable instrument of knowledge, stood in sharp contrast at the outset with the Newtonian idea of force. Yet, on the other hand, the form taken by Coulomb's law of magnetic and electrical phenomena seemed to show a perfect correspondence between them and the phenomena of gravitation, so that even in this realm the concept of "action at a distance" might assert its claims.

Thus it appeared not only permissible but obligatory to put this concept of force at the center of all interpretations of nature. This was most plainly and decisively done in the introductory observations of Helmholtz in the first formulation of the law of the conservation of energy. Here Newton's action at a distance was not only recognized as valid for the field in which it had been discovered but elevated to the dignity of a general axiom for the understanding of nature. All operations in nature are to be traced to attractive and repulsive forces, whose intensity depends only upon the distance between the mutually interacting points, for only thus is it possible to give full validity to the highest law of scientific investigation, the law of causality. The demand for a consistent explanation of events is never satisfied so long as we have not penetrated to the ultimate causes which operate according to an immutable law and therefore produce the same effect at all times and under the same external conditions.

The appointed . . . task of physics is thus to refer natural phenomena to unchangeable attractive and repulsive forces, whose intensity depends upon distance. The solution of this problem is at the same time the prerequisite for a thorough understanding of nature. . . . So if theoretical science is not to stop halfway on the road to comprehension, it must bring its views into accord with the postulates set up regarding the nature of the simple forces and their consequences. The work of science will have been completed only when phenomena have been traced back to the simple forces and when it can be shown also that the given account is the only possible one admitted by the phenomena. Then this would have been proven to be the necessary way of interpreting nature, and it would be the one to which objective truth should be ascribed.[8]

If this program, advanced by Helmholtz in the middle of the nineteenth century, could have been realized, it would have furnished a cosmology that would have been equally satisfying from both empirical and epistemological standpoints. Of course it would have been necessary to put up with the absurdity that seemed to reside in the idea of action at a distance, but once the idea was accepted for this purpose an extremely

[8] Helmholtz, Einleitung, *Über die Erhaltung der Kraft*, Ostwald's "Klassiker der exakten Wissenschaften" (Leipzig, W. Engelmann, 1889), I, 6 f.

simple and self-consistent system of physics would have been attained. All the complexity and all the qualitative differences of natural phenomena would have been brought ideally under one common head.

It was easy to overlook the fact that this simplicity had been merely postulated, not empirically proved. As far as the popular materialism was concerned, there were no scruples of that sort to hinder its constructions and proofs, for it had apparently grown out of natural science, though in truth it was actually but a remnant and later offshoot of dogmatic metaphysics. We need not go into the materialistic controversy here as it raged in the second half of the nineteenth century. Its origin and historical development have been exhaustively described by Friedrich Albert Lange.[9] Most of the doctrines that he analyzed so minutely, however, have left no permanent trace in either scientific or philosophical thought. Neither the opponents nor the defenders of materialism were theoretically equipped for the battle they attempted to fight. Often both thesis and antithesis stood on the same ground. How thoroughly skepticism and dogmatism were permeated by the same spirit is seen especially in the sort of criticism and refutation of materialism found in du Bois-Reymond, which could not help at every turn affirming implicitly just what it seemed explicitly to oppose and deny. Du Bois-Reymond meant to show the objective limits set for all knowledge of nature and to prove that there are definite realms of being that this knowledge can never penetrate, realms which remain world riddles, and for which not *ignoramus,* "we do not know," but *ignorabimus,* "we never shall know," are the right dicta.[10]

The sole basis for this assertion, however, is the assumption that mechanism represents the sole trustworthy and possible route to understanding and that outside it there can be no salvation for natural science. Still far in the future lay the notion that the questions of science itself could ever compel a transformation of the mechanistic cosmology. Even the more rigorous thinking of philosophy yielded place to this idea slowly and with reluctance. At first philosophers sought to follow the same path as Helmholtz and held that a complete and adequate understanding of nature could be reached only through an explanation of its mechanism, but then they wanted to establish the special position and pre-eminence of this sort of explanation on a priori and not solely empirical grounds. For this there was nothing else to do but define and form the general concept of cause in such a way that all natural phenomena would necessarily be reduced to pure phenomena of motion. This tendency appears most clearly in Wilhelm Wundt's *The Axioms of Physical Science and Their*

[9] F. A. Lange, *Geschichte des Materialismus* (Leipzig, J. Baedeker, 1887).
[10] E. du Bois-Reymond, *Über die Grenzen des Naturerkennens: Die sieben Welträthsel* (3. Aufl. Leipzig, Velt & Co., 1891).

Relation to the Causal Principle (1866). A comparison of his train of thought with the introductory remarks in Helmholtz' treatise on the conservation of energy shows how science, austere and aloof from the popular catchwords of the quarrel over materialism, conceived the problem. Wundt's book alone suffices for an insight into the deeper epistemological motives that underlay adherence to the mechanistic explanation of nature.

As the first of his six axioms of physics Wundt formulated the proposition that all cause in nature is concerned with motion. This theorem, to be sure, cannot be derived immediately from experience, which seems rather to contradict it, since all changes in objects that are open to direct observation have to do with their perceptible qualities, and as such these present an irreducible complexity and variability. Were we entirely dependent on the information furnished by our senses, therefore, every change in nature would have to be described by the statement that an object, that is, a collection of perceptible characteristics, had disappeared and that another object with qualities partly different had taken its place. That we do not stop here in our *scientific* interpretation of nature, but can refer the event to a fixed substrate and say that the identity of the object has been preserved during its various modifications, is not because of experience but primarily because of reflection over the evidence given by our senses. In this first step beyond mere observation all the following ones are implicitly included and from it they can be logically developed. The principle of identity—understood as a physical not as a logical principle —compels a transition to the mechanistic view and shows how this is not a fortuitous but a necessary factor in all our interpretations of nature.

Observation forces us to assume two objects, whereas thought will admit but one . . . The struggle would be endless were it not terminated by observation itself. There is one single case where an object does change before our eyes and yet still remains the same, and this is the case of motion. Here the change consists merely in alteration of an object's spatial relationships to other objects. Thus a difference in position is the only imaginable change in objects during which they remain identical.

If we would be saved from a flood of experiences or from Heraclitus' river of becoming, without consequent denial of becoming itself and a retreat to the motionless being of Parmenides, there remains but one escape: "We must trace every change back to the only conceivable one in which an object remains identical: motion." [11]

[11] W. Wundt, *Die physikalischen Axiome und ihre Beziehung zum Causalprinzip. Ein Kapitel aus einer Philosophie der Naturwissenschaft* (Erlangen, 1866), S. 125 ff.; and *Die Prinzipien der mechanischen Naturlehre* (2. ungeänd. Aufl. Stuttgart, F. Enke, 1910), S. 178 ff.

Here was a sort of transcendental deduction of the mechanistic view of nature that might have seemed highly satisfactory and convincing at first glance, since this explanation appeared to flow as a simple corollary from the chief fundamental concepts of all natural science: those of matter and causality. Grave doubts over its validity could not arise until scientific thinking ventured to undermine these basic ideas and until it broadened its criticism to include the ideas of matter and cause themselves, which lay at the very roots of classical physics. But such a venture was possible, of course, only when experience itself prompted and even demanded it.

In Planck's lecture before the Königsberg meeting of the Deutscher Verein Naturforscher und Ärzte in 1910, he described the various historical stages of this process, tracing the particular empirical motives that had compelled physics to change its attitude toward the mechanistic view and placing in the foreground the problem concerning the mechanics of the luminiferous ether. The more exactly its nature seemed to be understood, the more had it proved to be the "truly woebegotten child of the mechanistic view." For while the existence of a material luminiferous ether is a postulate of the view, the behavior of the ether certainly contrasts very strangely with that of all other known matter. Every barely imaginable suggestion and combination had been exhausted in an effort to establish its constitution until finally, after all endeavors had failed, a change in the whole intellectual orientation was effected and investigators began to submit to critical proof the assumption of its existence instead of continuing to examine into its nature. No longer did they ask about the constitution, the density, the elastic properties of the ether, or about its longitudinal waves, and so forth; they began to inquire what relations must subsist among the forces of nature when one says it is impossible to demonstrate any of the properties of matter in the luminiferous ether, and to wonder whether on general principles the ether would have to be denied that material substantiality and identity which earlier theory had to assume.[12]

But however impressive and decisive all these empirical considerations were, they might not have sufficed alone to shake the firmly constructed edifice of the mechanistic theory without the aid of other motives, which originated in purely methodological opinions on the scientific character of mechanics itself. Gustav Kirchhoff had already abandoned all claims that the mechanistic view could furnish an explanation of natural phenomena. He saw as its goal and object merely a complete description of the motions occurring in nature, given in the simplest possible fashion. His definition played an important role in theoretical discussions of the

[12] For further details see M. Planck, *Die Stellung der neueren Physik zur mechanischen Naturanschauung* (Leipzig, S. Hirzel, 1910): see also *Physikalische Rundblicke* (Leipzig, 1922), S. 38 ff.

concept and task of natural science.[13] It was regarded as a significant innovation, and many experimentalists and thinkers regarded it as a complete break with the tradition of classical physics.[14] From a purely historical standpoint, however, such a belief was hardly justified, since even in the debates about the Newtonian theory of action at a distance a similar definition had been reached. The first followers of Newton had disarmed criticism by saying that theoretical physics had no business to offer an explanation of the inner possibility of happenings in nature and that in this matter only a description should be striven for and attained.[15]

The decisive feature in Kirchhoff's definition, however, lies in another quarter. There had been no doubt in the eighteenth and nineteenth centuries that there is a sort of hierarchy of existence, which science must trace and copy in its structure of knowledge. In his Preface to the *Encyclopédie* and his *Elements de philosophie,* d'Alembert sketched this hierarchy from the simplest to the most complex phenomena. Beginning with logic, it proceeded to algebra and geometry, and finally reached in mechanics the first science of reality. That all other branches of natural science—astronomy, optics, hydrostatics, and empirical physics in its entirety —were erected on this foundation and wholly dependent on it for their validity was thought to be beyond dispute. But just toward the end of the nineteenth century serious doubts respecting this notion began to arise, because of the new problems with which physics was faced in thermodynamics, in optics, and in the theory of electricity. Is there really such a firmly established "lower" and "higher" in the order of natural events, and is it so certain that the only secure base for this imaginary pyramid is mechanics? If the task of theoretical physics is not to settle the nature of things; if it must be satisfied instead with description, with a systematic classification of phenomena, at least it is not restricted either in its methods or in the path that it may pursue. Here is no unilateral relationship of dependence as in the connection between "cause" and "effect"; no logical "earlier" or "later." On the contrary, pure correlation rules, whose simplest expression is to be found in the mathematical concept of "function." Once the physicist's idea of force has been recognized as merely a special case of the function concept, all necessity disappears of conceding to mechanical forces any sort of exceptional position, and there is no need to treat the phenomena of motion as "better understood," or "simpler," than any other phenomena.

This line of thought could be pursued in two different directions ac-

[13] G. Kirchhoff, *Vorlesungen über mathematische Physik* (2. Aufl. Leipzig, B. G. Teubner, 1877), I, 1.

[14] K. Pearson, "Cause and Effect—Probability," *The Grammar of Science* (2d ed. London, Adam and Charles Black, 1900), chap. iv, pp. 113 ff.

[15] For other examples see Cassirer, *Das Erkenntnisproblem,* II, 404 ff.

cording to the particular concept of knowledge and reality from which one started. Scientific phenomenalism takes it for granted first that all reality with which natural science has to do is nothing but sensory reality. The *esse est percipi,* "to exist is to be perceived," is here the obvious point of departure. What would be the relationship of physics to mechanics on this assumption and if one explains accordingly that color, sound, heat, pressure, space, time, and so on, as immediately experienced by the senses, are the true and only objects of physics, whose task is consequently nothing else but studying the manifold ways in which these elementary data are associated? The answer to this question was what Mach set out to give in his theory of knowledge. This is strikingly apparent even in one of his earliest works, in which there was already a fully developed program that he consistently held to and extended in his later writings.[16] What distinguishes his analysis and lends it a special significance at the outset is the fact that it stressed emphatically the difference between the claim to give a causal interpretation of nature and the postulate of the mechanistic view. We have seen that the boundary line between these two questions was obliterated by Helmholtz as well as by Wundt, both of whom endeavored simply to derive the axioms of mechanics from the general principle of causality. The aim of Mach's inquiry was to show why any such attempt must remain forever fruitless. The law of causality demands nothing more than certainty and determinateness in what happens; it says nothing, however, about one realm of events being in principle of a higher order than all others. Hence it is absolutely impossible to prove that all strict and actual causality must be of mechanical nature.

If there is any proposition in physics directly connected with the general principle of causality, as representing in a measure a concrete expression of it, this very general proposition alone is the one in question, viz., that work cannot be obtained from nothing, and not the other proposition that all causes in nature are mechanical ones. This principle of the conservation of energy, that is to say, the conviction that so-called perpetual motion is impossible, must indeed be deeply rooted, for it can be shown to have colored the thought of mankind long before it was explicitly formulated by science. This fact Mach endeavored to prove by examples from the history of mechanics, especially by the way in which the law of the lever and the fundamental laws of hydrostatics were deduced and formulated by Archimedes and Stevinus.

At first glance it may appear very surprising that the whole argument should have then assumed a very different character—that its center of gravity should have shifted from the systematic to the historical problem. But Mach took this step with full awareness of its implications and with-

[16] See the early lecture, *Die Geschichte und die Wurzel des Satzes von der Erhaltung der Arbeit* (Prag, J. G. Calve, 1872), S. 27.

out relinquishing in the least his general theoretical convictions. "There is a special classical education for the student of nature," he wrote, "which comprises a knowledge of the history of his science. Let us not lose track of the guiding hand of history. It has made everything and can change everything."

Here speaks an adherent of the modern theory of evolution, who is convinced that there can be no such thing as truth in itself. What a given proposition means and is, and how far it is objectively valid, can be determined only by tracing its origin and development. All truths, the logical and mathematical as well as the physical, have had their beginning and their growth, and none of them can advance the claim to be superior to and untouched by the stream of time as an "eternal truth." Every abstract theory has its roots in primitive and instinctive experiences which have forced themselves upon man in daily intercourse with his environment and which become more impressive throughout the centuries. From such beginnings, from the disappointment repeatedly suffered in consequence of attempts to get work out of nothing, man learned that perpetual motion is impossible. This persuasion cannot be grounded in mechanics, for it was felt long before the science had been developed. Tracing this sentiment and its origin back through history, we come to the real root of physical principles and discover at the same time why these principles have nothing to do with any sort of reflection on the nature and ultimate grounds of natural occurrences. Reflective thought and abstraction come only at the end, never at the beginning of science. They merely combine into formulas the precise results from thousands and thousands of single cases. Hence it is dangerous to base all physics on a mechanistic view and set this up as an axiom of the science. For whatever one may think of its value, it is a relatively late product after all, with no direct logical evidence in its favor, and it owes its plausibility to purely empirical, and to this extent accidental, factors. Mechanics is concerned with the physical world, that is, with what is given us in visible and tangible qualities, but we are not entitled, and nothing compels us, to give this series of qualities any privileged position in our cosmology. No such distinction is recognized in immediate experience, where qualities of all sorts intermingle and are seen to be indissolubly blended. There are other sensory perceptions entirely analogous with that of space, wrote Mach: the series of sounds, which corresponds to a space of one dimension. As a phenomenon it is exactly similar to the order of qualities that are seen or felt, and thus there is no reason, unless undemonstrable metaphysical assumptions are introduced, why it should not be given the same ontological value as the other. Yet we do not in fact think of everything as sound and represent molecular phenomena in terms of musical pitch or tonal relationships, though we have as much right to do so as to think of them in terms of space.[17]

The only safe course here is to remain within the ambit of appearances themselves and describe them simply as they present themselves, without seeking groundless explanations. Physics recognizes only the dependence of phenomena upon one another, and this can be established directly without any circuitous interpretations or hypothetical substratum. Even space and time require no special form of intuition for their defining; on the contrary, they can be reduced purely to determinations of content alone which in no way transcend sensory items like color, sound, and pressure.

As we recognize what we call time and space only through certain phenomena, spatial and temporal determinations are achieved only by way of other phenomena. When, for example, we express the positions of the heavenly bodies as functions of time, that is, of the earth's angle of rotation, we have merely found out that these positions depend upon one another . . . The same is true of space. We know the situation with respect to space through an effect on the retina, on our optical or other means of comparison, and actually the x, y, and z in the equations of physics are no more than convenient terms for these effects. Thus spatial determinations are also determinations of some phenomena through other phenomena. The present effort of physics is directed toward representing every phenomenon as a function of other phenomena and certain positions in time and space. If in the equations above we make substitutions in this fashion for the temporal and spatial positions, we have the result simply that every phenomenon is a function of other phenomena.[18]

Here we reach the point of view that Mach later called phenomenological physics, in contrast to mechanistic physics.[19] The science seems to have entered upon a new phase in its theoretical development, a phase that has often been regarded not only as a significant step forward but as a final and conclusive one. Yet one opponent after another has appeared, even within physics itself. Noted investigators like Boltzmann and Planck have rejected it vigorously, seeing in it an unjustifiable restriction of the concept of physical knowledge.[20] It may be said however that in one respect the new interpretation far surpassed the views that had ruled physics for so long and influenced its whole development. Mach might well have boasted that his elimination of the metaphysical idea of matter

[17] Mach, loc. cit.

[18] Ibid., S. 34 f.

[19] Mach, "Der Gegensatz zwischen der mechanischen und der phänomenologischen Physik," Die Prinzipien der Wärmelehre (Leipzig, J. A. Barth, 1896), S. 362 ff.

[20] L. Boltzmann, "Über die Unentbehrlichkeit der Atomistik in der Naturwissenschaft," Populäre Schriften (Leipzig, J. A. Barth, 1905), S. 141 ff. Planck, "Die Einheit des physikalischen Weltbildes," op. cit., S. 1 ff.

had freed the science of a long series of imaginary problems. He explained that the only real constant in things is the set of definite equations or relations, so that if actual substantiality is to be ascribed to any element of experience it must be ascribed to these constant relations. But then it will be necessary to expel all the naïve ideas of matter with which this concept has been commonly associated throughout the history of physics.[21]

In the first half of the eighteenth century these naïve ideas had not yet lost any of their force. For every separate class of phenomena a special material agent was assumed, and the number of these "imponderables" increased more and more. In addition to material light and material heat, magnetic and electrical matter was recognized. The theory of electricity had to struggle longest with this sort of notion and reached full scientific stature only after it had taken strides forward to emancipate itself. Whereas Franklin believed that one highly tenuous substance, which is distributed throughout all nature, is responsible for electrical phenomena, it was necessary later to postulate two different substances of opposite polarity in order to reconcile the facts of positive and negative electricity. The conflict between the one-fluid and the two-fluid theory lasted for many years without either side realizing the hypothetical nature of the electrical substance.[22] Sir Oliver Lodge, for example, continued to ascribe complete physical reality to it. Electrical waves, he declared, must be "waves of something," and the existence of this something was as certain as that of any physical object. "The evidence for the ether is as strong as the evidence for the air." [23]

It was this sort of thinking that Mach opposed so incessantly, hoping to strike it down by his criticism, but he was thereby driven far beyond his proper methodological goal, for his theory of knowledge recognized only one dimension of reality, that of the simple data of the senses such as colors, sounds, odors, and so on. These were the essential components out of which reality is built, and behind these elements no others were to be sought. Thus all that went beyond the establishment of sensory facts incurred the suspicion of "transcendence," and a sharp dividing line could no longer be drawn between the assumptions of physical theory and those of metaphysics. The obliteration of this boundary, especially striking in Mach's criticism of atomic theory, robbed his opinion of the greater part of its fertility. Boltzmann [24] rightly objected that he had not protested in the name of metaphysics or speculative natural philosophy against the re-

---

[21] Mach, "Der Substanzbegriff," *op. cit.*, S. 422 ff.

[22] For details see Rosenberger, *Die Moderne Entwicklung der elektrischen Prinzipien* (Leipzig, 1898).

[23] O. Lodge, *The Ether of Space* (London and New York, Harper & Bros., 1909), pp. 17 ff.

[24] L. Boltzmann, "Ein Wort der Mathematik an die Energetik," *Populäre Schriften*, S. 104 ff.

striction demanded by such phenomenological physics, but in the name of mathematics. As a matter of fact it was an extraordinary blunder, from an epistemological as well as a historical standpoint, for Mach to call modern atomic theory an attempt "to make a notion as thoroughly naïve and crude as that which holds matter to be absolutely unchanging the fundamental tenet of physics." [25] Even the atomism of antiquity was far removed from such naïveté, since it was in fact a sharp criticism of sense perception upon which this atomism was based and which was its starting point.[26]

Mach's restriction of phenomenological physics could be the more easily overlooked, however, since in other respects it was undeniably characterized by great methodological fertility. It freed physics of the burden of imponderables and limited its task to a knowledge of the laws associated with natural events. It did not have to depend upon definite ideas of substance for an exact formulation of these laws: the permanence of relations replaced the permanence of matter. In this connection the discovery of the principle of conservation of energy was an important circumstance; furthermore, in a purely methodological respect it represented a turning point in physical theory. Whereas Humboldt still continued to associate this principle directly with the mechanistic view of nature and endeavored to deduce it therefrom, Robert Mayer chose another path. He saw in the equivalence between heat and mechanical energy the nucleus of the principle, but had no intention of interpreting that as an identity. He wanted explicitly to leave out of consideration any question as to the nature of heat. All that is known with certainty, he believed, is merely that heat, motion, and kinetic energy can be converted one into the other in conformity with fixed numerical relationships; but there was reluctance to infer from this that kinetic energy and motion are identical, and no less reluctance in drawing a similar conclusion for heat. Thus Mayer was well justified in distinguishing sharply between his theory and all hypotheses of natural philosophy. "It would certainly have to be called a backward step," he wrote, "if an attempt were to be made to construct a world a priori. But when one has succeeded in connecting the innumerable events of nature with each other and deriving a supreme principle therefrom, then it is no ground for reproach if, after this has been carefully tested, it is used as a sort of compass to guide the investigator safely forth on the sea of particulars." [27]

[25] Mach, *op. cit.,* S. 428.

[26] On the epistemological assumptions in the atomism of antiquity see P. Natorp, "Demokrit," *Forschungen zur Geschichte des Erkenntnisproblems im Altartum* (Berlin, W. Hertz, 1884), S. 164 ff.

[27] R. Mayer, "Die organische Bewegung in ihrem Zusammenhange mit dem Stoffwechsel," *Die Mechanik der Wärme,* Zwei Abhandlungen (Leipzig, W. Engelmann, 1911), S. 9 ff.

These remarks by a discoverer of the law of conservation of energy foreshadow clearly and precisely the trend of philosophical thought that was later to bring the new science of energetics into general recognition and acceptance. At first glance the vehemence of its struggle with mechanics during the last decades of the nineteenth century is astonishing, for when the law of the conservation of energy is considered only as to content, it is found to hold nothing that would fall outside the views of mechanics or radically contradict them. This, the first law of thermodynamics, did not constitute the same difficulty for the mechanical view of nature as was the case with the second law and the idea of irreversible phenomena which followed from it. Historically, too, the law of the conservation of energy developed out of the principle of the conservation of kinetic energy as formulated in mechanics by Huyghens and Leibniz. Thus there was no real opposition between the assertions of energetics and those of mechanics, and it would have been just as reasonable to make the law of the conservation of energy supreme and deduce from it the mechanical axioms of the conservation of energy as, conversely, to make the mechanical view a basis for deducing the law of the conservation of energy. Planck chose the former course, expressly emphasizing, however, that the rights of the second were by no means to be gainsaid thereby.[28]

But toward the end of the century the situation underwent a complete change. After Ostwald's lecture at Lübeck in 1895,[29] the conflict between mechanics and energetics was waged with a vigor that seemed to exclude any chance of reconciliation between these two fundamental views. Both parties believed not only that they were in possession of scientific truth but that they were defending the only possible and solely justifiable concept of science.

"In the Lübeck controversy of 1895," says Georg Helm, who described thoroughly all its various phases,

the question was not really about atomism or about the plenum or about discrepancies in thermodynamics or about the grounding of mechanics upon energetics, for these were all mere details. In the final analysis it was about the principles of our knowledge of nature. Opposing the omnipotence claimed by the mechanistic method of reproducing experience there appears a new procedure that allows of far more immediate description yet at the same time attains the generality of concept which is indispensable for every useful theoretical interpretation of nature. If one regards energetics as having such a broad scope (and that is the only way one can do justice to what it is trying to do), the deci-

[28] M. Planck, *Das Prinzip der Erhaltung der Energie* (Leipzig, B. G. Teubner, 1887), S. 135 ff.

[29] W. Ostwald, *Die Überwindung des wissenschaftlichen Materialismus* (Leipzig, Veit & Co., 1895).

sion is easy. The choice is simply between scholasticism on the one hand and energetics on the other.[30]

Not since the controversies over the validity of Newton's idea of force acting at a distance had minds been so engaged and agitated by a dispute over method. The very manner in which the battle was waged makes it clear that it was not primarily concerned with empirical results, since there was no difference of opinion between the two sides in respect to the authenticity and fundamental significance of the law of conservation of energy. Instead there was the feeling in both camps, just as in the polemic between Leibniz and Newton, that it was again a matter of principle; the argument was over definitions of the concept and the task of scientific knowledge.

There were prominent investigators who took their stand with classical mechanics, and who were convinced like Huyghens that one must either explain a phenomenon on mechanical grounds or abandon once for all any hope of understanding it. Energetics made this mode of apprehension wholly inadequate and inadmissible. Ostwald's lecture on the conquest of scientific materialism introduced a real iconoclasm, whose first commandment was: "Thou shalt not make unto thee any graven image, or any likeness of anything. . . ."[31]

In order to understand this opposition it is necessary to go back to its roots in the theory of knowledge. The conflict was essentially between two different motives, each one indispensable in the construction of the edifice of scientific knowledge. The exclusion of either was not to be thought of, though there was room for argument as to which should be accorded the central position and real supremacy. At times the concept of space, at other times the concept of number, took the lead. Galileo said that truth lies open before us in the great book of nature, but that only those can find it who are familiar with the characters in which it is inscribed. These are of a geometrical kind: lines and angles, triangles, circles, and other figures. No natural process can be understood unless it can be expressed geometrically. In modern philosophy this ideal of knowledge had received its logical justification. In Descartes it was the idea of extension that possessed the character, above all other ideas, of being clear and distinct. The physical object must be completely reducible to spatial determinations if any exact knowledge of it is ever to become possible. Matter was thus transformed and taken up into space, and all changes in it had to be traced back to purely spatial changes. Geometry and mechanics were accordingly declared the true and only foundation for physics, an idea

[30] G. Helm, *Die Energetik nach ihrer geschichtlichen Entwicklung* (Leipzig, Veit & Co., 1898), S. 366.
[31] Ostwald, *op. cit.,* S. 22.

that remained in almost full force until the middle of the nineteenth century. Then, however, an intellectual movement set in that may be compared in a way with the arithmetization of mathematics, which occurred at the same time.[32] The center of gravity of theoretical scientific knowledge began to shift, number taking the position formerly conceded to space, which made the previous mechanistic schemata of doubtful value. Ought it not to be possible to determine natural phenomena mathematically without such schemata and thus to gain a rigorous knowledge of them? Robert Mayer had already asked this question and answered it in the affirmative. He explained that it was enough to connect the different natural processes with one another without changing them qualitatively and thus abolishing their obvious dissimilarities, but yet in such a way that the connection would be subject to general quantitative rules and that the transition from one province to another would occur always according to fixed and constant numerical relationships. The ascertaining of these numerical equivalents would then be the sole aim of the empirical interpretation of nature, and all beyond that would be at best only a work of supererogation. Once strict numerical relationships have been discovered between the various classes of natural phenomena, all that can be expected and demanded of knowledge has been attained, and over and above this we cannot go. "Precise delimitation of the natural limits of human inquiry is an end that has practical value for science, whereas the attempt to penetrate by hypotheses to the inner recesses of the world order is of a piece with the efforts of the alchemists." All our reliable and established knowledge of natural events is contained in our mathematical knowledge: "One single number has more real and permanent value than an expensive library of hypotheses."[33]

In its further advance energetics held to this view and endeavored consistently to broaden it. With Rankine, who was the first to speak of a science of energetics, its development from the standpoint of the theory of knowledge was already in view. He emphasized that research in physics could set up a twofold goal and strike out into one of two paths. Either it could try to get behind events and discover their underlying substratum or remain content with a classification of appearances in order to determine solely their common factors and the fixed relationships between them. The second plan appeared preferable from a methodological standpoint, since it did not involve the necessity of leaving the firm ground of experience and introducing assumptions that could not be proved. Instead of attributing the various kinds of physical phenomena to motions and forces no instances of which are ever given but which are merely in-

[32] Cassirer, *op. cit.*, Chap. IV, p. 59.
[33] R. Mayer, "Mayer an Griesinger," *Kleinere Schriften und Briefe* (Stuttgart, J. G. Cotta'schen Buchhandlung, 1893), S. 222 ff.

ferred, it would suffice to stop at simple comparison and eventually reach principles that hold equally for all cases and so represent the ultimate discoverable relationship between facts.[34] In such statements Rankine had no intention of disputing the mechanistic view of nature as a whole; indeed he himself even set up a definitely mechanistic hypothesis on the intrinsic nature of bodies.[35] But though he did not deny himself such hypotheses, he wanted to define their limits more sharply than they had been set in the past. The later development went far beyond this view, and it was thought finally possible to build up a natural science which would be wholly free of hypotheses. But not all the proponents of energetics could hold strictly to this position. Helm rejected with decision the idea that energy is an indestructible substance shifting from place to place and declared such a notion entirely useless and unwarranted, since energy is never more than an expression of relationships. "For general theoretical physics," he emphatically stated,

there exist neither atoms, nor energy, nor any kind of similar concept, but only those experiences immediately derived from direct observation. Therefore I believe the most valuable feature of energetics to be that it is far better able than the older theories to adapt itself straightway to experience, and I see in attempts to attribute substantial existence to energy a hazardous departure from the original clarity of Robert Mayer's views.[36]

But other noted champions of energetics were much less cautious here. Ostwald often spoke of energy as though it were to be taken not only as *an* actuality but as *the* actuality, the thing of things and the source of all dynamic effect. Even in this respect he would not place it over matter, of which we never have a direct but only an indirect knowledge, whereas of energy we have direct perception.

What we hear originates in work done on the ear drum and the middle ear by vibrations of the air. What we see is only radiant energy, which does chemical work on the retina that is perceived as light. When we touch a solid body we experience mechanical work performed during compression of our finger tips and, in suitable cases, of the solid body itself. . . . From this standpoint the totality of nature appears as a series of spatially and temporally changing energies, of which we obtain knowledge in proportion as they impinge upon the body and especially upon the sense organs fashioned for the reception of the appropriate energies.[37]

[34] W. J. M. Rankine, "Outlines of the Science of Energetics," *Miscellaneous Scientific Papers, Proceedings of the Philosophical Society of Glasgow*, III (London, C. Griffin & Co., 1881), No. 4 (1855), 209.

[35] For details see Helm, *op. cit.*, S. 110 ff.

For Rankine's place in the history of energetics see A. Rey, "L'Energétique de Rankine," *La Théorie de la physique chez les physiciens contemporains* (Paris, F. Alcan, 1907), II, chap. i, 49 ff.

[36] Helm, *op. cit.*, S. 362.

[37] Ostwald, *Vorlesungen über Naturphilosophie* (Leipzig, Veit & Co., 1902), S. 159 f.

In our representation of the role of energetics and phenomenological physics as a whole in the theory of knowledge of the nineteenth century there appear, apart from differences among individual thinkers in developing their fundamental ideas, some positive accomplishments and also some obvious limitations in them. The fruitfulness of the movement lay, above all, in resolutely dispensing with all ontological elements in physics. The metaphysical idea of substance was attacked in all its various forms, and the scientific object was resolved into a system of relations and functional connections.[38] In this respect J. B. Stallo's book, *The Concepts and Theories of Modern Physics,* published in 1881, was of special importance. The German edition was introduced with a preface by Mach, who praised the work because it had recognized and definitely removed the scholastic, metaphysical elements that still clung to the older physics.[39] Of course Stallo did not stop here, but on the strength of his theoretical convictions furiously attacked certain empirical theories besides, such as the kinetic theory of gases and the entire theory of the atomic constitution of matter, professing to see even in these nothing but a hidden metaphysics. This onslaught was possible only because Stallo had slipped imperceptibly from logical criticism of the concept of substance to an entirely different problem. In his attempt to be a consistent empiricist he became a psychologist who strove to confine physics to the realm of "phenomena of consciousness." His own thesis of the relativity of all knowledge attained thereby a wholly different character. The proposition that "objects and their properties are known only as functions of other objects and properties," and that in this sense relativity is necessarily predicated of all objects of knowledge, was transformed into this other, quite distinct, proposition, that what is present in the mind in the act of thinking is never a thing but always a state of consciousness, and so, in the final analysis, even physics has to do only with the description and classification of such states of consciousness.[40] This psychologism is the hereditary malady, so to speak, of all "phenomenological physics": the phenomenon, in the sense of the object of physical knowledge, is resolved into a series of elements and states of consciousness.

There was nothing original in the idea that an object is nothing absolute but consists entirely of relationships: The *Critique of Pure Reason* had enforced the point again and again and with the strongest possible emphasis. "Matter," said Kant,

is *substantia phaenomenon.* Whatever is intrinsic to it I seek in all parts of the space that it occupies and in all effects that it exerts, which, after all, can never

---

[38] For details see Cassirer, *Substanzbegriff und Funktionsbegriff,* chap. iv.

[39] J. B. Stallo, *Die Begriffe und Theorien der modernen Physik* (Leipzig, J. A. Barth, 1911), S. xii.

[40] Stallo, *ibid.,* Kap. ix, S. 126 ff.

be anything but phenomena of the outer sense. Thus I have nothing absolute but merely something comparatively internal which, in its turn, consists only of external relationships. But what appears to the mere understanding as the absolute essence of matter is again simply a fancy, for matter is never an object of pure understanding; but the transcendental object that may be the ground of this appearance called matter is a bare Something, whose nature we should never be able to understand even though someone could tell us about it. . . . The observation and analysis of phenomena press toward a knowledge of the secrets of nature, and there is no knowing how far they may penetrate in time. But for all that we shall never succeed in answering those transcendental questions that reach out beyond nature, though all nature were to be revealed to our gaze.[41]

In respect to the exclusion of these transcendental questions, phenomenalistic physics took exactly the same position as the critical philosophy of Kant. The difference between them is not the thesis of the relativity of knowledge but the way in which physics seeks to establish this thesis. The foundations of the phenomenalism ultimately go back not to the logic of physics but to anthropological and psychological considerations, which appeared to demand that what we call an object of knowledge be reducible to an aggregate of simple sense data, a mere "bundle of perceptions." For Kant, however, the object, even when understood as object of "appearance," was never such a "rhapsody of perceptions." It depended rather upon a "synthesis" into which the pure concepts of the understanding entered as necessary conditions.

But in trying to eliminate even these conditioning factors and to make of physical experience a mass of sense data, the chief defenders of energetics became more and more deeply involved in contradictions. The underlying reason was that Mach and other champions of energetics, while attacking mechanism in physics, still remained wholly in bondage to its assumptions so far as their psychology was concerned. It was and remained a psychology of elements. It was only Gestalt psychology that caused any change in this respect, by virtue of the concept of "wholeness" (*Ganzheit*), which when it gained acceptance in physics as well as in psychology placed the two sciences in a new relationship.[42] Before this clarification came to pass, the phenomenalistic view was in constant peril of being limited by its sensationalistic concept of physical knowledge. This danger was especially apparent in criticisms of the atomic idea, which was regarded with the most profound distrust at best as a purely fictitious and auxiliary hypothesis that must be dispensed with as speedily as possible once its service had been rendered. The escape from such a narrow sensationalistic system was not due to considerations of the theory of

[41] Kant, *Kritik der reinen Vernunft* (2. Aufl.), S. 888 f.

[42] See Wolfgang Köhler, *Die physischen Gesialten in Ruhe und im stationären Zustand* (Braunschweig, Philosophische Akademie Erlangen, 1924).

knowledge but to imperative demands from within physics itself. The wholly empirical proofs of atomism eventually broke down the last stronghold; they had been accumulating one after the other—Boltzmann's establishment of the kinetic theory of gases, the investigations on Brownian movement, Helmholtz' proof of the atomic nature of electricity, and Laue's discovery of crystal diffraction. Even Ostwald, who had been the most active champion of the battle against atomism, had to give up in the end, declaring that experimental proof of the atomic structure of matter had at last been attained.[43]

But although such a transition from "hypothesis" to rigorous physical "theory" had been possible, the relation of hypothesis to theory had to be examined anew from a purely epistemological standpoint and the connection between the two more firmly established. The purely abstract features encountered everywhere in physics throughout its development could not be treated merely as convenient experiments; they had to be recognized and confirmed in their distinctive character. Even when one continued to speak of the fundamental concepts of theoretical physics as symbols, in order to avoid from the first any danger of ontological interpretation, there was a necessity of attributing to these very symbols themselves a theoretical meaning and therewith an "objective" content. Far from being merely arbitrary additions to what was given by direct observation they became essential factors with which alone an organization of the given, the fusion of the isolated details into the system of experience, was possible.

The first great physicist actually to complete this turn of affairs and at the same time to grasp the full measure of its philosophical implications, was Heinrich Hertz, with whom began a new phase in the theory of physical methods. In order to understand the change and assign to it its rightful place in the history of physical thought, one should really examine it in connection with Hertz's experimental investigations. In his *Researches on the Propagation of Electrical Force* he had applied himself to the testing of Maxwell's theory of light. He succeeded in producing experimentally the electromagnetic waves that Maxwell had described in theory, and demonstrated that they possess all the known properties of light, such as reflection, refraction, interference, and so on. Thus the question of the nature of light, which had occupied physical speculation for so long and given rise to two opposing theories—the wave theory and the emission theory—was clarified. The electromagnetic theory, according to which electrical waves differ from heat and light waves only in their length, was speeded on its way to final victory.

But it might have been argued that one riddle had merely been substituted for another, since the nature of electromagnetic phenomena was

[43] W. Ostwald, *Grundrisse der allgemeinen Chemie* (4. Aufl. 1909).

no more easy to understand than that of optical phenomena. An objection like this can be disposed of only by proving that it contains a significant misunderstanding of the meaning and purpose of a physical theory.[44] It was such a challenge, no doubt, that led Hertz to the reflections later set down with systematic rigor in the introduction to his work *The Principles of Mechanics*. Maxwell himself, still feeling the need of a mechanistic statement and interpretation of his theory, had successively constructed a number of entirely different models of the ether.[45] But Hertz no longer asked which of these was the "right" one. He declared that Maxwell's electromagnetic theory of light was nothing but the system of Maxwellian differential equations and that no objective content need be sought in it over and above that already expressed there.[46] When we can develop deductively determined consequences from Maxwell's theory and find them verified by experiment, said Hertz, then the proof of its validity is furnished and no more is possible, nor is there any point in trying to achieve more. This view is fully presented and justified in the following preliminary observation:

It is the first and, in a way, the most important task of natural science to enable us to predict future experience so that we may direct our present activities accordingly. . . . But our procedure in deriving the future from the past, and thus achieving the desired foresight, is always this: We set up subjective pictures or symbols of the external objects, and of such a type that their intellectually necessary consequences are invariably symbols again of the necessary consequences in nature of the objects pictured . . . Once we have succeeded in deriving symbols of the desired kind from the totality of past experience we can develop from them in a short time, as from models, consequences that would appear in the external world only after a long time, or as a result of our own manipulations. . . . The symbols of which we speak are our ideas of things; with these objects they have one essential conformity, which lies in fulfillment of the practical demand we have mentioned above, but it is not necessary to their purpose that they have any further sort of resemblance to things. In fact we do not even know and have no way of discovering whether our ideas correspond with objects in any other way than just this one fundamental relationship.[47]

At first glance these remarks seem to contain nothing different from and to prove no more than what had been emphasized by phenomenological physics in its various aspects. They appear to confirm Mach's theory,

[44] Planck, *Das Wesen des Lichts* (2. unveränd. Aufl. Berlin, J. Springer, 1920).

[45] See Poincaré, "La Théorie de Maxwell et les oscillations Hertziennes," *Scientia* (November, 1907).

[46] H. Hertz, *Untersuchungen über die Ausbreitung der elektrischen Kraft* (Leipzig, J. A. Barth, 1892), S. 28.

[47] Hertz, *Die Prinzipien der Mechanik in neuem Zusammenhange dargestelli* (Leipzig, J. A. Barth, 1894), S. 1 f.

that transformation and adaptation are an integral part of all scientific thinking. By adaptation to relationships in the external world certain ideas take form in the mind, and each fresh experience adds a new feature until finally a more complete correspondence is achieved between these ideas and external phenomena.[48] Upon closer examination, however, it turns out that the concept of symbols is employed by Hertz in quite another sense and that it has a function to fulfill in the construction of physical theory that is entirely different from the one assigned by Mach. For the latter, the "reality" that the physicist has to describe is only the sum of simple sense data: sounds, colors, smells, tastes. Theory accordingly will better accomplish its task the more completely it succeeds in conforming to these data and expressing them simply as they exist, without arbitrary changes or addition. Even the general propositions of a theory can serve no other purpose. They always refer ultimately to an individual in the Aristotelian sense; they point to individual facts and endeavor to express them in all their concrete precision, in their *here* and *now*. They cannot, of course, dispense with general terms, but these are only convenient mnemonics, providing the dissimilar and the complex with one linguistic sign and so making it more easily reproducible. Hence wherever general concepts or principles are encountered in a physical theory they are but convenient devices for expression.[49]

Because the capacity to comprehend and remember details is limited, the material must be arranged in order. For instance, if we knew for every period of time the space traversed by a falling body we might be well content. But what a prodigious memory it would take to carry the pertinent table of *s* and *t* in our heads! Instead of so doing we employ the formula $s = \dfrac{gt^2}{2}$, that is to say, the principle by which we can find the appropriate *s* for any given *t*, and this provides a complete, convenient, and compendious substitute for the table. This principle, this formula, this "law" has not one iota more of factual value than the isolated facts taken together, its worth lying merely in its convenience. It has utilitarian value.[50]

As an empiricist Hertz was certainly not inferior to Mach, as the whole nature and tenor of his research shows, and for him too there was not the slightest doubt that every idea employed by physical theory would eventually have to be confirmed by concrete observation. But he was convinced that not every single element of a theory is susceptible or in need of such verification. This is only necessary for the whole; for an entire

[48] Mach, "Über Umbildung und Anpassung im naturwissenschaftlichen Denken," *Populär-wissenschaftliche Vorlesungen* (S. verm. und durchges. Aufl. Leipzig, J. A. Barth, 1908), Kap. xiv, S. 248 ff.

[49] Mach, "Die ökonomische Natur der physikalischen Forschung," *Populär-wissenschaftliche Vorlesungen*, Kap. xiii, S. 215 ff.

[50] Mach, *Die Geschichte und die Murzel des Satzes von der Erhaltung der Arbeit*, S. 31.

system of theoretical propositions. Thinking was thereby given an entirely different significance and assured of a much wider scope than in Mach's doctrine, which held that the validity of any definite idea can be proved only when it is identified as a copy of a definite "impression." The fundamental concepts of physics, according to Mach, are the product of and the passive impressions left by the effects of objects upon the sense organs, whereas for Hertz they are the expression of a highly complex intellectual process—a process in which theorizing holds full sway in order to attain to its goal through experience and therein to find confirmation or justification. Accordingly Hertz held fast to the possibility and necessity of a "pure natural science" in the sense of Kant—an idea that Mach and the phenomenalistic physics which he represented could only reject with horror.

Hertz begins with an entirely free sketch of thinking, with a comprehensive system of physical concepts and axioms which are introduced at first as pure hypotheses only in order to compare their consequences with the concrete facts of reality. "Experience remains wholly foreign to the considerations in the first book," he wrote regarding the definitions of time, space, and mass with which he prefaced his system of mechanics. "All the statements there set down are a priori judgments in the sense of Kant. They rest on the laws of inner intuition and forms of the inner logic of the person stating them, and have no connection with his external experience other than these intuitions and forms may have with it." [51] Thus for Hertz the fundamental concepts of theoretical physics were patterns of possible experiences, whereas for Mach they were copies of actual experiences.

The logic of physics received herewith a new and highly characteristic form. Above all it appeared that fundamental concepts are not established from the first with entire precision but may vary freely within certain limits. Hertz undertook an audacious alteration in the system of classical mechanics when he ventured to banish its central and basic idea and substitute other abstract definitions for it. Classical mechanics, whose various stages of development are signalized by the names of Archimedes, Galileo, Newton, and Lagrange, was founded upon the ideas of space, time, force, and mass, with force introduced as the antecedent and independent cause of motion. The complete system seemed wholly to satisfy all possible demands for logical rigor, and from its basic concepts the principles and laws of motion were strictly deduced in perfect order. Yet more exacting criticism was able to discern certain difficulties and inconsistencies that could not be removed within the confines of the system. These logical discrepancies justified and encouraged the attempt to carry out the reform that was proving more and more urgently necessary, not only in regard to

[51] Hertz, *op. cit.,* S. 53.

details but respecting the whole system itself. Then investigators were led to that second representation of mechanical events that set up energetics in place of the Newtonian system. The start was made here also from four independent basic concepts, whose relations to one another were supposed to form the content of mechanics. Two of them, space and time, are mathematical in character while the other two, mass and energy, were introduced as physical realities that are present in given amounts, indestructible, and not susceptible of increase. The idea of force did not appear among these elements but was brought in, if at all, as a mathematical artifact and somewhat as though it were a simplification or an ancillary item that was unnecessary though it might prove convenient. But even this system, Hertz meant to show in detail, was not absolutely satisfactory and had certain serious flaws. Thus the way was open for his real task, which was to prove that besides the system of Newton and that of energetics there was possible a third constructive view of the principles of mechanics. This differed radically from the others in starting with only three independent basic concepts: time, space, and mass. This "third picture" allowed, as the work of Hertz demonstrated, a thoroughly consistent development of all the fundamental laws established by classical mechanics. It could not conflict with any of the basic phenomena and therefore was just as "true" as either of the first two representations. But it was more satisfactory and more to the point because it had definite methodological advantages in so far as it contained, in addition to the essential features, a smaller number of relations that were supernumerary or without any content and thus as a whole it was simpler.[52]

Through this attitude, expressed in his *Principles of Mechanics,* Hertz originated a demand that went far beyond the problems in question. The task of physical theory was now posed in another way. In the view represented by Mach and Ostwald the relation of physical theory to physical facts had hardly yet become a problem. Theory was defined merely as an adaptation to facts and hence as a simple reproduction of them. Accordingly a physical law or principle had no independent cognitive value comparable to that of immediate perception, and certainly none above it. It merely repeated in abridged form, as a convenient verbal summary, the knowledge that perception furnished directly and, consequently, better and more faithfully. A law is no more than a catalogue of isolated facts, a principle no more than a register of laws. The implication of this was the strange corollary that the necessity of thinking in general concepts and laws did not represent a special virtue of the human mind but actually originated in its weakness. An intellect broad and inclusive enough to grasp all details as details would require no such roundabout method— nor would there be any "science" for it. "If all single facts, all separate

[52] Hertz, Einleitung, *op. cit.,* § 1–3, S. 5 ff.

phenomena, were as directly accessible to us as we demand that knowledge of them be," Mach expressly declared, "science never would have arisen." [53]

If physical theory had actually no aim other than to describe definite, individual facts as faithfully as possible, it would have to be confessed that so far it had accomplished this task very poorly, for even in its most important theorems it not only turns its back upon these facts but directs its gaze upon something "that has never occurred." The law of inertia proposes to describe the motion of a body that is not acted upon by any external forces, though the assumption that such a condition is ever realized in nature is absurd. Whence this urge to pass from considerations of the real to considerations of the unreal, even of the impossible? Is there any sense in entertaining such notions as that of an "ideal gas," or a "perfectly black body," when we are aware that these correspond with no empirical facts? Mach's theory actually did not dispute the right to introduce ideal elements like these into physics, for they form an integrating part in the "experimental thinking" without which physics, as Mach emphasized, cannot complete its edifice.[54] Yet from the standpoint of his general theory of knowledge it is doubtful in the extreme whether experimenting with mere thoughts of things rather than with the things themselves is ever justifiable.

The Hertzian system of mechanics represents experiment of this sort in the grand manner, for it resolved upon a free variation of the basic concepts of mechanics in which even its once fundamental idea, the idea of force, was sacrificed. The spontaneity inherent in all theory was herewith brought out into clear view. To be sure, the freedom was not to be unbridled license, for a theory can be proved valid only through the fact that its inferences lead to results that correspond with experience. But it was shown that no single component of any theory of nature, such as the idea of force or that of mass, can be separated out in order to seek an objective correlate for it and thence to decide as to its validity and truth. The process of verification was proved to be much more complex. It was no longer demanded of the single concepts hypothetically set up in a theory that they should reproduce concrete and empirically demonstrable facts; their part was really performed when it could be shown that in their totality, in their mutual interrelations, they represented a symbol of reality in such a way that "their intellectually necessary consequences" would always be "symbols of the necessary consequences in nature of the objects represented."

A continuation and development of this train of thought is to be found

[53] Mach. *op. cit.,* S. 31 f.
[54] Mach, "Über Gedankenexperimente," *Erkenntnis und Irrtum* (Leipzig, J. A. Barth, 1905), S. 180 ff.

in Poincaré's investigation of the nature of scientific concepts and hypotheses.[55] Here the problem was broadened in so far as it related directly to Poincaré's interpretation of the meaning of mathematical hypotheses. In respect to the non-Euclidean geometries he wished to show that in establishing a system of mathematical axioms we are not bound to experience, in the sense that we can draw from experience a decision as to which of the various systems, all equally possible from the standpoint of logic, corresponds to "real" space. Experience is unable to give such a decision, and accordingly the "truth" of any one geometry cannot depend upon it. No geometry is "truer" than another, though one may be more suited to the purpose of experience or, in other words, prove a more useful instrument for a systematic description of its given facts.[56]

But this freedom in forming ideas and hypotheses, according to Poincaré, does not stop with mathematics. It must be extended to physics in so far as this science, in the form of theoretical physics, makes use of mathematics and so actually becomes the same type of knowledge. The "scientific fact" of physics differs from "brute fact" precisely in this respect, that it is not limited to the information from perception but expresses the data in the new language of mathematical symbols. Only so is a transition from one kind of fact to the other made possible.[57] This reasoning shows how the axioms of physics are connected with the world of facts; no one axiom can be asserted to be in itself the simple description of any isolated fact given in experience. That every physical principle owes its establishment to the stimulation which we have received from experience is true beyond all question, but the universality attributed to the principle can never be derived from experience alone. *The raising of any principle to universality is always a free act of scientific thought.* In this fundamental point of view Poincaré agrees with what Hertz said, that the symbols we construct for ourselves of external objects not only depend upon the nature of these objects but owe their form to "the inner logic of the one making the assertion." This logic calls for another and closer connection between phenomena than what meets us immediately in observation. It teaches us that we must reconstruct the conditioned assertions, which are all that we are entitled to make on the ground of observation, in such fashion that they take on the character of absolutely universal and to that extent unconditioned assertions. According to Poincaré this reconstruction is the truly basic feature in the formation of all physical theory, and it has become more and more apparent in the modern development of the science.

The older physics was for the most part a physics of symbols in *this*

[55] H. Poincaré, *La Science et l'hypothèse* (1902); *Science et méthode* (1909); *La Valeur de la science* (Paris, E. Flammarion, 1905).

[56] See *The Problem of Knowledge*, pp. 43 f.

[57] For further details see Poincaré, *La Valeur de la science*, troisième partie, chap. x, § 3, p. 221 ff.

sense: it tried to represent the nature of every object or event investigated in a corresponding mechanical model, whose single items passed as replicas of the details and properties of the object. Modern physics has increasingly renounced this procedure, and from a physics of literal pictures has become a physics of principles. Its development in the nineteenth century was signalized by the discovery and precise formulation of several principles, such as Carnot's principle, the principle of the conservation of energy, the principle of least action, and so on. A principle is neither a mere synopsis of facts nor solely an epitomization of single laws. It contains in its meaning the claim of "always and universally," which experience as such is never warranted in making. *Instead of deriving a principle directly from experience we use it as a criterion of experience.* Principles constitute the fixed points of the compass that are required for successful orientation in the world of phenomena. They are not so much assertions about empirical facts as maxims by which we interpret these facts in order to bring them together into a complete and coherent whole.

Poincaré insisted that the selection of these reference points is not imposed on us by objects but originates in the free choice of theoretical thinking, though he definitely refuted the extreme nominalistic and skeptical conclusions that many followers wished to draw from his premises.[58] Freedom in the construction of physical hypotheses and theories is not caprice, in his opinion, for the relationships expressed in them are subject to constant verification by experience and are confirmed in their objective validity by it. Only the language of physical theories and the symbols applied to experience proved to be variable factors, but this changeableness does not exclude the continuity and the logical coherence of these theories; on the contrary it turns out to be a means of actually keeping them intact.

This symbolic character of all physical knowledge was emphasized by Duhem even more strongly than by Hertz or Poincaré himself. Duhem thought it pure theoretical naïveté to believe that even a single proposition made in physics can be regarded as describing a result of direct observation. No judgment in theoretical physics ever relates directly to those "elements" in which Mach, in his "phenomenological physics," saw the essence and meaning of all reality. Duhem's criticism of this interpretation is more searching than that of either Hertz or Poincaré, for he proceeds on the assumption that if physical sensationism is ever to be displaced the lever should be applied more fundamentally. What the Machian system could not adequately explain was not primarily the general principles but rather the particular statements of physics. Between the two types of assertion there is not the wide gap ordinarily assumed. They are inseparably bound together and in some measure have an ultimate solidarity. As far as meaning and truth value are concerned, the judgment of fact cannot be

[58] See especially *La Valeur de la science*, p. 213 ff.

divorced from that of principle, for there is not a single factual conclusion that does not contain an implicit assertion of principle. Every judgment concerning an individual case, in so far as it purports to be a proposition in physics, already includes a *whole system* of physics. It is not true, therefore, that the science consists of two strata, as it were: simple observation and the results of measurement being in the one, theories built upon these in the other. Observation and measurement prior to all theory, and independent of its assumptions, are impossible. Nothing of the sort is ever given as a fact; it is rather a theoretical abstraction which upon critical analysis turns out at once to be pure illusion.

The distinction between "brute fact" and "scientific fact" was drawn still more rigorously by Duhem than by Poincaré. Between the two there is a difference not only in degree but actually in kind. No physical proposition, be it ever so simple, is to be understood merely as a sum of observed facts, an aggregate of such observations as are carried out in everyday life. On the contrary, ordinary observations and those of physics move on entirely different planes and belong therefore in wholly different spheres. When a physicist imparts the results of an experiment undertaken to discover or test a definite law of nature, he cannot give them in the form that he would employ in presenting the series of sense impressions received during the course of his experiment. The latter would be a psychological report but in no way a presentation of his experimental findings. The scientific statement would not describe the ocular, auditory, or tactile sensations of an individual observer in a particular physical laboratory but would state an objective fact of quite another sort—a fact that could be made known, of course, only if an appropriate language, a system of definite symbols, had been created for its communication. What is told is not that while making his readings the observer suddenly noticed one or another sensation within himself, but that an electric current of given intensity passed through a magnetic field, or that the pressure, volume, and temperature of a gas varied in this way or that under certain experimental conditions. In order to understand the meaning of this evidence, in order to define exactly what an electric current is, or pressure, volume, or temperature, mere reference to the data of simple observation is never adequate. On the contrary, it is realized upon closer examination that the very use of such terms involves highly complex theoretical assumptions, and that a whole system of physical judgments is therefore implied. Every time instruments of measurement are employed there is presupposed a theoretical designation of the phenomena in terms of such judgments. In order to give a strict explanation of what is meant by the *volume* or the *pressure* of a gas it is necessary to go back not only to the principles of arithmetic and geometry, but to the axioms of general mechanics as well as to the most abstruse theories of hydrostatics, electricity, and so on.

"What a physicist gives as the outcome of an experiment is not a report on the isolated facts that he has ascertained but an interpretation of these facts, or in other words their transposition into an ideal, abstract, symbolic world constructed on theories that he regards as established." A law of physics is a symbolic relationship, whose application to concrete reality demands a knowledge of a whole system of theories which one assumes to be valid.[59]

This granted, it will be realized that the process of verification of a theory signifies something other than what empiricism in its usual form admits, and it is a much more complicated process. The decisive experiment, which Bacon called the *experimentum crucis*, becomes impossible, since the theoretical can never be separated from the factual in such a way that the former stands on one side and the latter on the other. Inasmuch as even the simple determination of a physical fact implies a whole set of theoretical statements and is significant only in relation to this whole, the truth or falsity of a physical theory can never be determined by measuring it against the world of facts as though this represented self-contained reality independent of all assumptions of the theory. A theory can be tested only by means of another theory; a physical system can never be compared with the "exact" data of observation if we wish to discover its truth value but only with another system, with a whole set of theoretical principles and theorems.

This is the same view that we encountered in the writings of Hertz and Poincaré, but it gains a special importance and more precision in Duhem. It is generally assumed that every hypothesis employed by physics can be accepted on its own merits and separately tested by experience, and that after its value has been established by manifold and varied experiments it will receive its final place in the system. But this is not true. Physics is not a machine that can be taken apart. One cannot test every piece individually and wait until it has stood this sort of testing before putting it into the system. Physical science is a system that must be accepted as a self-contained whole, an organism of which no single part can be made to work without all the others, even those farthest removed, becoming active —some more, some less, but all in some precise degree. When the functioning is blocked in any way the physicist must try to guess from the behavior of the whole which part is at fault and in need of repair, with no possibility of isolating and testing it separately. Given a watch that will not go, the watchmaker removes all its parts, examining them one by one until he finds which was out of place or broken, but the physician cannot dissect a patient in order to make a diagnosis; he must guess at the seat and cause of the disease merely by studying a disturbance that affects the

[59] P. Duhem, *La Théorie physique* (Paris, Chevalier et Rivière, 1906), deuxième partie, chaps. iv, v, p. 233 ff.

whole body. The physicist resembles the latter when he has a defective theory before him which he has to improve.[60]

The word *symbol,* which both Hertz and Duhem had to employ in order to establish their views of the nature of physical theory, itself contains plenty of new epistemological difficulties. Hertz did not hesitate to call the symbols of physics "inner illusions" (*innere Scheinbilder*). But the question arises immediately how these "illusions" can bring us nearer the truth; how it is possible by their aid not only to combine present experiences but even to make valid hypotheses about an unknown future. The problem of induction now looms once more with all its difficulties and appears capable of solution only if we accept with Hertz the supposition that "there is a certain accord between nature and our minds." Experience teaches that the postulate can be met, he explained, and therefore such a rapport actually exists.[61]

But here we run the risk of being caught in that well-known epistemological circle that Hume disclosed in his criticism of the theory of causality: the axiom of the "uniformity of nature" is derived from experience, yet it appears to be the necessary presupposition of the validity of every inductive inference. The difficulty can be met in a certain sense if the concepts of physics are regarded as nothing but direct models or reproductions of objects, for while even in this case there is no necessity of any identity between prototype and copy, still a high degree of similarity between the two may be asserted, on the strength of which the one may be substituted for the other in practice. But the strictly symbolic character of physical concepts puts an end to this similarity, too, for the signs have a wholly different structure from that which they indicate and belong, as it were, to an entirely different world. For symbols in the sense employed by Hertz and by Duhem, no connection with reality, such as was demanded by earlier theories, is either necessary or possible. Here a particular symbol can never be set over against a particular object and compared in respect to its similarity. All that is required is that the order of the symbols be arranged so as to express the order of the phenomena.

This conception made its way but slowly and against strong opposition. The mechanistic view of nature demanded that every hypothesis shall be capable of verification by direct observation, and the demand would not be satisfied until all the various details of the picture had been completely filled in. "I am never content," wrote William Thomson,

until I have constructed a mechanical model of the object that I am studying. If I succeed in making one, I understand; otherwise, I do not. Hence I cannot grasp the electromagnetic theory of light. I wish to understand light as fully as possible, without introducing things that I understand still less. Therefore I

[60] Duhem, *op. cit.,* p. 307 f.
[61] Hertz, *op. cit.,* S. 1.

hold fast to simple dynamics for there, but not in the electromagnetic theory, I can find a model.[62]

And even Maxwell himself, who contributed most to the supplanting of this older view, was at first still in the toils of it. "The complicated structure that Maxwell ascribed to the ether in the earliest version of his theory," remarked Poincaré, "made his system strange and repellent. One could almost believe that one were reading the description of a factory, with its cogwheels, its drive shafts bending under the strain of transmitting motion, its governors, and its belts." [63] The renunciation of this way of making things plain in sensible form came reluctantly, but when it was made the surprising result emerged that physics was thereby nearer its real goal of unification.

The last step in this direction was the development brought about by the general theory of relativity and the quantum theory. It required a far greater sacrifice in regard to the sensible representation of nature but brought the fullest measure of compensation for this sacrifice. The general theory of relativity showed that even the hypotheses upon which geometry is founded are not fixed once and for all, but are subject in principle to the same sort of variations as those that can be observed in the axioms of physics. There resulted a solidarity of the geometrical and physical principles, yielding a theory not composed of distinct and separate elements but an integrated one where the principles mutually penetrate each other, and this total theory can be compared with experience and either corroborated or rejected.[64]

Previously it had been necessary only to concede logical possibility to the non-Euclidean geometries, which were without sensible representation and consequently, it was believed, without any relevance to physics, so that the new geometry and physics were kept absolutely apart. Now this barrier, too, fell with the construction of the Einstein theory of gravitation, which explained how all former definitions of the space-time continuum by means of rigid measuring rods, watches, light rays, and paths of inert bodies might satisfy the laws of Euclidean geometry in narrow and restricted fields, but that on the whole a more comprehensive theory of space needed to be set up.[65]

The progress of the quantum theory exhibits the same characteristic process of transformation. The first models of atoms seemed to satisfy the demand for sensible representation in the most gratifying way. They were

[62] W. Thomson, *Lectures on Molecular Dynamics and the Wave-theory of Light* (Baltimore, 1884), p. 270.

[63] Poincaré, "Théorie de Maxwell . . . ," *Scientia* (November, 1907), p. 7 f.

[64] See Chap. III, p. 53.

[65] For details see Max Born, "Die allgemeine Relativitätstheorie Einsteins," *Die Relativitätstheorie Einsteins und ihre physikalischen Grundlagen,* "Naturwissenschaftliche Monographien und Lehrbücher," III (2. umgearb. Aufl. Berlin, J. Springer, 1921), 218 ff.

believed to afford a more or less direct *view* of the atomic world, and the microcosm appeared in exactly the same form as the macrocosm. The atom became a planetary system in which the planets were electrons revolving around a central body, the nucleus.[66] But the simplicity of this picture was lost as the theory developed, and it was Niels Bohr himself, one of the earliest creators of the atomic model, who warned against overvaluing it as a representation. In his essay of 1925, "Atomtheorie und Mechanik," he expressed the conviction that the general problem of the quantum theory was not concerned with a modification of mechanical and electrodynamic theories that could be explained on the basis of ordinary physical concepts but involved a radical denial of the space-time ideas by means of which a description of natural phenomena had previously been attempted.[67] Atomic physics cannot be constructed "without resignation of the wish for sensuous presentation." [68]

Quantum mechanics achieved herewith a character wholly different, in epistemological respects, from that of classical physics and mechanics. It required the development of new symbolic methods. Heisenberg relied on a new algebra, for which the commutative law of multiplication was not valid and in which the symbolic character of the theory was strikingly evident in the appearance of imaginaries in the law of commutation.[69] So the quantum theory retained indeed a mathematical schema, but this could not possibly be interpreted as a simple connection of objects in space and time. On the other hand, it was Schrödinger's hope, in his doctrine of wave mechanics, to be able to achieve an even closer union with space-time intuition. But here, too, new problems immediately arose, since the wave process is not embedded in the three-dimensional space of co-ordinates but in an extended space, where the number of dimensions is equal to the number of degrees of freedom in the system and thus essentially different from three-dimensional, ordinary space.[70]

So Heisenberg insisted,

the atom of modern physics can be symbolized only through a partial differential equation in an abstract space of many dimensions. . . . *All* its qualities are inferential; no material properties can be directly attributed to it. That is to say, any picture of the atom that our imagination is able to invent is for that very

[66] For details see, for example, A. Sommerfeld, "Das Wasserstoffspektrum," *Atombau und Spektrallinien* (4. umgearb. Aufl. Braunschweig, F. Vieweg & Sohn, Akt.-Ges., 1924), Kap. ii, S. 73 ff.

[67] N. Bohr, "Atomtheorie und Mechanik," *Atomtheorie und Naturbeschreibung* (Berlin, J. Springer, 1931), S. 22.

[68] "Wirkungsquantum und Naturbeschreibung," *ibid.,* S. 64.

[69] W. Heisenberg, *Die physikalischen Prinzipien der Quantentheorie* (Leipzig, S. Hirzel, 1930), S. 48, 78 ff.

[70] For details see Bohr, "Das Quantenpostulat," *op. cit.,* S. 50; and Reichenbach, "Ziele und Wege der physikalischen Erkenntnis," *Handbuch der Physik* von Geiger und Scheel (Berlin, J. Springer, 1929), IV, 77.

reason defective. An understanding of the atomic world in that primary sensuous fashion . . . is impossible.[71]

But here we stop, having already passed beyond the limits of our purely historical discussion.[72] The problems that now emerge do not yet lend themselves to simple historical review, for they are still in flux. They have been touched upon here merely because they show that the advance of physical thought which had led to the recent revolutionary results of atomic physics has been proceeding more steadily, on the whole, than is generally realized. Physics would hardly have accepted the consequences of the new theories, which conflict so strikingly with the findings of direct observation, had it not been encouraged and enabled to do so by a change in the idea of knowledge that had grown out of the classical system. In this fact we see how the concrete work of research, and reflective thought on the theory of knowledge which accompanied it, have constantly interacted and stimulated each other in important and fruitful ways.

[71] W. Heisenberg, "Zur Geschichte der physikalischen Naturerklärung," *Wandlungen in den Grundlagen der Naturwissenschaft* (6. Aufl. Leipzig, S. Hirzel, 1945), S. 36.

[72] For a statement of the epistemological problems of modern atomic physics see Cassirer, *Determinismus und Indeterminismus in der modernen Physik,* S. 1–265.

E. Flower : NORMS AND INDUCTION

P<small>ROFESSOR</small> *Elizabeth Flower, of the Department of Philosophy, University of Pennsylvania, in her essay prepared for this volume, indicates the epistemological problem raised by the common judgment that factual and normative statements are the products of distinct modes of knowledge. Dr. Flower examines the role of judicial proceedings as offering material for the conclusion that legal theories, like predictive empirical theories, are cognitive, and suggests that ethical theories can be developed in similarly cognitive modes.*

• Among the discussions of our day few are more popular than those which contrast its science with its morals.[1] The histories and philosophies of these enterprises emphasize their distinctiveness. Science, at least as ordinarily portrayed, unfolds in a self-correcting and antiseptic fashion. Its course is marked by the almost steady refinement of explanations and their replacement by progressively more adequate ones, by public and accepted criteria of advance, and by the confidence that incompatible theories can be mashed. On the other hand morals and law are frequently depicted as rationalizations in struggles for power or as adjuncts to the interplay of cultural forces or psychological drives. Even the history of jurisprudence and ethical theory is often so regarded. We are there met by a succession of explanations which, though magnificent, are just as often contradictory, by the inability of later theories to build systematically on earlier ones, and by appeals to the authority of a Plato or an Aristotle, a Locke, a Kant, or a Bentham.

Part of the legacy of such a disparate tradition is the present lack of agreement on objectives, measures of achievement, or subject matter in ethics. Justice Stone makes a similar comment about law: "It would not seem too severe to describe jurisprudence as a chaos of approaches to a chaos of topics." [2] Most discouraging of all, at least for the status of normative inquiries, genuine achievements in the philosophy of science not only seem inapplicable to evaluative and normative judgments but appear to exclude them as legitimate and corrigible elements in explanation. The question is put: Suppose the consequences of alternative actions could be known, would such knowledge alone provide the sufficient or even relevant grounds for a choice of which ought to be done? Much of the recent literature answers negatively. From factual or *is* statements (from calculations of risk or from preferential orderings), it is not possible to derive genuine normative or *ought* statements. The first are cognitive; their truth or falsity, or the probability of these values, is determinable by empirical methods. On the other hand, ethical statements are supported by emotive or persuasive reasons rather than by evidential ones. Both morals and law are thought to need a special logic, to face unique kinds of decisions, or to use language distinctively.

What makes the non-cognitive character of ethical and legal judgments more plausible is the manner and substance of our daily disputes. Can anyone believe that rational resolutions are sought for international disagreements or even that the latter are regarded as problems to be solved? Further, democracy, justice, and the public good are claimed as justifica-

[1] Part of this paper was read at the Philosophy Colloquium, Columbia University. I am particularly indebted to Professor A. Leo Levin of the Law School of the University of Pennsylvania and to Professor Thomas A. Cowan of the Law School of Rutgers University.
[2] Stone, H., *The Province and Function of the Law*, Harvard, 1950, p. 16.

tions for quite incompatible policies. Even in domestic matters, for example the Bollingen Award to Ezra Pound or the graver segregation issue, opponents often enough seem agreed both on what are the facts and which facts are relevant and yet disagree both on the resolution and the decisiveness of the factors. And one century's views can be altered radically by the next. Thus in the nineteenth century *Plessy vs. Ferguson* interpreted "equal" to mean "equal and separate," while a twentieth century decision, *Brown vs. Topeka,* takes "equal and separate," to imply "desegregation." At the same time others such as Wechsler suspect that other constitutional problems are involved than the simple problem of guaranteed equality. He raises the question in the Oliver Wendell Holmes Lecture for 1959, *Toward Neutral Principles of Constitutional Law:*

> Given a situation where the state must . . . choose between denying association to those individuals who wish it or imposing it upon those who would avoid it, is there a constitutional basis demanding that the claims of association should prevail . . . ? The denial by the state of freedom to associate . . . is a denial that impinges equally on any group or race that may be involved.

Just as this issue can be construed as a question of the definition or the criteria of "equal" (and of the ordering of the guarantees of equality and free association), so the debate over the Bolingen Award may be said to turn on the appropriate construction of "aesthetic"—can the excellence of lyric poetry be judged independently of (an admittedly) foul content? However, for sceptics such disagreements have been held to be attitudinal —to be matters of affection, "inclinations more properly felt than judged of." It is urged by them that the reasons offered as to what consequences will follow, say, on one or another interpretation of equality are logical; whereas, the reasons that support the preference of one set of consequences over another are not only different but are not even evidential.

There is force to arguments such as these. But if we take the problem to be one of determining the legitimacy of normative judgments and not that of motivation then there is cause to challenge the profitableness of the dichotomy between the normative and the descriptive or factual—at least in so far as this implies a corresponding divorce between the noncognitive and the cognitive. What is at stake is not whether the distinction can be made, for of course it can; the issue is whether it can be maintained without excluding much of what is interesting in theory construction generally and whether it has not withdrawn critical moral and legal matters from investigation. Some of the considerations which weaken the distinction are related to the problems of definition and ordering mentioned above, but it is to be noted, even here, that the reasons predicting the consequences of an interpretation—of equality, aesthetic, or intelligence (or acid or diamond or resonance for that matter)—appear to be different from those reasons offered in defense of the interpretation.

The history of this dichotomy has generally been focused on four issues: Is there so fundamental a difference between the aims of ethical theory and of explanation generally that one cannot seek a common method? Is there something so distinctive about the data of ethics and related value fields as to disqualify them as elements of explanation? Is there something distinctive in the way in which the data are organized or developed into theory? And finally, is there a unique problem for the way in which the principle of morals and law, as well as other normative enterprises, are justified in contrast to the way in which fundamental principles of empirical science are established?

The problem about the data is not the primary concern of this paper, and yet it is important to remember how much of the conflict among legal and, particularly, ethical theories has turned on one choice or another. Thus egoists differ from altruists and idealists from empiricists at the start, and even among those of the latter persuasion, G. E. Moore spoke of an indefinable moral property, Dewey of value experiences, Hobbes of pleasure and pain, Ayer of the emotive use of language, Smith of propriety, and Hume of sympathy and humanity. Now surely, to ask what is *the* data of ethics is misleading if this is taken to mean some absolute commitment. Traditionally at least, psychological priority has often been mistaken for logical primacy, and many who supposed they had got hold of an original moral experience could not have established it as such on their own grounds nor defended it against competing claims. Surely primitives, or less formally, starting points are elected and not predestined—and elected, just as premises are, for their role in explanation. In any case, for the purpose of this paper it is sufficient to agree with Sidgwick that judgments about ethical matters are made and are made on all levels of generality from the most particular statement, "this is wrong," to the highest ordered principle of an ethical theory. The problem of bringing order to such commitments persists whatever the philosophic position.

The main interest here is the organization and elaboration of the data and its justification. We start trivially and somewhat afield with examples that illustrate two rather different kinds of enterprizes. We are all familiar with how important is a lawyer's ability to predict correctly what will not come under fire, or, if tested, what the holding will be. If the case is to be heard, he will take into account the effect of his presentation on the behavior of the trier. Thus it might have been possible to predict the position of a Frankfurter or of a Holmes on sports cases from what one knows of their concern about sports, and what kinds of argument might be persuasive to them. Indeed, there is a famous jest, "if you have no case, insult the judge." (That is, you can expect to benefit by a judge's effort to be fair if he is angry.) This effort to understand and to utilize the extra-legal considerations which influence or cause a judge's behavior is sometimes called "gastronomic" jurisprudence; it says in effect that a psychological knowledge of the judge's behavior can be utilized to increase the likelihood of a favorable decision.

On the other hand, the judge is attempting to do something quite different, namely, to decide what is a valid holding in terms of his past experience, his knowledge of the judicial process and his insight into the present case. Even if the judge learns of the odds on his behavior, still such information is relevant only as he seeks to avoid bias. It is also clear that the reasoning which supports the attorney's prediction is vastly different from that to which the judge appeals to support his decision. And even where the "same" data appear they are utilized in different roles. Of course, the restriction to the judge's decision is a matter of simplicity of presentation. Similar remarks, though more complex, are clearly appropriate when applied to a jury or to any citizen engaged in predicting or explaining why the legislative body made certain legislation in contrast to his critique of it.

These pairs of examples have important parallels with the anthropologist's account of what a person (or persons) values or thinks ought to be done and the latter's effort to decide what is valuable or what ought to be done. Such cases also illustrate what are ordinarily taken to be factual, empirical, or scientific judgments as contrasted with normative or valuative ones, and it is precisely this contrast and the apparent lack of a bridge between them that is at issue. Yet is the situation so transparently simple? Are not these examples also paralleled by the contrast of predictive enterprises and problem-solving whatever the area of inquiry? Sell's tests on the atmospheric effects of premises, their negativity, universality, etc., allows him to predict with amazing accuracy the errors that students will make in completing syllogisms as well as which of legitimate conclusions will be favored.[3] The student of course is little helped by the knowledge that his behavior is subject to psychological analysis, and his task, as is the case with the judge, is to draw valid conclusions. Strictly, of course, there is no theoretical reason why the behavior of logicians could not similarly become the object of psychological investigation and prediction, but the mathematician and the logician are still concerned with "interesting" and significant deductions.

The illustrations need not be limited to the formal sciences but may be found equally in empirical undertakings. The learning of a language seems to depend on forging generalizations which are very difficult to make explicit in grammar but which serve as norms for sentences that are

[3] Sells, S. B., Koob, H. F., "The Atmosphere Effect," *J. Ed. Psych.*, 1937, 28, pp. 514–518.

judged as legitimate in the corpus; also the reports of complex kinship and allied relations rest on a similar sense of correctness on the part of the informant. In contrast the empirical linguist or the anthropologist aims to formulate an explanation which will explain the base reports and predict future ones. Yet when the theory is well assured, it frequently forces a reconsideration of the very data from which it was derived. The role of musical analysis is unexpectedly analogous. There are various ways of describing musical relations and these are licenses for repetition. Yet the insights gained locate areas for innovation and often unseat canons that were thought to be inviolable.

Of course the enterprises of the judge, the moralists, and the logician differ from the accounting of their behavior in psychological or anthropological terms; the latter seeks to explain or predict what happens and the former to derive right or valid conclusions. The relation between these kinds of tasks is as intimate as it is difficult to state, for critique seems bound to an understanding of judgments actually made, and there are dangers in seeking for more extensive (or special) connections than those which would appear between any allied investigations. Still, as above, there are those who object that the relation can not be a logical one since, at least with the judge and the moralist, their undertakings are "meaningless" or non-cognitive.

The most frequent objections to the cognitive character of ethical and legal statements in this context are two. Ayer long ago argued [4] that to say a man's actions are wrong is not to say what they are; it adds no fact or detail to the description of his behavior. "Wrongly" expresses a resolution not to imitate actions so designated and to discourage others from doing them. But "wrong" seems to function as "illegal" (or "illegal in Utah"), "correct," "economical," or "is kin to"; it indicates the relevance of a context which overlaps (and possibly is wider) than that of physical description. Very different materials may be relevant to different descriptions or explanations. Left-handedness, for example, may be of interest to a geneticist, or, in a very different way, to a psychiatrist. Generally it would be of little interest to a Court, though it might be. Almost always it would be of no concern to a micropathologist. The effort to determine formal criteria of relevancy is rather like trying to identify the victim before the crime; it would save a lot of trouble, but it is difficult. The adequacy or truth of one description or explanation need not necessarily be purchased at the expense of another where different materials are relevant. Surely there are adequate histories written in psychological, economic, or anthropological dimensions, and it seems over-demanding to require a super explanation that embodies all of them. The case may well be the same with the conflict

[4] Ayer, A. J., "On the Analysis of Moral Judgments," *Horizon*, XX, 117, 1949, pp. 175–188.

of morals and science; the contrast may lie in a difference in the task. Indeed, there is an interesting series of experiments [5] which show how the same spatio-temporal event is assigned a different role according to whether the subject assumes a gambling situation or a problem-solving one (i.e., to find a pattern in the stimuli presented). Perhaps then it would be worthwhile to see whether the history of morals and of law might not properly be understood as increasing in explanatory power, as progressing in an orderly and self-correcting fashion. But this is just what the judicial process in common law appears to be.

The second objection is a more serious one, and it concerns the role, or lack of one, of prediction. This is illustrated in both classes of examples and it was of course critical to the question of verification which ruled out value-statements as legitimate. The distinction between predictive and non-predictive theories must not be minimized, nor do I think it need be to challenge the cognitive status of moral and legal judgments. It is interesting that some ethical theories such as Bentham's theory of expectation which are close to law often use predictive elements and emphasize how these systems generate norms of expected behavior. Yet even if a sharp distinction between predictive and nonpredictive enterprises is urged, still it is clear that the kinds of reasons which are offered in the constructing of a theory, e.g. for greater predictive power, are as different from those which support a given prediction as the reasons which support factual judgments are different from those supporting normative ones. A more serious way of putting this issue asks whether predictive theories do not make similar commitments in the forging of their key concepts as do normative theories. Prediction is not always a critical concern even for empirical theory. Such considerations as simplicity, generality, connectedness, and other systematic concerns are crucial for both kinds of theory construction. The critical case here is how concepts are changed, and it is suggested here that the differences between moral and legal theory are not significantly different from those factors which forge empirical theory. An appropriate place to look for the physiology of theory development is the judicial process.

Ethics and morals have many differences, but they seem incidental to issues of the systematization of knowledge, and what differences there are that are relevant here seem to be largely to the institutional character of law, that is, to the control of evidence and inference by the structure of a trial and to the relatively greater precision guaranteed by tradition, corpus, and a "fixed" vocabulary. The outcome of the adversary method of inquiry in law is decisional and relative to rather specific data. The black and white of a verdict, however, frequently obscures its genuine proba-

[5] Goodnow, J., "Determinants of Choice-distribution in Two Choice Situations," *Am. J. Psych.*, 1955, 68, pp. 106–116.

listic character (even the dramatic change of the Nine Old Men under the threat of court packing by Roosevelt is not nearly so dramatic when it is remembered that the shift at first was from a six-three to a four-five). Of course, opposing conclusions in ethics frequently depend neither on differences of principle nor of fact but on differences in the assaying and weighing of facts admitted to be relevant, but this can scarcely be regarded as distinctive of attitudinal disagreement since this difference in weighing is characteristic of all manner of scientific debate.

Until the end of the nineteenth century the prevailing conception of the judicial process in American law was mechanical. The major premise was thought to be the appropriate legal principle, the minor premise, a statement of the facts, and the conclusion, the disposition. Attack by legal realists, pragmatists and others then made it clear that the common law was no depository of major premises, and worse, that for any desired conclusion sophistically proper premises could be found. Such legal theories have, of course, their counterpart in ethical theory. Now what is it that a judge has to decide? He has at hand no single appropriate legal concept. He must decide on the basis of precedent what is the precedent and whether the case before him is sufficiently like those defined by the precedent—that is to say, since any case is like any other in some respects, whether the present one exhibits sufficiently appropriate characteristics to be joined under the principle to the class of base cases. When all goes well and there is sufficient similarity, the appeal to *stare decisis* decides one instance to be like the others; a little uneasiness about the kinship encourages him to avoid straining the precedence by singling out some unlikeness or disqualifying property; finally, genuine discontent leads him to the change or withdrawal of the principle. Of course this last category includes many of the dramatic innovations and reversals such as Cardozo's far-reaching holding in *Macpherson vs. Buick*.

The pressures which make for the dynamics and the growth of judicial process lie in the necessity to confront new cases, in considerations of consistency and simplicity, in the search for higher order generalizations with power, etc. There is a constant and mutual adjustment of principles and commitments of varying degrees of specificity. The development of the "right of privacy" from early cases involving residual ownership in letters is an excellent though extended illustration. For present purposes let us streamline a series of cases. "Theft" was defined as "the abstraction of corporeal property without the consent of the owner" and it seemed an adequate enough statement of the identifying characteristics of theft until some ingenious fellow tapped a municipal power line. Strictly, of course, he had "abstracted" no "corporeal property"; but his use of the power was clearly akin to that of more ordinary materials which fell within the definition. The courts of appeal sympathized with this latter and strained to define electricity as corporeal, but they had to give way to a commitment of physics. In the long run they extended the scope of theft, and the defendent was liable.

Once again let us compare such considerations with those of admittedly empirical nature. The development of the notion of theft was forged under pressures that are clearly germane to the development of non-moral conceptions. Suppose that we have two definitions of "slum": the one, an architect's criteria in terms of the hardware, the sanitary conditions, the space per person, etc.; the other, a sociologist's definition weighting heavily such matters as family cohesion, juvenile delinquency, interest in and attachment to the home, etc. Now it is clear that the application of these different criteria would result in widely different policies. Is there a way of legislating between such definitions? A compromise definition is after all just one more candidate. Even more removed from morally charged issues are the decisions about what factors are important in "intelligence," or what is an "acid" or even what are appropriate limitations on "is pure" or "is soluble." What we seem to have are principles which are derived from examinations of particular cases and then these principles become normative and may well exclude some of the base cases or themselves be replaced in favor of some more adequate principle for systematic or other reasons.

This is of course one way of regarding the process of induction. At least it agrees with one contemporary account. In *Fact, Fiction and Forecast* Nelson Goodman writes:

> The real inadequacy of Hume's account lay not in the fact that he described how inductive judgments are made, but that his description was incomplete. Regularities in experience give rise to habits of expectation and thus it is predictious conforming to past regularities that are normal or valid. But Hume overlooks the fact that some regularities do and some do not establish such habits; that predictions based on some regularities are valid, while predictions based on others are not.[6]

Goodman, in contrast to Hume:

regards the mind as in motion from the start, striking out with spontaneous predictions in dozens of directions, and gradually rectifying and channeling its predictive processes. We ask not how predictions come to be made, but how—granting they are made—they come to be sorted out as valid and invalid. Literally, of course, we are not concerned with describing how the mind works but rather with describing or defining the distinction it makes between valid and invalid projections.

But these generalizations or postulates—at least those of highest order —in ethics and law traditionally have been thought to demand some spe-

---

[6] Goodman, N., *Fact, Fiction and Forecast*, Harvard, 1955, p. 75.

cial justification or to require some special guarantee. Their explanatory role is easily forgotten; they are placed beyond criticism and recall, and, when they are entrenched and buttressed by social and religious beliefs, they appear as unabridgeable commitments. And yet it seems to me that our problem in morals lies precisely here. If we regarded our high-order moral generalizations as hypotheses to which the richness of experience and increased scientific knowledge were relevant then we might come to seek common goals and common ways of resolving conflicts.

Various philosophers have approached agreement lately that the problem of establishing fundamental principles of logic, of induction, or of morals and law presents similar difficulties. Thus Feigl says:

The justifying principles (*justificantia*) for the establishment of knowledge-claims have been retraced to their ultimate foundations in the rules of inference and substitution in deductive logic. We cannot, without vicious circularity, disclose any more ultimate grounds of validation here. Similarly the rules of maximal probability in inductive inference form the ultimate validating basis of all empirical reasoning. Correspondingly, the supreme norms of a given ethical system provide the ultimate ground for validation of moral judgments.[7]

But the issue need not be stated thus. There is clearly something suspicious about the effort to ground ultimates in something "higher," for to succeed is simply to make what was ultimate, penultimate. The need for such justification has seemed more crucial in the history of legal and ethical theory, doubtless due to the more obvious claims on behavior. Goodman suggests that inductive and deductive arguments are justified by their conformity to logical rules, but it is to valid rules. But rules are valid if they yield correct inferences. "The process of justification is the delicate one of making mutual adjustments between rules and accepted inferences. And in the agreement achieved lies the only justification needed for either."[8] Equally with the normative, it is notorious that appeals to justice, to the greatest good for the greatest number, to self-realization, or even to uniformity in nature are little help in specific instances—but judgments on a multitude of cases are valueless to carry us to the next one. Perpetual and mutual correction of principles and instances under pressures of changing circumstances constitute moral enlightenment and justification.

[7] Feigl, H. "Validation and Vindication" in *Readings in Ethical Theory*, ed. Sellars and Hospers. N. Y. 1957, pp. 433–444.
[8] Goodman, N., *op. cit.*, p. 67.

F. H. Parker : ON THE BEING OF
FALSITY

PROFESSOR *Francis H. Parker of Haverford College observes in this essay that a serious omission characterizes realist ontologies of falsity, that the underlying epistemic scheme of such a metaphysic has failed to account sufficiently for the kind of being possessed by the concept without a referent in intention. This exposition of the lacuna in realist epistemology seeks not to fill but to delineate it so that approach may be taken to evaluate the process of knowing in a total context. Dr. Parker has prepared this contribution especially for the present volume.*

• That the problem of error is the peculiar and special stumbling block of every realist epistemology has long been a common philosophical saying. But most realists, myself included, have, I am now convinced, never taken this sufficiently seriously. While being convinced in their own minds that no other theory can account for truth, that other theories can at best account only for error, realists have rejected the putative corollary that no realist theory can account for error, that realism can account *only* for truth. Essential to the definition of epistemological realism is the thesis that the objects of cognition are independent of being cognized. Does this not mean, however, that independence from being cognized characterizes *all* objects of cognition, false as well as true ones? And does this not rule out the possibility of error by making erroneous cognition identical with veracious cognition?

"Not at all!" objects the monistic or "neo-" realist. Sticking consistently to the realist thesis that things cognized exist objectively and independently of the cognitions of them, the monistic or "neo-" realist grants—in fact insists—that this independence characterizes erroneous objects just as much as veracious ones. But this does not rule out the possibility of error by making erroneous cognition identical with veracious cognition, he claims, for illusory objects are objects of a very different kind from veracious ones. While it is true that the peculiarity of erroneous objects does not consist in any alleged subjectivity or mentality, in being "all in your head," illusory objects do have a peculiarity which is both wholly objective or cognitively independent and yet which serves to distinguish them adequately from veracious objects so as to account for the possibility of error. Different monistic realists have, of course, defined this objective essence of falsity in different ways. It may be a peculiarity of the physical world—"contradiction in nature,"[1] or "physical reduplication,"[2] or a "projectively indiscernible"[3] quality. Or it may be something other-worldly, a non-physical quality, a "subsistence" or an "unreality," but if so this other-worldliness "is no more subjective than reality."[4] Thus, in either case:

The objective universe contains not only the straight stick, but also the bentness; not only the parallel rails, but also the convergence; not only the rustling of the curtain, but also the flimsy ghost; not only the existent poisons, but also the imagined ones of the dream and the hallucination.[5]

False awareness does not, therefore, differ from true awareness with respect to the *awareness;* rather false awareness differs from true awareness

[1] E. B. Holt *et al., The New Realism,* Macmillan, 1912, p. 361 (Holt).
[2] *Ibid.,* p. 304 (Holt).
[3] *Ibid.,* p. 458 (Pitkin).
[4] *Ibid.,* p. 367 (Holt).
[5] Edward G. Spaulding, *The New Rationalism,* Holt, 1918, p. 378.

in having a special and peculiar kind of *object*. True cognition is thus a cognition of an objective, independent *true* or *real* thing; false cognition is a cognition of an objective, independent *false* or *unreal* thing.

A realist who reflects critically on this monistic, "neo-" realist conclusion must find it unsatisfactory, however, for it makes a false cognition just as true a cognition *of its own very peculiar object* as a true cognition is of its normal, mundane object. The difference between seeing pink elephants and seeing gray ones is, on this "neo-" realist theory, not essentially other than the difference between seeing large elephants and seeing small ones. In all four cases the proper object is apprehended exactly as it is, and isn't this what truth means? "The net outcome seems to be," as the "critical" realist Arthur K. Rogers said,[6] "that we are wrong in supposing illusion illusory; it is as good a fact as anything else," though it has a peculiar object.

The "critical" realist therefore concludes that the "neo-" realist theory leads to the abolition of error. From this conclusion the "critical" realist infers that the object of a false cognition cannot be independent of the cognition, as is the object of a true cognition. Hence he concludes that realism's defining thesis—that objects of cognition exist independently of being cognized—applies only to true cognition, not to false. Thus "critical" realism's stand on the status of true and false objects is a dualistic one. For "critical" or dualistic realists, whether they be of the modern–Cartesian or of the classical–Aristotelean variety, the objects of erroneous cognition only appear to be independent and objective; they are in fact subjective and mind-dependent. Their *esse* is *percipi;* they are *entia rationis*. The objects of erroneous belief are " 'ideas' or 'essences'—not at all to be identified with supposed reality";[7] "nothing else (relevant) exists but the mental fact—[nothing] external to the organism."[8] In erroneous cognition "what exists as an object of knowledge exists merely and solely *as an object, not as a subject*."[9] By false perceptions we mean "perceptions which do not intentionally reiterate things as they exist outside our psychic life."[10]

Thus the "critical" realist accounts for falsity by saying that the objects of false cognition are not really, realistically, independent of their apprehensions at all. Of course, the objects of erroneous awareness do *appear* to

[6] Durant Drake *et al.*, *Essays in Critical Realism*, Macmillan, 1920, p. 134.

[7] *Ibid.*, p. 142 (Rogers).

[8] Durant Drake, "That Elusive Doctrine of Essence," *Philosophical Review*, XXXVII (1928), pp. 56–57.

[9] Frederick D. Wilhelmsen, *Man's Knowledge of Reality*, Prentice-Hall, 1956, p. 179. I am indebted to this book for helping me see the deficiencies of my own account of error, as well as bringing clearly to my mind the way in which to formulate the distinction between having the truth and knowing the truth. On this distinction see p. 305 below.

[10] *Ibid.*, p. 176.

be just as objective and independent as the objects of veracious ones, and this fact must be accounted for. We must say that the objects of *bona fide* false cognitions are given *as being* independent and objective, but we cannot now, as "critical" realists, allow this merely apparent and presumptive independence to be a real and actual independence and objectivity. Thus we may distinguish falsity from truth, as the present author has been in the habit of doing, as follows: While,

the truth of a proposition consists in the coincidence of a merely terminal, judgmental, dependent act of existing with a non-terminal, extra-judgmental, independent act of existing . . . the falsity of a proposition consists in the failure of the merely terminal, dependent act of existing to coincide with any nonterminal, independent act of existing. . . . A true proposition presumes to, and actually does, terminate in an independent, extra-judgmental act of existing, while a false proposition merely presumes to do this and does not actually succeed in it.[11]

Dualistic or "critical" realism thus succeeds, where "neo-" realism does not, in distinguishing error from truth. But essentially involved in this dualistic account of error is a crucial problem which, I have now come to believe, has not been solved and which has perhaps not even been clearly seen. This problem, put in the simplest terms, is that the above-sketched "critical" realist account has, as it stands, no place for the fact that the sincerely deceived person is aware of his object *as independent of his awareness of it,* just as much as the undeceived person is. To tell the person suffering *bona fide* error that he only thinks he sees a ghost in the graveyard because there really isn't any there, that the ghost that he really sees is only in his head, is to tell him that he is lying; and this is both, on the one hand, outrageous, and also, on the other hand, destructive of anything for him to be sincerely mistaken about. It is no good telling the sincerely deceived person that the object of his awareness has, in the more technical terms just quoted, only a terminal, judgmental, dependent existence in fact or actuality, for *his* object patently and ineluctably has also a non-terminal, extra-judgmental, independent existence. While his erroneous object does, indeed, have a dependent, judgmental status—as does also the true object—the object which the sincerely deceived person contemplates is *also* something existing *in rerum natura* independently of his awareness. To say that there is no such real, independent thing is to say that there is nothing relevant for him to be (falsely) aware of, and this is to say that his false awareness is no awareness at all. If, on the other hand, his false awareness is a genuine awareness, then to say that his object is really the cognitively dependent, judgmental object which alone is allowed to exist, is to make his cognition *true,* since *this* object exists as he

[11] *The Return to Reason* (John Wild, editor), Regnery, 1953, p. 172.

apprehends it. In brief, I have come to the conclusion that the above-sketched dualistic or "critical" realist account of error implies that a false proposition is meaningless, or else that it is true.

This statement must seem dogmatic and unjustified, however—and probably even unclear. To clarify and defend this thesis, let us assume the role of "critical" realists and undertake a very cautious search for the locus of false being, to see whether the "critical" realist can handle falsity in his own terms, and to see that the problem of the independence of false objects is indeed an inescapable problem. Let us begin, however, by putting this allegedly inescapable problem out of our minds and by trying to approach the problem of falsity with a clean slate.

(I)

All our results would be wasted if it should turn out that our subject, falsity, is itself non-existent, so a preliminary moment spent on a demonstration of the existence of falsity will show that there really is something here for realism to explain, as well as lay the foundation for our search for the essence of falsity. While the fact that others disagree with us is usually sufficient to convince us of the reality of falsity and error, the philosopher tends to be ill at ease until he feels that he has logically coercive evidence for the reality of his starting point. Logically coercive evidence unfortunately always involves premises, however, and the truth of every such premise ultimately depends on definitions which are themselves conditioned by data or intuitions, as well as by the obstinacy of the human will. Still, the so-called laws of logic or general metaphysical principles, and especially the principles of excluded middle and non-contradiction, are more often accepted than the principle that whoever disagrees with us is in error. This being so, our choice of such metaphysical or logical principles as the sole premises for our demonstration of the fact of falsity—as well as for other demonstrations later—may put the philosophical conscience at ease and get us started on our task.

There is such a thing as falsity, says the principle of excluded middle. For there is such a thing as a proposition distinguishing truth from falsity, and if this proposition is true, then there is such a thing as falsity distinct from truth; and if this proposition is false, then again there is such a thing as falsity. There is such a thing as falsity, echoes the principle of non-contradiction. For there are pairs of mutually contradictory propositions, and one of these must be false and the other true. Having thus reassured ourselves of the genuineness, and even inescapability, of our enterprise, let us be off.

Our task is to localize the essence of falsity—a task made necessary by the impracticability of dealing with every last example of falsity ranging from perceptual illusion through mathematical error to dramatic impossibility. The general locale of falsity must be the proposition or statement or judgment, since a cognition is false only in virtue of some proposition or judgment which it contains. "Centaur," "rain," and "square root of minus two" are not in themselves false, nor are the images △ , □ , and ○ . It is not the words, phrases, and concepts which are false (or true), but rather the propositions in which they inhere; and the same is true, though perhaps less obviously, of sensory images, whether immediate, remembered, or conjured up in imagination. Such propositions are often, of course, not expressed. They are doubtless often not even verbalized in imagination, achieving only the form of a psychophysical set, attitude, attention, or expectancy—an acting as if a certain proposition were true: running forward on the desert as if the mirage were an oasis, shrieking with terror as if the tombstone were a ghost, or reaching for the moon as if it were made of green cheese. Yet a proposition is always implicit in every experience which can meaningfully be called true or false, and it can therefore always be explicated and expressed. And since it is in virtue of this proposition, and of it alone, that an awareness is or can be false, we can and must abstract away from the particular cognitive context of the proposition and the particular significance of its constituents in order to get at the heart of the problem of falsity. While there, of course, are many and extremely diverse modes or types of false cognition, such as hallucination, illusion, delusion, inconsistency, literary incredibility, being false to one's wife or to one's subject matter, etc., it is the falsity as such which all these and other cases exemplify that is our concern here. And it is perhaps now clear that the general locale of falsity is the proposition.

But what is it about a false proposition which makes it false? We might answer, of course, that all propositions are divided into two (or more) classes, that one of these classes is the class of false propositions, and that a particular proposition is false because it is a member of this class. But this is, of course, unhelpful, and it is, in addition, positively misleading in suggesting that the falsity of a proposition is due to or springs from each and every one of its parts conjointly and indifferently. For the same item may be a component of a true proposition as well as of a false one—"Squirrels are mammals" and "Squirrels are molluscs," for example. So falsity is not a characteristic attaching simply to certain propositions taken as unanalyzed wholes. It is rather something to be discovered only in and through a careful analysis of the total structure of the proposition.

How shall we set about such an analysis? Every proposition or judgment is analyzable into two terms related by a certain relation. True, one of the terms may be hardly more than a reference to existence or thinghood: *"It's* a ghost!," *"There* is an oasis," *"That* is made of green cheese," "Martians *exist."* While it is important in some contexts to regard these so-called existence propositions as having only one term, the fact that a second term can always be supplied to form a proposition which is equivalent in truth-value, though perhaps not synonymous, with the original ("Martians are *real*," "*What you call a tombstone* is a ghost," etc.) permits us, for present purposes, to regard all propositions as subject-predicate ones.[12] This being so, let us see if we can discover, within the structure of the subject-predicate proposition, the locus of falsity by analyzing the epistemology of each of these three components: the subject term, the predicate term, and the relation between them.

Is the source of the falsity of the proposition the subject term? Certainly not when it is taken just as such, as a single term, for we have seen that only propositions are true or false, that a term in isolation is neither true nor false. "Elephants, true or false?" makes no sense, though of course it does if it tacitly contains a proposition: "There are elephants—true or false?" So the subject of a false proposition, just as a subject, as a term, is as good as the subject of a true one.

More than that, it is also the case as a distinct fact that the referent of the subject term must even be known *truly*. It seems impossible to say, for example, that the proposition, "*That elephant* is pink," is false unless "that elephant" is truly known just as it is. Error is always a mistake *about something unmistaken,* just as disagreement is always *about something agreed on.* Ralph Barton Perry once put this beautifully: ". . . The object which one's knowledge is *about* has in some sense to be infallibly identified before the cognitive act can be either true or false. The questionableness of cognition is relative to the indubitableness of its object." [13] Or, as Santayana once put it, "Even to fall into error and misconceive its object the cognitive process must first select that object unequivocally . . . by designating some true circumstance that will suffice to identify it." [14]

This true knowledge in and by the subject term is also manifest in the fact that it is always possible to explicate from any proposition of the form "S is P" another proposition of the form, "There is S," and this in spite of the dicta of contemporary logicians about existential import—in spite of these dicta because the truthful apprehension of the referent of the subject term in a false proposition does not mean that that referent necessarily exists *really,* or *physically,* or in any other particular mode of being. Nor, apparently, need the referent of the subject term exist in the mode of being in which the user of the false proposition thinks it exists—or at least so it now seems. It may well be that the elephant which is truly known through the subject term in our false proposition is only a fictional one, for example, while the deceived proposer may happen to think that it

[12] Actually, as we shall see, my thesis does not depend on this analysis of propositions; it is only a convenient approach.
[13] *Philosophical Review*, XXX (1921), p. 400, in his review of *Essays in Critical Realism.*
[14] *Essays in Critical Realism*, p. 166.

exists *in rerum natura*. If this should happen to be so, then that implicit proposition, "There is S" or, "There is an elephant," would itself also be a false proposition, since in this case there would not in point of fact be an elephant in the sense in which the deceived proposer tacitly proposes that there is. But even in this case the falsity cannot be due to the subject term as such, since in that implicit proposition, "S exists" or, "There is S" or, "That elephant exists," the subject term "S" is once again, as in our original proposition, both on the one hand *infallible,* as the simple conceptual apprehension of a quiddity, and also on the other hand *true,* in so far as it is the subject of *another* and *second* implicit proposition to the effect that "S (in the proposition "S exists") exists." In any event, therefore, the elephant, the referent of the subject term, does exist somewhere or somehow, or else when the speaker speaks about "it" he is speaking about just nothing at all, falsely speaking about nothing at all, and therefore not speaking falsely at all.

As the object of a term, therefore, as the object of a simple concept, that is, the elephant is *infallibly conceived*. And as the object of an implicit proposition intending it as existing in some mode of being or other, at least in the mode of the possible or conceivable, the elephant is even *known truly*. This being so, the referent of the subject term is, for the realist, cognized as it is independently of the cognition of it and unchanged by that cognition, whether the cognition be *via* the term alone just as a concept and its object a mere quiddity apprehended infallibly, or whether the cognition be *via* another proposition, implicit in the original proposition, and its object that quiddity as truly existing in some mode or other, at least in the mode of the conceptual. Consequently all the characteristics of truth, as it is viewed both realistically and commonsensically, attach to the subject term as a cognition; and hence the subject term cannot as such be the source of the falsity of the proposition in which it occurs. "Those railroad tracks really converge," for instance, cannot be a false proposition unless those very railroad tracks themselves are both infallibly conceived and truly known.

If the source of the falsity of a proposition is not to be found in its subject term, perhaps it is to be found in the predicate term. But surely this cannot be the case either, for if pink is not accurately identified, then the proposition, "That elephant is pink," for example, is not even meaningful, let alone false. So the predicate term, like the subject term, must, as a concept, as a simple apprehension of a quiddity, be infallible; it must signify its object, a characteristic abstracted from any act of existing, just as it really is in itself independently of its being signified. "Pink," taken alone, can no more be false than "that elephant" can—though of course neither, taken alone, can be true either. But just in order to have a proposition in the first place of which it is then meaningful to say that it is false (or true), the quiddities signified by the constituent terms must be grasped infallibly.

Moreover, the referent of the predicate term, again like the referent of the subject term, must even be *known truly*. For just as with the subject term so also with the predicate term, it is always possible to explicate from any proposition of the form "S is P" another proposition of the form "There is P" whose truth is presupposed by the meaningfulness, and therefore by the falsity, of the original proposition, "S is P." Once more, of course, we needn't say—or at least so it now seems—that the referent of the predicate term exists *really, in rerum natura,* nor even in any other mode of existence in which the proposer may think it exists. If "S is P (really)" is false because P exists only conceptually, and if the relevant intended tacit proposition is "P exists (conceptually)," then this second, tacit proposition is true, and P is not only infallibly conceived but also truly known. And if P should happen, in point of fact, to exist in some other mode of being than the conceptual, then, while the tacit proposition "P exists (conceptually)" might then be said to be false, there would in that case be *another* tacit proposition, "P exists (x-ly)," which would be true. And so on. So in any case the referent of the predicate term exists in some fashion or other, and it is both infallibly conceived and truly known as it exists. Once more, then, as in the case of the subject term, the possibility of falsity on the part of the proposition as a whole requires and presupposes both an infallible, simple, conceptual apprehension of the object of the predicate term as a quiddity abstracted from an act of existing and also a truthful, propositional knowledge of the object of the predicate term as that very quiddity as existing in some mode or other. To quote Perry again, "The questionableness of cognition is relative to the indubitableness of its object." [15]

It therefore seems sufficiently clear that we cannot say that the falsity of the proposition is traceable to either of the two constituent terms as such. For in each of these terms there is, and must be in order to have a proposition at all, let alone a false one, both an infallible, conceptual apprehension of a quiddity as a sheer possibility abstracted from any and every mode of existence and also a truthful, propositional knowledge of that very same quiddity as existing in some mode of existence or other, at least in the mode of the thinkable. Of course, all this says nothing whatsoever about the *kind* of existence which either or both of these infallibly conceived and truthfully known quiddities may happen to have in point of fact, nor anything at all concerning whether the mode of existence which they happen to have is or is not the same mode of existence which they are intended as having either in the original "S is P" proposition or in any of the tacit "There is S (or P)" propositions. Still, each infallibly and truth-

[15] *Loc. cit.*

fully apprehended object has *some* status, some mode of being—or else the false proposition is a proposition about nothing at all and therefore no proposition. Moreover, as infallibly and truthfully apprehended, each object is, for the realist, quite independent of the cognition of it; and it therefore conforms entirely to the requirements of a realist account of its being known as it really is (however that may be) in itself.

If the source of the falsity of a proposition is not discoverable in either of its two terms taken in isolation, however, perhaps it is discoverable in the relation between these two terms; perhaps, that is to say, it is a function of the proposition taken as a whole and, more specifically, of the peculiar propositional relation existing between the two terms. This possibility we must now explore.

What is the relation between the subject and the predicate in a false proposition, between "that elephant" and "pink," for example? *As* the *object* of the propositional *intention,* especially of the verb, the relation between subject and predicate is exactly as proposed. That is, *as intended* the relation is as intended—a tautology—identity in an affirmative proposition and duality in a negative one. The *intended* relation between that elephant and pink, for example, is one of identity—"That elephant *is* pink"—and consequently that elephant and pink *must* be identical *as intended,* for otherwise there would be nothing at all intended and hence no intention. But in *this* context there is obviously no error, for the relational complex is exactly as it is intended: the elephant is intended as pink, and *as intended* it *is* pink. For error to occur the relational complex cannot, it would now seem, really be as it is intended as being; the referents of the subject and predicate terms must really be dual when apprehended as identical and really identical when apprehended as dual. But what can be the *nature* of the difference between the intended complex and the real complex?

Since to be different from the real would be, seemingly, to be unreal, one might be tempted to say that the intended complex is simply unreal, that it doesn't exist at all. Thus some "critical" realists take the position that an illusory object "has absolutely no existence of any sort." [16] But the more we think about it the more we see that this position is untenable, since, if taken strictly and seriously, it would mean that the deceived person is not aware of anything at all, that the person who sees pink elephants doesn't see pink elephants, for his illusory object "has absolutely no existence of any sort." Hence *some* ontological status must be given to the illusory object; but this status must be, for the "critical" realist, a status different from the status of independent reality which he has reserved for the objects of veracious cognition. What can this status be, and how can we describe it?

We might describe this status very bluntly as simply *being subjective,*

[16] Durant Drake, *Mind and Its Place in Nature,* Macmillan, 1925, p. 177.

being "all in your head," being totally dependent on the very act of cognizing the object possessing that subjective status. This is the position most
frequently taken by the "critical" or—as we may call them in connection
with their view of falsity—subjectivistic realists. As we saw in our introductory preview, however, this position does not do justice to the fact that
the illusory object *seems* to be just as objective and independent, to the
mind of the deceived person, as a veracious object does. Hence we must
qualify the position and say that the *intended* or *apparent* or *presumptive*
object, in a false cognition, *is independent,* while adding, to keep our
realism a "critical" or dualistic or subjectivistic one, that the real or actual
object—that intended object as seen from outside the perspective of the deceived person—is subjective or dependent on the act of cognizing it. This
is the line the present author has taken previously. According to this
modified view,[17] the key to the nature of falsity lies in the recognition that
the terminus of an immaterial, immanent, relational act may have two
facets or statuses. In the first place, it has its status just *qua terminus,* and
with respect to this status it is, *qua terminus,* a necessary part of the relational act and hence dependent upon that relational act. Now every relational act, since it is relational, has a terminus *qua terminus*—if it did not,
it would not be relational. And hence every intention intends something,
namely the terminus *qua terminus.* Hence every false proposition intends
an act of existing insofar as an act of existing is the terminus of that relational propositional act. But though an essence in an act of existing is always the terminus of every proposition, true or false, it is never intended
as being a terminus; that is, it is never intended in its *capacity* as the
terminus, but rather as being *independent* of that intention or relation.
But while a proposition never intends its terminus merely as being a terminus, yet it may nevertheless be merely that; what the proposition intends
may be merely its terminus *qua terminus.* And when this situation occurs,
the proposition is false; it is deprived of its full completion because the
terminus that it intends not merely *qua terminus* is in fact merely a terminus. That is, what it intends is merely a terminus, yet it does not intend
it merely as such. Truth consists in the presumptive independence of a
propositional object being also a factual independence, and falsity consists
in the lack of this.

All of my repeated and varied attempts to work this thesis out into a
detailed and tenable theory of falsity have, however, been stopped by the
same insurmountable barrier: the inescapable fact (as it now seems to me
to be) that the object of a false cognition must exist independently of that
cognition simply because that is what is sincerely intended. The conclusion has therefore come to seem inescapable that the above subjectivistic

17 The remainder of this paragraph is quoted, with some omissions, from *The Return to
Reason,* pp. 171–172.

or dualistic or "critical" realist account of falsity does not really see or deal with the problem of the proper being of what is falsely intended, and that such an account even implies, in fact, that a false proposition is no proposition at all. Each new skirmish or maneuver comes up against the same insurmountable barrier, as we shall now see.

(II)

This insurmountable obstacle is the fact that the object that is meant or intended in *bona fide* false cognition is not at all the judgmental, dependent, and merely presumptively independent object; the intended object is rather something really and actually independent of that cognition. The person genuinely experiencing a mirage and being deluded by that experience is referring to a real, independent, extra-mental oasis, for example. Hence it does no good to tell him that what he sees is really merely heat waves and that the oasis which he thinks he sees exists only in his mind. It is true, of course, both that he is seeing heat waves and that the oasis he sees is in his mind. But the point is that neither of these true realities is what *he means,* is what he is *referring* to. And there *is* something that he means and is referring to, namely the oasis, for otherwise his cognition could not be called false.

This much, as thus put, might readily be granted; but the essential point implicit in this is somewhat harder to see. This essential point is that the oasis which we must allow to exist since it is being referred to is one which is objective and independent of the deceived person's cognition of it. This must be granted for the same reason that it must be granted that the oasis he sees exists—namely, that otherwise what *he* intends is non-existent, in which case his intention of it must also be non-existent, and this destroys the falsity. "What do you see, Mr. X?" "I see an oasis." "But there isn't any real, independent oasis existing there in nature, since you are experiencing a mirage; so the oasis you see is only in your mind." "Are you calling me a liar? The oasis that I see is not at all mental or subjective; it is not an oasis-in-mind that I see but a real-oasis-existing-independently-of-my-mind-in-nature. You say that there isn't any such thing. But how is it then that I see it? There *must* be a real, independently existing oasis there, for otherwise I couldn't see it and then you couldn't say that I am experiencing a mirage!" The object in every authentic case of false cognition is thus something *not as*-intended but rather something *as not*-intended.

If we cling to the subjectivistic or "critical" realist account of error, therefore, we are faced with a paradox: What is intended (the independent object of the genuine false cognition) is not intended (because, for the "critical" realist, such an independent object does not exist). What is meant can't be meant. But paradoxes rest on ambiguous terms, so the terms "object" and "intention" must be ambiguous here. Let us use the terms "object" and "intention" for what the deceived person is aware of and his awareness of it, respectively, and the terms "subject" and "reference" for what the undeceived person is aware of and his awareness of it, respectively. Thus the deceived person's mistake consists in the fact that he thinks he is referring to a subject whereas he is really only intending an object. But this way of putting it is obviously only verbally different. If, on the one hand, there is in false cognition *only* an "object," then, if the false cognition is *false* it is not a *cognition,* since the "subject" that it falsely "refers to" doesn't exist to be cognized, and if the false cognition is a *cognition* it is not *false,* but *true,* since the only thing there to be cognized, the "object," is cognized as it is. And if we say, on the other hand, that there must be in false cognition a "subject" as well as an "object," since the deceived person is really *thinking* of his "object" *as* a "subject," then once more the cognition is not false but true, since it is of an independently existing "subject" and this is our definition of truth. How can a person refer to a subject when there isn't any subject to refer to? The answer seems inescapable: He cannot. We must try again.

Perhaps the difficulty lies in defining falsity in terms of non-existence. May we then not escape the difficulty by conceiving of falsity in some other way—as logicism's incoherence, for example, or, with Berkeley, as the fact that the false object is what is not perceived by God? Just a moment's reflection should convince us, however, that nothing essential is changed in these alternative formulations, for falsity is then *otherness,* and otherness is non-existence in a relative sense.[18] For Berkeley the false is defined as that which is other than what God perceives, and for logicism it is what is other than a constituent of a coherent system. But both kinds of otherness are cases of non-existence in a relative sense: *this* (the false) is *not that* (the truth). Furthermore, there is even an *absolute,* non-relative kind of non-existence involved in these accounts of falsity. For what is falsely intended is not simply the *thing which* is other, the "this"; what is falsely intended is the *identity* of the "this" which is other with the "that" from which it is other—what is intended is the "this-that"—and *this* object lacks existence *absolutely.* The "this" which is falsely intended may be *something* and thus have some ontological status—which ontological status is necessary in order for it to be the object of a cognition at all —even though it is not the "that" which is the reality or existence or truth. But what is intended in a *bona fide* case of error is the "this-that," the identity of the presumptively independent object, in "critical" realist

18 This seems to me to be the essential character of the solution of the problem of falsity which Plato ultimately arrives at in the *Sophist* after his negative conclusions in the *Theaetetus.* And this present essay seems very similar to Plato's struggle with the problem except that Plato's final conclusion seems to be, in the language of this essay, the dualistic or "critical" realist one which is here rejected.

terms, with the actually independent one; and this "this-that" cannot, for the "critical" realist, exist in *any* sense, not even as a something which is not something else. For even though this "this-that" object might be claimed to be a judgmental or conceptual or subjective something, *this* something is not what is *meant* or *intended* in the false proposition; and it is the something which is *meant* which cannot be, according to the "critical" realist, if the proposition is to be false. But, again, if this something that is meant cannot, by hypothesis, exist, how can it be meant? If it can be meant it must be, and if it cannot be it cannot be meant—and therefore, *a fortiori,* not falsely meant. Thus no way of construing falsity can dodge the fact that falsity is, from a "critical" realist standpoint, non-existence of some kind or other. And hence our problem continues to plague us: How can that which does not exist at all still exist to be something that the deceived person is aware of?

The situation is getting desperate, but let us make a new start. Falsity must be conceived thus: the false object is not what *it itself* claims to be. All falsity is thus falsity to *self,* duplicity, self-alienation. This definition, we note, seems to offer as a bonus an initially plausible account of *conative* types of falsity, such as being false to oneself, not being "to thine own self true," being false to one's friend, lying, etc. Thus the object of erroneous cognition *is* not what *it* seems. But what kind of being is seeming? Not just *intentional* being, not just judgmental, cognitively dependent being, for then we are back in the original difficulty: the sincerely deceived person means to refer to the real, independent object. The false object *is,* and *must* be, independently real because that is what is really intended. But the false object must also, for the "critical" realist, *not* be independently real because it is *falsely* intended, and that is the meaning of falsity. Once more our problem returns: how can the object both be and not be independently real?

Let us try, in final desperation, one last gimmick. Can we not solve our problem in a way analogous to the Thomist solution of the problem of universals, through the use of the concept of an "absolute nature" or "neutral entity"? In the context of the problem of universals a nature is in itself absolute and neutral with respect to unity and multiplicity, so a nature may take on either or both or neither of these two conditions without itself being altered. It may be multiplied and individuated by being actualized in matter without being unified through being known, or it may be unified through being known without being multiplied and individuated by being actualized in matter, or it may be neither multiplied nor unified when it is neither known nor actualized in matter. In like manner why may we not say that the thing intended in false cognition is in itself a neutral entity, neutral, now, with respect to independence from or dependence upon the cognition of it? Thus, when I believe, falsely, that there is an oasis before me, I am not meaning to say that this oasis, my intended object, is either independent of or dependent upon my cognition of it; this thought simply does not cross my mind. Now this oasis certainly exists in some sense in itself, and if I say that the existence it has is simply a neutral existence, an existence in itself, then I do not have to say, what the "critical" realist cannot say, that my false object exists independently and objectively. If it should happen to have independent, not merely judgmental, existence, then my cognition of the oasis would be true. But if the cognitively neutral existent which is my object happens to have, in addition to its own neutral existence, a dependent, judgmental, cognitive existence, then my cognition of it is false. That is, *status relative to a given intention is not itself an object of that intention.* Hence the object of a false cognition can lack *cognitively independent* existence, so that the cognition may indeed be false, without lacking *every* kind of existence, so that it can still *be* an object of a false cognition. Consequently we do not have to say that the authenticity of the illusory experience of the oasis, for example, requires that the oasis have real, cognitively independent existence when the fact that the experience is illusory requires, for the "critical" realist, that it not have such existence. All that we now have to say is that the oasis *is, period, neutrally* with respect to cognitively independent or dependent status or existence. Thus the object of a false cognition exists *as intended* because it is intended as simply being what it is, as an oasis if an oasis, as a pink elephant if a pink elephant, and not as "cognitively independent." And yet it lacks the kind of existence which, for the "critical" realist, is the essence of truth, namely cognitively independent existence. Hence the object of a false cognition exists as intended and yet does not exist truly.

Ingenious as this last attempt may be, however, it arises out of desperation and it does not really solve our problem any more than the previous attempts did. It is, indeed, only a verbal solution, because the "neutral," "simple," "in itself" kind of existence that the intended object of a false cognition has, on this view, is clearly none other than the real, independent existence *in rerum natura* which our "critical" realist approach has been trying all along to quash. While it is doubtless true, in first or unreflective intentions, that "status relative to a given cognition is not itself an object of that cognition," it is true only explicitly, not implicitly. The person experiencing the oasis mirage does not *say,* in the *first* instance, that the oasis which he is experiencing exists independently of his experience of it; he merely says, "I see an oasis" or "There is an oasis" or just "Water!" or even nothing at all, putting his energy rather into running for the water. But when the veracity of his experience is questioned, he will then—if he has the strength and can temporarily overcome his thirst—explicate from his oasis object a real, cognitively independent existence in nature: "Do you really see an oasis? I don't believe there's really any oasis there." "Yes, I see a real oasis, right there in the [real, independently existing] desert." "Come now! That can't be! The map says we're miles from water. Your oasis is all in your head!" "Are you calling me a liar? How can you see what I see? I tell you I see a real, objective, independently existing oasis! So there must *be* one!" In sum: real, cognitively independent existence is what is *meant* by the existence which the intended object has in authentic false cognition,[19] though the deceived person usually doesn't say so explicitly; and so, once more, the object must really have this kind of existence just in order to be intended as such.

The same conclusion is manifest in an analysis of the meaning of "knowing the truth" combined with a comparison of such knowledge with *bona fide* false cognition. In merely *having* but not knowing the truth, in knowing something that is true but not knowing *that* it is true, the knower is not explicitly aware of the fact that his object has existence independently of his cognition of it. But in *knowing* the truth, in knowing that his object is known truly, the knower is explicitly aware of the fact that his object exists independently of his knowledge of it—even though, of course, the ordinary person might not use this language. "Whales are mammals." "Are you sure?" "Certainly I'm sure; it's the truth and I know it." "But some people don't think so; some people call them fish." "I don't care what some people think. Whales are mammals no matter what *anybody* thinks!"

Now every genuine case of erroneous cognition presents itself to that erroneously cognizing mind as identical with a case of true cognition. That is, a person who is truly and sincerely deceived or mistaken is unaware of the fact that he is mistaken; if he were aware of that fact he would thereby have conquered his error, no longer be deceived, and be aware of a truth: that he was mistaken and that the opposite of what he had first believed is in fact the truth. Just like a person cognizing truly, the person cognizing falsely first merely *has* the "truth" (falsely) and is not aware of the fact *that* he has the "truth" (falsely), and thus, as we have just seen, is not explicitly aware of the cognitively independent existence that his (falsely) intended object has. But, once more just like a person knowing truly, when a mistaken person apprehends (falsely), in a second, reflective act, *that* his object is apprehended "truly," he is explicitly aware of the fact (falsely, the "critical" realist says) that the object of his awareness exists independently of his awareness of it. "Whales are fish." "Are you sure? The zoologists say they're mammals." "I don't care what the zoologists say. I know that whales are fish no matter what a zoologist or anybody else says!"

[19] This must be slightly qualified to yield the more precise definition of independence given below on p. 307 ff.

We have, in sum, two premises and a conclusion: (1) The theoretical, realist premise: True cognition consists in apprehending an object that is independent of that apprehension of it; and, consequently, knowing that one's cognition is true is, at least tacitly, knowing that the object apprehended is independent of that apprehension of it. (2) The phenomenological, common-sense premise: False cognition is, from the inside, to the person experiencing it, identical with true cognition. (3) The conclusion: False cognition is, as such, from the inside, to a person experiencing it, an apprehension of an object which exists independently of that apprehension of it; and falsely knowing that one's cognition is true is therefore, at least tacitly, apprehending the independent existence of that object.

Thus our last maneuver, like the earlier ones, has failed to surmount the obstacle of the independent being of what is falsely intended. Many other maneuvers are of course possible, but this obstacle now seems to me to be truly insurmountable by a "critical" or dualistic or subjectivistic realism. That this conclusion has not been granted by "critical" realists is due to the fact, it seems to me, that many of them, myself included, have not seen clearly or taken seriously the fact that every authentic false cognition is an intention of its object *as* real and cognitively independent. If as the result of the analysis here attempted, we now see this fact clearly, we also see that statements like the following are false: "In the false judgment, we *intend* the term of the relation of knowledge *merely as a term* . . . the relation has not been referred to extra-mental reality . . ."[20] This is simply not the case, as I hope the foregoing analysis has amply shown. The person sincerely making a false judgment is intending what he intends *not* merely as terminating his judgment but *as* existing *independently* in *extra-mental* reality. To deny this is to misdescribe the false judgment as well as to destroy its falsity—the latter since the deceived person would then be judging truly what he is judging. And we should also now see clearly that statements like the following are even self-contradictory: ". . . while a proposition never intends its terminus merely as being a terminus, yet it may nevertheless be merely that . . . what it intends is merely a terminus, yet it does not intend it merely as such."[21] This statement is self-contradictory because an intention of a non-existent independent object is an intention of nothing at all, and hence a non-existent intention. And many other examples of such false descriptions and self-contradictions may be found in other "critical" realist writings, whether the "critical" or dualistic realists be of the classical, Aristotelean variety or of the modern, Cartesian variety.

The results of the foregoing analysis may now be summarized. The "critical" or dualistic or subjectivistic account of error which grants to the

[20] Wilhelmsen, *op. cit.*, p. 179.
[21] Parker in *The Return to Reason*, p. 172.

object of erroneous cognition only a cognitively dependent or subjective existence is untenable because: (a) Either it makes false propositions *true,* if it asserts that the intended object of a *bona fide* false cognition is the merely judgmental, cognitively dependent existent, since this existent is then grasped exactly as it is, as a judgmental, cognitively dependent existent. (b) Or else it makes false propositions *meaningless* or *non-existent,* if it asserts that the intended object of a genuine false cognition is a non-judgmental, cognitively independent existent, for this independently existing object is declared, by the "critical" realist, to be non-existent, and an intention of a non-existent object is a non-existent or meaningless intention. The inescapable fact confronting realist epistemology is the fact that *the object of a bona fide false cognition does and must possess existence independent of that cognition.* And this inescapable fact is contradicted by the thesis essentially defining the "critical" or dualistic or subjectivistic realist account of error.

(III)

Then why not abandon realism? If realism must maintain that the objects of false cognition have the same cognitively independent existence possessed by the objects of true cognition, then isn't realism forced to populate objective reality with ghosts, goblins, and gremlins? But is this not simply fantastic? And is it not far removed from the common-sense realism from which philosophical realism claims to spring and to which it wants to be true? More importantly, does not the granting of independent, objective status to the objects of erroneous cognition actually make all false cognitions true, as we saw at the beginning that "neo-" realism's "pan-objectivism" makes error "as good a fact as anything else," [22] even granting that it has a very peculiar object? If, that is to say, we can not account for error in terms of a "critical," dualistic realism, it is also the case, just as the "critical" realists maintain, that we cannot account for error on the basis of a monistic, "neo-" realism either. And if this be so, maybe it is realism itself that is at fault. So shouldn't we abandon realism entirely?

To abandon realism, however, would be, I am convinced, to go from Scylla to Charybdis. For, as our opening maxim forecast, if realism can not account for error, at least it alone can account for truth. And the arguments in support of the thesis that realism alone can account for truth are still, to my mind, completely convincing. The defining core of realism's view of truth is the proposition that every truly known object exists independently of the knowledge of it. It must be noted at once,[23] however, that this independence possessed by objects of veracious cognition does

[22] *Essays in Critical Realism,* p. 134 (Rogers).
[23] Cf. *The Return to Reason,* pp. 153–154.

not mean that the thing known is necessarily independent of *every* cognition, or independent of *mind* or *mentality,* for many of the things truly known, such as ideas and purposes, are themselves mental and mind-dependent. Nor does the cognitive independence of veraciously apprehended objects mean that they are necessarily independent of the *physical conditions* of their apprehension, since the condition of the sense organs, the sensory media, and the central nervous system, for example, clearly make a difference to what is apprehended. This last proviso means, incidentally, that the uncertainty principle in physics in no way contravenes the realist thesis. Nor, finally, does this cognitive independence mean that things truly known are necessarily independent of cognitively mediated *practical* activities; all artefacts, indeed, depend on physical actions which are directed and controlled by awareness. No, the independence definitive of realism's account of truth means the independence of the object truly known from the *awareness* of *it*. An entity possesses cognitive independence if and only if it in no way depends, for either its existence or its character, upon *its awareness*—upon *that precise act* whereby *it* is *known*.

The most compelling arguments for the realist's thesis that the objects of true knowledge are independent of their being cognized are, to my mind, indirect arguments—arguments for the impossibility of the opposite view.[24] The usual form taken by the opposition to realist independence is the proposition that the object of true knowledge is dependent upon the mind by virtue of the fact that it is constructed by cognition out of certain given materials, the raw materials of sensation. Now this means that to know truly any entity, x, is to transform x into x'. But this is to assert that the true knowing of x is not a true knowing of *x itself* at all, but rather of non-x (x'). And this is surely self-contradictory. At this point, however, the opposition will protest that x is not an object of true knowledge at all before its transformation by the mind, that x is only the material for an object of true knowledge. It is rather x', the constructed object, the "phenomenon," which is the object of true knowledge; and as soon as we see this, the opposition continues, the contradiction vanishes. If this be so, however, in what way is the mentally constructed phenomenon truly known, according to this theory? Since the constructed object or phenomenon is by hypothesis the object of true knowledge, and since true knowing is regarded as an activity of constructing, then we must say of the original construct that it too is altered or constructed, or better

---

[24] The author intends to prepare a demonstration of realism which will include a more detailed presentation of such arguments. The reason for presenting arguments in favor of realism's account of truth in an essay on falsity is that it is important to demonstrate that the problem of the cognitive independence of the object of false cognition is a problem *for realism.*

re-constructed, by the act of knowing *it,* into a *different* object—x″. But then, once more, truly to know x′ is not truly to know *x′*, but rather x″— and so on. In each case there is a contradiction, and the contradiction is continued in an infinite regress away from it. This theory thus makes the mind like the donkey reaching for the carrot: every step it takes to grasp the object of true knowledge succeeds only in pushing it out of reach.[25]

At this point, however, the opposition may again object that for any given object of true knowledge the constructing process occurs only once, and that after it has once occurred to produce an object, phenomenon, or construct, why then that constructed object is just simply known. By saying this, the opposition concludes, we stop the regress and avoid the contradiction. This is, indeed, just what Kant, for example, seems to say. But the point to be noted is that this is to declare that in the very act itself of truly *knowing* the object, the mind does not act upon or alter the object; and the object therefore remains independent of the act whereby it is truly *known*. This does avoid the contradiction, but only by conceding the point. Thus we must say, to avoid the contradiction, that the object of true knowledge is unaltered by and independent of that precise act whereby it is truly known.

There is also a second contradiction to be found in this opposition theory, the contradiction involved in the knowledge of something in principle unknowable. To restrict the objects of true knowledge to phenomena constructed by the mind out of the raw materials of sensation is to maintain that there are things which are both by hypothesis unknowable, on the one hand, and also actually known, at least to a certain extent, on the other hand. For one like Kant who believes that the raw materials of sensation are caused by or due to some transcendent, ultimate thing-in-itself, it is this trans-empirical thing-in-itself which is by definition unknowable and yet at the same time known to be the transcendent source of the raw material for objects of knowledge. For one like the positivist who refuses—as Kant also would have refused, had he been consistent—to speak of any source or cause of the sensory raw material, it is this sensory raw material itself which is in principle unknowable and yet at the same time known to be the raw material for objects of knowledge.[26] But if we truly know that this transcendent unknowable is the material for objects of true knowledge or the source of such material, then surely we truly know something about it. And if, on the other hand, we know only the phenomenal objects constructed out of this raw material, then surely we cannot, without contradiction, say that there exists any material from

[25] Cf. the form of this argument given in "A Realistic Appraisal of Knowledge" in this volume, p. 37.
[26] Note as evidence for this statement the difficulties which positivists and other analysts have had with so-called protocol or ostensive propositions.

which these phenomenal objects are constructed, or any source of this material.

The same contradiction of knowing the unknowable occurs in a different area if this constructivist theory maintains that there is more than one constructive and thus truly knowing mind or cognitive agent. In the first place, but falling just short of contradiction, such a "pluralistic constructivism" implies solipsism, since the difference between these cognitively constructive minds means that their cognitively constructed objects are different, and then each such mind is by definition confined to its own constructed objects. In the second place, this solipsistic position is in fact self-contradictory, for it maintains that the mind knows something, namely that there is another constructive mind which is different from the mind which knows it, which it cannot know because its knowledge is by definition restricted to its own constructed objects. Hence the constructivist view is driven to the position that there is only one such constructive, truly knowing mind—a *Vernunft überhaupt*. But even such a general mind must still, as we have just seen, either fall short of ever knowing its object truly, by repeatedly changing it into a different object in the attempt to know it, or else know its once constructed object unaltered and independent, which concedes the realist thesis.

In sum, the theory which denies the cognitive independence of the object of true knowledge by making it a mental construct out of the raw materials of sensation—whether or not these raw materials are said to be caused by trans-empirical things-in-themselves, and whether or not there is more than one constructive mind—contradicts itself by knowing things which are by hypothesis unknowable and also by having a knowledge without an object.

These difficulties might lead one to adopt a second and more extreme version of the non-realist position—the version, namely, that the object of true knowledge is cognitively dependent not only with respect to its *form,* which the mind imposes upon the raw material of sensation, but also with respect to the very *matter* or *content* of the object. This more extreme version maintains, that is to say, that the object of true knowledge is *wholly* dependent upon the act whereby it is known, that true cognition *completely creates* its object, rather than merely constructing or producing it. But this more extreme, creativist view is subject to the very same difficulties which we have just seen to be involved in the less extreme constructivist view.

In the first place, such a more extreme view cannot consistently maintain that there is more than one such cognitively creative mind, for the same reason, which we have just seen, that there cannot consistently be more than one cognitively *constructive* mind—namely, that this would be to know unknowables. This more extreme, creativist version of the cognitive act is therefore driven, like the constructivist version, to the position that there is only one such truly knowing mind: the absolute mind. And of course it cannot maintain, as Berkeley does, for example, that there are other, *non*-creative, "finite" minds in addition to the one cognitively creative mind, since then these other, non-creative minds either gain true knowledge by constructing their objects—which is ruled out both by the present hypothesis and by our previous arguments—or else they know realistically, leaving their objects unaltered and independent—which concedes the point. No, there must now be only one truly knowing mind, and its knowing acts must be completely creative of its objects.

This position, however, is self-contradictory in just the same way, essentially, as the constructivist view was first seen to be. Since, on this creativist view, there exists no object to be truly known until after the cognitively creative act has occurred, *that* still non-existent object cannot be what is truly known. But may it not be truly known after it has once been cognitively created? No, since then, once more, *it* could not be the object of true knowledge because, this time, the cognitively creative knowledge of *that* object is now in the past, is now non-existent, and therefore not an existent cognition of *that* object at all. So it must be a *second* created object which is the object of true knowledge, and a *second* cognitively creative act which is the true knowledge of it. Once again, however, this cannot be the case, since this second object doesn't even exist to be known until *after* the second cognitively creative act has occurred. And so on, *ad infinitum*. On this creativist view, in short, when there is a (creative) act of knowing there is no object to be known, and when there is an object to be known there is no (creative) act of knowing it. Once more, therefore, we are in an infinite regress with cognition always thrusting its object away from itself—though behind itself now instead of in front of itself—but never ever reaching an object of true knowledge.

At this point, however, the creativist may take the same position which we saw that the constructivist finally takes; he may say that for any given object of true knowledge the creating process occurs only once, and that after it has once occurred to create an object, why then that created object is just simply known. By saying this, the creativist declares, we stop the infinite regress and avoid the contradiction. But as we saw before, this qualification concedes realism, since thus to qualify the position is to say that in the very act itself whereby the object is truly known it is not created and therefore is and remains independent of the act whereby it is truly known.

Hence to assert that the object of true knowledge is dependent upon the cognitive act, either for its form or for its total being, is to contradict oneself. We must therefore conclude, I am convinced, that truth can be accounted for only by realism, that the object of true knowledge must be independent of the act whereby it is truly known. But if only realism can account for truth, and if, as the analysis in Part (II) seemed to show, realism can account *only* for truth, perhaps we should conclude not that realism is true but that there is no such thing as truth. After all, a statistical study would probably show that there are far more false beliefs than true ones, so isn't error more important to explain than truth, and may not truth even be non-existent?

This will not do, however, for the existence of some truth is inescapable.[27] While the proposition, "There is no truth," is not itself *logically* self-contradictory, the *assertion* of this proposition is *psychologically* self-contradictory, or self-destructive. For the assertion that there is no truth is the assertion that that assertion is not true; this is the real point of value in Descartes' *cogito*. The only alternative to asserting that there is truth is, in Aristotle's terms, to be a vegetable, for to think anything at all is to think that there is something which is true. Moreover, we saw in Part (I) that error itself essentially involves truth, that "the questionableness of cognition is relative to the indubitableness of its object."[28] Thus not only is truth inescapable in itself, but also the very attempt to escape a theory of truth by substituting for it a theory of error is *eo ipso* a confrontation with the necessity for a theory of truth. Hence there is truth for epistemology to explain, and realism, defined essentially as the thesis that the object of true knowledge is independent of the act whereby it is truly known, is, I am still convinced, the only acceptable explanation of this truth.

Realism therefore cannot be rejected even though it seems unable to explain error. Realism thus seems like a woman: you can't live without her even if you can't live with her. The object of true knowledge is, realistically, independent of the knowledge of it; and the object of false cognition must, we have seen, be given the same independence as the object of true knowledge. So the problem of the independence of the object of false cognition is an inescapable problem for epistemology and thus for realism.

(IV)

The aim of this essay is simply to show that this is a problem which realists cannot dodge, and that it has been neglected by realist epistemologists. It is not the aim of this essay to attempt any solution of the problem —and, indeed, I do not at present find any satisfactory solution. At the same time, the results of our investigation indicate that there are two types

[27] Compare the formulation of this point made in "A Realistic Appraisal of Knowledge" in this volume, p. 19.

[28] Perry, *loc. cit.*

of solution which must be rejected and that there is one remaining area which needs to be explored.

In the first place, the "critical" or dualistic type of realist account of error must, we have seen, be rejected because, in the simplest terms, it is contradicted by the existence of propositions which are *sincere, meaningful,* and *false*. The heart of the account of falsity given by the "critical" or dualistic version of realism is the thesis that the object of false cognition has only a cognitively dependent, judgmental, intentional, mental, or subjective existence. But the ineluctable fact which this essay has tried to make clear is that this thesis is not and cannot be true. It *is* not true because the object intended, meant, or referred to in every authentic instance of error is patently a real, independent, extra-mental, objective existent. To deny this is phenomenologically false; to grant it while denying that there is any such independent existent is self-contradictory. And the "critical" or dualistic thesis *can*not be true, for if it were then the false, cognition *could* only refer to the subjective, mental, dependent existent; and if this were so and the false cognition were also a genuine cognition, then it would be a cognition of that sole existent as it is and hence not be false at all, but true. But there are false cognitions, as has been demonstrated. Hence any possible realist explanation of error must be of the "neo-," monistic, objectivistic type; it must, that is to say, grant that the object of *bona fide* false cognition exists just as independently of that cognitive act as the object of veracious cognition does of its cognitive act, for the simple reason that it is, in each case, this independently existing object that is intended.

However, and in the second place, we saw at the beginning of this essay that the account of error given by the twentieth-century school called neo-realism does not clearly distinguish error from truth. The object of an erroneous cognition is, according to that school, apprehended as it is in itself—or at least it is apprehended as it is in itself just as much as the object of veracious cognition is—though, of course, the accurately identified object of erroneous cognition is a very peculiar one. But this account forces us to conclude, as we saw that the twentieth-century school called critical realism did in fact conclude, that a false cognition is then just as true a cognition as a true cognition is.

Monistic, "neo-" realism is correct in saying that the objects of erroneous cognition have the same independent existence that the objects of veracious cognition have, but its identification of the essence of falsity with an intrinsic peculiarity of the object turns false cognition into true cognition of erroneous objects. Dualistic, "critical" realism, correctly seeing that such cognition is not erroneous cognition at all, makes the mistake of saying that the independent objects of erroneous cognition are non-existent; and in doing this it makes erroneous cognition no cognition at all.

Thus we learn that the essence of falsity is to be identified neither with a peculiar characteristic intrinsic to the object, as the "neo-" realist maintains, nor with status relative to the cognitive act, as the "critical" realist maintains. The essence of falsity must be something cognitively independent and objective, but it must not be, as with "neo-" realism, an intrinsic property of objects. Can we at present go further than this? One last step seems warranted by our investigation: the objective, independent essence of falsity must lie, apparently, in some extrinsic relation borne by the object of false cognition *to something else which is likewise objective and independent*. This final step seems unavoidable since our investigation seems to have eliminated all other types of alternative. Our analysis has shown that the essence of falsity must involve a relation of the object of false cognition to something else other than itself, rather than merely some property intrinsic to that object. And it has also shown that to make this relation a reference of the object back again to the subjective cognition would be once more to run up against the same insurmountable barrier of the cognitive independence of what is falsely intended. Such an objective relation or reference of the object to some other objective thing or property is thus an area which needs to be explored by attempts to discover the essence of falsity. But beyond this conclusion the results of our investigation do not, apparently, permit us to go.

Following up this last conclusion, however, we might be bold enough to take a further step and say that the essence of falsity consists in a truthful knowledge of an independently existing object *combined with* an *ignorance* of the just admitted real, independent relations of the object to other extrinsic, real, independent things or properties. In this case truth and falsity would be defined as follows: A cognition is true to the extent that the things or properties to which the cognized object is really, independently related are themselves objects of that self-same cognition. And a cognition is false to the extent that the things or properties to which the independently existing cognized object is really independently related are *not* themselves objects of that self-same cognition. Falsely to apprehend the railroad tracks as converging, for example, would then be to apprehend a convergence which really exists independently of that cognition but at the same time to fail to apprehend such other factors, to which that convergence is really related, as the unequal distances from the observer's eyes of the various points along the tracks. Falsely to perceive an oasis on a desert would be to apprehend an oasis which really exists independently of that cognition but at the same time to fail to grasp the relation between that apprehended oasis and such things as the heat waves and the deluded person's desire for drink. Believing that one is Napoleon would be (for all of us other than Bonaparte himself) to apprehend something really existing independently of that belief and, in the same act, to fail to apprehend the relation between that objective "one's being Napoleon" and one's own really and objectively psychotic condition. And so on. Thus falsity would be ignorance, but a special kind of ignorance, not simply ignorance as such. It would be ignorance of what the cognized object really involves, and it would be an ignorance essentially involved in an act not *merely* of ignoring but also of knowing.

It might be objected that such a solution commits us to the skeptical view that there is no truth at all, since every possible object is related to every other thing in reality and since we certainly do not possess the omniscience which this solution's definition of truth, as a knowledge of *all* the relations and relata of a given thing, would thus require us to possess. A moment's reflection should show, however, that this solution does not in fact thus commit us, for this solution does not necessarily imply that "every possible object is really related to every other thing in reality." This proposition is an ontological one requiring the support of ontological evidence and argument; it does not follow from the presently considered theory of falsity taken alone.

A seemingly contrary objection might also be leveled against this solution, the objection, namely, that it commits us to the absolutistic view that there is *only* absolutely certain truth about absolutely everything, since every possible object is "internally" or essentially related, like the flower in the crannied wall, to every thing else in reality, and since, as we have seen earlier, we certainly do have *some* true knowledge of *something*. Once more, however, it should be clear that we are not thus committed by the solution under consideration, since that solution does not imply that the objective relations essential to falsity are relations which are "internal" or essential to the thing falsely cognized. Again, the theory of "internal" relations is an ontological thesis requiring the support of ontological evidence and argument; it does not follow from the solution being considered. More than that, this absolutistic conclusion would apply to *any* and *every* theory of truth and error, given the theory of "internal" relations. Hence it follows neither peculiarly nor even at all from the solution under consideration.

Such a possible solution would not, therefore, commit us to either skepticism or absolutism. But it does possess another defect which is, I believe, very simple and yet very fatal. That defect is simply the theory's essential identification of falsity with ignorance, for ignorance is not the same thing as falsity. To say that someone is ignorant of the relations of his object to other things is not at all the same thing as saying that he is *mistaken,* either about those relations or about his object. The object itself, apart from its relations, he cognizes truly—and this is granted by the solution under consideration. And his ignorance of the object's relations, which ignorance, combined with the true knowledge of the object itself, is for this solution the essence of falsity, is just simply no cognition at all. In short, the part of the cognition that has an object is a true cognition, and the part of the cognition that has no object is for that reason not a cognition at all. To be *mistaken* about the object's relations, the mistaken person would have to cognize those relations *themselves,* as we have seen; but this would mean, according to the solution under consideration as well as to the other solutions we have considered, that he is not mistaken at all.

Thus this bold further step seems clearly unacceptable, and we can therefore, apparently, draw from our investigation only the three following conclusions: (1) An acceptable theory of falsity must recognize as an ineluctable fact that the object of false cognition exists independently of that cognition. (2) An acceptable theory of falsity must not define the essence of falsity as any peculiar property intrinsic to the object of false cognition. And finally, since there seems to be no other remaining locale for falsity, (3) the clue to the essence of falsity should be sought in some extrinsic relation which the independent object of false cognition bears to some other cognitively independent thing beyond it.

A. Nemetz : METAPHYSICS AND METAPHOR

D<small>R</small>. *Anthony Nemetz of the Department of Philosophy, The Ohio State University, offers in an essay, prepared especially for this book, an investigation of the point of tension in philosophic discourse between necessity or universality, on the one hand, and multiplicity or cultural relativity, on the other. The epistemic modes of comprehending or conceptualising by analogues—metaphors—that constitute the premises of various philosophic schemes are analysed with respect to their metaphysical judgments. For a further discussion of metaphors, or linguistic configurations, in the act of knowing, the reader should consult Prof. Nemetz's article: "Metaphor: Daedalus of Discourse,"* THOUGHT, *XXXIII, no. 130 (1958), pp. 417–42.*

• The most cursory reading of the history of philosophy suggests that consensus on any philosophic position seems in the nature of the case to be impossible. And, perhaps, this is as it should be, for reality surely cannot be circumscribed in any final set of human propositions or concepts; nor does our experience of reality constrain us to explain experience in any fixed manner. Here, then, are the two roots of philosophic pluralism —the richness of nature and the liberty of reason. To say, however, that philosophy is pluralistic is by no means to abandon philosophy to a relativism of insight or culture, for relativism implies that philosophers have abandoned or ought to abandon the quest for unqualified universality and necessity in expression. And if the ideal of universality is abandoned, philosophy, like pottery, becomes a vestigial fragment in the complex of cultural history; and if the search for necessity is curtailed by axiomatic postulation, philosophy abdicates its presumptive right to love wisdom and becomes instead the institutionalized head of pragmatic knowledge.

Needless to say, acceptance of either consequence, i.e., seeing philosophy discussed as purely cultural aspiration and explanation, or viewing the task of philosophy as the codification of scientific discourse and precise expression, results in abandoning any traditional notion of metaphysics. But it is equally fateful to metaphysics either to insist that cultural differences have no part in the selection of problems and in the emphasis of their statement, or to insist that metaphysical necessity can be articulated in a form which is neither ambivalent nor ambiguous.

With regard to the place of cultural differences in philosophy, an example may be more convincing than its supporting argument. "Faith seeking to understand" surely involves a metaphysic which was absolutely unavailable to the Greeks, and certainly the metaphysic resulting from this view was contingent on Christian culture. What I am insisting on is simply that the principles and problems of metaphysics are perennial and, nonetheless, that metaphysics has a genuine history. Furthermore, if what makes history is the succession of events, then the history of metaphysics must depend not on the perennial problems but on the diverse ways in which metaphysical problems have been and can be addressed. To ignore the history of metaphysics even with the laudable motive of presenting perennial truth is to run the risk of pretending that the truth can be at any one time wholly stated. And this in turn seems to me to be at least an unconscious kind of relativism.

Granting the importance of history in the understanding of metaphysics, there remains the more formidable question of stating or understanding a given metaphysical view. For metaphysics unlike any other discipline does not and cannot proceed in univocal terms. Aristotle insisted that any particular science was expanded from the principles through the apposition of extreme terms, all of which must be univocal. But how can metaphysics as a discipline be expanded since it is not concerned with "one aspect of being"? How can its principles be univocal if its subject matter is being as being? Moreover, since no special discipline can vindicate its own principles it remains for metaphysics to be the critic of the principles of the particular sciences. Here the difficulty becomes acute. Metaphysical inquiry must be applicable to the special sciences, but metaphysical expression cannot be univocal, for if it were, it would be a special science. In sum, how can metaphysical inquiry be applicable to the special sciences, especially when the principles of the special sciences are under scrutiny, without in some sense being ambivalent or ambiguous?

Traditional metaphysics beginning with Plato and Aristotle has always maintained a ready answer to the dilemma of metaphysical expression: metaphysical discourse must be analogical. The history of metaphysics since the Greeks reveals profound differences on what is to be regarded as the ground of the basic analogy: differences as to the mode of analogizing and differences as to the criteria for determining what is analogous. Yet if there is any agreement whatever in metaphysics, it surely includes the admission that there is an absolute need for analogical discourse in metaphysics. But why such a need? And what does analogical discourse accomplish which univocal forms of discourse cannot?

I think it begs the question to say that metaphysical discourse must be analogical because reality is analogous. Segments of reality may indeed be analogous; and it is true that discourse ought in some way to clarify our experience of reality. But so to base the reason for analogical discourse may be to confuse expediency or facility with necessity. An example may point up the difficulty. According to St. Thomas the transcendentals (*res, unum, aliquid, verum, bonum*) are admittedly basic terms in metaphysics which serve as the basis for specific analogies. Furthermore, the fact that the transcendentals are convertible terms makes possible continuing analogical discourse. Lastly, Aquinas does insist that the transcendentals are predicable of the primary content of mind which is being (*ens*) and that the knowing mind is in its own mode identical with the external reality. This of course means that for Aquinas all real things are in some way analogous. But I don't think this settles the matter.

For although truth is primarily the relation of 'adequation' between mind and its object, Aquinas does assert that truth belongs also to things and to discourse. The point I'm trying to make is that truth like reality is analogous and more. Discourse like truth is analogous. In sum, it seems that it makes no causal difference whether one says that analogical discourse is necessary because reality is analogous, or whether one says that when reason attempts to discursively account for its own pluralism, the result is necessarily analogical.

This last assertion needs clarification, because I think the metaphysics of knowledge centers on the question of how reason can account for its own inherent pluralism. The term pluralism here has two meanings: 1. it may refer to the way in which reason divides and interrelates the parts of knowledge, given a metaphysics; 2. it may equally refer to the fact that reason is at liberty to formulate diverse metaphysical systems (witness the history of philosophy). In asking the question, Why is analogical discourse necessary? I am indifferently looking at both senses of pluralism, but for purposes of exemplification I want to restrict myself to the kinds of knowing as found in Aquinas. There is little point in reviewing in detail the several acts of the mind which Aquinas distinguishes, nor is there any advantage here in restating the divisions of the sciences. Let all this be gainsaid (not because it is so clear, but rather because the difficulties will not further illuminate the problem at hand). The issue which is important here is the difference between knowing objects and the knowledge of the transcendentals.

To know a physical object means, I take it, to grasp its essence or at least partially to understand its essential constitution. But what does it mean to have knowledge of a transcendental? The transcendentals are clearly not 'supra universals,' nor are they akin to Platonic ideas, nor are they formally analytic. Yet St. Thomas asserts: 1. they severally apply to each object soever, and; 2. that they are predicable each of the other. Consequently, with respect to knowing they must be synthetic. But precisely what do they add to our knowledge? The transcendentals cannot add to our knowledge in the way that a universal adds to knowledge, because they are convertible each with the other and no two distinct universals are convertible. Nor can they add to our knowledge in the way that common axioms, like non-contradiction, add to our knowledge, because they individually are simple terms. And they cannot add to our knowledge in the sense that formal rules of logical construction add to our knowledge because they are directly predicable of physical objects, which is not true of the rules of logical construction.

As I see it, then, only one answer remains possible, namely, that the transcendentals are in principle the primary terms which are to be used in describing the knowledge of knowledge. And it is because of the modal identity between knowledge and object known that they are also descriptive of the object known. Even this is not altogether accurate, because it seems to imply a priority of knowing over the known which of course Aquinas would deny. Hence, a clearer statement of just how and what the transcendentals add to our knowledge requires some further reflections on the predicational role of the transcendentals.

What does it mean to say that *'aliquid est verum'* or conversely, that *'verum est aliquid'*? (I concede that *res est bonum* is more likely, but the likelihood of use is not decisive here.) In content these propositions are immediately seen as differing from propositions of the form, 'Two on the nose' is a horse; or, Horses are mammals. These latter propositions have predicates which are specific or generic, and such predicates do not convert with their subjects. It is true that in an essential definition, the *definiendum* is convertible with the *definiens,* but this is the case because they are conceptually equivalent. Hence, because transcendentals are convertible they are neither specific nor generic terms, and because of their singleness, they cannot be the defining phrase of anything. Why then are they convertible if the ordinary condition of convertibility is equivalence and no two transcendentals are equivalent in this way?

Equivalence, of course, may be purely a semantic identity as in the case of A = A. But this certainly cannot hold of the transcendentals since presumably they are described differently. Perhaps the fact that the transcendentals are also predicable of objects may be of importance here. Aristotle notes that in certain cases, a cause, effect, and subject may be "reciprocally predicable." [1] Aristotle's case in point deals with the expansion of a special science, and his solution depends on seeing the role of definition in demonstration. Aristotle is, of course, not speaking of unqualified convertibility when he talks about reciprocal predication. But I mention this point because the transcendentals are not only convertible with each other but are also predicable of universals and particulars. To the extent that they are predicable of universals and particulars, they seem to function like the relation of a universal to a particular. And this relation is surely causal in the sense that the universal is the cause of our knowledge of particulars. It is true of course that particulars are the cause of coming to know the universal, but there is a great difference between the causes of learning and the causes in the order of explanation and science. (Aristotle carefully distinguishes these two orders in distinguishing between prior to us and prior by nature.) And our concern here surely is the order of explanation. In sum, because the transcendentals are predicable of both particulars and universals, they must function in some fashion like a universal, and this would be causal in nature. This of course does not explain the convertibility of the transcendentals, but it does give a clue to that problem. For apart from synonymity and conceptual equivalence which have been rejected, a causal relation seems to me the only remaining possible ground for justifying convertibility of terms.

Simply pointing to the kind of reciprocal predication which holds among subject, cause, and effect unfortunately does not solve the problem with respect to the predicability of the transcendentals. And this for a good reason. The reciprocal predication mentioned depends on the cause

[1] Aristotle, 99a16–23.

being appropriate to the subject, i.e., the cause must involve the essential constitution of the subject and, therefore, be univocal if it is to connect the subject with the effect. But this certainly is not the function of a transcendental. For while the transcendentals are mutually convertible, separate and distinct causes are not so convertible for the reason that even when an effect has a plurality of causes, those causes must be serially or hierarchically ordered, and this excludes unqualified convertibility. Consequently, if it is granted that the transcendentals are mutually convertible, and that they function in some causal sense, other than the causal function in the special sciences, only one conclusion seems plausible. The transcendentals must be causal aspects or causal functions among which no absolute priority can be established. I have added the negative qualification of no absolute priority simply because I think that if an absolute priority of one transcendental over another were asserted the mutual convertibility of the transcendentals would fall.

In this connection I should add that the distinction between *in se* and *per aliud* which St. Thomas makes in grouping the transcendentals does not seem to me to be a distinction of absolute priority; rather, it seems to be only an analytic device for the derivation of the meaning and the definition of the several transcendentals. How can there be an absolute priority between *res* and *verum?* One could of course argue from the history of human knowledge that *res* must be prior, but that, I submit, would threaten the notion that "all truths are true in virtue of one truth." Negatively stated, I think that absolute convertibility and absolute priority are simply incompatible notions. The solution then is to say that although one can assert a priority of one transcendental over another, it follows that the assertion of priority will always be relative to the purposes of discourse, and consequently the priority itself is only intentional or logical.

In sum, then, the transcendentals are causal aspects among which only relative priority can be established. But what do the transcendentals cause, or of what are they causal aspects? The answer must take direction from the fact that they are predicable of the knowledge of objects, but that the knowledge of essence, however fragmentary, is not predicable of the transcendentals. This means that the transcendentals are not independent of the knowledge gained through experience. But it also means that the transcendentals are in some sense more universal than the knowledge of nature. I hesitate to use the term, "more universal," because it is obviously ambiguous. The transcendentals are, of course, not universals in the ordinary sense of genus and species. But the fact that they are predicable of universals needs to be explained.

The distinction between first and second substance or the distinction between first and second intention is of value here. For second substance or second intention refers to the way in which primary substance is understood or exists in the understanding. In other words, second intentions or second substances are the understood content of primary substances. To predicate, then, a second substance of a primary substance, e.g., man of Socrates, is simply to assert a relation between a sense experience and its intelligible content; or more generally, predication is a terminological expression of a factual relation between a mind and an object. Consequently, if the transcendentals are predicable of second substances or second intentions and are causal in nature, then their primary function must be to contribute to our knowledge of universals. But how?

I can find only one way of expressing the contribution that the transcendentals make to the knowledge of universals, i.e., the transcendentals are the modalities of conceptual knowledge. The transcendentals express the contribution which the knowing mind can make to knowledge naturally come by. That contribution consists precisely in presenting aspects under which the universal can be viewed. And the effect of the aspect presented by a given transcendental, e.g., *bonum,* is to provide the discursive means for both continuing the examination of the grounds of a particular concept as well as for providing the connectives between the distinct kinds of knowledge, e.g., knowledge through faith and through reason. Consequently, the reason that every transcendental is predicable of any universal (and *a fortiori* of every singular) is that as a causal function it expresses a modality of the natural content of mind both as content of mind and as existing entity.

The term, modality, ordinarily connotes aspects of existence, and I so intend it here. However, since the problem under discussion is metaphysical knowledge, the aspects of existence are qualified by the nature and purposes of the inquiry. In other words, modality here has reference to the meaning of universality and necessity in metaphysics as opposed to the universality and necessity of the special sciences. The example of the transcendentals in St. Thomas was intended to show that the very significance of universality with respect to metaphysical knowledge has been modified. For the sake of emphasis I should like to repeat in what I think that modification consists. If one looks to the basic propositions in metaphysics, then the applicability, extension, or inclusiveness of those propositions comprehends all the basic propositions of the special sciences, because metaphysical propositions are primarily modal statements expressing in a synoptic way the causal interplay between mind, its objects, and the expression of knowledge. For example, the law of non-contradiction holds equally of fact, thought, and expression and yet is expressed in a single formula. And if one looks to the transcendentals as basic metaphysical predicates, then the shift from the basic predication in the special sciences becomes obvious. For the transcendentals are predicates which generalize on the predicate of a mode of existence. For example, the predicate, *bonum,* directs the view of an understood content by specifying a relation to the appetite. In sum, basic metaphysical predication consists in an expression of intellectual direction to the modal ways in which the mind can view its own content. Put in other terms, metaphysics as a discipline expands by successively adding modal views, whereas the special sciences expand either by generic expansion of the predicates or specific limitations of the subject. Thus the controlling factor in the expansion of a special discipline is the essential constitution of the selected subject, whereas the controlling factor in the expansion of a metaphysic is an intellectual insight which turns on the multiplicity of modes in which the subjects of all sciences can be viewed.

The question of comparing the universality appropriate to the special sciences with the universality appropriate to metaphysics has thus far been limited to the problem of predication. But the question of predication cannot be discussed without assuming a relation among expression, thought, and existence—a relation which is and must be expressed propositionally, and held to be necessary. Needless to say, the principles which govern predication in the special sciences will differ from those which regulate metaphysical propositions. And consequently, the concept of necessity in metaphysics will differ from the meaning of metaphysics in the special sciences.

To document this assertion one need only consider how St. Thomas justifies the predication of essence or more generally, the use of universals as predicates. Aquinas is clear enough about the nature of a universal with regard to the knowledge of nature. The universal is implicit in the singular object and is abstracted by a natural process. But what is there about the object and about the mind which allows for such abstraction? However this question is ultimately answered, the answer must have the status of an assumption. All I mean here is that ultimate answer cannot be self-evident in the same sense as a primary principle in the *De Anima,* for the simple reason that the first principles of the particular disciplines are established on principles which themselves are not principles of a particular discipline. The principles by which particular sciences are established are, I take it, metaphysical principles.

True enough, metaphysical principles can be examined and tested, and evidence for their truth can be submitted. For example, abstraction is certainly a psychological principle. If one asks: What is the ground for holding to such a principle? the answer will consist in a principle stating that there is an identity between the principles of physical constitution and the principles of the intelligibility of constituted objects. The doctrine that the form both makes things to be what they are and makes them intelligible is familiar enough. But notice something most interesting—the claim for the identity of the principle of physical specification and the ground of the intelligibity of a natural object. Now this principle is certainly not intended to be a tautology; nor is the predicate intended to define the subject. What then is intended by the 'identity'? The usual way of explaining this is to say that there is a singleness of the reality but a plurality of the modes of its existence. And that the identity consists simply in the affirmation of the unity of reality with its modes. It certainly is admitted that to exist as external reality is distinct from existing as understood. But that which exists in both instances is identical.

However that may be, it certainly is the case that the identification of the principle of constitution with that of intelligibility is not self-evident. But it does furnish us with both a principle by which to determine evidence as well as a principle which integrates and directs inquiry. The function of this principle is thus twofold: 1. it is terminal in the sense that no more universal principle can be adduced to justify it; 2. it is methodological in the sense that the necessity found in principles and demonstrations concerned either with knowledge or nature are dependent on the necessity inherent in this principle of identification.

What kind of necessity does this principle have? To begin with, the meaning of necessity here must differ from the meaning of necessity in the particular disciplines. Consider the two loci of necessity in a discipline such as the *Physics*. There is first the necessity inherent in the basic truths or primary principles, and, secondly, there is the necessity proper to the conclusion of a demonstration. I do not want to elaborate on the differing shades of meaning which the term, necessity, has in the two cases as much as I want to point to a common feature to both instances. Both the self evidence of the basic truths of *Physics* and the conclusiveness of demonstrations in that discipline presuppose and must presuppose the univocal use of the terms involved. But to say that 'to be' is 'to be intelligible' is certainly not univocal as when nature is defined as a principle of rest and motion. In defining nature there is of course an identity between an essence and its verbal formula, and here an absolute univocalness does obtain. But the identification of the principle of constitution with that of intelligibility is by no means such an identity and consequently cannot be univocal in expression. This of course does not mean that the expression is equivocal. It is rather to say that there is an ambivalence in the expression. For those who have traditionally divided meanings into univocal, equivocal, and the analogical, the point I am getting at may seem trivial; yet I want precisely to avoid saying that the principle of identification, the formal ground of constitution with that of intelligibility, is analogical in character.

Before explaining this last assertion, it might be well to restate in summary my argument. The question at issue is: Why should metaphysical discourse be analogical? The answer I have proposed initially looks to the marks of all philosophic discourse, namely, universality and necessity and asks whether the universality proper to metaphysical predication and the necessity peculiar to metaphysical principles differs from the universality and necessity found in the principles of the particular disciplines. The examples of the transcendentals and the principle of identity indicated that there is and must be a difference. But how to state that difference is the problem. The approach that I have used focused on the character of predication in metaphysics with special emphasis on the relation of the meanings between subject and predicate. All primary principles in philosophy, whether in metaphysics or in the special sciences, assert an identity between the subject and the predicate, e.g., defining nature as a principle of motion and rest, or defining the soul as the first act of a body. But the identity which is asserted in the principles of the special sciences is an identity of a subject with its nature or an identity of a nature with its verbal formula. Although such identities clearly involve at least two modes of existence, yet the mark of the special sciences is that they assume the principles on which such identity can be based and argue only to the development of a single mode. For example, Aristotle certainly insists on the identity of thought and nature. And yet the *Physics* and the *De Anima* are distinct even if related disciplines. How is this to be explained, if not by seeing that the identity which is assumed in both cases is treated *qua* thought in the *De Anima,* but *qua* nature in the *Physics?*

In short, the individual or particular sciences are such precisely because their expansion is limited to a single mode of existence, and the primary predicational terms are all taken from that mode. The consequence of restricting the view of a subject matter to a single mode of existence is that the principles of the particular science are unqualifiedly univocal. For example, if one regards the principle of non-contradiction as a basic metaphysical proposition the case is clear. Certainly the case of non-contradiction applies equally to propositions, to natures, and the judgments, but it is a single statement which must be assumed but not investigated by the special sciences. And the reason that the special sciences are unable to investigate this principle is precisely because their investigations are limited to a single mode or aspect of existence.

Now I think that all philosophers must concede that the principle of non-contradiction is necessary, but they certainly do not agree that it holds indifferently for all the modes of existence to which Aristotle applied it. Philosophers may well agree that it applies to language, but deny it of existence. What I am getting at, is the fact that in order to philosophize, more than one principle is required. Or another way of putting the same point is to say that all philosophers require some principle of identity or non-contradiction in order to philosophize, but they differ radically on the selection of the basic modes which are identified. Thus Plato selected thought and action as his basic modes (knowledge is virtue); Berkeley selected existence and perception (to be is to be perceived); and St. Thomas certainly looked to existence and thought (to be is to be intelligible).

The point of introducing these examples is twofold. In the first place if one asks what is the basic difference among metaphysics, I would reply that the difference consists primarily in positing a principle of identity which is composed of differing modes of existence. And since metaphysics is the critic of the particular sciences, it is the difference in the primary modes which accounts for the differing approaches to the perennial problems. Moreover, the selection of the primary modes also determines what kind of necessity can be asserted to hold in the case of the particular disciplines. It seems reasonable to me that Plato found so much difficulty in making 'becoming' intelligible precisely because he selected behaviorial action as one of his primary modes, and found no way of identifying behavior with natural process.

The character, then, of the necessity proper to metaphysical principles is almost paradoxical. For the necessity of metaphysical principles is the source of the necessity of the special disciplines. Yet there seems to be no *a priori* reason which dictates the modal content of the principle of identity. In other words in the special sciences there is a one to one correspondence between the necessity of the principles and the consequent certitude of the philosopher. (Although, as Aristotle said, "It's hard to know when we know.") [2] But metaphysics presents a unique challenge, namely, trying to find those modes which when identified will most adequately establish the necessity required for successful philosophizing. The metaphysician knows the magnitude of his task; he knows that his basic propositions must embrace the totality of the philosophic enterprise. And he is aware that whatever the modes of existence which he selects as primary, he cannot state them in a univocal fashion.

This challenge introduces the second reason for bringing in the examples of Plato, Berkeley, and Aquinas. When Plato says that knowledge is virtue, he is stating in the form of an identity the modes of existence which he regards as primary. Yet this axiom is certainly not to be understood as an univocal statement. Plato certainly does not intend virtue to be the definition of knowledge; nor does he intend knowledge and virtue to be conceptually equivalent, no matter what else is said about the highest level of dialectic. How, then, to describe an axiom such as Plato's?

I want to call such basic metaphysical propositions metaphors. By metaphor I mean a proposition which asserts an identity of two modes of existence and which consequently can only be explicated by employment of two modes of verification. It should be clear that I am not using meta-

[2] Aristotle, 76a26.

phor to mean an ornamental figure of speech or to designate a variant mode of analogy. On the contrary, the reason for calling basic metaphysical propositions metaphors is to distinguish between analogizing as the method of argument proper to metaphysics and the ground for that method.

This essay began by asking why is metaphysical discourse analogical, and what does it accomplish which univocal forms of discourse cannot? I think that an answer can now be given. Granted that analogizing is a method of argumentation in which the basic structure is a parallelism of propositions which establish similarity or proportion, one should ask why such parallelism is required. Because the basic metaphysical propositions assert an identity of modes of existence, no single line of univocal argument can in the nature of the case explain or explicate the metaphysical proposition. And without the plurality of modes of existence, no metaphysical proposition can be architectonic with respect to the special sciences. Consequently only through analogies can metaphysics as a science be developed.

The history of metaphysics, however, shows that philosophers disagree on almost every aspect of analogy. And I hold that this disagreement reflects, more than anything else, a fundamental disagreement regarding what shall be taken as the primary modes of existence, the basic metaphor. Conversely, the basic metaphor determines the appropriate kind of analogies and analogizing for any metaphysician. For example, I think that St. Thomas' philosophic disagreement with Plato stems from the fact that he regards existence and intelligibility as the basic modes, rather than knowledge and behavior. And this difference in principles of identity has profound consequences in the systematic problems which arise and in judgments about the adequacy of proposed solutions.

It might be well if I indicated what philosophic purpose an analysis such as I propose will serve. As I indicated at the outset of this paper, I hold both that any metaphysic must in the nature of the case be only an approximation of the truth, and therefore, that philosophy is of necessity pluralistic. But I hold equally that every philosopher has the obligation to try to discover a more universal formulation of basic metaphysical propositions and, therefore, that the philosopher's task is one of intellectual synthesis. What I am proposing, then, is in no sense a meta-metaphysics; rather, what I have in mind is a propaedeutic to the ultimately personal task of philosophizing—a task which can be enormously aided by an enriched understanding of the history of philosophy, above all by a comprehension of the philosophy of knowledge.

J. Maritain : MAN'S APPROACH
TO GOD

I$_N$ this essay based upon a lecture delivered at Marquette University in 1950, Professor Jacques Maritain considers the typical way in which the modern mind may arrive at a knowledge of the Infinite. The essay is divided into three parts. In the first, Professor Maritain describes the particular form that the knowledge of God which the human intellect naturally possesses is assuming in our modern mental climate: a new approach which is but a new form of the eternal relation to the Absolute Being. The second point is that this natural knowledge of God is conceptual knowledge through analogy. These considerations lead finally to a statement of the possibility of an immediate apprehension of the Divine Essence —in which the intellect, through beatific vision, not only knows but sees that which it loves.

• It is of human reason's search after God, or of the manner in which the human intellect approaches the mystery of God, that I shall try to explain in the first part of my essay.

Physics is today reigning unchallenged over our minds and culture. Its progress and achievements are actually wonderful and deserve deep admiration. What is badly needed is not to disparage physics and accuse it of atomizing us, but to be aware of its very nature, its true field of knowledge and its limitations. What is badly needed is to supplement physics with another type of knowledge, concerned with grasping being for its own sake. What is badly needed is a renewal of metaphysics.

No doubt there is no continuity between the world of physics and the world of metaphysics. The modern image of the atom—each day more complicated, more mysterious and more fecund in practical applications—is a mathematical image or ideal entity founded *in re,* which gives us an invaluable symbolical or phenomenological knowledge of *how matter behaves,* but cannot instruct us philosophically or ontologically about *what matter is.* Yet the fact remains that the conceptions of modern science and the extraordinary progress of micro-physics provide the human intellect with a scientific imagery, an imaginable or supra-imaginable picture of nature which is incomparably more favorable to the edification of a philosophy of nature and more open to the deepening labor of metaphysical reason than the old Newtonian physics. The opportunity is now given for that reconciliation between science and wisdom for which the human mind thirsts. What we are longing for is a rediscovery of Being and by the same token a rediscovery of Love.

This means a rediscovery of God. The *"existential"* philosophies which are today in fashion are but a sign of a certain deep want to find again the sense of Being. This want is now unfulfilled, for these philosophies are still enslaved by irrationalism and seek for the revelation of existence, for ontological ecstasy, in the breaking of reason, in the experience of Despair and Nothingness, of Anguish or Absurdity. True existentialism is the work of reason.

Because the primary reality grasped by the intellect is the act of existing as exercised by some visible or tangible thing; and because it is the intuition of being—disengaged for its own sake, and perceived at the summit of an abstractive intellection—it also is the intuition of being—even when it is distorted by the error of a system, as in Plato or Spinoza—which causes a human intellect to enter the realm of metaphysics and be capable of metaphysical intelligence.

Once a man is awakened to the reality of existence and the true life of Reason, to the intelligible value of Being, once he has really perceived this tremendous fact, sometimes exhilarating, sometimes disgusting and maddening, namely: I *exist*—he is henceforth taken hold of by the intuition of Being and the implications it involves.

Precisely speaking, this prime intuition is both the intuition of *my* existence and of the existence of things; but first and foremost of the existence of things. When it takes place, I suddenly realize that a given entity, man, mountain, or tree, exists and exercises that sovereign activity *to be* in its own way, totally self-assertive and totally implacable, completely independent from *me*. And at the same time I realize that I also exist but as thrown back into my loneliness and frailty by such affirmation of existence in which I have positively no part, to which I am exactly as naught. So the prime intuition of Being is the intuition of the solidity and inexorability of existence and, secondly, of the death and nothingness to which *my* existence is liable. And thirdly, in the same flash of intuition, which is but my becoming aware of the intelligible value of Being, I realize that the solid and inexorable existence perceived in anything whatsoever implies—I don't know in what way, perhaps in things themselves, perhaps separately from them—some absolute, irrefragable existence, completely free from nothingness and death. These three intellective leaps—to actual existence as asserting itself independently from me; from this sheer objective existence to my own threatened existence; and from my existence spoiled with nothingness to absolute existence—are achieved within that same and unique intuition which philosophers would explain as the intuitive perception of the essentially analogical content of the first concept, the concept of Being.

Then a quick, spontaneous reasoning, as natural as this intuition (and, as a matter of fact, more or less involved in it) immediately springs forth, as the necessary fruit of such primordial apperception and as enforced by and under its light. I see that my Being, first, is liable to death and, second, that it depends on the totality of nature, on the universal whole whose part I am and that Being-with-nothingness, as my own being is, implies, in order to be, Being-without-nothingness. It implies that absolute existence which I confusedly perceived as involved in my primordial intuition of existence. The universal whole, whose part I am, is Being-with-nothingness, from the very fact that I am part of it; so that finally, since the universal whole does not exist by itself, there is another, separate whole, another Being, transcendent and self-sufficient and unknown in itself and activating all beings, which is Being-without-nothingness—that is, Being by itself.

Thus the inner dynamism of the intuition of existence, or of the intelligible value of Being, causes me to see that absolute existence or Being-without-nothingness transcends the totality of nature and compels me to face the existence of God.

This is not a new approach to God. It is the eternal approach of man's reason to God. What is new is the manner in which the modern mind has become aware of the simplicity and liberating power, the natural and somehow intuitive characteristics of this eternal approach. The science of the ancients was steeped in philosophy. Their scientific imagery was a pseudo-ontological imagery. Consequently there was a kind of continuum between their knowledge of the physical world and their knowledge of God. The latter appeared as the summit of the former, a summit which was to be climbed through the manifold paths of the causal connections at play in the sublunar world and the celestial spheres. The sense of Being that ruled their universal thought was for them too usual an atmosphere to be felt as a surprising gift. At the same time the natural intuition of existence was so strong in them that their proofs of God could take the form of the most conceptualized and rationalized scientific demonstrations and be offered as an unrolling of logical necessities, without losing the inner energy of that intuition. Such logical machinery was quickened instinctively by the basic intuition of Being.

We are in a quite different position now. In order to solve the enigma of physical reality and to conquer the world of phenomena, our science has become a kind of Maya—a maya which succeeds and makes us masters of nature. But the sense of Being is absent from it. Thus when we happen to experience the impact of Being upon the mind it appears to us as a kind of intellectual revelation, and we realize clearly both its liberating and its awakening power and the fact that it involves a knowledge which is separated from that sphere of knowledge peculiar to our science. At the same time we realize that the knowledge of God, before being developed into logical and perfectly conceptualized demonstrations, is first and foremost a natural fruit of the intuition of existence and forces itself upon our mind in the imperative virtue of this intuition.

In other words, we have become aware of the fact that human reason's approach to God, in its primordial vitality, is neither a mere intuition, which would be suprahuman, nor is it that artlike philosophical reasoning by which it is expressed in its achieved form, each step of which is pregnant with involved issues and problems. Human reason's approach to God in its primordial vitality is a *natural* reasoning, that is, intuitivelike or irresistibly vitalized by, and maintained within, the intellectual flash of the intuition of existence. Then the intuition of existence, grasping in some existing reality Being-with-nothingness, makes the mind grasp by the same stroke the necessity of Being-without-nothingness. And nowhere is there any problem involved, because the illumining power of this intuition takes hold of the mind and obliges it to see. Thus it naturally proceeds, in a primary intuitive flash, from imperative certainty to imperative certainty. I believe that from Descartes to Kierkegaard, the effort of modern thought—to the extent that it has not completely repudiated metaphysics and if it is cleansed of the irrationalism which has gradually corrupted it—tends to such an awareness of the specific *naturality* of man's knowledge of God, definitely deeper than any logical process scientifically developed. It tends to the awareness of man's spontaneous knowledge of God and of the primordial and simple *intuitivity* in which it originates.

Finally, the rediscovery of the value of existence not only means the rediscovery of God. It also means the rediscovery of Love. For when the intuition of Being and Existence takes place in me, it normally carries along with itself another intuition, the intuition of my own existence or my Self, the intuition of Subjectivity as subjectivity. Now Subjectivity, in so far as it is subjectivity, is not an object presented to thought but rather the very wellspring of thought—a deep, unknown and living center which superabounds in knowledge and superabounds in love, attaining only through love its supreme level of existence, existence as giving itself.

This is what I mean: Self-knowledge as a mere psychological analysis of phenomena more or less superficial, a wandering through images and memories, is but an egotistic awareness, however valuable it may be. But when it becomes ontological, then Knowledge of the Self is transfigured, implying intuition of Being and the discovery of the actual abyss of subjectivity. At the same time it is the discovery of the basic generosity of existence. Subjectivity, this essentially dynamic, living, and open center, both receives and gives. It receives through the intellect, by superexisting in knowledge. It gives through the will, by superexisting in love; that is, by having within itself other beings as inner attractions directed toward them and by giving itself to them, in other words, by spiritually existing in the manner of a gift. And "it is better to give than to receive." The spiritual existence of love is the supreme revelation of existence for the Self. The Self, being not only a material individual but also a spiritual personality, possesses itself and holds itself in hand in so far as it is spiritual and in so far as it is free. And to what purpose does it possess itself and dispose of itself, if not for what *is better,* in actual existence and absolutely speaking, that is, to give itself? Thus it is that when a man has been really awakened to the sense of being or existence, and grasps intuitively the obscure, living depth of the Self and Subjectivity, he discovers by the same token the basic generosity of existence and realizes, by virtue of the inner dynamism of this intuition, that love is not a passing pleasure or emotion, but the very meaning of his being alive.

And not only does he know, by virtue of his primordial intellectual grasping of existence, that God exists and is absolute Being, is self-subsisting *Esse.* He also knows that because of this very fact God is absolute ontological generosity, self-subsisting Love; and that such transcendent Love causes, permeates, and activates every creature, which in answer loves God more than itself. Thus love for God, the natural and universal eros, is the very virtue and innermost vitality in which all beings desire and love, act and strive.

That God is Love itself, subsisting Love, is, as I just said, a truth which can be naturally known by the human intellect with its natural forces alone, by virtue of its primordial grasping of existence. Yes, but in actual fact the human intellect did not attain this truth by means of its natural forces alone. The aid of revelation was necessary. If the revelation made to Moses of the Divine Name, "I am that I am," taught reason from above what it could have, but had not in fact, discovered, this is far truer of the revelation made to St. John, "God is love." Note, however: in view of the relationship in which creatures stand to God, the affirmation that God should not only be loved but that He loves—I mean with the distinctive *madness* of love—and that there can be relations of friendship, mutual self-giving, community of life, and the sharing of a common bliss between God and His creatures implies the supernatural order of grace and charity. And it is this supernatural truth and this experience which lead the reason to understand what is meant by the statement that God is Love, in so far as it enunciates a truth of the natural order, which concerns God regarded in Himself, even though no creature existed. The most resplendent manifestation of the Divine glory within the scope of our reason is that love, which presupposes understanding and is above all a superflux, an ultimate superabundance of the life of spirits, is in God identical with His essence and His existence. In this sense Love is His Name par excellence—it is His gospel Name.

Thus it is that being as being is superabundant, and that God, Who is at the peak of being, is Superabundance in pure Act, or absolute ontological generosity. In token of this fact we have two other truths, but ones which deal with the supernatural order and can be known only by revelation: namely, that God is indeed One and Incommunicable, but with a generosity which is of His very essence and which requires within Himself the Trinity of Persons and renders the Incarnation possible. God is a Trinity of Persons—such is His intimate life, and He is so accessible to human nature that He can be the Person in whom the nature of a man subsists.

So we are confronted with one knowledge of God which depends solely on reason and the natural forces of the human intellect, and another knowledge of God which is knowledge by faith and deals with the supernatural order.

Knowledge by faith is obscure and in an imperfect state, because faith believes and does not see. Faith, which is a gift of God, implies the action of divine grace which innerly inspires and illumines the intellect and moves the will; it is the adherence of the intellect to truths and realities which are above the range of reason, and are believed as spoken and witnessed by the word of God, the Prime Truth itself. So the *mode* of knowledge by faith is imperfect, but its *object* is more valuable than anything reason can know since its object is the hidden treasure involved in the very essence of God and His own Knowledge of Himself.

On the contrary, knowledge of God as afforded by reason is clear and obvious knowledge, springing forth from the first intuition of being with cogent force. Be it either merely spontaneous or philosophically elaborated, its *mode* is luminous, not obscure. But the *object* it attains is God known only as through His effects, or as the primary Cause of things, which can be made manifest by the same ideas through which things are first known—God known not in Himself, but in the mirror of things, God in the analogical community of His being with the being of creatures.

No doubt faith also is knowledge through analogy as regards the *means* or the human *concepts* it uses. But analogy, there, does not determine the very content offered to knowledge, or the formal objectivity with which God faces the intellect, and which is the divine essence itself, the inner mystery of God as known to Himself. In faith analogy, or rather superanalogy, deals with the signs and means that bring such an object within our understanding. To express the mystery of the Trinity, for example, it is necessary to make use of the concepts of Father, and Son, and Spirit, of generation and procession, concepts which were first supplied to us by creatures, and which God Himself uses in making Himself known to us through His Son who tells of Him, and through His Church which guards and explains the word of the Son: analogical concepts by means of which *lumen fidei,* the light of faith, reaches the inwardness of God. They are the *outward silver,* as St. John of the Cross put it, by means of which we grasp the pure gold of divine reality. Let us say, then, that faith dwells in the divine fountain-head itself, in the heart of the Increate, but that God has laid His hand over her eyes.

But merely rational and natural knowledge of God dwells in the created world, and from there gazes—without seeing it in itself—at the inaccessible source toward which all perfections of created things converge, and whose pure light natural reason can only grasp as broken in the multiplicity of those perfections. In the rational and natural knowledge of God the analogical process is the very measure and rule of knowledge. God is not attained in the name of His Selfhood and incommunicable nature, or of the indivisibility of His pure and simple essence, but only to the extent that He is manifested in the reflected hues and analogical participations which things proportioned to our reason offer us. His essence is not attained as such, but only to the extent that creatures speak of it from themselves, to our intellect. Thus not only is the *mode* of this

335   *J. Maritain*

kind of knowledge human, but its very *object* is proposed to the mind and constituted as the aim of knowledge only insofar as it condescends, so to speak, to human reason through the mirror of sense-perceivable things and through the analogy of being.

I should like to dwell a moment on this natural knowledge of God, either spontaneous or philosophical, and to give a few indications of its analogical character.

In all things that we see and touch there are certain objects of thought, brought out by our intellectual power of conceptual apprehension, which are called *transcendental* objects of thought because they transcend and overflow any genus and category; they know no bounds. Such is, first of all, being—our first object of thought. Such objects of thought as being, unity, truth, beauty, imbibe each and every thing, including the very differences through which things are distinct from each other. As a result, these transcendentals, which are restricted to no thing whatever, imply in their very notion neither limitation nor imperfection; and they are ascribed to things essentially varied—to a man, to a color, to a physical energy, to a spiritual power—in an analogous, not a univocal manner. In each one of those things they do not signify one single generic or specific nature, but something intrinsically varied, namely a similarity in relations between similar terms, for instance: the essence of man is to his own existence as the essence of the color blue is to its own existence.

Thus it is that such notions can be ascribed to God: being, truth, or beauty are limited and imperfect in things, but they do not imply any limitation or imperfection in their very notion. They therefore can and must be ascribed to the one who is infinite and infinitely perfect—the prime cause of every being and every beauty is really being, the very act of existing subsisting through itself—and is really true, and truth itself, beautiful, and beauty itself.

Being, truth and beauty do not imply any community of essence in the various things that exist, and are true, and are beautiful. They can therefore be ascribed to God without jeopardizing in any way the absolute and infinite difference in essence between God and the things in which we first deciphered these notions. They imply between God and things no univocal identity whatsoever, only *analogous* community.

Let us now point out that our knowledge of God—and this is true for the super-analogy of faith-knowledge as well as for the analogy of reason-knowledge—does not only proceed through analogy. It must be added that this analogy is uncontaining, *uncircumscriptive.* The concepts and names which designate perfections pertaining to the transcendental order do not vanish, do not fly into pieces; they keep their proper significance when applied to God. But although coming into effect far better in God than in things, they neither enclose nor embrace the divine reality; they leave it uncontained and uncircumscribed. *What is signified* by our analogous or polyvalent concepts pertains to God, and in a better way than to things. But *the manner in which we conceive them,* with the limitations it inevitably involves (since we have received those concepts from creatures), the *modus significandi* does in no way pertain to God. God is truly *Ipsum esse per se subsistens,* Being itself subsisting through itself, but He does not suffer any of the circumscribing marks implied in our manner of conceiving being, insofar as we conceive being as distinct from goodness, truth, or beauty. God exists, but He does not exist as do any of the existing things. God is good and just and merciful, God knows, God loves; but He is not good, just, or merciful, he does not know or love as any of the beings are or do which have taught us what is goodness, justice or mercy, knowledge or love. In the very degree to which they make the divine essence known to us, our concepts, while keeping their proper meaning, are absorbed into its abyss. In God *what is signified* by them breaks loose—we don't know how—from our *manner of conceiving.* The divine essence is known in some fashion—and truly known—but it does not surrender itself; its own mystery remains intact, unpierced. To the very extent to which we know it, it escapes our grasp, infinitely transcends our knowledge. As St. Thomas put it after Augustine and Boethius, "Whatever form our intellect may conceive, God escapes it through His own sublimity."

Through the natural forces of our intellect we know that God exists, as primary Cause of things; we know God in and by His effects, but we do not know Him in and by His essence.

Now it is but normal that knowing a reality—and the most important one—from the outside and by means of signs, we have a desire to know it *in itself,* or to grasp it without intermediary. So we have a natural desire to *see* in His essence that very God whom we know through His creatures.

Yet such a longing to know the first Cause in its essence is a longing which does not know what it is asking for—like the sons of Zebedee when they asked to sit on the right and left hand of the Son of Man— because to know the first Cause in its essence, or without the medium of any other thing, means ceasing to know it through its effects, or insofar as it is Cause and first Cause, that is, ceasing to use the very way through which our intellect has come to know it and is facing it. To know the first Cause in its essence is in reality something which transcends all the forces of any created or creatable nature, it is identical to possessing the deity intuitively, in a vision in which the divine essence itself plays within our mind the part of our concepts as means of grasping intelligible objects; to know God in His essence is to know God divinely, as He is known to Himself, it is to know Him as He knows us, in His own uncreated light. To see God is supernatural, is even at the peak of the supernatural order. To see God is possible only for a divinized mind, for a mind whose subjective intellectual power is proportioned to God by that supreme participation in God's life which is called *lumen gloriae,* the light of glory, for a mind whose objective intentional determination depends on nothing created, not an impressed form or fecundating germ, not a mental concept or expressed fruit, not an idea, but on the divine essence itself. Such perfect intuition is so supernatural that through it man becomes God intentionally, in the pure spirituality of this eternal intellectual act, and that through it man possesses beatitude and enters God's very joy, an absolute happiness which, with respect to our merely natural possibilities, we could not dare to dream of. And the longing to see God, when it is a desire which knows what it is asking, when it tends to God *as God*—this longing is a supernatural longing rooted in supernatural faith, and distinct from the natural desire, tending to God *as first Cause,* of which I spoke a moment ago. It is grafted on this natural desire to see the first Cause, and it also perfects and superelevates our natural desire for happiness, now become desire for bliss. But in itself it is supernatural; and it is as supernatural desire proceeding from divine grace, that it longs for the vision of God as for an aim which we really can reach and without which the end for which we are cut out would be frustrated.

Thus it is that faith is a movement toward vision. Thus it is that in the dynamism of our grace-given energies, faith, which by itself can only believe but neither penetrate nor experience, demands to be vitally complemented by other supernatural virtues—the gifts of the Holy Spirit—which, thanks to the connaturality of love, make faith penetrate and experience the divine reality, and so to speak give eyes to faith—*fides oculata.* For "where love is, there also are eyes." So divine contemplation is here below a token and shadow, an experienced promise of vision.

We are co-natured with God by charity. The things of God having been thus intimately joined with us, made ours, bred into our bones by the love of charity, the property of the gift of wisdom is to make use of this love to make it grow into an *objective means* of knowing, in such a way that we not only experience our love, but it is God Himself whom we experience through our love. As John of St. Thomas put it:

It is by the very virtue of the giving of God to us, and of the union with Him which love experiences, that mystical wisdom attains divine things (rendered, by love, more one with us, more immediately touched and tasted), and makes us perceive that what is thus felt in love is higher and more excellent than any consideration of the power of Knowledge.

And again:

Charity attains God immediately in Himself, and becomes one with that very reality which in faith is not seen. . . . So by virtue of this union by which love adheres immediately to God, the intellect is raised by a certain affective experience to the point of judging of divine things in a higher manner than is possible for the obscurity of faith, because the intellect penetrates and knows that there is *still more* hidden substance in the things of faith than faith itself can manifest, and because it finds there *more* to love and to taste in love; and from this *more* which is hidden there, as the intellect knows through love, the intellect judges of divine things in a higher fashion, by a special instinct of the Holy Spirit.

We see, then, that mystical wisdom penetrates the things of God by an experience of love which bears on that very substance which is hidden in faith. It is in the very degree to which divine reality is hidden to us—absolutely transcendent with respect to any concept or idea—that this secret wisdom experiences it. Truly Thou art a hidden God, a Saviour God: all the more saviour and vivifier as He is hidden. The man of contemplation cherishes these dark shadows of faith because he knows that they are fecund, because he knows, he feels, that only in them can he intimately taste and judge by experience the depths of his God. Here we are at the root of the doctrine of St. John of the Cross: "Seek Him in faith and love," he says. "Like a blind man these two guides will lead you, by roads you do not know, up to the secret of God. . . . He is hidden in you, why do you not hide yourself like Him in order to know Him and to feel Him. If a man wants to find something hidden, he must hide himself in entering its hiding place, and when he has found it he is hidden like it. . . . Always you must hold Him to be hidden, and serve Him by hiding yourself."

In such an experience the concepts are not suppressed; but all distinct concepts keep silent, they sleep, as the Apostles slept on the Mount of Olives. And the confused concepts which intervene, and which may remain wholly unperceived, play a merely accidental part. It is the connaturality of charity which plays the essential part and is the formal and decisive means of knowledge. The light of God-given contemplation is the ardor of love gleaming in the dark. That is why this supreme wisdom, this supernatural knowledge of love, is described as a giving up of knowledge and an unknowing, *a ray of darkness for the intellect.* As St. Thomas puts it, quoting the Pseudo-Dionysius, "at the summit of our knowledge we know God *as unknown."* He is known as unknown, *tamquam ignotus cognoscitur,* as infinitely transcending any human or angelic knowledge; that is to say, He is known precisely as God, in the incomprehensible depths themselves of His deity, in the infinite splendor of His glory which is darkness to our created eyes, He is actually known—while remaining unknown and inscrutable. All particular representations have vanished away, the soul has given up everything, and given up itself, it is dispossessed, it is naught.

In killing me Thou hast changed death into life, St. John of the Cross says. And again:

To win that which you know not
You must go the way which you know not

To win that which you are not
You must go the way where you are not

To win the knowledge of all
Wish to know nothing.

Is contemplation the right word to express this supreme knowledge of God through union with God? There is probably no adequate word. Then "they are two in one single Spirit and love." Then the God of faith is experienced by his reverberation, His implanting in love, as the God of the beatific vision, in addition to being seen, will also be thus tasted in the life to come: for mystical experience, begun here on earth, will keep on existing—inferior to vision, but joined with it—in the eternal homeland.

I have tried to explain these things at greater length in a book—*Les Degrés du Savoir* [a new and correct translation of which is now available]. Now I should like to add that for the Christian philosophy of life contemplation—I mean that supernatural contemplation of which I just spoke, and which would be better called entrance into the very states of God, of God Incarnate—is not the business only of specialists or the chosen few. It is a promise to all men. Compared with the pre-Christian world, this was an astounding revolution in the *spiritual order*. Greeks and Jews, masters and slaves, men and women, poor and rich (but the poor, first), souls who have known evil and souls (if there be such) who have not, whatever their condition or race, whatever their scars,—all are called to the feast of divine Love and divine Wisdom. That wisdom calls them all, it clamors in the public places and in the roadways. All without exception are called to perfection, which is the same as that of the Father who is in heaven; from near by or from afar, all are called to the contemplation of the saints, not the contemplation of the philosophers, but to loving and crucified contemplation. All without exception.

Let us not forget that God-given contemplation, not being confined to the intellect, being the fruit of love and love-connaturality with God, asks to overflow in activity and enter the sphere of action, by virtue of the abundance and generosity of love, which consists in giving oneself. Thus it is that inspired wisdom, unlike that of the philosophers, is not only speculative, but practical as well; it is not a self-sufficing contemplation, but one which, as St. Paul puts it, walks toward them that are without, redeeming the time. As a result this contemplation requests to have certain men especially dedicated to it in a uniquely contemplative state of life, but it also requests to spread over the world and attract to itself all men, provided they have the will to enter the ways of the spirit, whatever their state of life may be. For in whatever work they are engaged, their action can, at least as regards the *manner* in which it is done, spring from the superabundance of contemplation, if their soul habitually makes room for the divine inspiration.

Moreover, if we define mystical life as a coming of the soul under the regimen in which those gifts of Grace, called in sacred terminology gifts of the Holy Spirit, predominate (so that henceforth the soul is docile to the spirit of God, who, dispossessing it of itself, takes it into His own charge), then it is clear that every soul is called—at least in a remote way —to mystical life *thus defined*. Why is this so? Because all are called to the perfection of love. And that perfection cannot be attained without the radical purifications and substantial remoldings which are the mystical life's sacrificial privilege.

We must observe furthermore that among the inspiring gifts which we have learned to enumerate from Isaiah, some, like those of Counsel, Force, and Fear, mainly concern action, while others, like those of Intelligence and Wisdom, are mainly related to contemplation.

It follows that souls which have entered upon the ways of spiritual life will behave in very different manners, each according to its calling. Some will be favored in a pre-eminent manner with the highest gifts, those of Wisdom and Intelligence; these souls will represent mystical life in its normal plenitude and will have the grace of contemplation in its typical forms, be they arid or comforting. In the case of other souls it will be primarily the other gifts of inspired freedom; their life will be indeed a mystical and dispossessed life; but it will be such preeminently in relation to their activities and works, and they will not have the typical and normal forms of contemplation.

They will not be, for all that, deprived of contemplation, of participating in and experiencing lovingly the divine states. For St. Thomas teaches us that all the gifts of the Holy Spirit are connected and therefore cannot be present in the soul without the gift of Wisdom—though, in the case we are dealing with, it will be exercised in a less apparent way, and in an atypical, attenuated, or discontinuous mode. The contemplation of the "active" souls will be *masked* and unapparent, but they will have contemplative graces; perhaps they will be capable only of falling asleep when they cease moving, and mental prayer will bring them only headaches. Mysterious contemplation will not be in their way of praying but in the grace of their behaviour, in their sweet-minded hands, perhaps, or perhaps in their way of walking, or in their way of looking at a poor man or at suffering.

It should perhaps be added that contemplative life is superhuman, whereas the active life is connatural to man and better adapted to the equilibrium of his natural energies. It appears that the forms of contemplation to which souls faithful to grace will actually attain most often, will not be the typical one, where the supernatural sweeps away everything at the risk of breaking everything, but rather the atypical and masked forms which I have just mentioned, where the superhuman condescends in some measure to the human and consorts with it.

We see, then, with what nuances and distinctions we should understand the crucial doctrine of every single soul being called to contemplative graces. Each is called, if only in a remote manner, to contemplation, *typical or atypical,* apparent or masked, which is the multiform exercise of the gift of Wisdom, free and unseizable, and transcending all our categories, and capable of all disguises, all surprises.

BIBLIOGRAPHY FOR PART IV

Aaron, R. I., *The True and the Valid*, Oxford University Press, London, 1955.

Acton, H. B., "Man-Made Truth," *Mind*, n.s., XXXXVII (1938), pp. 145–58.

Adler, M. J., "Knowledge and Opinion," *Art and Prudence*, Longmans, Green and Co., New York, 1937, pp. 231–63.

Alston, W. P., "Pragmatism and the Theory of Signs in Peirce," *Philosophy and Phenomenological Research*, XVII (1956), pp. 79–88.

Aveling, F., "Universals and the 'Illative Sense,'" *The Dublin Review*, CXXXVII (1905), pp. 236–71.

Ayer, A. J., "On Particulars and Universals," *Proceedings, Aristotelian Society*, n.s., XXXIV (1933–34), pp. 51–62.

———, Whiteley, C. H., Black, M., "Truth by Convention: A Symposium," *Analysis*, Oxford, 1936–37, pp. 17–22; 22–28; 28–32.

———, "Basic Propositions," *Philosophical Essays*, The Macmillan Co., London, 1954, pp. 105–24.

Baillie, J. B., "Truth and History," *Mind*, n.s., VII (1898), pp. 506–22.

Balthasar, N., "Intuition humaine et expérience métaphysique," *Revue Néo-scolastique de Philosophie*, XXXXI (1938), pp. 262–66.

Bartolomei, T. M., "Thought and Language," *Philosophy Today*, I, No. 1 (1957), pp. 48–53.

Beardsley, M. C., "Artistic Truth," *Aesthetics*, Harcourt, Brace and Co., New York, 1958, pp. 367–99.

——, "Literature and Knowledge," *Aesthetics*, Harcourt, Brace and Co., New York, 1958, pp. 400–53.

Beck, L. W., "Self-Justification in Epistemology," *The Journal of Philosophy*, XXXXV (1948), pp. 253–60.

Beck, M., "Are Value Judgments Unscientific?" *The Philosophical Review*, LIV (1945), pp. 65–71.

Bell, E. T., *The Search for Truth*, The Williams and Wilkins Co., Baltimore, 1934.

Bergmann, G., "Remarks Concerning the Epistemology of Scientific Empiricism," *Philosophy of Science*, IX (1942), pp. 283–93.

Bilsky, M., "Truth, Belief, and the Value of Art," *Philosophy and Phenomenological Research*, XVI (1956), pp. 488–95.

Biser, E., "The Countenance of Truth," *Philosophy Today*, I, No. 2 (1957), pp. 89–94.

Bixler, J. S., "The Problem of Religious Knowledge," *The Philosophical Review*, LI (1942), pp. 574–86.

Black, M., "The Semantic Definition of Truth," *Analysis*, VIII, No. 4 (1948).

Bliss, H. E., "The System of the Sciences and the Organization of Knowledge," *Philosophy of Science*, II (1935), pp. 86–103.

Bochenski, I. M., *Die Zeitgenössischen Denkmethoden*, Francke, Bern, 1954.

——, "Philosophy of the Idea," *Contemporary European Philosophy*, University of California Press, 1956, pp. 72–99.

Bradley, F. H., "On Appearance, Error and Contradiction," *Mind*, n.s., XIX (1910), pp. 153–85.

——, "On Truth and Coherence," *Mind*, n.s., XVIII (1909), pp. 329–42.

Broad, C. D., "The Philosophical Implications of Foreknowledge," *Aristotelian Society*, Supplementary XVI (1937), Harrison and Sons, Ltd., pp. 179–209.

Buchler, J., *Toward a General Theory of Human Judgment*, Columbia University Press, New York, 1951.

Caldin, E. F., *The Power and Limits of Science; A Philosophical Study*, Chapman and Hall, London, 1949.

Carnap, R., *Logical Foundations of Probability*, University of Chicago Press, Chicago, 1950.

Carlile, W., "Reality and Causation," *Mind*, n.s., IV (1895), pp. 82–91; 213–24.

Carritt, E. F., *An Introduction to Aesthetics*, Hutchinson's University Library, London, 1949.

———, *Philosophies of Beauty*, The Clarendon Press, Oxford, 1931.

Cassirer, E., "Psychology and Epistemology," *The Philosophy of the Enlightenment*, tr. by F. C. A. Koelin and J. P. Pettegrove, Princeton University Press, Princeton, 1951, pp. 93–133.

Cattaui, G., "Bergson, Kierkegaard, and Mysticism," *The Dublin Review*, CXCII (1933), pp. 70–8.

Cauchy, V., "The Nature and Genesis of the Skeptic Attitude," *The Modern Schoolman*, XXVII (1949–50), pp. 203–21; 297–310.

Chatalian, G., "Induction and the Problem of the External World," *The Journal of Philosophy*, XXXXIX (1952), pp. 601–7.

Chaudhury, P. J., "Truth and Error," *Review of Metaphysics*, VIII (1955), pp. 569–73.

Chisholm, R. M., "Epistemic Statements and the Ethics of Belief," *Philosophy and Phenomenological Research*, XVI (1956), pp. 447–60.

Collingwood, R. G., Taylor, A. E., Schiller, F. C. S., "Are History and Science Different Kinds of Knowledge?" *Mind*, n.s., XXXI (1922), pp. 443–66.

Copleston, F., "On Seeing and Noticing," *Contemporary Philosophy*, The Newman Press, Westminster, Md., 1956, pp. 77–86.

Cousin, D. R., "Carnap's Theories of Truth," *Mind*, n.s., LIX (1950), pp. 1–22.

Cunningham, F. A., "*Certitudo* in St. Thomas Aquinas," *The Modern Schoolman*, XXX (1953), pp. 297–324.

———, "Judgment in St. Thomas," *The Modern Schoolman*, XXXI (1954), pp. 185–212.

D'Arcy, M. C., "The Claims of Commonsense," *The Dublin Review*, CLXXXI (1927), pp. 161–78.

———, "Belief and Religious Experience," *The Nature of Belief*, Sheed and Ward, London, 1945, pp. 167–200.

De Burgh, W. G., "Aesthetic Knowledge," *Knowledge of the Individual*, Oxford University Press, London, 1939, pp. 22–41.

Delesalle, J., "L'affirmation de l'être et la connaissance intuitive," *Revue de Philosophie*, XXXVIII (1938), pp. 38–70.

Demos, R., "The Spectrum of Knowledge," *The Philosophical Review*, LVI (1947), pp. 237–57.

Dewey, "The Dilemma of the Intellectualist Theory of Truth," *Journal of Philosophy, Psychology and Scientific Methods*, VI (1909), pp. 433–4.

De Wulf, M., "La notion de vérité dans la critériologie du Cardinal Mercier," *Revue Néo-scolastique de Philosophie*, XXI (1914), pp. 231–6.

Drewitt, N., "Faith and Mysticism," *The Thomist*, II (1940), pp. 59–87.

Ducasse, C. J., "Is Scientific Verification Possible in Philosophy?," *Philosophy of Science*, II (1935), pp. 121–7.

Elton, W., ed., *Aesthetics and Language*, essays by W. B. Gallie, A. Isenberg, B. Lake, G. Ryle, etc., Philosophical Library, New York, 1954.

Féraud, L., "Le Raisonnement fondé sur les probabilités: essai d'analyse épistémologique," *Revue de Métaphysique et de morale*, LIII (1948), pp. 113–38.

Foerster, H. von, *Cybernetics*, Transactions of the Eighth Conference, March 15–16, 1951, Macy Foundation, New York, 1952.

Furry, W. D., "The Aesthetic Experience: Its Nature and Function in Epistemology," *Monograph of the Psychological Review*, Review Publishing Co., Baltimore, 1908.

Garnet, A. C., "Arthur Pap's Analysis of Necessary Propositions," *The Philosophical Review*, LIX (1950), pp. 370–4.

Gendreau, B., *La certitude, sa notion et son dynamisme selon St. Thomas d'Aquin*, Université de Montréal, 1950 (Diss.).

Gledhill, A. W., "Statistical Truth," *Blackfriars*, XXX (1949), pp. 329–35.

Grabmann, M., "Scientific Cognition of Truth," *The New Scholasticism*, XIII (1939), pp. 1–30.

Hinshaw, V. C., Jr., "The Pragmatist Theory of Truth," *Philosophy of Science*, XI (1944), pp. 82–92.

Hoenen, P., "A Field of Research in Scholasticism," *The Modern Schoolman*, XII (1934), pp. 15–18.

Hoijer, H., ed., *Language in Culture*, University of Chicago Press, Chicago, 1954.

Holt, E. B., "Error," *The New Realism*, The Macmillan Co., New York, 1912, pp. 357–73.

———, "Illusions of Perception and Thought," *The New Realism*, The Macmillan Co., New York, 1912, pp. 303–56.

Jaspers, K., "Philosophy and Science," *Way to Wisdom*, tr. by R. Manheim, Yale University Press, New Haven, 1951, pp. 147–67.

Joachim, H. H., "'Absolute' and 'Relative' Truth," *Mind*, n.s., XIV (1905), pp. 1–14.

Johnstone, H. W., "Argument and Truth in Philosophy," *Philosophy and Phenomenological Research*, XVIII (1957), pp. 228–36.

Jolivet, R., *Essai sur le problème et les conditions de la sincérité*, Vitte, Paris, 1950.

Kaplan, A., "What Good is 'Truth'?," *Philosophy and Phenomenological Research*, XV (1954), pp. 151–69.

Kattsoff, L. O., "Logic or the Psychology of Language," *Philosophy and Phenomenological Research*, XVI (1955), pp. 108–12.

Keeler, L. W., *The Problem of Error from Plato to Kant*, Gregorianum, Roma, 1934.

———, "St. Thomas' Doctrine Regarding Error," *The New Scholasticism*, VII (1933), pp. 26–57.

Kremer, R., "La connaissance historique, son objet et sa nature," *Revue Néo-scolastique de philosophie*, XXIV (1922), pp. 93–118.

Lechner, R., *The Aesthetic Experience*, Henry Regnery Co., Chicago, 1953.

Lévêque, R., *Le problème de la vérité dans la philosophie de Spinoza*, Istra, Strasbourg, 1923.

Long, M., "Truth," *The Spirit of Philosophy*, W. W. Norton and Co., New York, 1953, pp. 266–92.

Lossky, N., "Absolute Criterion of Truth," *Review of Metaphysics*, II (1949), pp. 47–96.

Lottin, J., "Le calcul des probabilités et les régularités statistiques," *Revue Néo-scolastique de philosophie*, XVII (1910), pp. 23–52.

Lotz, J. B., "Metaphysical and Religious Experience," *Philosophy Today*, II, No. 2 (1958), pp. 240–9.

Malcolm, N., "Russell's Human Knowledge," *The Philosophical Review*, LIX (1950), pp. 94–106.

Mansion, S., *Le jugement d'existence chez Aristote*, Desclée de Brouwer, Paris, 1946.

Maritain, J., "Digression sur la phénoménologie et sur les 'méditations cartésiennes'," *Rivista di Filosofia Neo-scolastica*, Milano, XXIV (1932), pp. 13–23.

———, "On Knowledge Through Connaturality," *Review of Metaphysics*, IV (1950), pp. 473–81.

Marling, J. M., "The Dialectical Character of Scientific Knowledge," *Philosophical Studies* in honor of V. R. I. Smith, O.P., The Newman Press, Westminster, Md., 1952, pp. 3–13.

Marrou, H. I., *De la connaissance historique*, Editions du Seuil, Paris, 1954.

Mays, W., "Can Machines Think," *Philosophy*, XXVII (1952), pp. 148–162.

McAllister, J. L., *The Nature of Religious Knowledge in the Theology of Charles Hodge*, Duke University, Durham, 1957 (Diss.).

McCall, R. J., "St. Thomas on Ontological Truth," *The New Scholasticism*, XII (1938), pp. 9–29.

McKeon, R., "Dialogue and Controversy in Philosophy," *Philosophy and Phenomenological Research*, XVII (1956), pp. 143–63.

McNabb, V., "Faith and Reason," *Blackfriars*, XIII (1932), pp. 327–32.

———, "On Evidence," *Blackfriars*, XVIII (1937), pp. 165–70.

Merrill, W. S., "Relativity of Knowledge: A Brief Critique," *The New Scholasticism*, XVII (1943), pp. 79–86.

Metcalf, W. V., "The Reality of the Unobservable," *Philosophy of Science*, VII (1940), pp. 337–41.

Metz, A., "Probability and Reality," *Philosophy Today*, I, No. 2 (1957), pp. 128–32.

Miéville, H. L., "Des constituants formels de l'idée de vérité et de leur signification ontologique," *Dialectica*, VII, No. 2 (1953), pp. 99–138.

———, "Réflexions sur le problème de la tolérance considéré dans son rapport avec l'idée de vérité," *Revue de Théologie et de Philosophie*, XXVI (1938), pp. 308–25.

Miller, D. L., "Two Kinds of Certainty," *Philosophy of Science*, VII (1940), pp. 26–35.

Milmed, B. K., "Theories of Religious Knowledge from Kant to Jaspers," *Philosophy*, XXIX (1954), pp. 195–215.

Montague, W. P., "Truth Substantial and Existential," *The Ways of Things*, Prentice-Hall, New York, 1940, pp. 262–80.

———, "Mysticism," *The Ways of Knowing*, The Macmillan Co., New York, 1948, pp. 54–68.

Moore, G. E., Joseph, H. W. B., "Indirect Knowledge," *Proceedings, Aristotelian Society*, IX (1929), pp. 18–50; 51–66.

Morris, C. W., "The Predication Theory of Truth," *The Monist*, XXXVIII (1928), pp. 386–401.

Nabours, R. K., "The Masquerade of ESP," *Philosophy of Science*, X (1943), pp. 191–203.

Nagel, E., "Truth and Knowledge of the Truth," *Philosophy and Phenomenological Research*, V (1944–45), pp. 50–68.

Newman, J. H., "Implicit and Explicit Reason," *Essays in Philosophy*, ed. H. Peterson, Pocket Library, New York, 1959, pp. 172–93.

Nicolas, J. H., "Le problème de l'erreur," *Revue Thomiste*, LII (1952), pp. 328–57; 528–66.

Noone, J. B., *The Form and Meaning of Knowledge in Mathematical Physics*, Fordham University (1954) (Diss.).

Oakeley, H. D., "Epistemology and the Logical Syntax of Language," *Mind*, n.s., XXXXIX (1940), pp. 427–44.

Panniker, R., "The Existential Phenomenology of Truth," *Philosophy Today*, II, No. 1 (1958), pp. 13–21.

Pap, A., "Are All Necessary Propositions Analytic?," *The Philosophical Review*, LVIII (1949), pp. 299–320.

———, *Elements of Analytic Philosophy*, The Macmillan Co., New York, 1949.

Parker, D. H., "Knowledge by Acquaintance," *The Philosophical Review,* LIV (1945), pp. 1–18.

———, "Knowledge by Description," *The Philosophical Review,* LIV (1945), pp. 458–88.

———, "Is There a Third Kind of Knowledge?," *The Philosophical Review,* LIX (1950), pp. 221–9.

Patri, A., "Sur la nature de la vérité," *Revue de Métaphysique et de Morale,* LIX (1954), pp. 290–301.

Perkins, M., "Notes on the Pragmatic Theory of Truth," *The Journal of Philosophy,* XXXXIX (1952), pp. 572–87.

Poteat, W. H., "What is a Poem About?," *Philosophy and Phenomenological Research,* XVII (1957), pp. 546–50.

Prall, D. W., *Aesthetic Analysis,* Thomas Y. Crowell Co., New York, 1936.

Quick, O., "Knowledge, Action and Religion," *Philosophy,* XII (1937), pp. 208–21.

Rader, M., *A Modern Book of Aesthetics,* Revised Edition, Henry Holt & Co., New York, 1952.

Ramsperger, A. G., "Absolute Truth, Relative Reality and Meaningful Events," *The Journal of Philosophy,* XXXXVIII (1951), pp. 29–34.

Randall, J. H., *The Role of Knowledge in Western Religion,* Starr King Press, Boston, 1958.

Raymond, P., "La théorie de l'induction. Duns Scot, précurseur de Bacon," *Etudes Franciscaine,* XXI (1909), pp. 113–26; 270–79.

Reichenbach, H., "Are Phenomenal Reports Absolutely Certain?," *The Philosophical Review,* LXI (1952), pp. 147–59.

Régis, L. M., *L'opinion selon Aristote,* Vrin, Paris, 1935.

Reiser, O., "Logic, Cybernetics and General Semantics," *General Semantic Bulletin,* no. 16 and 17 (1955), pp. 57–62.

Rogosin, H., "Telepathy, Psychical Research and Modern Psychology," *Philosophy of Science,* V (1938), pp. 472–83.

Russell, B., "Le principe d'individuation," *Revue de Métaphysique et de Morale,* LV (1950), pp. 1–15.

Santayana, G., "That Which is Denied and May be Absent is Not Truth but Knowledge of Truth," *The Realm of Truth,* Charles Scribner's Sons, New York, 1938, pp. 122–24.

Sellars, R. W., "A Correspondence Theory of Truth," *The Journal of Philosophy,* XXXVIII (1941), pp. 645–54.

———, "The Meaning of True and False," *Philosophy and Phenomenological Research,* V (1945), pp. 98–103.

———, "Epistemology and the New Way of Words," *The Journal of Philosophy,* XXXXIV (1947), pp. 645–60.

Sheldon, W. H., "The Criterion of Reality," *Review of Metaphysics,* I (1948), pp. 3–38.

Sidgwick, H., "Criteria of Truth and Error," *Mind,* n.s., IX (1900), pp. 8–25.

Smith, V. E., "Cognitive Aspects of the Heisenberg Principle," *The Thomist,* XII (1949), pp. 474–99.

Solomon, J., "Is there an A Priori Knowledge?," *Mind,* XV (1890), pp. 260–65.

Stace, W. T., "The Problem of Unreasoned Beliefs," *Mind,* n.s., LIV (1945), pp. 27–49; 122–47.

———, "Are All Empirical Statements Merely Hypotheses?," *The Journal of Philosophy,* XXXXIV (1947), pp. 29–38.

Stirling, J. H., "Kant has *not* Answered Hume," *Mind,* X (1885), pp. 45–72.

Strong, E. W., "William Whewell and John Stuart Mill: Their Controversy about Scientific Knowledge," *Journal of the History of Ideas,* XVI (1955), pp. 209–31.

Stuart, H. W., "Knowledge and Self-Consciousness," *The Philosophical Review,* XXXXVI (1937), pp. 609–43.

Swabey, M. C., *The Judgment of History,* Philosophical Library, New York, 1954.

Taylor, R., "Knowledge and Certainty," *Review of Metaphysics,* VII (1954), pp. 679–80.

Thompson, M. H., "J. S. Mill's Theory of Truth: A Study in Metaphysics and Logic," *The Philosophical Review,* LVI (1947), pp. 273–92.

Toohey, J. J., "Reality and Truth," *The Philosophical Review,* XXXXVIII (1939), pp. 492–505.

Trethowan, I., *Certainty, Philosophical and Theological,* The Docre Press, Westminster, 1948.

Tsanoff, R. A., "Professor Bordin on the Nature of Truth," *The Philosophical Review,* XIX (1910), pp. 632–38.

Turning, A., "Computing Machinery and Intelligence," *Mind,* n.s., LIX (1950), pp. 433–60.

Van Riet, G., "La doctrine thomiste du jugement," *Revue Philosophique de Louvain,* XXXXVI (1948), pp. 97–108.

Verbeke, G., "Connaissance de soi et connaissance de Dieu chez Saint Augustin," *Augustiana,* annus IV, Fasc, 3–4, 1954, pp. 495–515.

Vier, P. C., *Evidence and its Function According to John Duns Scotus,* Franciscan Institute, St. Bonaventure, New York, 1951.

Walsh, F. A., "The Humanistic Theory of Error," *The New Scholasticism,* IV (1930), pp. 337–48.

Waters, B., "Particulars, Universals and Verification," *Philosophy of Science,* VII (1940), pp. 81–91.

Watts, N. H., "Poetry and Science," *The Dublin Review*, CXCVII (1935), pp. 295–310.

Weiss, P., "The Quest for Certainty," *The Philosophical Review*, LV (1946), pp. 132–51.

Weitz, M., "Analytic Statements," *Mind*, n.s., LXIII (1954), pp. 487–94.

White, V., "Thomism and Affective Knowledge," *Blackfriars*, XXIV (1943), pp. 8–16, 126–32; XXV (1944), pp. 321–28.

Whitehead, A. N., *Adventures of Ideas*, The Macmillan Co., New York, 1933.

Whorf, B. L., "The Relation of Habitual Thought and Behavior to Language," *Language, Thought, and Reality*, ed. J. B. Carroll, The Technology Press, M.I.T., John Wiley & Sons, Inc., New York, 1957, pp. 134–59.

Wild, J., "Is There a World of Ordinary Language?," *The Philosophical Review*, LXVII (1958), pp. 440–76.

Williams, D., *The Ground of Induction*, Harvard University Press, Cambridge, 1947.

Williams, G., "On Our Lack of Certainty as to the Truth of Any and All Propositions," *The Philosophical Review*, XXXXVIII (1939), pp. 632–37.

———, "Absolute Truth and the Shadow of Doubt," *Philosophy of Science*, XV (1948), pp. 211–24.

Wilson, N. L., *The Concept of Language*, University of Toronto Press, Toronto, 1959.

Winn, R. B., "The Distinction Between Truth and Knowledge," *The Personalist*, XIV, no. 3 (1933), pp. 185–95.

Wolf, L. O., "Mr. Russell's Theory of Truth," *The New Scholasticism*, V (1931), pp. 234–47.

———, "Mr. Russell's Theory of Facts," *The New Scholasticism*, V (1931), pp. 342–54.

Wolz, H. G., "The Universal Doubt in the Light of Descartes' Conception of Truth," *The Modern Schoolman*, XXVII (1949–50), pp. 253–79.

Zink, S., "Poetry and Truth," *The Philosophical Review*, LIV (1945), pp. 132–54.

Part V : THEORIES OF

KNOWLEDGE

R. B. Perry : THE CARDINAL PRINCIPLE OF IDEALISM

THE *late Ralph Barton Perry (1876–1957), longtime Professor of Philosophy at Harvard, was one of the most influential teachers and scholars on the American scene. His thorough exploration of the contributions to philosophic thought made by William James has made* THE THOUGHT AND CHARACTER OF WILLIAM JAMES *(1935) the definitive biography and critical study of that writer. Perry's* GENERAL THEORY OF VALUE *(1926) and* REALMS OF VALUE *(1954) are, and will remain, important additions to moral philosophy. The present essay, from his comprehensive investigation,* PRESENT PHILOSOPHICAL TENDENCIES, *reveals his ability to distinguish between apparently similar but basically differing epistemological schemes and, therefore, is an essential guide to the problem of idealism in its modern dimensions and extensions. Reprinted by permission from* PRESENT PHILOSOPHICAL TENDENCIES, *George Braziller, Inc., New York, 1955, pp. 113–34.*

• 1. "The constant presupposition is that a spiritual life which is a unified whole is at work in the depths of our soul." These words, written by Rudolph Eucken,[1] admirably express the *message* of idealism to modern times. Idealism is a form of spiritualism in which man, the finite individual, is regarded as a microcosmic representation of God, the Absolute Individual. Man's spiritual nature is a revelation of the *principle* of reality, and his ideals an intimation of the *perfect* and *eternal* reality. So that, but for his limitations, man would be God; and taken together with the balance of spiritual life, which compensates for these limitations, he *is* God.

But a characterization of idealism in terms so general as these, while it helps to define its place among religious and ethical motives, throws little light upon its technical philosophical meaning. To understand this it is necessary to examine its method and proofs. And we then discover that idealism rests fundamentally upon a theory of *knowledge*. The supremacy of spirit is argued from the theory of the priority of the knowing consciousness itself, over all with which it has to do. All things, it is contended, are primarily 'objects'; and to be object means necessarily to be 'for' something, to be in some sense the expression or creation of a 'subject.' The so-called 'external world' being in this manner reduced to knowledge, and knowledge being construed as spiritual, the supremacy of spirit is established. This is the reply of idealism to naturalism; and the justification which idealism affords to the religious belief that the world at large is governed in the interest of goodness.

The assertion of *the priority of the cognitive consciousness,* the assertion that *being is dependent on the knowing of it,* may, then, fairly be regarded as the cardinal principle of idealism. Only in the light of this principle can either the applications of idealism, or its own inner dialectical movement, be comprehended. I shall attempt in the present essay to throw this principle into bold relief, by examining its origin, and formulating its fundamental proofs.

2. Modern idealism, defined in the light of this principle, may be clearly distinguished from ancient idealism, or Platonism. Platonism is primarily the culmination of a tendency which manifested itself among all the pre-Socratics: a tendency of which the central motive was the assertion of the superiority of systematic or well-grounded knowledge to mere opinion. Thus Parmenides distinguished between "the unshaken heart of persuasive truth," and "the opinions of mortals in which is no true belief at all." Heraclitus remarked that the truth differed from opinion in being one and universal. "Though wisdom is common, yet the many lives as if they had a wisdom of their own"; just as "the waking have one and the same world, but the sleeping turn aside each into a world of his own." [2]

[1] *The Life of the Spirit,* trans. by F. L. Pogson, p. 100.
[2] Burnet's *Early Greek Philosophy,* pp. 184, 140.

Similarly with Plato, philosophy is primarily a means of escape from the relativity and conflict of opinion. The philosopher is "he who has magnificence of mind and is the spectator of all time and all existence"; who "will not rest in the multiplicity of individuals which is an appearance only, but will go on—the keen edge will not be blunted, neither the force of his desire abate until he have attained the knowledge of the true nature of every essence by a kindred power in the soul." True knowledge is marked by the kind of object which it discovers or seeks, "the absolute, eternal, and immutable," or "the things themselves," which, like the absolute square and the absolute diameter of mathematics, "can only be seen with the eye of the mind." And this insistence on the objectivity and permanence of truth is united with the speculative interest in completeness of truth. The knowledge of the philosopher will be not only unerring in point of certainty, but also unlimited in point of sufficiency and generality. Thus Plato represents also that philosophical tendency which has come latterly to be termed 'absolutism.'[3]

So far, in this summary of Plato, no provision has been made for the moral element. Plato's 'absolute' is defined as *the good,* and in the order of the sciences, ethics is elevated even above mathematics. "The excellence or beauty or truth of every structure, animate or inanimate, and of every action of man, is relative to the use for which nature or the artist has intended them."[4] In other words, for Plato *the teleological categories are fundamental.* And this motive doubtless tended to contradict his rationalism, and to create a certain affinity between him and those very sophists who were his dearest foes. The fact remains, however, that so far as method was concerned, ancient idealism was opposed, not to physical or mathematical science, but to the laxity of common sense.[5] This is proved by Plato's high esteem for mathematics as a means of intellectual discipline, through which the philosopher might be emancipated from personal bias and the evanescent chaos of immediate experience, and brought to apprehend definite conceptions and fixed principles.

3. This rationalistic motive—critical, scientific, and speculative—which dominated constructive philosophy among the ancients, found a more complete expression many centuries later in Spinoza. But in Spinoza it is so far freed from all connexion with teleology as to provoke a wholly different alignment of forces. In the famous Appendix to Part I of the *Ethics,* it is argued that an explanation of nature in terms of final causes is necessarily anthropomorphic. Man is virtually attempting to account for the absolute origin of things in terms of that value which they have for *him.*

[3] Cf. Chapter VIII, especially pp. 167, 169–172, *Present Philo. Tendencies.*

[4] Plato's *Republic,* Jowett's translation, 479, 486, 490, 510, 601.

[5] This was largely due to the fact that the physical and mathematical sciences themselves were not wholly free from teleology. The mechanical ideal of science was not yet developed.

He assigns as reasons for the being of things those reasons which would have moved *him* to create them. And where he can find no such reason he simply imputes one to God's inscrutable wisdom. "Such a doctrine," says Spinoza, "might well have sufficed to conceal the truth from the human race for all eternity, if mathematics had not furnished another standard of verity in considering solely the essence and properties of figures without regard to their final causes."[6] It will be observed that Spinoza prizes mathematics, not only for its exactness, but also for its dispassionateness, for that very character that led Plato to subordinate it to ethics. The philosopher of Spinoza is not the guardian of the State, representing the good of the whole rather than the good of any part, or even the lover of the absolute good, but the witness of those inexorable necessities which make no allowance for human ideals.

Thus in the rationalism of Spinoza the teleological principle, derived through Plato and Aristotle from the humanism of the Socratic age, and reinforced by the Scriptural account of the creation and of God's dealings with man, is replaced by the principle of *mechanism*. Science has now become identified in men's minds with the quantitative laws of motion. The Copernican revolution had further emphasized the meaning of the mechanical theory and brought out its essentially de-anthropomorphic character, by removing the Earth from the centre of the stellar system, and reducing man's historical career to a peripheral and incidental feature of the cosmos. Man was now of small account in that world which he had once been led to believe was contrived for his especial comfort and salvation. If the religious attitude was to be maintained with such a philosophical background, only two possibilities seemed to remain. Either, as in the case of Spinoza himself, the religious consciousness must be reduced to the reason's approval of truth; or religion as a whole must be conceived with Hobbes[7] as a secular institution, used to pacify disorderly men, and sharing the pettiness which under the mechanical philosophy attaches to all human affairs. But religion of the former type must be as rare as the spirit of renunciation and the capacity for intellectual mysticism; while religion of the latter type is a mere convention imposed by cynical enlightenment upon servile ignorance. Hence, not without reason, Spinoza and Hobbes were singled out and anathematized as the great prophets of irreligion.

Spinoza and Hobbes do not, it is true, adequately represent the rationalism of the seventeenth and eighteenth centuries. It was on the whole characteristic of these centuries to believe that religion, even Christian orthodoxy, could be established by strictly rational means.[8] But Spinoza and

---

[6] Elwes's translation, Vol. II, p. 77. The *Ethics* was first published in 1677.
[7] Cf. his *Leviathan* (1651), Ch. XII.
[8] Cf. above, pp. 32–34.

Hobbes represent the rationalistic spirit of this age in its freest and purest expression, and their philosophies typify its logical trend. To keep one's eye single to things as they are, to yield one's mind only to facts and necessities, seemed to lead in the end to the belittlement of man and the disallowance of his spiritual claims.

4. We are now prepared to understand the service which modern idealism offered to religious belief. True religion required to be defended, not, as in the days of Socrates and Plato, against the prejudices and blindness of unthinking men, *but against the claim of science to have alienated the world from man.* Faith and revelation had been left unsupported in their demand that the world should be subordinated to spirit. That nature which religion had conceived to be the handiwork of God, or the stage-setting of the moral drama, or at most merely the principle of negation in the spiritual life, threatened to swallow up both man and God. A new philosophy must redeem nature from mechanism and restore its spiritual centre. It must not be supposed that this was the conscious aim of the idealists and their forerunners, or that the tendency was not in large part due to purely theoretical motives. But it is this that accounts for the great human importance of idealism, for its stimulating power and widely diffused influence. And it is in this sense that idealism is revolutionary. Kant, for example, compared his theory of knowledge with the Copernican revolution in astronomy. He proposed to assume that "the objects must conform to our mode of cognition" rather than that "our knowledge must conform to the objects," just as Copernicus, "not being able to get on in the explanation of the movements of the heavenly bodies, as long as he assumed that all the stars turned round the spectator, tried, whether he could not succeed better, by assuming the spectator to be turning round, and the stars to be at rest." [9]

But Kant did not point out the fact, nor has its importance ever been sufficiently recognized, that the idealistic revolution was virtually a *counter-revolution,* through which the spectator again became the centre of the system. Nor did this counter-revolution either begin or end with Kant. It is a movement of epochal proportions, supported by a wide diversity of thinkers, and dominating philosophy from the time of Berkeley down to the present day. Its central motive is the restoration of the supremacy of spirit. Its distinguishing characteristic as a philosophy of religion is its subordination of nature to God by means of a preliminary reduction of nature to knowledge. Science is to be allowed a free hand in nature; and having annexed nature, its title is to be transferred to mind. That very mechanical cosmos which had served to belittle man, is now made to glorify him through being conceived as the fruit of intelligence.

---

[9] *Critique of Pure Reason* (1781), Max Müller's translation, second edition, p. 693.

God, the discarded hypothesis of science, is enthroned again as the master-knower of whom science itself is only the imperfect instrument.

Thus, while the burden of idealism is a religious interpretation of nature, its cardinal principle is a theory of knowledge. For the purposes of technical philosophy it consists in a single proposition, to the effect that knowledge is an originating or creative process. Idealism's claims can be substantiated only provided it is true that *to know is to generate the reality known*. It must be proved that the being and nature of things are conditioned by their being known. In what follows, the attempt will be made, amidst the confusing motives which attend the history of idealism, to keep this cardinal principle constantly in view, and to sift and test the evidence with which it has been supported. And first, let us consider the manner in which Descartes and Locke, the forerunners of idealism, prepared the ground for Berkeley, its founder.

5. The strategy of idealism depends on the adoption of a certain initial standpoint.[10] The world must be viewed under the form of knowledge. Although the precise significance of the fact cannot yet be made clear, it *is* a fact that everything that can be mentioned, such as the sun, gold, or Napoleon I, can be classed as an element of knowledge, or *idea*. This generalization does, it is true, require a qualification, the importance of which will shortly appear. Elements of knowledge, or ideas, imply a knower, which is not itself an idea, but which confers the character of idea on what it possesses. With this amendment, we may say that it is possible to regard the world of all mentionable things, even the Copernican plurality of worlds with their inflexible mechanical necessities, as comprehended under the knower and his ideas.

Descartes [11] adopted this standpoint only provisionally, but the difficulty he met in extricating himself from it demonstrated its dialectical possibilities. When you record the knower and his ideas, or all knowers and their ideas, what is there left to account for? Descartes, of course, thought that there were at least two things still to account for, namely, God and nature. If asked whether these too were not ideas, he would have replied, not *merely* ideas—for they exist also in their own right. Nevertheless, from the Cartesian standpoint, God and nature are *primarily* ideas, that being the most certain thing about them. That there are such ideas is indubitable; that they are more than ideas remains somehow to be proved from what is known of them as ideas. The existence of God must be argued from the idea of God, and the existence of nature from the idea of nature.

The characteristic difference between Descartes and Locke lies in the fact that the former seeks to establish existence (as something other than

---

[10] The dialectical importance of this starting-point will appear later. Cf. below, pp. 127–128.

[11] Cf. his *Discourse on Method* (1637), and *Meditations* (1640), *passim*.

the knower and his ideas) first in the case of God, while the latter seeks to establish it first in the case of nature. Let us consider the procedure of Descartes. He believes that he escapes from the circle of the knower and his ideas, through the peculiar character of the idea of God. He here employs the traditional 'ontological' proof, according to which the idea of an infinite and perfect being implies the existence of its object; and further argues that the idea of God possesses so high a degree of meaning as to require a being of like degree to account for it. Once the existence of God was established and the circle broken, Descartes thought it safe to infer that other "clear and distinct" ideas, such as the ideas of nature, were also representative of existence.

Let us turn to the case of Locke. Nominally, he follows Descartes and proves God before he proves nature. But logically he follows just the reverse order. Albeit with a certain becoming hesitation, he sets aside the ontological proof of God, and prefers those proofs that carried more weight with Englishmen and deists of the eighteenth century.[12] God's existence is proved from the necessity of an eternal and intelligent first cause of nature. The problem of existence must, then, be first solved with reference to nature. And here Locke's distrust of intellectualism leads him to define a new criterion. The ideas, he asserted, that are most significant of existence, are not those that are most clear and distinct, or most full of meaning, but those which are directly imprinted on the mind by an *external cause*. Existence is to be inferred, not from the import of ideas, but from the circumstances of their origin. It is not a question of proving the trustworthiness or representative validity of illuminating ideas; but of proving the extra-mental source of vivid and forceful ideas, that are beyond the mind's control. The unique case of such ideas is the sense-impression.[13]

Owing to this difference of procedure between Descartes and Locke, there came to prevail two notions of the relation between existing nature and the idea of nature. According to the Cartesian procedure, existent nature is essentially that which *corresponds* to the idea of nature. According to the empirical procedure of Locke, on the other hand, existent nature is essentially the *cause* of the idea of nature. In the first case existent nature must resemble the idea, and the real difficulty is to distinguish it therefrom. In the second case existent nature need not resemble the idea, and the real difficulty is to give it any real character or meaning at all. We are now prepared to understand the form which idealism first assumed in the writings of Berkeley.

[12] Cf. Locke's *Essay Concerning Human Understanding* (1690), Bk. iv. Ch. X, § 7.
[13] Cf. *op. cit.*, Bk. iv, Ch. XI, § 1. "No particular man can know the existence of any other being, but only when, by actual operating upon him, it makes itself perceived by him."

6. Berkeley, like Descartes and Locke, begins with the assumption of the knower and his ideas and feels the difficulty of establishing the existence of anything else. But Berkeley parts company with his predecessors, and with common-sense, in concluding that the difficulty is insuperable and the attempt to overcome it gratuitous. He asserts, in short, that all existence may adequately be comprehended under the knower and his ideas; and in this assertion modern idealism first sees the light.[14]

With Berkeley, as with Locke, the question primarily concerns nature. Is there an existent nature over and above the idea of nature? The answer may be formulated as a dilemma. If, as Descartes would have it, existent nature agrees with the ideas of nature, then what is the difference? But if, as Locke suggests, existent nature does not agree with the ideas of nature, then what is it, and how can it be proved? Furthermore, why must a thing be other than idea in order to exist? In the case of nature, Berkeley asserts, it would appear that *esse est percipi*.

Berkeley's argument is too well-known to require detailed restatement, but it is highly important to discover just what it proves. That Berkeley believed that he had established idealism is beyond question; his whole religious philosophy depended on a reduction of nature to spirit. But it is certainly true of much of Berkeley's argument that, while it serves to refute the dualism of Descartes and Locke, it nevertheless does not establish idealism. There is a halting-place short of that theory, where the issue is altered, and where new alternatives arise and diverge. Consistently with our purpose of disentangling the cardinal principle of idealism, and of isolating the evidence offered in support of it, we must therefore separate Berkeley the idealist from another Berkeley, who is simply the vanquisher of dualism.

The dualistic position is thus summarized by Hylas, the *advocatus diaboli* in Berkeley's well-known dialogue: "To speak the truth, Philonous, I think there are two kinds of objects:—the one perceived immediately, which are likewise called *ideas;* the other are real things or external objects, perceived by the mediation of ideas, which are their images and representations. Now, I own ideas do not exist without the mind; but the latter sort of objects do."[15] In attacking this position Berkeley first shows that whatever answers to the name of a natural object, such, for example, as "tulip," is perceived immediately, and hence is idea. Its color is seen, its shape and size both seen and felt, its odor smelt, and so with every quality or element that is attributed to it. What, then, is the "real" or "external" tulip "without the mind?" And what ground is there for af-

<hr>

[14] Berkeley's *Principles of Human Knowledge* was published in 1710. Malebranche, Norris, and Collier should be credited with original contributions to this doctrine, but Berkeley gave it its prominence and classic form.

[15] *Dialogue between Hylas and Philonous* (1713), Fraser's edition, Vol. I, p. 414.

firming it? There are, Berkeley believes, only two conceivable alternatives, both of which are untenable.

In the first place, one may contend, after the manner of Descartes, that an idea, if it be clear and distinct, is a trustworthy likeness of something that exists "without the mind." But how can a thing that is in its substance or essence non-mental be like a thing that is essentially mental? Surely a copy which must necessarily miss the essence of the thing copied is no copy at all. Does it mean anything to speak of absolutely invisible color, or inaudible sound? In general, does it mean anything to speak of an object that is like ideas in all particular qualities and attributes and yet possesses a fundamentally and radically different nature? By means of these and similar considerations, Berkeley shows that a non-mental world which corresponds with the mental world but never coincides with it, is both arbitrary and meaningless. And is it not also gratuitous? This raises the question in the form in which it presents itself to Locke.

For, in the second place, it may be contended that certain ideas, sensations, namely, have an extra-mental cause. They are forced upon the mind and are not of its own making. In this Berkeley is empiricist enough to agree with Locke. But what *is* the cause? If it be conceived as matter, then it reduces itself to an unknown substratum, because everything that is known of matter is, as we have seen, contained within ideas. And why should a cause, to which none of the properties of matter can be attributed, be regarded as material at all? Since here it is not required that the extra-mental reality shall be like the ideas, but only that it shall be their cause, why should it not be conceived after the analogy of the only cause of ideas with which we are directly acquainted, namely, will or spirit? In this case, matter or physical nature would simply coincide with perceptions caused by God. There would be no matter behind appearance, no duplication of known matter through the assumption of a likeness or prototype of it, and no discrediting of knowledge through the assumption of an unknown and unknowable essence.

7. Now without doubt Berkeley meant to assert that whatever is content of ideas, such as matter in the above sense, is *necessarily* or *essentially* ideal; its *esse* is *percipi*. But this does not follow from the argument as thus far outlined. For it is entirely possible that the real tulip should be, as Berkeley argues, identical, element for element, with the idea of tulip, and yet not require to be perceived in order to be. It is only necessary to conceive of idea as an *office,* or *relationship,* instead of as a kind of substance.[16] It is then possible to suppose that a thing may *occupy* that office or relationship, and thus *assume* the status of idea, without being *identified* with it.

The principle involved is a very common one, and never disputed in

16 The view adopted by pragmatism.

its more familiar applications. Thus when a citizen of the United States becomes President, the citizen and President are identical. There is no 'presidential' entity substituted for the citizen—no correspondence or representation. The simple fact is that a citizen, without forfeiting his citizenship, may assume the status of President. But no one would think of contending that therefore being President is a condition of citizenship, or that citizens are essentially presidential, or that there can be no citizens that are not presidents. Similarly, tulips may be known, and when known called 'ideas of tulips.' There is, as Berkeley justly contends, no substitution or representation, no duplication or mystification. The tulip simply assumes a certain status, definable by the special relationship *percipi,* and involving no forfeiture of its nature or identity. But this does not at all imply that whatever assumes the status of idea, *must* be idea in order to be at all, or that there are no things that are not ideas. The confusion doubtless arose from a convention to the effect that mind and nature are different 'substances,' or different domains, lying wholly outside of one another, and therefore mutually exclusive in their content.[17] It would follow from such a supposition that whatever belongs to mind or to nature belongs to it absolutely and irrevocably. But once this supposition is abandoned, there is nothing whatsoever to prevent a thing's belonging *both* to nature and to mind; in which case it is impossible to argue that because a thing belongs to mind it therefore owes its existence to the fact.

Now the doctrine which results from the rejection of the dualism between idea and existence, but which stops short of idealism, deserves independent recognition and a name that shall distinguish it. For it is accepted by contemporary thinkers of opposing schools and can therefore be eliminated from most present-day controversy. The phrase 'epistemological monism' has the virtue of suggesting that the doctrine in question is essentially a doctrine about knowledge, and not about being or existence, and also of suggesting that the doctrine arose historically as a refutation of dualism.[18] Epistemological monism means that when things are known they are identical, element for element, with the idea or content of the knowing state. According to this view, instead of there being a fundamental dual division of the world into ideas and things, there is only the class of things; ideas being the sub-class of those things that happen to be known. That which is commonly called the 'object' of knowledge merges, according to this view, with the idea, or is the whole thing of which the idea is a part. Thus when one perceives the tulip, the idea of the tulip and

[17] Descartes is mainly responsible for the prominence of this notion in modern philosophy; but it probably arose mainly from the emphasis given to "the inner life" by introspective Christianity.

[18] This doctrine is discussed more fully in *Present Philosophical Tendencies, loc. cit.,* p. 308 ff.

the real tulip coincide, element for element; they are one in color, shape, size, distance, etc. Or, if one so desires, one may reserve the name of 'real tulip' for the whole of the tulip, as distinguished from whatever portion of it is actually embraced within the idea. But in this doctrine nothing whatsoever is asserted or implied of the tulip, except as respects this particular question. Whether it be essential or accidental to the tulip that it should be perceived, and thus become an idea—whether all tulips are ideas—is a wholly different question which must be decided on different grounds. And it is an answer to this second question which constitutes the cardinal principle of idealism. We may now turn to that principle as it is formulated and defended in the philosophy of Berkeley.

8. Berkeley only infrequently isolates his strictly idealistic arguments, but the passages in which he does so are of the greatest historical importance. In the dialogue to which we have already referred, we read:

That the colors are really in the tulip which I see is manifest. Neither can it be denied that this tulip may exist independent of your mind or mine; but, *that any immediate objects of the senses—that is, any idea, or combination of ideas—should exist in an unthinking substance, or exterior to all minds, is in itself an evident contradiction.*[19]

Now we shall understand Berkeley's meaning if we can apprehend this "evident contradiction." "The tulip which I see" is idea, and it belongs to the essential character of ideas that they should be in mind; hence it is contradictory to assert that "the tulip which I see" is exterior to mind. If all redundancy and equivocation is eliminated, this amounts to the assertion that a tulip *when* seen, or defined as seen, is not a tulip unseen. But what Berkeley sought to establish was virtually the proposition that the tulip which I see can never be unseen, and this does not follow. For it is not contradictory to assert that the tulip which I see today was unseen yesterday, or that many tulips are "born to blush unseen" forever. Berkeley's error lies in his inferring that because the tulip *is* seen, therefore its being seen is its essential and exclusive status.

Berkeley's reasoning at this point is so characteristic of idealistic reasoning in general as to make it worth our while to generalize it. It does not occur to him, apparently, that a natural body, like a tulip, can belong both to the order of ideas and *also* to another and independent order. In other words, he assumes that an identical element can belong to only one complex. But, as a matter of fact, such is not the case. The letter *a,* for example, is the second letter of the word 'man,' and also the fifth letter of the word 'mortal'; and it enters into innumerably many other words as well. It possesses, in other words, a *multiple* and not an *exclusive* particularity. And the false assumption to the contrary gives rise to a specious argument. For

[19] *Op. cit.,* Fraser's edition, Vol. I, p. 406. (The italics are mine.)

having found an entity, like the tulip, in the mental context, where it is named 'idea,' and having assumed that it can belong to only one context, Berkeley thereupon *defines* it as idea, and concludes that it is such exclusively. But this is as though, having found the letter *a* in the word 'man,' we should propose to define it as 'the second letter in the word man' and so to preclude its occurring in any other word.

This specious argument, involving the assumption of 'exclusive particularity,' may be conveniently described as 'definition by initial predication.'[20] It consists in regarding some early, familiar, or otherwise accidental characterization of a thing as definitive. I may, for example, owing to the accident of residence, first learn of Columbus through the fact that the Columbia River was named for him; but it does not follow that 'the man the Columbia River was named for' may be substituted for 'Columbus' in historical science, for the obvious but sufficient reason that this characterization is not adequate. Similarly, Columbus is 'the man I am now thinking of'—the fact is not to be impeached; but to treat him as such in all subsequent discourse would be to assume that his being thought of by me was the most distinctive thing about him; which is, of course, contrary to fact. Now idealists habitually construe things as 'thought of,' and accordingly name them 'objects of thought,' or 'ideas.' But while, as we have seen, it is proper to say that it is the thing itself, and not a duplicate or representation of it that *is* thought of, it does not follow that to be thought of, or otherwise known, is either necessary or important for things. And it is precisely this which idealism must prove if it is to justify itself. It must prove that to classify things as ideas, objects of knowledge, or experiences, is *the most fundamental disposition that can be made of them.* To classify them thus at the outset, and then to *prefer* this classification to the many other possible ones, is simply to assume the very thesis under discussion.

9. Berkeley's argument assumes a different form in the following passage taken from the *Principles of Human Knowledge:*

But, say you, surely there is nothing easier than for me to imagine trees, for instance, in a park, or books existing in a closet, and nobody by to perceive them. I answer, you may so, there is no difficulty in it. But what is all this, I beseech you, more than framing in your mind certain ideas which you can call *books* and *trees,* and at the same time omitting to frame the idea of any one that may perceive them? But do not you yourself perceive or think of them all the while? This therefore is nothing to the purpose; it only shows you have the power of imagining, or forming ideas in your mind; but it does not show that you can conceive it possible the objects of your thought may exist without the mind.[21]

[20] Cf. also below, p. 133.
[21] Fraser's edition, Vol. I, p. 269.

In other words, one cannot conceive things to exist apart from consciousness, because to conceive is *ipso facto* to bring within consciousness.
It is to this argument that Berkeley appeals in the last resort, and his procedure is here again so typical as to deserve to be ranked with "definition
by initial predication" as one of the fundamental arguments for idealism.

The argument calls attention to a situation that undoubtedly exists, and
that is one of the most important original discoveries that philosophy has
made. *No thinker to whom one may appeal is able to mention a thing that
is not idea,* for the obvious and simple reason that *in mentioning it he
makes it an idea.* No one can report on the nature of things without being on hand himself. It follows that whatever thing he reports does as a
matter of fact stand in relation to him, as his idea, object of knowledge, or
experience. In order to avoid making inferences unawares, it is necessary
to have a name for this situation just as it stands. It will be convenient to
call it *"the egocentric predicament."* [22]

This predicament arises from the attempt to discover whether the cognitive relationship is indispensable to the things which enter into it. In order
to discover if possible exactly how a thing is modified by the cognitive relationship, I look for instances of things *out* of this relationship, in order
that I may compare them with instances of things *in* this relationship. But
I can find no such instances, because "finding" is a variety of the very relationship that I am trying to eliminate. Hence I cannot make the comparison, nor get an answer to my original question by this means. But I cannot conclude that there are no such instances; indeed, I now know that
I should not be able to discover them if there were.

Again, with a view to demonstrating the modification of things by the
cognitive relationship, I examine the same thing before and after it has
entered into this relationship with some knower other than myself. But
in making the comparison, I institute this relationship with myself, and
so am unable to free the thing *altogether* from such relationships.

Again, within my own field of consciousness, I may attempt to define
and subtract the cognitive relationship, in order to deal exclusively with
the residuum. But after subtracting the cognitive relationship, I must still
"deal with" the residuum; and "dealing with" is a variety of the very relationship which I sought to banish.

Finally, just in so far as I do actually succeed in eliminating every cognitive relationship, I am unable to observe the result. Thus if I close my eyes,
I cannot see what happens to the object; if I stop thinking, I cannot think
what happens to it; and so with every mode of knowledge. In thus eliminating all knowledge, I do not experimentally eliminate the thing known,

[22] I have formulated and criticised this argument more fully in an article entitled "The
Ego-centric Predicament," *Jour. of Phil., Psych., and Sc. Methods,* Vol. VII, 1910, No. 1. A
part of what follows is reprinted from that article. Cf. also below, pp. 133–134.

but only *the possibility of knowing whether that thing is eliminated or not.*

This, then, is "the ego-centric predicament." But what does it prove, and how does it serve the purpose of idealism? It should be evident that it proves nothing at all. It is simply a peculiar methodological difficulty. It does, it is true, contain the proposition that *every mentioned thing is an idea.* But this is virtually a redundant proposition to the effect that every mentioned thing is mentioned—to the effect that every idea, object of knowledge, or experience, is an idea, object of knowledge, or experience. And a redundant proposition is no proposition at all. The assertion that an idea is an idea conveys no knowledge even about ideas. But what the idealist requires is a proposition to the effect that *everything is an idea,* or that *only ideas exist.* And to derive this proposition directly from the redundancy just formulated, is simply to take advantage of the confusion of mind by which a redundancy is commonly attended.

It may be argued, however, that the ego-centric predicament is equivalent to an inductive proof of the proposition that all things are ideas. Every observed case of a thing is a case of a thing observed. Neglecting the redundancy, which is sufficient of itself to vitiate the assertion, we remark that the induction proceeds entirely by Mill's "method of agreement," which is invalid unless supported by "the method of difference," that is, the observation of negative cases. But the ego-centric predicament itself prevents the observation of negative cases. It is impossible to observe cases of unobserved things, even if there be any. In other words, there is a reason *connected with the conditions of observation* why only agreements should be observed. But where this is the case the method of agreement is worthless, and the use of it is a fallacy. Thus, I cannot conclude that English is the only intelligible form of speech simply because whomsoever I understand speaks English. On the contrary, my peculiar situation, as one acquainted only with a single language, is sufficient to discredit my results. If I should discover that I had been wearing blue glasses, I would at once discount the apparent blueness of everything that I had seen. And similarly, the general circumstance that in observing I am compelled to supply the very element whose real ubiquity or necessity I am attempting to discover, must itself be discounted or corrected, if I am to draw a true conclusion. In so far as the idealistic conclusion depends on that circumstance itself, it is fallacious.

10. A study of the later development of idealism will disclose the fact that it relies mainly, if not entirely, on the Berkeleyan proofs—'definition by initial predication,' and 'argument from the ego-centric predicament.' Despite the fact that present day idealism prefers to attribute its authorship to Kant, some idealists expressly credit Berkeley himself with having established the cardinal principle. "The truth is," says one writer,

that Berkeley gave the *coup de grace* to all forms of materialism, when he proved, or led the way to the proof, that matter (so-called physical reality) is a compound of qualities, and that every quality turns out to be an elemental form of consciousness, a way of being conscious.[23]

But it is more usual to find Berkeley's proofs restated, with slight variations to match the shade of the particular idealism which the author represents. For the cardinal principle lends itself to various interpretations. In its general form this principle asserts the priority of the cognitive consciousness, and it is therefore capable of as many diverse formulations as there are diverse conceptions of cognition. Thus there may be perceptual, rational, or volitional idealists, according as knowledge is held to consist essentially in perception, reason, or volition. And Berkeley's proofs are capable of corresponding formulations.[24] It will throw further light on the meaning of Berkeley's proofs, and illustrate their wider significance, if we have set before us a single contemporary instance of each.

The use of "definition by initial predication" appears, for example, in the common habit among idealists of adopting what is called *the standpoint of experience*. This standpoint being once adopted, and the meaning of experience formulated, idealism needs no further proof. Thus Professor Baillie writes: "We must start, in other words, from the whole of experience as such. . . . Now we take experience as a whole when we look upon the subject-mind, in which alone experience exists, as the centre to which all forms of experience refer and round which they gather. . . . Experience always implies a relation between two distinct elements: the one is that for which something is, and the other the something which is presented. These are the so-called subject and object." [25] But nowhere does this author show why we should start with experience in this sense, or why having so started we should regard that particular aspect of things as essential and definitive.

When idealists do raise these last questions, they employ, as a rule, the argument from the 'ego-centric predicament.' We *cannot avoid* the standpoint of experience, if we are to have anything before us at all, or eliminate the relation to a thinking consciousness, if we are to think. "Find any piece of existence," says Mr. Bradley,

take up anything that anyone could possibly call a fact . . . and then judge if it does not consist in sentient experience. . . . When the experiment is made strictly, I can myself conceive of nothing else than the experienced. Anything, in no sense felt or perceived, becomes to me quite unmeaning. And as I cannot try to think of it without realizing either that I am not thinking at all, or that

[23] M. W. Calkins: *The Persistent Problems of Philosophy*, p. 400; cf. pp. 118–132.

[24] Some of these diversities are discussed in *Present Philo. Tendencies, loc. cit.*, especially pp. 158–62.

[25] J. B. Baillie: *Idealistic Construction of Experience*, pp. 105, 108.

I am thinking of it against my will as being experienced, I am driven to the conclusion that for me experience is the same as reality. . . . You cannot find fact unless in unity with sentience.[26]

But all this proves no more than that *finding* is finding; no amount of reiteration or verbal alteration can ever make it prove what the idealist wants it to prove—namely, that *being* is finding, that in order to be or to be what they are, things *must* be found.

It is doubtless true that idealism has had a long and eventful history since Berkeley, and there are many who would maintain that idealism did not begin its history until after Berkeley. But to any one who refuses to permit the issue to be confused, it must be apparent that the theory with which Berkeley startled the world in 1710 is essentially the same as that which flourished in the nineteenth century in the form given it by Fichte and Hegel. It is essentially the same, in that the agreement is far more important than the difference. The two theories agree in asserting that the cognitive consciousness is the universal condition of being, or that *to be is to be either knower or known;* they differ in what they conceive to be the fundamental properties of consciousness and the nature of truth. But it is the principle in which they agree from which both theories derive their philosophy of religion and to which both have owed their popular influence. And this principle obtains both its simplest statement and its original arguments in the writings of Berkeley.

[26] F. H. Bradley: *Appearance and Reality,* pp. 145, 146.

J. O. Wisdom : POSITIVISM

P<small>ROFESSOR</small> *J. O. Wisdom, of The London School of Economics, here takes issue with a criticism leveled against Positivism by W. T. Stace, Emeritus Professor of Philosophy at Princeton University. In commenting on Professor Stace's article, Professor Wisdom explores the bases, terms, extensions, and relations of Positivism, and provides an argument against a serious point at issue in modern epistemology. Reprinted by permission from* <small>MIND</small>, *n.s., LIV (1945), pp. 65–70. It must be noted that Professor Wisdom in a subsequent note (ibid., p. 288) regretted that he failed to notice that Professor Stace applied the Principle of Observable Kinds in two different fields. It relates not only to what is observable, in which case Professor Wisdom maintains that it is a tautology, but also to natural laws in which case, according to Professor Wisdom, it is not a tautology but rather an attractive criterion of significance.*

• In an attractively presented paper ("Positivism," MIND, n.s., Vol. LIII, No. 211, 1944) Prof. W. T. Stace puts forward the following contentions: (*a*) Positivism entails a principle of significance † which he calls the "Principle of Observable Kinds" ††; (*b*) this Principle is neither an arbitrary stipulation nor an inductive generalisation based upon a fair sample of facts selected without bias; (*c*) nor is it a development of Empiricism; (*d*) it is in fact false; and, as an appendix, (*e*) the correct principle of significance would admit as significant many statements that positivists reject as not being so. It will be convenient to discuss these points in the order (*c*), (*b*), (*d*), (*a*), (*e*).

(*c*) In §§ 11, 12 Prof. Stace wishes to show that Positivism is not a legitimate development of Empiricism, *i.e.* that the arguments that support Empiricism do not support Positivism or rather the Principle of Observable Kinds. He does this not by stating these arguments and showing that they lend support in the one case and not in the other, but by pointing out what he holds is an essential difference in the fundamental assertions of the two positions.

If Empiricism means that all *knowledge* is based upon experience, it concerns the distinction between statements that can be known to be true and those about which we can never find out whether they are true or false. But Positivism is concerned with criteria of significance of statements. Thus Empiricism is concerned with knowledge and Positivism with significance; hence the two are essentially different and there can be no way of deriving one from the other.

If Empiricism means that all *ideas* are based upon experience, we have a criterion of meaning of *words*. But Positivism is concerned with criteria of significance of *statements*. Hence his conclusion is as before.

Now Prof. Stace thinks that positivists rest their case upon the second of these interpretations. But they surely have the first in mind also (in fact I think they have in mind the first solely), for they would interpret it as a criterion of significance, on the grounds that statements about which we

† EDITOR'S NOTE: "The characteristic thesis of positivism, as the term will be here understood, seems to run something like this: 'A set of words purporting to express a factual proposition P is significant only if it is possible to deduce or infer from it, in combination if necessary with other premises, some proposition or propositions (at least one) Q1, Q2, Q3 . . . etc., the truth or falsity of which it would be logically possible to verify by direct observation. If no such directly verifiable deductions from P are possible, then the set of words purporting to express P is non-significant, and P is not really a proposition at all but a pseudo-proposition.' I shall call this the *Positivist Principle,* and I shall refer to any philosophy which maintains it as positivism." W. T. Stace, "Positivism," p. 215.

†† EDITOR'S NOTE: *"The Principle of Observable Kinds.*

A sentence, in order to be significant, must assert or deny facts which are of a kind or class such that it is logically possible directly to observe some facts which are instances of that class or kind. And if a sentence purports to assert or deny facts which are of a class or kind such that it would be logically impossible directly to observe any instance of that class or kind, then the sentence is non-significant." Ibid.

can never tell whether they are true or false are thereby without significance.

However this may be, it is surely in the spirit of Empiricism to include within it, though we cannot deduce from its historical forms, this application of significance to statements as well as to words. It is difficult to see why Prof. Stace denies this merely because of the sharp distinction, which he makes for another purpose, between the meaning of words and the significance of statements (pp. 215-6).† These considerations about Empiricism do not, of course, constitute Prof. Stace's basic argument; and therefore they can no more provide a refutation of his general view than he can establish it by means of them.

(b) Prof. Stace considers that the Principle of Observable Kinds, and therefore Positivism, cannot properly be obtained by inductive generalisation (§ 10), because positivists that have regarded it as such appear to have based it upon a non-random sample of statements, selected unfairly in two different ways: they appear to have based it on scientific statements only, which ignores philosophical kinds and others; and even then on only certain classes of scientific statements. I do not know what view positivists have taken about the status of their principles or whether they themselves are clear about it in their own minds; but it seems reasonable to regard Positivism as an inductive generalisation so far as it is based on scientific statements, and as an arbitrary definition of "significance" so far as non-scientific statements are concerned. This procedure would be unobjectionable if Positivism were trying to state the fundamental principles of science. If, however, it is trying to confute speculative philosophy, it would be doing something like trying to demonstrate to children that there are no fairies, which cannot be done. Positivism, taken beyond its scientific application, is simply an assertion of attitude—"I do not believe in the transcendent." With regard to Prof. Stace's other charge, that Positivism is based upon an unfair sample of *scientific* statements, this would be true, if it were correctly represented by the Principle of Observable Kinds; that it is not true will be urged in (d) below.

(d) Does the Principle of Observable Kinds, and does Positivism, cover such scientific concepts as gravitation? Consider the statement, "The attraction between equal masses is inversely proportional to the square of the distance between them." For Positivism, it has significance because in

† EDITOR'S NOTE: "I wish to distinguish between the *meaning* of a word and the *significance* of a sentence. In common language we speak both of the meaning of a word and of the meaning of a sentence. But the meaning of 'meaning' in the two cases is quite different. For the meaning of a sentence is something to which the predicates true or false apply. The meaning of a sentence must be either true or false. But the predicates true and false do not apply to the meanings of words. A single word, such as 'red,' is neither true nor false. To mark this distinction I shall call what is in common language called the meaning of a sentence its significance. I shall confine the word meaning to meaning in the sense in which single words have meaning. Sentences have significance, words have meaning." *Ibid.*, pp. 215-6.

conjunction with statements of a directly verifiable kind it leads deductively to a directly verifiable statement. The same holds good for statements about electrons without giving them the phenomenalistic interpretation that Prof. Stace supposes positivists to have adopted (p. 227).†
The Principle of Observable Kinds, on the other hand, would not allow that such statements were significant. Hence, it would seem, positivists would agree with Prof. Stace that this principle was false. A positivist might hold, however, that it was false if applied universally, but that it was true of some classes of statements. This point will be taken up in the independent discussion given below. With reference to the previous paragraph, it is clear that, though the principle cannot be an inductive conclusion based upon a fair sample of scientific statements, Positivism itself may quite well be so based.

(*a*) It follows from (*d*) that, if the Principle of Observable Kinds fails to apply to a certain class of scientific statements to which Positivism does apply, then the Principle is not entailed by Positivism. If this is correct, there must be a mistake in the argument by which Prof. Stace tried to prove the entailment. He develops an argument (§ 7) in which P is a statement whose significance is to be tested and Q a statement that verifies it, by distinguishing the case where P leads to Q by a deductive inference from that where P leads to Q by a causal inference; and he is able to show the entailment quite clearly for the latter. His argument with regard to the former *might* hold if P was a statement such as "Water boils at 100° C"; but he seems to have overlooked such statements as the Newtonian one about attraction, and here the entailment plainly does not hold. He would doubtless reply with his *ad hominem* argument (p. 225): "It is notorious that positivists take the view that logical deduction is linguistic transformation. Therefore it does not lie in their mouth to object that the facts stated in P might be of a wholly different kind from the facts stated in Q." If Prof. Stace were right about this, he would have put his finger on a fundamental contradiction in Positivism. But, though the argument might hold against all statements other than those illustrated by attraction, against this kind I cannot see its force. P need not state a fact at all. There is nothing in the language thesis, so far as I can see, to suggest that, if "Q" asserts Q, there must exist a P to be asserted by "P."

(*e*) Prof. Stace's own criterion of significance is as follows: (i) ideas

† EDITOR'S NOTE: "For it is not at all certain that there are not highly respected scientific hypotheses which allege the existence of unobservables. It is at least arguable that the electron hypothesis is of this kind. It is at least arguable that scientists themselves attribute no observable characteristics whatever to the electron, whether in the way of primary or secondary qualities. They certainly do not attribute secondary qualities to it. And as to primary qualities, it is doubtful whether the space-time of which they speak has any of the characters of perceived spaces and times. Of course positivists can and do *interpret* the electron hypothesis so as to *make* it conform to their principles. They can and do interpret it as a construction out of sense-data." *Ibid.*, p. 227.

must conform to the Principle of Empiricism; and (ii) words standing for them must be assembled in sentences according to rules of logical syntax (§ 13). This he states would allow statements about unknowable physical objects, and the like, to have significance—"There exists a physical object which it is logically impossible to observe, having intrinsic qualities which we can never perceive, and which is causally related to our sense-data" (p. 237), but he has not noticed that an unknowable physical object does not pass the first part of his own criterion. Positivists would probably not accept the criterion, because a narrow Empiricism that required each separate word to have meaning would not allow significance to statements such as our Newtonian example.

A comment should be added on Prof. Stace's definition of the Positivist Principle (p. 215): the word "factual" should, I think, be deleted. This is important. His definition, as it stands, is in keeping with his omitting to discuss statements like the Newtonian one.

In order to clarify the meaning and application of the Positivist Principle, it is desirable to distinguish three classes of statements: (1) those statements that can be understood prior to their verification; (2) those that cannot; and (3) those about which this feature is debatable. This is not a precise or fundamental description, but the examples that follow will show what classes of statements are meant.

(1) The first may be illustrated by the statement that there are mountains on the other side of the moon. This may be verified not directly but in principle; we know what the experience would be like of finding mountains on the other side of the moon and what the experience would be like of finding no mountains there; we know what sort of experience is relevant to the truth or falsity of the statement. The Principle of Verifiability involved here is equivalent, it seems to me, to the Principle of Observable Kinds. We are not confronted here with the paradox that the meaning of a statement about the present or the past is given by statements about the future; for statements about the future are merely relevant to, or constitute evidence for, the existence of meaning but do not contain, define, determine, prescribe, or confer meaning. Thus the principle, "The meaning of a statement is determined by its verification," is false for statements of this kind if it is interpreted by "The meaning of a statement is the method of its verification."

(2) The next type of statement may be illustrated by "Jehovah is angry." We cannot verify it in principle; we do not know what the experience would be like of finding it true or false; we do not know what sort of experience would be relevant to its truth or falsity. The principle here used is *not* equivalent to the Principle of Observable Kinds. In what sense, then, can it be verified? As a result of questioning someone who asserts that Jehovah is angry, we may find that there is simply one test that he has

in mind, namely that it is thundering. Hence, according to this principle, "Jehovah is angry" is equivalent to, "It is thundering." Here the meaning of the statement *is* determined by its verification or *is* the method of its verification. This has a parallel in the work of some archaeologists: suppose we dig and find a bronze axe, may we say that it belongs to the Bronze Age? Dr. Daniel's comment is that this "is almost saying no more than that it is made of bronze, which is perilously near saying nothing at all" (G. E. Daniel, *The Three Ages: An Essay on Archaeological Method,* Cambridge, 1943, p. 40); that is to say, according to one usage, if an excavation is classified as being of the Bronze Age, this is verified simply by finding bronze objects.

(3) The third kind of statement is illustrated by the Newtonian example already given. It is not susceptible to the kind of treatment just described. It must be dealt with according to the Positivist Principle, that, from a conjunction of it with statements that are significant according to the Principle of Verifiability used in (1) or that satisfy the Principle of Observable Kinds, we can *deduce* a statement that is significant by this same standard. Here, again, the meaning of the statement is determined by its verification, though whether or not this has the sense of being given by the method of its verification is a matter requiring further discussion.

Positivists write as if one and the same Principle of Verifiability covered all three of these clases of statements. Whether this is the intention of any of them I do not know, but it seems to me plain that it ought not to be.

For brevity let us refer to the three kinds of statements as the screened-mountain, the Jehovah, and the gravitation cases.

The first point to notice is that, since the Principle of Observable Kinds applies only to the screened-mountain case, this Principle is *a tautology;* for all statements to which it applies are members of the class of observable kinds. In other words we cannot use this Principle to distinguish significant from non-significant statements, for we have to know something about a statement before we can apply the Principle to it, namely that it falls within the class of observable kinds. Hence for this class of statements we have, not a principle, but a predicate-label, either "observable kind" or "verifiable." Prof. Stace's formulation of the Principle of Observable Kinds is clearly of value in making it possible to bring out this point and in leading to the distinction between the screened-mountain case and the others.

The Positivist Principle—provided that in Prof. Stace's formulation (p. 215) "factual proposition" is replaced by "general scientific hypothesis"—seems to be quite definitely the correct criterion of significance with the gravitation case. Is the Jehovah case in the same position? With it, additional premises are not required to lead deductively to a directly verifiable statement. One might therefore suppose that it was related to the gravitation case as immediate inference is to mediate—not a sufficiently important difference to warrant separate consideration of the two cases. But with the Jehovah case verification performs two functions: it acts as a *test* of significance, and it provides the *meaning* of the statement; and the question arises whether the same is true of the gravitation case. Here the verification certainly reveals the *existence* of significance; but opinions may differ about whether or not it also shows what that significance is. Some positivists seem to hold that it does, and their interpretation of the gravitation case may conveniently be thought of as phenomenalist. On this view, there would be no essential difference between this kind of statement and the Jehovah kind.

Arguments can be found, however, to show that the gravitation statement cannot rightly be regarded as of the same type as the Jehovah, or interpreted phenomenalistically, *i.e.* that its verification confirms only the existence of significance and does not prescribe what that significance is. Two are here offered. (i) Verification of the gravitation case consists in general in statements about the future, and no doubt its actual truth has an indefinite reference to the future. But, after the occasion of its first verification, it may be said to have a meaning, because, though its verification may continue, its verifiability has been established. Thus it seems preferable to say not that its meaning lies (phenomenalistically) in future verification but that the existence of its meaning is guaranteed by its having proved verifiable or amenable to empirical testing. This treatment would require the gravitation and Jehovah cases to be placed in different categories. (ii) The positivist treatment of the Jehovah statement makes it *synonymous* with its verification; we have two sets of words having the same use; and there is no value in using the one instead of the other—in fact the Jehovah statement is apt to be misleading in a way its verification is not. On the other hand the gravitation case is not synonymous with any of its verifications. Here in fact the difference is that between the types of verification appropriate to categorical and hypothetical statements.

The positivist may ask for a criterion of meaning in this sense in which it is independent of its verifications though not independent of being verifiable. I suggest that "meaning" means *the possibility of obtaining verifications.*

This part of the discussion may be expressed by saying that there are different levels of verification: verification of a hypothetical statement would consist in deriving from it a categorical statement which would have a verification in a different sense, *i.e.* which would be an instance of an Observable Kind (where this phrase refers not to terms but to statements). Less precisely, verification of a hypothetical would consist in relating it to Observable Kinds.

Thus, it seems to me that positivists have confused in one formula two criteria of significance (if we disregard the screened-mountain kind): one applicable to scientific hypotheses and the other to speculative philosophy. This amounts to an arbitrary decree that speculation must conform to the principles of science. However one may sympathize with this aim, it cannot be proved. The speculative philosopher will always maintain that the Jehovah statement has a significance over and above what is contained in its verification. The issue may be amplified as follows.

All that the positivist is entitled to say is that speculative statements cannot be brought into relation with any sense-experience. To this the speculative thinker's reply is one of agreement, for he never meant them to be relatable to sense-experience.

The speculative philosopher would maintain, however, that his statements, though not relatable to sense-experience, were relatable to experience in a wider sense.

The positivist may then deny that this Experience affords evidence of anything objective, *i.e.* deny that it is an experience *of* anything. But the speculative philosopher would refuse to accept this.

The positivist would have no grounds for his denial; he can give only an arbitrary definition of what avenues of experience lead to the objective. On the other hand, the speculative logician cannot prove his contention either.

This is a complete impasse, which philosophy cannot overcome.

The following way of dealing with this stalemate may be suggested. The speculative position cannot be disproved; all that can be said is that one should no more attempt to disprove it than attempt to disprove the existence of fairies where children are concerned. Children have experiences that are described in terms of fairies; a good fairy will fulfill all a child's hopes—to-morrow; speculative philosophers have experiences that are described in terms of a harmonious Absolute in which all conflict is overcome. With the power both of the fairy and the Absolute, "it must be, therefore it is."

A. C. Benjamin : THE ESSENTIAL PROBLEM OF EMPIRICISM

A. *Cornelius Benjamin, John Hiram Lathrop Professor of Philosophy at the University of Missouri, here explores the implications and extensions of the approach to the objects of the mind that is called empiricism. The meaning of such terms as "experience," "fact," "mind," "derivation," and "verification," as they relate to the process of knowing, and the major divisions of active and passive empiricism in that epistemic scheme, are noted by him. In his book* OPERATIONISM *published by Charles Thomas, Springfield (1955), Professor Benjamin has explained further the categories suggested in this essay. Reprinted by permission from* PHILOSOPHY OF SCIENCE, *X (1943), pp. 13–17.*

• Every natural scientist, I should suppose, is an empiricist. But to say this is not to assert that he is consciously such. Very few scientists would presumably consider themselves qualified to state even what is involved in the term, and still fewer would be willing to admit that they are adherents of the position. One might say that natural scientists, in their general outlook, presuppose—in one of the many meanings of this term—the empirical point of view. This probably means that if one could make clear to them what is meant by the term, and if one could convince them that it is proper for scientists to take sides on philosophical issues, they should probably be willing to call themselves empiricists. Expressed otherwise, the general temper and spirit of natural science are those which philosophers tend to identify with the empirical outlook.

Unfortunately, however, empiricism is not at all easy to define. A first approximation to a definition is a simple matter. Empiricism is that theory of knowledge which maintains that experience is the sole source and the sole guarantee of knowledge. This looks harmless enough, and seems to say exactly what we want to say. Negatively it tells us that empiricism disclaims abstract and speculative methods, deductive techniques, innate ideas, and all "anticipations of experience"; positively it informs us that empiricism leans heavily on sense observation, laboratory techniques, and inductive generalization. It seems to distinguish empiricism sharply from rationalism, mysticism, intuitionism, and pragmatism, yet it does not identify empiricism with a narrow positivism which would exclude hypotheses and theories from the consideration of the scientist.

But the definition proves, upon examination, to suffer under two important ambiguities. The first of these concerns the term "experience." This aspect of the definition has often been discussed, and I shall not consider it here.[1]

The second defect is more difficult to express, and I shall devote the present article to an examination of it. Because it is not stated in the definition it is often overlooked, and many think that there is no special difficulty in being a consistent and thoroughgoing empiricist. The point concerns the role of the individual in the acquisition of knowledge. Knowledge is made up of ideas, and ideas come from experience. Is this, however, an accurate and precise or only an elliptical manner of speaking? Do ideas come from experience alone, or from experience plus an active experiencer? Is the individual merely the recipient of the ideas, contributing nothing except the *tabula rasa* upon which experience writes its message, or does the individual in some sense create the ideas through a modification of the stuff of experience? Let me attempt to distinguish these two

[1] I have treated this problem in an article in *The Philosophical Review*, Vol. LI, no. 5, pp. 497–502.

interpretations of empiricism by designating the former "passive empiricism," and the latter "active empiricism."

Empiricists have on the whole, I think, tended to favor passive empiricism. At least this was the emphasis in the earlier formulation. Bacon, while not unmindful of the other side of the issue, laid great stress on the passivity of the investigator—man should "listen" to nature. To be sure, there is activity even in listening, for attention is selective; to listen is often very tiring. But there is no contribution of the individual in the sense that he "modifies" that which he is observing. In fact just such activity must be avoided, because if something is done in the process of creating the idea it cannot "correspond" to its object and can no longer "represent" it. Error arises precisely because the knowing process is "transforming." Therefore ideas which merely reflect the objects which occasioned them are true and all other ideas are false. The simplest interpretation of this view of empiricism is to say that ideas of objects are caused by objects. It is the objects which are active not the individuals in whom the ideas are produced.

Passive empiricism runs into two very important difficulties. The first of these is the fact that objects which cause our ideas are in many cases not the objects to which those ideas refer. Or, according to an alternative formulation, objects sometimes cause ideas which refer to those objects themselves and sometimes cause ideas which refer to other objects. For example, I may be observing a red sunset, and this may cause me to think of the idea "red sunset." Now this idea clearly both is caused by and refers to the actual sunset. But I may be observing a red sunset and think of the idea "clear weather tomorrow." This idea is likewise caused by the sunset but it obviously does not refer to the sunset. To generalize, ideas of the future, while they are caused by present objects, cannot refer to present objects but must refer to objects which do not yet exist. Past objects involve essentially the same difficulty; my idea of Julius Caesar is probably not produced by Julius Caesar at all but by certain statements in historical books, yet the idea refers to the individual who no longer exists. Ideas of hypothetical and conjectural objects offer the same problem; we cannot say that these ideas are caused by the objects to which they refer because these objects are not clearly and indubitably given in the here and now. When we generalize still further we find our position expressible in a dilemma. Either ideas of objects are directly and uniquely caused by objects, in which case we must assume that the past and the future, together with certain other possible realms, all exist in some sense in the present, or a plurality of indirect modes of causal operation must be assumed, in which case our empiricism becomes strained. Either a multiplicity of realms of objects, or a multiplicity of modes of causal operation.

The second difficulty of empiricism is the fact of error. If ideas of objects are caused by objects then erroneous ideas must be caused by erroneous objects. If I look at a dog and mistake it for a bear, there must be an erroneous bear which causes me to have the idea. The only alternative seems to be to suppose that a dog has two modes of causal operation—one which produces a correct idea, the idea of a dog, and the other which produces an erroneous idea, the idea of a bear. Either of these possibilities seems to strain the logical faculties. The one populates the world with false objects, the other gives every object two modes of causal operation which are, so far as we can tell, equally possible in any situation.

Difficulties of these kinds have, I believe, led most empiricists to abandon passive empiricism in favor of a more active type. Active empiricisms are all forms of operationism. There is much of operationism in Locke, Mill, and Mach, though the term is not used, and the formulation is not clear-cut. Common to all these positions is the recognition that ideas are caused not merely by objects but by objects plus knowers. Knowing is an active process in which the investigator makes his own contributions. Given an idea, therefore, the route for the determination of its meaning involves an appeal to two elements—the world and the individual, in a great variety of possible modes of combinatory action.

The way in which this theory avoids the difficulties of passive empiricism is clear. Operations are the source of both novelty and error. An idea may refer to something which did not cause it because the reference of an idea is contributed by the individual; thus, although the realm of objects which may cause ideas is very limited, the realm of objects to which ideas may refer is very extended. Mind is in some sense creative. Further, erroneous ideas are a commonplace occurrence simply because of this activity of the individual; true ideas are caused simply by objects, but false ideas are caused by the mind operating upon objects. Hence we need not suppose the world to be inhabited by erroneous objects; we have only to account for erroneous objects in terms of erroneous activities of the knowing mind.

This is certainly a step in the right direction, and an active empiricism thus seems to me to be much more satisfactory than a passive form. But the problem of novelty and error is not really solved—it is merely located. Operations produce both novelty and error. But novelty we want, and error we do not want. How, then, are operations distinguished, and how can we select the desirable operations and reject the undesirable ones? Unless we have some technique for making this selection, the appeal to operations helps not at all. There is always a tendency to solve problems in terms of well chosen words; "operation" is such a word, and leads many to believe that the difficulties of a thoroughgoing empiricism have been adequately met. They cannot be met, I believe, until the notion of operation is subjected to further analysis.

An operation is an act performed upon something and producing a certain result. But two important types of operation must be distinguished. On the one hand are operations which are automatic, spontaneous and uncontrolled. These operations just occur, like eating when we are hungry or resting when we are tired. While they produce results, we do not in general know their mode of causal operation, nor do we deliberately and consciously select them with a view to achieving their appropriate results. No question as to whether we shall or shall not perform them arises, and they are not usually evaluated with a view to their effectiveness in achieving results. On the other hand are operations which are conscious, deliberate, and controlled. Operations of this kind are known to produce results of a certain kind and are selected because of this capacity. They are normative and instrumental in character; there are right and wrong ways of using them.

Now the essential limitation of present day empiricism (and consequently the problem of future empiricism) lies in the fact that only a part of the knowing processes has been adequately described in terms of operations of the latter type. The area of thinking to which these operations apply is, in fact, that of the *verification* of ideas as opposed to that of the *derivation* of ideas. This much of thinking seems to be more or less under deliberate control, there is a right and wrong way of doing it, and we may choose that method which is best adapted to achieving the results we desire. Deductive logic has its rules, and hypotheses can be tested through the wise application of these rules. Thus so far as verification is concerned we know how operations produce results, and we are in a position to select those operations which will eventuate in truth rather than in error. Consequently, our operationism becomes a *specific* operationism; we are not obliged to say merely that ideas come through undesignatable operations. To a great extent the operations are describable and statable according to rules.

But what of that other extensive area of thinking—the processes concerned with the *derivation* of ideas? The empiricists have given us a logic of the *testing* of ideas but no logic of the *acquisition* of ideas. We get ideas but we do not know how. They seem to appear suddenly in our minds without our being aware how they come, and without our being able either to produce them at will or to determine their character in advance. Geniuses seem to get ideas, others do not, and that seems to be the end of the matter; as to the foundations of genius we are essentially ignorant.

The surprising feature of present day empiricism is its complacency in the presence of this fact. The empiricist insists upon an operational formulation of his position, yet he professes that a great many of the operations are unknown. He claims that ideas are operationally defined—in fact, unless they are operationally defined they are essentially meaningless—yet he admits his inability to specify what these operations are. Even more significantly, he forgets that until an idea has acquired meaning it cannot be verified; while the manner of verification becomes part of the meaning of an idea, it cannot determine the meaning of that idea in the first place. Thus the empiricist in resorting to unconscious and unstatable operations is acknowledging the basic unintelligibility of his position; he is admitting that he is committed to vagueness and confusion in the expression of ideas.

I am not claiming that the problem of genius must be solved before empiricism can be made tenable. I am merely protesting against the disposition on the part of most empiricists to disregard the problem. They claim either that the problem is unimportant or that it is psychological rather than logical. I have tried above to point out its importance—the solution to the entire problem of meaning is dependent on it. And to deny its logical status is merely to dodge the issue. Regardless of who solves the problem, the issue must be met. It is unfortunately true that psychologists have not been able to throw much light on the problem. Whether this is due to the incompetence of the psychologists or the complexity of the task is not our concern here. I am attempting to show merely that if we are to be consistent and thoroughgoing empiricists we must at least wrestle with this problem.

As the merest suggestion I offer the following list of operations which must be defined and clarified before empiricism can be satisfied with its solution to the epistemological problem: naming, generalizing (describing, characterizing, correlating), abstracting (isolating), associating, ordering, serially interpolating and extrapolating, analyzing, synthesizing, analogizing and negating. This list is not by any means complete. The essential problem of empiricism is precisely that of drawing up such a list, differentiating each member from the others, and assuring oneself that the list is exhaustive.

E. Gilson : VADE MECUM OF A
YOUNG REALIST

Iɴ the following essay, the eminent historian of mediaeval philosophy, Professor Etienne Gilson warns the unpracticed realist against letting the idealist put him on the defensive in controversy. Since the ability of the mind to grasp reality, however mistakenly, is axiomatic, it remains for the idealist to establish his position. If the realist is drawn into the web of criticizing not the process whereby the mind apprehends things, but the very power to apprehend them, the idealist then has him at his mercy. But, as Professor Gilson points out, the idealist must forever remain a prisoner of his own abstractions. Authorized translation by W. J. Quinn, University of Notre Dame, from LE RÉALISME MÉTHODIQUE (Cours et Documents de Philosophie, Collection publiée sous la direction d'Yves R. Simon), Chez Pierre Téqui, Paris, pp. 87–101.

• The first step on the path of realism is to perceive that one has always been realistic; the second is to perceive that, whatever one does to become otherwise, one will never succeed; the third is to ascertain that those who do pretend to think otherwise, think in realistic terms as soon as they forget to act their part. If one then wonders why, the conversion is almost complete.

Most of those who say and believe that they are idealists would rather not be so, but they can see no alternative. One points out to them that they will never escape from their thought and that a "beyond thought" is unthinkable. If they decide to seek a response to this objection, they are lost in advance, because all the objections of the idealist to the realist are formulated in idealistic terms. Why should it be astonishing, then, that the idealist always brings back the victory? The idealist's solution of the problem is always implied in his questions. The realist must therefore be accustomed, from the very beginning, to refusing any discussion on a terrain which is not his own, and to judging himself in no difficulty because he cannot respond to some questions, surely insoluble, which, for him, are not even posed.

One must begin by being wary of the term *thought* itself because the greatest of the differences between the realist and the idealist is that the idealist thinks while the realist knows. For the realist, to think is only to organize some previous acts of knowledge or to reflect on their content. He would never conceive of making thought the point of departure of his reflection, because a thought is possible for him only where there first exists some knowledge. Because the idealist goes from thought to things, he is unable to know if his starting point corresponds or not to an object. When he asks the realist how to rejoin the object in departing from thought, the latter must hasten to answer that it cannot be done and that this indeed is the principal reason for not being an idealist. Realism however departs from knowledge, that is to say from an act of the intellect which consists essentially in seizing an object. Thus, for the realist, the question does not pose an insoluble problem, but a pseudo-problem, which is something entirely different.

Each time that the idealist calls upon us to answer the questions which are posed by thought, we can be sure that he speaks in the name of the Spirit. For him, the Spirit is that which thinks; as for us, the intellect is that which knows. One must therefore avoid, as much as possible, compromising himself with this term. This is not always easy because it has its legitimate meaning. However we live in a time when necessity demands that we first retranslate into realistic language all the terms which idealism has borrowed from us and corrupted. An idealistic term is generally one used by the realist to designate the spiritual conditions of knowledge, but henceforward considered as engendering its own content.

The knowledge of which the realist speaks is the living and experienced unity of an intellect and an apprehended reality. This is why a realistic philosophy bears always on the very thing which is apprehended and without which there would be no knowledge. Idealistic philosophies, on the contrary, since they stem from thought, very quickly succeed in choosing science or philosophy as the object of it. When the idealist truly thinks in idealistic terms, he realizes under its perfect form the essence of "the professor of philosophy"; while when the realist truly thinks in realistic terms, he is in accordance with the authentic essence of the philosopher. It is the philosopher who speaks of things but the professor of philosophy who speaks of philosophy.

Just as we do not have to go from thought to things (knowing, as we do, that such an enterprise is impossible), so also we do not have to ask ourselves if a "beyond thought" is thinkable. It is possible that a "beyond *thought"* is unthinkable, but it is certain that all *knowledge* implies a "beyond thought." The fact that this "beyond thought" is given to us by knowledge only in thought does not prevent its being a "beyond." But the idealist always confuses "being given in thought" and "being given by thought." For him who starts from knowledge, a "beyond thought" is so conceivable that there is only this kind of thought for which he can have a "beyond."

It is by a similar error that the realist wonders how one can, in starting with the ego, prove the existence of the non-ego. For the idealist, who does start with the ego, this is the normal, and even the only possible way of posing the question. The realist must be twice wary of it: first, because he does not start with the ego; next, because for him, the world is not a non-ego (which is nothing), but an "in-itself." An "in-itself" can indeed be given in knowledge; a non-ego, to which reality is reduced by the idealist, can be neither seized by knowledge nor proved by thought.

One should be no more disturbed by the classical objection of the idealist against the possibility of attaining an "in-itself," and above all, of having a true knowledge of it. You define true knowledge, says the idealist, as an adequate copy of reality; but how can you know that the copy reproduces the thing such as it is in itself, since the thing is given to you only in thought? The objection is meaningful only for idealism, which posits thought before being. Since it can no longer compare the two successfully, it wonders how another could do so. The realist, on the contrary, does not have to wonder whether things do or do not conform to the knowledge which he has of them, since knowledge, for him, consists in being assimilated to things. In an order where the proportion of the intellect to the thing, which the judgment formulates, supposes the concrete and living correspondence of the intellect to its objects, it would be absurd to require of knowledge that it guarantee a conformity without which it cannot even exist.

One must always remember that the impossibilities in which idealism wishes to corner realism are the work of idealism itself. When it defies us to compare the thing known with the thing itself, it only manifests the internal evil which eats away at it. For the realist, there is no "noumenon" in the sense in which the idealist understands it. Knowledge presupposes the presence of the thing itself to the intellect. There is no need to suppose, behind the thing which is in thought, a duplicate, mysterious and unknowable, which would be the thing of the thing in thought. To know is not to apprehend a thing as it is in thought, but, in thought, to apprehend a thing as it is.

It is not sufficient to establish that everything is given to us in thought to conclude rightly that we should necessarily go from thought to things and that it is impossible to proceed otherwise. As a matter of fact, we do proceed otherwise. The awakening of the intelligence coincides with the apprehension of things which, as soon as they are perceived, are classified according to their most manifest analogies. From this fact, which has nothing to do with any theory, theory itself must take rise. This is what realism does, following the similar example of common sense; this is why all realism is a philosophy of common sense.

This does not mean that common sense is a philosophy. Rather, every healthy philosophy presupposes it and has confidence in it, even at the risk of appealing, each time that it will be necessary, to a common sense anywhere from badly informed to better informed. Such is the procedure of science, which is not a critique of common sense, but of its successive approximations of reality. The history of both science and philosophy testifies that common sense is capable of discovery, thanks to the methodic use which it makes of its resources. One must therefore invite it to examine critically and ceaselessly the conclusions which it has obtained, which is not to invite it to renounce itself, but to remain itself.

The word "invention," like many other words, has been contaminated by idealism. To invent means *to find,* not *to create.* The inventor resembles the creator only in the practical order, especially in that of either utilitarian or artistic production. Every activity of the intelligence therefore consists in its function of *speculating* on reality: if it does create, what it creates is never an object, but a way of explaining the object at the very interior of this object.

This is also why the realist never demands that his knowledge engender an object without which it would not exist. Like the idealist, he makes use of his reflection, but the realist maintains it within the limits of the given reality. The starting point for his reflection must therefore be being, which is actually for us the beginning of knowledge: *res sunt.* If we penetrate the essence of the object itself which is given to us, we orient ourselves towards a science which is crowned by a metaphysics of nature; if we penetrate the conditions in which the object is given to us, we orient ourselves towards a psychology which is crowned by a metaphysics of knowledge. The two methods are not only compatible, they are complementary, because they rest on the primitive unity of subject and object in the act of knowledge, and every complete philosophy implies the consciousness of this unity.

Nothing prevents the realist then from proceeding, by way of reflective analysis, from the object given in knowledge to the intellect and to the subject which knows. Indeed, on the contrary, he has no other method at his disposal to assure himself of the existence and nature of the knowing subject. *Res sunt, ergo cognosco, ergo sum res cognoscens.* The realist is not distinguished from the idealist because the former rejects this analysis while the latter accepts it. Rather, the realist refuses to take the final term of his analysis for the principle engendering the analysis. Granted that the analysis of knowledge leads us to an "I think," it does not follow that this *Cogito* is the first principle of knowledge. Granted that every representation is, in fact, a thought, it does not follow either that there is only one thought, or even that the "I think" conditions all my representations.

All the strength of idealism comes from the coherence with which it develops the consequences of its initial error. One would therefore be very mistaken to reproach it for its lack of logic. Quite the contrary; it is a doctrine which can live only by logic, since the order and connection of ideas here replaces the order and connection of things. The *saltus mortalis* which precipitates a doctrine is anterior to the doctrine, and idealism can justify everything by its method, save idealism itself. And the reason is simply that the cause of idealism is not idealistic, it is not even epistemological: it is ethical.

Prior to every philosophical explanation of knowledge comes the fact, not only of knowledge itself, but also of the ardent desire of men to understand. If reason is too often content with summary and incomplete explanations, if it sometimes does violence to the facts, deforming them or passing over them when they embarrass it, this is precisely because its passion for understanding prevails over its desire to know, or because the ways of knowing which are at its disposal are powerless to satisfy it. The realist is no less exposed to these temptations than the idealist, and he yields to them no less often. The difference is that the realist surrenders to them against his principles while the idealist posits in principle that such a surrender is legitimate. At the origin of realism then there is a resignation on the part of the intellect to depend on the reality which is the cause of its knowledge; at the origin of idealism, there is the impatience of a reason which wishes to reduce reality to cognition in order to be sure that its knowledge allows nothing to escape it.

If a part of idealism has often tied itself to mathematics, it is precisely because that science, whose object is quantity, extends its jurisdiction over the whole of material nature, inasmuch as materiality depends on quantity. However, if idealism has sought its justification in the triumphs of mathematics, the latter owes nothing to idealism. The mathematical sciences are in no way bound to it, and they justify it all the less insofar as the most completely mathematicized physics maintains all its constructions at the very interior of the experimental facts which they interpret. After vain efforts to render a new fact assimilable to the theory, every mathematical physics will reform itself in order to fit the theory to the fact. The idealist is rarely a scientist and still more rarely a man of the laboratory; yet it is the laboratory which furnishes the mathematical physics of tomorrow with the data it will have to explain.

The realist therefore should have no fear that the idealist will confound him with scientific thought, because every scientist, as such, thinks in realistic terms, even if, in philosophy, he believes himself to be an idealist. A scientist will never begin by defining the method of the discipline he is going to establish. It is even by this characteristic that one can most surely recognize the false sciences: they are preceded by their methods. In truth, the method should be deduced from the science, not the science from the method. This is why no realist has ever written a *Discourse on Method:* he must know things themselves before he can understand how he knows them; he must apprehend each order itself of things before he can grasp the ways of knowing these orders.

The most dangerous method of all is the "reflective method." The realist is content with "reflection." When reflection becomes a method, it is no longer the intelligently directed act it should be, but a reflection which substitutes itself for reality, a reflection whose order becomes that of reality itself. When it is faithful to its essence, the "reflective method" supposes always that the final term of the reflection is also the first principle of our knowledge. It naturally follows from this that the last term of the analysis must contain virtually the totality of the analysis. Finally, whatever one cannot rediscover in starting from the ultimate term of the reflection either does not exist, or can be legitimately treated as non-existent. Thus, one is led to exclude from knowledge, and from reality itself, the very thing without which knowledge would not exist.

The second characteristic by which one can recognize the pseudo-sciences engendered by idealism is that, in taking their departure from what they call thought, they commit themselves to defining truth as a particular case of error. Taine has rendered a great service to good sense by defining sensation as a *true* hallucination, because he has shown by this where logic necessarily leads idealism. Sensation then becomes the same thing as an hallucination, when this hallucination is really not a true one. One must not let himself be impressed, therefore, by the famous "errors of the senses," nor be astonished by the fact that the idealists make much of them. They are people for whom the normal can be only a particular case of the pathological. When Descartes is jubilant in establishing that even the insane cannot deny this first principle, "I think, therefore I am," he aids us greatly in seeing what happens to reason when it is reduced to such a first principle.

One must then consider as errors of the same order, the arguments based on dreams, on the illusions of the senses, and on madness, which the idealist has borrowed from the skeptics. He who is dreaming does not feel himself different from he who is awake, but he who is awake knows himself very different from he who is dreaming. He even knows that it is because he has previously had sensations that he can afterwards have what are designated as hallucinations, just as he knows that he would never dream anything if he were not previously awake. That some of the mentally ill deny the existence of the exterior world, or even (with all due respect to Descartes) their own existence, is no reason to consider the certitude of our existence as a particular case of "true delirium." These illusions are not disquieting to the idealist only because he doesn't know how to prove that they are illusions; they must not unnerve the realist, who alone knows that they are truly illusions.

We should not take seriously the reproach addressed to us by certain idealists that our theory of knowledge condemns us to infallibility. We are simply philosophers for whom the truth is normal and error abnormal. Nor does this mean that the truth is not, for us, just as difficult to attain and conserve as perfect health. It is not because the realist cannot make a mistake that he differs from the idealist. The difference is first of all that, when he does fail, it is not a thought unfaithful to itself which errs, but rather a knowledge unfaithful to its object. Above all, the realist is wrong only when he betrays his principles, while the idealist is right in the exact measure that he is unfaithful to his.

To say that all knowledge is the seizure of the thing as it is does not at all mean that the intellect infallibly grasps the thing such as it is, but that it is only when it does so that there is knowledge. This signifies still less that knowledge exhausts, in a single act, the content of its object. That which knowledge grasps of the object is real, but reality is inexhaustible, and even when the intellect has discerned all its details, it still collides with the mystery of the object's very existence. It is the idealist Descartes who believes he can seize, infallibly and at a single glance, the whole of reality. The realist Pascal well knows how naïve this pretension of the philosopher is: "To comprehend the principles of things, and from this, by a presumption as infinite as their object, to arrive at knowing all." The virtue proper to the realist is modesty in knowledge; and if this is not what he practices, it is what he is, by profession, bound to practice.

The third characteristic by which one can recognize the pseudo-sciences which idealism generates is the need they feel to "found" their objects. In reality, they are not sure that their objects exist. For the realist, whose thought bears on being, the Good, the True, and the Beautiful are fully real, since they are only being itself, willed, known, and admired. But from the moment when thought is substituted for knowledge, these transcendentals begin to fluctuate as in a vacuum, without knowing upon what to rest themselves. This is why idealism spends its time in "founding" morality, knowledge, and art, as if what man must do were not inscribed in the nature of man, the manner of knowing in the very structure of our intellect, and art in the practical activity of the artist himself. The realist never has anything to found, but he has to discover constantly the foundations of his operations; and it is in the nature of things that he finds them: *operatio sequitur esse.*

Thus one must be also cautious to turn himself away from any speculation on "values." Values are nothing other than transcendentals which have separated themselves from being and try to substitute themselves for it. The "founding of values" thus becomes an obsession for the idealist; but for the realist, nothing.

It is extremely difficult for a man of our times to refuse to become a "critical spirit." Nevertheless, to such a denial must the realist be resigned, for the critical spirit is the end point of idealism, and there one finds it again, no longer as a principle or a doctrine, but as the will to serve a cause. The critical spirit actually expresses the resolution to submit the facts to a suitable treatment in order that nothing in them any longer offer resistance to the spirit. The procedure to follow in order to be successful in this is to substitute everywhere the point of view of the observer for that of the observed. This negation of reality will be pursued, if necessary, to its most extreme consequences. Indeed, the more alive the resistance opposing this process will be, the more will the idealist be determined to ignore it. The realist, on the contrary, must always recognize the object as the cause of knowledge and treat it with the deepest respect.

To respect the object of knowledge is, before all else, to refuse to reduce it to what it would have to be in order to be submitted to the rules of a type of knowledge arbitrarily chosen by us. There is no reason to condemn introspection because it does not permit us to reduce psychology to the status of an exact science. It may be that its object is such that psychology should not become an exact science, at least if it wishes to remain faithful to its object. Human psychology such as a dog knows it, must be at least as sure as our science of nature; and our science of nature is nearly as penetrating as human psychology such as a dog knows it. Behavioral psychology is thus perfectly wise in adopting the dog's point of view towards man, for as soon as consciousness enters upon the scene, it reveals so many things that the infinite divergence between a science of consciousness and consciousness itself bursts upon the eyes. If our organism were conscious of itself, who knows if biology and physics would still be possible to us.

The realist should always maintain, then, against the idealist, that to every order of reality there must correspond a certain manner of approaching and explaining this reality. Having then refused to deliver himself to a critique prior to knowledge, he will find himself free, and much freer than the idealist, to deliver himself to a critique of knowledges, in measuring them by their objects. The "critical spirit" criticizes all, save itself; the realist, because he is not a critical spirit, never ceases to criticize himself. He will never believe that a psychology which places itself outside of consciousness at the outset, in order to know it better, gives him the equivalent of consciousness. Nor will he believe, with Durkheim, that the true savages are in books; or that the social reduces itself to a constraint accompanied by sanctions, as if the only society we have to explain were that of Leviticus. He will no more believe that historical criticism is in a better position than the witnesses invoked by it in order to know what has happened to them and to discern the exact meaning of what they themselves have said. This is why realism, in subjecting knowledge to its objects, places the intelligence in the most favorable conditions for discovery. Indeed, even if it is true that things have not always occurred as their witnesses have believed, the relative errors which they might have committed are of little matter next to those in which our fancy will involve us if we reconstruct, according to our own estimation, facts, feelings, or ideas which we have not experienced.

Such is the freedom of the realist, for we have a choice: either we defer to the facts and are free from our thought or we are free from the facts and enslaved to our thought. Therefore, let us turn ourselves towards the things themselves which knowledge apprehends and towards the relation of our cognitions to the things which they apprehend. In regulating itself better and better by these things, philosophy can progress anew.

It is also in this spirit that it is suitable to read the great philosophers who have entered before us on the way of realism. "It is not in Montaigne," writes Pascal, "it is in me that I find all that I see there." Likewise: "It is not in Saint Thomas or in Aristotle, but in things that the true realist sees all that he sees in them." He will therefore not hesitate to quote these masters as his authority, because, for him, they are only guides towards reality itself. And if the idealist reproaches him, as one of these has just amiably done, with "clothing himself richly with the hand-me-downs of truth," his response will be quite ready: it is still better to be clothed richly in the hand-me-downs of truth from others, as the realist feels in need of doing, than to refuse to do so, and, like the idealist, go naked.

H. U. von Balthasar : MAN CREATES MEANING IN ENCOUNTER

D<small>R.</small> *Hans Urs von Balthasar, who has contributed to the understanding of contemporary philosophic problems in such works as,* DIE WAHRHEIT *and* DIE APOKALYPSE DER DEUTSCHEN SEELE, *in this essay investigates the engagement of man and what he encounters—an engagement that results in both the discovery and the creation of meaning in knowledge, an engagement that is both the duty and the completion of the knower. Reprinted by permission from* SCIENCE, RELIGION AND CHRISTIANITY, *translated by Hilda Graef, The Newman Press, Westminster, Maryland, 1959, pp. 31–39. Copyright 1958 by Burns, Oates and Wasbourne, Ltd.*

• Before Leibniz expressed it, St Thomas knew that the human mind possesses the key to the meaning of things, not by the presence in it of innate ideas, but by directing on things its own intellectual light as the means of apprehending all being. This light is spiritual; hence, despite its receptivity for the finite, it is active and spontaneous without restriction. It can thus be capable of spiritual interpretation only because it is the medium of meaning as such, into which the "objective" can enter, and, bringing its meaning with it and revealing it, can attain to its true and objectively intended meaning. This total and universal *a priori* of meaning is difficult to grasp; but it can be in some way elucidated if it be approached from its more easily intelligible preliminary, namely, from organic sensibility and specific sense qualities. Colour is only in the eye, sound is only in the ear; both sense organs apply this medium so that those things can develop and find themselves in it which the Creator has evidently prepared, invented, and willed for it. It is irrelevant that the lower existed in time before the higher, receptive element that offered it space. Even the formal conception of applying and spreading a medium introduces us into a sphere beyond realism and idealism, before ascending to the distinctively intellectual and spiritual. For things are not what they are and are meant to be—in this case coloured and sounding—outside the sense organ, as if this were a mere photographic plate passively reflecting what is already wholly there "outside"; nor is the form of the things simply subjective, put on the formless and unknowable material of a "thing in itself" as a means of bringing it into orderly categories; but they find their own objective essence in the medium of their mutually open subjectivities. If, at the level of sense experience, this offering of space (*Raumbieten*) is still purely natural and necessary, at the level of the human mind it is supported and characterized by a person in a way which is at the same time inescapably rational and voluntary; the space of meaning thus opened is a personal space. That is why knowledge that occurs in this space cannot be interpreted by any defective case but solely by the highest, adequate and fully valid one, that is by the meeting of another person. For this is not a special case of knowledge beside others, but that which gives direction to all other cases of intellectual or sense knowledge which are below it, because they are inferior in depth of meaning; they all are, at least inchoatively, forms of meeting and letting meet, and thus of the being-for-another of the world's creatures.

A theory of knowledge that resolutely starts from the case that sets the norm of all knowledge, i.e. the meeting between persons, saves itself a good many false problems. These appear necessarily where the higher is approached from the lower, where the meeting person is ranged among the "objects as such" or "things" and thus can never appear in his own right. However, we do not here mention this true centre of the theory of knowledge in order to develop a detailed personalism, but to elucidate every case from the highest standpoint. In order to fulfil the conditions of objective knowledge, every personal meeting demands an unrestricted openness of one's own person, on principle; this means an advancing of meaning that is not conditioned (*eine nichtnur-bedingte Vorstreckung von Sinn*), concretely a preparedness to admit another and let him assert himself, to love objectively and unselfishly; and this form of personal openness cannot be missing from any other form of knowledge. In other words: there is no "purely theoretical" attitude of knowledge that would not be at least in its root also a wholly human and true (*gesamtwahrheit-lich*) attitude. Man as a whole performs his act and is responsible for it; indeed, in his intellectual and spiritual acts he is always present as a whole and appears in them in his indivisible essence. To all things and beings that appear in the cosmos he opens himself as that wherein meaning can be found; offering himself as a medium where, in the light of the human spirit, he certainly proves himself as that which is in principle capable of all truth and of being changed into all things and conditions (*anima quodammodo omnia*). But he is so not primarily in order to dominate, but to render a service constantly renewed by a human existence fully understood and affirmed.

To an epoch in which anthropology has been recognized as the key to philosophy, it is self-contradictory to foster an intelligence that approaches things from a merely rationalistic and technical point of view; indeed it completely misunderstands its own being. This is the point of the warnings sounded by all those contemporaries who understand the situation, however different their views may otherwise be: by Scheler or Heidegger or Jaspers, by Bernanos or Buber or Aldous Huxley. No technical achievements can dispense us from the necessity of gaining this insight; even though things may ever more rapidly jump through all the hoops we extend to them, may ride all bicycles, and by their readiness to obey, hypnotize, rather than be hypnotized by, their trainer. Admittedly, man's success with things is due to man, to the right use of his reason that is *a priori* in relation to them; yet he should never forget that his reason is always the reason of a man, of one who wholly offers and gives himself because he cannot do otherwise, because in this freely accepted duty he is burdened with the responsibility for the destiny of the world. In the meeting between man and things the latter answer in proportion as man opens and surrenders himself; there is no other, less exacting way of creating truth, today less than ever. In the cosmological period a certain naïve realism and objectivism was still adequate, inasmuch as the measure of truth was primarily situated in the embracing cosmic order. In the anthropological period the highest objectivity can be attained only by the highest personal risk of man himself; for he cannot attain to what he is, that is the free and understanding spirit above nature, in any other way save by the ever renewed use of his freedom by which he, far from being made in advance, is always newly designed and realized. It is indeed consoling that this freedom that risks itself has a highest and freest master above and within itself, whose providence directs even the risk; but this does not for a moment absolve man from taking it. For God's providence is not a "natural order," nor a Hegelian "world spirit" to which the human spirit could simply entrust itself, expecting to be conveyed by this higher reason to the invisible goal. In the game of the world the stake is no less than man himself.

The practical consequences of this affect every sphere of knowledge. Detailed work on individual departments and their immanent laws (such as Dilthey, Spranger and Nicolai Hartmann have undertaken) may indeed be valuable, yet human life cannot be so confined; in whatever sphere the individual be engaged, he must always act in his entirety. The dignity of the scholarly and scientific attitude demands that every scientific judgment should be pronounced with the universal idea of man in view, and, consequently, as coming from, and pointing towards, man. It must come from the man who is given the responsibility for this judgment; he can never escape it by imagining that in this case he is called in merely as a theoretician, an aesthetic expert or a sociologist; he is asked always as the indivisible, freely responsible person that he is. It must point towards man, whom he will then invariably consider in his judgments and actions. This does not only envisage the practical point of view, as being concerned with the possible consequences of a truth, with inventions and their application, social measures, and so forth. It is also important theoretically, in the way an individual judgment fits into the total truth about man. Thus we may prove the result of a piece of research to be misleading merely by applying it to the human context, even though in isolation it cannot be impugned. For example, the well-known American statistics on the sexual behaviour of man and woman is conspicuously divorced from any anthropological framework: the *sexual* behaviour of men is always a *human* sexual behaviour, and thus has a meaning and importance which the expert must have explicitly and constantly in view if he is not to miss the mark. This holds good also if the "object," in this case American man, probes himself no more deeply than his questioner. If he had been questioned more deeply and adequately, the investigation would perhaps have yielded more correct and objective results than the "object" could have produced if left to himself.

To give another example: take the examination of a great work of art belonging to the past, say a poetic work of Goethe or Schiller. It is evident that the person who examines it must possess the necessary aesthetic equipment, both objective, scientific knowledge and subjective, delicate sensitiveness for aesthetic values, and that the examination has to start from these. Yet it is certain that the poet did not mean to create a work that was to be confined to the world of aesthetic values, but that he wanted to express his own humanity in the language of art, and, even more, to touch other men by putting before them the highest and most exacting ideal of man. Hence, even in the perspective of the poet, the aesthetic aspect is transcended by the integrally human. On the other hand, the interpreter cannot be satisfied with understanding and evaluating this transcendence in its historical setting. He has to communicate with the poet in the universal idea of man which is the intellectual sphere common to them both, and to deliver his own aesthetic judgment in function of this conception of which, in the final analysis, even aesthetic values depend. Thus it is in no way a violation of the functions of a critic for Guardini to question whether Rilke can really take full responsibility as a man for what he says about life and man in his *Duinese Elegies*, which, as he says himself, are meant to be philosophical and religious statements. The same applies to Reinhold Schneider, who asks the same question of the great creators of culture of German Idealism, for example of Schiller with regard to his *Wallenstein*, or of Kleist, Brentano, and others. This is no dreary application of moral standards to aesthetic values; but it does mean that the latter are anchored in a deeper and more comprehensive sphere which the aesthetic world must reflect, if it would not be irresponsibly degraded to some kind of beautiful make-believe and thus unwillingly would bear witness to a negation of philosophy.

This does not mean that the critic of the great works of the past should judge them by the standards of the present or even of his own limited subjectivity. On the contrary, we are concerned with an ever fresh encounter on the personal plane; the more deeply the enquirer questions, the richer is the meaning he elucidates; further, the more profound the man or the work of the past are in themselves, the more significant and intimate will be the communication. The enquirer will first humbly and willingly receive whatever can be learned from the object itself, even the categories according to which it must be considered, in order to be instructed by the object itself before himself pronouncing a judgment. Nevertheless, breadth of mind does not mean refusal to take up a definite attitude, and liberality is not a shirking of responsibility.

In medieval philosophy, the categories of encounter existed only in rudimentary form, because the "thou" remained subsumed under the abstract notion of the object. Even in Idealism they were not developed, because this was concerned with a perpetual encounter of the abstract ego or of the objective and absolute spirit with itself. In principle the equation of anthropology and philosophy is reached with Kant; in his posthumous handbook of logic the content of philosophy is characterized by the fourth, concluding question: "What is man?" Feuerbach's anti-Hegelian manifesto (*Principles of the Philosophy of the Future,* 1843) declares point-blank: "Modern philosophy makes man the sole and universal object of philosophy; that is, it makes anthropology the universal science." Marx and Nietzsche agreed with him; nevertheless, it is only in the twentieth century that this "man" is no longer seen as a materialistic or evolutionary phantom, but as the concrete human being, the individual person within the community. Martin Buber has described the advent of dialogic thought in his postscript to the *Dialogic Writings* (1953) and in his *Problem of Man* (1947). As a representative of the dialogical religion he was predestined to further this idea. According to his universalistic conception of Judaism, this religion is explicitly and obviously what man as such represents in a hidden and fragmentary way. This view allows him to find parallels in the most varied Christian thinkers, in the works of Ebner and Mounier, Gabriel Marcel, Emil and August Brunner, of Scheler and Jaspers. In Catholic circles, the practical wisdom of Peter Lippert gained the idea ready admittance, in that he made the encounter with the personal God in the human "thou" of Jesus Christ the primary case of knowledge at its simplest. In the second volume of his *Philosophy,* Jaspers intensified considerably the idea of communication. What for Kant was still outside the sphere of philosophy, now became the starting point of every serious theory of knowledge, namely an object that cannot be constituted by the categories of the knowing subject, and precisely as such must be the knowable that is to be known (not a "thing in itself"), in other words, the human person in his freedom and responsibility. The freedom of the other must be admitted, and this implies the impossibility of anticipating its decisions and self-revelation. But this can happen only where one's own reason is more than an isolated capacity of knowing, but is rooted in an equally free and responsible totality of the person.

However, this is not enough. The encounter of such an alien freedom within the sphere of one's own personal freedom cannot be suffered to take place as between two sovereign and absolute quantities, either of which could be aware of the other's sovereignty by reason of its own (in the way a ruler receives another of equal rank in his own territory with the same honours he knows to be due to himself). Such a "pluralism" of subjects would only be a relapse into a solipsistic theory of knowledge that built up everything alien from logical conclusions or psychological analogies of one's own enclosed and self-contained ego. The very capacity of letting a "thou" appear in its uniqueness and personal dignity, can be situated only in that region of the ego where, transcending itself, it is responsible to an absolute "Thou." If it were otherwise, the ego would always take its own intellectual light as the standard by which to measure the "thou," and precisely for this reason this "thou" could never appear before and in him in his free, independent being. The personal knowledge of a co-ordinated "thou" can take place only in the sphere where both created persons know themselves responsible before the eternal "Thou" and meet each other before the veiled throne of the eternal judge. Every spiritual person receives his highest dignity and freedom from his relation to God; for a person cannot be viewed and recognized in any other way. For as knowable, the person is himself only where he is freely responsible before the Eternal One, and he can be recognized by the ego only because this, as knowing, is open in principle before the absolute "Thou" (*cogito, ergo sum*). The knowing ego has not two windows, one towards God and one towards man; but because God looks into its window (and only thus is a window constituted) it can look out of the window towards a human "thou," and through this on to other beings and objects in the world.

Inter-subjectivity is the crux of all philosophy. It is, however, ruled out from the beginning if a philosophy starts with an abstract ego that has to manoeuvre itself out of its prison by syllogisms, or with a total ego in the idealistic sense, of which the individual consciousness would be but an "empirical" limitation. We are far from identifying God with inter-subjectivity, let alone with the absolute ego of the Idealist; nevertheless, we must admit that a true encounter can take place only in God and in his sight. This means it can happen only where created persons share in God's uniqueness and freedom, because they are open to God and hence, in principle, also to each other, without the one being entitled to call the other to judgment before the tribunal of his own knowledge and freedom. A theory of knowledge dealing with the meeting between human beings can only be established on a religious basis. This is the price that has to be paid if man is no longer regarded (cosmologically) as one "nature" among other natures, that is in the abstract as one "subject of knowledge" among other such subjects that are to be treated in an equally abstract way. It is true, his openness to the world makes him the creator of meaning (*Sinnstifter*) for the latter, and this not only in the sense still prevalent in the Middle Ages, as one whose abstract capacity enables him to read and elicit ready-made meanings that God has placed in things. Yet he cannot create these meanings autonomously, as if he were an absolute spirit, but only as one responsible to God to the very roots of his whole person, one ready to serve and listen. He is given the task to rule creation in precisely the measure as he fulfils this ideal. In exactly the measure as he listens to God, he can speak to the world an essential word on behalf of God, and he can also really hear his neighbour and, listening, can see him (*loquere ut videam te*—"speak so that I may see thee"). And beginning to see what the other is and ought to be before God, he can become a neighbour to him, giving help and creating meaning. In this alone consists understanding. The knowledge of partial truths, of individual spheres of creation and of the history of the world and mankind, as well as the investigation of the material world in its usefulness for man, in short, whatever wants to share in the act of understanding, it all remains enclosed in that all-embracing form of it which gives all knowledge its meaning. It may be somewhat humiliating for the history of the spirit that this elementary law should have needed thousands of years to dawn on us. It is nevertheless consoling that the *kairos* of this understanding is just this present time, which, in other respects, is decried as wickedly materialistic and utilitarian, and which indeed decries itself as such. But making the real living human being the centre of philosophy will have its consequences. It is simply a law of man's life that he must look for his God and for his neighbour, and in doing so can neither behave as an absolute ego nor as an abstract subject, but only as an ego conversing with its thou by question and answer. And this law will make itself heard above all the noise of machines. Here, too, lies the ultimate solution of the struggle between the warring ideologies of the Eastern and the Western worlds, which, from the point of view of the philosophy of history, are already reconciled in principle.

BIBLIOGRAPHY FOR PART V

Abbot, F. E., "Scientific Philosophy: A Theory of Human Knowledge," *Mind*, VII (1882), pp. 461–95.

Adorno, T. W., *Zur Metakritik der Erkenntnistheorie; Studien über Husserl und die phänomenologischen Antinomien*, Kohlhammer, Stuttgart, 1956.

Aicher, S., *Kants Begriff der Erkenntnis verglichen mit dem des Aristoteles*, Reuther & Richard, Berlin, 1907.

Alejandro, J. M., *La gnoseologia del doctor Eximio y la acusacion nominalista*, Universidad Pontificia, Comillas, 1948.

Apostel, L.; Mandelbrot, B.; Morf, A., *Logique, Langage et théorie de l'information*, Presses Universitaires de France, Paris, 1957.

Aybar, B., *El Realismo Intuitivo*, Universidad Nacional de Tucuman, Tucuman, Argentina, 1954.

Ayer, A. J., *Language, Truth and Logic*, Dover Publications Inc., New York, 1953.

Balz, A. G. A., "Where Ignorance is Bliss," *The Monist*, XXXX (1930), pp. 146–55.

Baker, R. R., "Naturalism of Roy Wood Sellars," *The New Scholasticism*, XXIV (1950), pp. 3–31; 153–73.

Barker, H., "Notes on the Second Part of Spinoza's Ethics," *Mind*, n.s., XXXXVII (1938), pp. 417–39.

Bayer, R., *Epistémologie et logique depuis Kant jusqu'à nos jours*, Presses Universitaires de France, Paris, 1954.

Beare, J. I., *Greek Theories of Elementary Cognition*, Clarendon Press, Oxford, 1906.

Becker, O., *Plotin und das problem der geistigen aneignung*, W. de Gruyter & Co., Berlin, 1940.

Bennet, C., "For a Thomistic Epistemology," *Proceedings*, American Catholic Philosophical Association, XXII (1947), pp. 122–31.

Berkeley, G., "Are Things Different From Ideas," *Readings in Philosophy*, ed. J. H. Randall, J. Buchler, E. Shirk; Barnes & Noble, New York, 1946, pp. 77–100.

——, *Principles of Human Knowledge*, ed. with analysis and Appendix, by T. E. Jessop, Brown, London, 1937.

Bérubé, C., "La connaissance intellectuelle du singulier matériel au XIIIᵉ siècle, *Franciscan Studies*, XI (1951), pp. 157–201.

Blyth, J. W., *Whitehead's Theory of Knowledge*, Brown University, Providence, R. I., 1941 (Diss.).

Bonansea, B. M., *The Theory of Knowledge of Tommaso Campanella*. Exposition and critique, The Catholic University of America, 1954 (Diss.).

Bourke, V. J., "Intellectual Memory in the Thomistic Theory of Knowledge," *The Modern Schoolman*, XVIII, No. 2 (1941), pp. 21–24.

Bourquard, L. C., *Doctrine de la connaissance d'après Saint Thomas d'Aquin*, P. Lethielleux, Paris, 1877.

Boyer, C., "Pourquoi et comment s'occuper du scepticisme?" *Revue de Philosophie*, XXXI (1925), pp. 225–45.

Brandt, R. B., *The Philosophy of Schleiermacher*, Harper & Brothers, New York, 1941.

Bridet, L., *La Théorie de la connaissance dans la philosophie de Malebranche*, M. Rivière, Paris, 1929.

Britton, K., "The Paragon of Knowledge," *Philosophy*, XXIX (1954), pp. 216–30.

Butts, R. E., *Husserl's Criticisms of Hume's Theory of Knowledge*, U. of Pennsylvania, Philadelphia, 1957 (Diss.).

Caldwell, W., "The Epistemology of Ed. V. Hartman," *Mind*, n.s., II (1893), pp. 188–207.

Carr, H. W., "Bergson's Theory of Knowledge," *Proceedings*, n.s., *Aristotelian Society*, IX (1909), pp. 41–60.

Carré, M. H., *Nominalists and Realists,* Oxford University Press, London, 1946.

Cator, G., "The Euclidean Theory of Knowledge," *Mind,* n.s., XXXVII (1928), pp. 210–14.

———, "Subjectivism and Solipsism," *The Dublin Review,* CXXXIII (1903), pp. 67–81.

Charles, P., "Etudes sur les théories de la connaissance," *Revue de Philosophie,* XVI (1910), pp. 60–73; 183–93; 294–305; 393–422.

Child, A. H., *Making and Knowing in Aristotle, Vico, and Dewey,* University of California Press, Berkeley, 1953.

Chisholm, R. M., "Sextus Empiricus and Modern Empiricism," *Philosophy of Science,* VIII (1941), pp. 371–84.

———, "Sellars' Critical Realism," *Philosophy and Phenomenological Research,* XV (1954), pp. 33–47.

Church, R. W., *Hume's Theory of Understanding,* Cornell University Press, Ithaca, 1935.

Corotti, A., "Intorno al problema della conoscenza in Democrito," *Sophia,* Anno III, No. 1, 1935.

Creaven, J. A., "Personalism, Thomism and Epistemology," *The Thomist,* VIII (1945), pp. 1–26.

Croce, B., "Dewey's Aesthetics and Theory of Knowledge," *Journal of Aesthetics and Art Criticism,* XI, No. 1 (1952), pp. 1–6.

Crocker, L. G., "The Problem of Truth and Falsehood in the Age of Enlightenment," *Journal of the History of Ideas,* XIV (1953), pp. 575–603.

Cronin, J. F., *Cardinal Newman: His Theory of Knowledge,* The Catholic University of America, Washington, D. C., 1935 (Diss.).

Dady, Sister Mary R., *The Theory of Knowledge of St. Bonaventure,* The Catholic University of America, Washington, D. C., 1937 (Diss.).

Day, S. J., *Intuitive Cognition, A Key to the Significance of the Later Scholastics,* The Franciscan Institute, St. Bonaventure University, New York, 1947.

De Boer, J. J., *The Theory of Knowledge of the Cambridge Platonists,* Methodist Publishing House, Madras, 1931.

De Vogel, C. J., "Stoic Theory of Knowledge," *Greek Philosophy,* III, E. J. Brill, Leiden, 1959, pp. 115–27.

———, "Scepticism," *Greek Philosophy,* III, E. J. Brill, Leiden, 1959, pp. 184–230.

Dewey, J., "The Experimental Theory of Knowledge," *Mind,* n.s., XV (1906), pp. 293–307.

———, Bentley, A. F., *Knowing and the Known,* Beacon Press, Boston, 1949.

Enriques, F., de Santillana, G., *Le problème de la connaissance. Empiricisme et rationalisme grecs,* Herman & Cie., Paris, 1937.

Efros, I., "Saadia's Theory of Knowledge," *Jewish Quarterly Review,* XXXIII (1942–43), pp. 133–70.

Farrer, A. M., "The Extension of St. Thomas' Doctrine of Knowledge by Analogy to Modern Philosophical Problems," *The Downside Review,* LXV (1947), pp. 21–32.

Feys, R., "Guillaume d'Ockham, théoricien de la connaissance," *Revue Philosophique de Louvain,* XXXXVI (1948), pp. 188–201.

Fireman, P., *Perceptualistic Theory of Knowledge,* Philosophical Library, New York, 1954.

Fisch, M. H., "Alexander Bain and the Genealogy of Pragmatism," *Journal of the History of Ideas,* XV (1954), pp. 413–44.

Fitch, R. E., "An Experimental Perspectival Epistemology," *The Journal of Philosophy,* XXXVIII (1941), pp. 589–600.

Fleckenstein, N. J., *A Critique of John Dewey's Theory of the Nature and the Knowledge of Reality in the Light of the Principles of Thomism,* The Catholic University of America, Washington, D. C., 1954 (Diss.).

Friedman, M. S., "Martin Buber's Theory of Knowledge," *Review of Metaphysics,* VIII (1954), pp. 264–80.

Fritz, A. D., "Malebranche and the Immaterialism of Berkeley," *Review of Metaphysics,* III (1949), pp. 59–80.

Garnett, C. B., "Kant's Theory of *Intuitus Intellectualis* in the Inaugural Dissertation of 1770," *The Philosophical Review,* XXXXVI (1937), pp. 424–32.

Gerhard, W. A., "Epistemology of Thomas Hobbes," *The Thomist,* IX (1946), pp. 573–87.

———, "Preface to a Science of Phenomena," *The New Scholasticism,* XXVI (1952), pp. 195–228.

Gibson, J., *Locke's Theory of Knowledge and Its Historical Relations,* Cambridge University Press, 1917.

Gouhier, H., "Introduction à la théorie thomiste de la connaissance," *Revue des Cours et Conférences,* XXXIII (1931–32), pp. 481–93; 648–53; 707–13; Deux. série, pp. 29–32; 248–63.

Hartung, F. E., "Operationism as a Cultural Survival," *Philosophy of Science,* XI (1944), pp. 227–32.

Haserot, F. S., "The Meaning of Rationalism," *The Journal of Philosophy,* XXXXIV (1947), pp. 205–16.

Hill, T. E., *Contemporary Theories of Knowledge* [in preparation].

Hill, W. H., "Peirce's Pragmatic Method," *Philosophy of Science,* VII (1940), pp. 168–81.

Hislop, I., "Introduction to St. Bonaventure's Theory of Knowledge," *Dominican Studies,* II (1949), pp. 45–55.

Hofstadter, A., "The Myth of the Whole: A Consideration of Quine's View of Knowledge," *The Journal of Philosophy,* LI (1954), pp. 397–417.

Hooper, S. E., "Whitehead's Philosophy: Propositions and Consciousness," *Philosophy,* XX (1945), pp. 59–75.

Jansen, B., "Marechal's Theory of Dynamic Cognition," *The Modern Schoolman,* XIII, No. 2 (1936), pp. 34–7.

Johnstone, H. W., "Knowledge and Purpose," *The Journal of Philosophy,* XXXXVII (1950), pp. 493–501.

Jones, P. C., "Idealism and Its Relation to Science," *Philosophy of Science,* VIII (1941), pp. 142–46.

Kagey, R., "Reality and 'the Real' in Bradley," *The Monist,* XXXXIV (1934), pp. 238–47.

Keeler, L. W., *Sancti Augustini Doctrina de Cognitione,* Gregorian University, Rome, 1934.

Kelly, T. R., "Meyerson and the Epistemological Paradox," *The Monist,* XXXXIV (1934), pp. 296–305.

Klausner, N. W., "The Epistemology of A. C. Strong," *The Journal of Philosophy,* XXXXII (1945), pp. 683–94.

Kleinz, J. P., *The Theory of Knowledge of Hugh of St. Victor,* The Catholic University of America, Washington, D. C., 1944 (Diss.).

Kremer, R., *La théorie de la connaissance chez les néoréalistes anglais,* Louvain, 1928.

Lafleur, L. J., "Epistemological Functionalism," *The Philosophical Review,* L (1941), pp. 471–82.

Lévèque, R., *L' "élément historique" dans la connaissance humaine d'après Cournot,* Les Belles Lettres, Paris, 1938.

Lewis, H. D., "Naive Realism and a Passage in the *Theaetetus,*" *Mind,* n.s., XXXXVII (1938), pp. 351–56.

MacKenzie, J. S., "The Theory of Knowledge," *Mind,* n.s., V (1896), pp. 396–410.

MacKennon, D. M., "Kant's Agnosticism," *Blackfriars,* XXVIII (1947), pp. 256–62.

MacPartland, J., "Aristotle and the Spectator Theory of Knowledge," *The Journal of Philosophy,* XXXXII (1945), pp. 291–93.

Maziarz, E. A., "Russell and Human Knowledge," *The New Scholasticism,* XXIII (1949), pp. 318–25.

McKeon, R., "Thomas Aquinas' Doctrine of Knowledge and Its Historical Setting," *Speculum,* III (1928), pp. 425–44.

McNabb, D. G. C., *David Hume: His Theory of Knowledge and Morality,* Hutchinson's University Library, London, 1951.

Malcolm, N., "Discussion: Bertrand Russell's Human Knowledge," *The Philosophical Review,* LIX (1950), pp. 94–106.

Marcel, G., "On the Ontological Mystery," *Philosophy of Existence,* Philosophical Library, New York, 1949, pp. 1–31.

Maritain, J., "A propos des cahiers du P. Maréchal," *Revue Thomiste,* n.s., VII (1924), pp. 416–25.

Maund, C., *Hume's Theory of Knowledge,* The Macmillan Co., London, 1937.

Meyerson, E., *Du cheminement de la pensée,* 3 vols., Alcan, Paris, 1931.

Miller, J. W., "Descartes's Conceptualism," *Review of Metaphysics,* IV (1950), pp. 239–46.

Montague, W. P., "Mr. A. C. Strong's Creed for the Sceptics," *The Journal of Philosophy,* XXXV (1938), pp. 572–80.

Moore, G. E., "The Refutation of Idealism," *Mind,* n.s., XII (1903), pp. 433–53.

Moreau, J., *Réalisme et idéalisme chez Platon,* Presses Universitaires de France, Paris, 1951.

Morrow, G. R., "The Theory of Knowledge in the Seventh Platonic Epistle," *The Philosophical Review,* XXXVIII (1929), pp. 326–49.

Murphy, A. E., "Dewey's Epistemology and Metaphysics," *The Philosophy of John Dewey,* ed. P. A. Schilpp, Tudor Publishing Co., New York, 1951, pp. 193–225.

Noël, L., "The Realism of St. Thomas," *Blackfriars,* XVI (1935), pp. 817–32.

Norris, O. O., "A Preamble to an Organismic Theory of Knowledge," *Philosophy of Science,* I (1934), pp. 460–78.

Parkin, A., "Platonic Theory of Knowledge," *Manitoba Arts Review,* IV, No. 2 (1945).

Parkinson, G. H. R., *Spinoza's Theory of Knowledge,* Clarendon Press, Oxford, 1951.

Perry, C. M., "Epistemology Re-examined," *The Philosophical Review,* XXXX (1931), pp. 444–58.

Perry, R. B., "The Philosophy of William James: II. Theory of Knowledge," *Present Philosophical Tendencies,* George Braziller, Inc., New York, 1955, pp. 356–68.

———, "A Realistic Theory of Knowledge," *Present Philosophical Tendencies,* George Braziller, Inc., New York, 1955, pp. 306–28.

Popkin, R. H., "Berkeley and Pyrrhonism," *Review of Metaphysics,* V (1951), pp. 223–46.

———, "David Hume: His Pyrrhonism and His Critique of Pyrrhonism," *The Philosophical Quarterly,* I (1950–51), pp. 385–407.

———, "David Hume and the Pyrrhonian Controversy," *Review of Metaphysics,* VI (1952), pp. 65–81.

———, "The Skeptical Precursors of David Hume," *Philosophy and Phenomenological Research,* XVI (1955), pp. 61–71.

Prichard, H. A., *Kant's Theory of Knowledge,* Oxford University Press, London, 1909.

Randall, J. H., "David Hume, Radical Empiricist and Pragmatist," *Freedom and Experience,* Cornell University Press, Ithaca, 1947, pp. 289–312.

Régis, L. M., "Father Maréchal: Thomistic Critique and Kantian Critique," *Epistemology,* The Macmillian Co., New York, 1959, pp. 93–104.

Ritchie, A. D., "Errors of Logical Positivism," *Philosophy,* XII (1937), pp. 47–60.

Ryan, J. A., "Two Essays on American Critical Realism," *Revue de l'Université d'Ottawa,* VI (1936), pp. 102–28; 262–96.

Ryan, J. H., "The Problem of Knowledge from the Point of View of Dualistic Realism," *The Philosophical Review,* XXXV (1926), pp. 399–415.

Sellars, R. W., "A Clarification of Critical Realism," *Philosophy of Science,* VI (1939), pp. 412–21.

Shien Gi-Ming, "The Epistemology of Buddhism, Taoism, and Confucianism," *Philosophy,* XXVIII (1953), pp. 260–64.

Smith, G., "A Date in the History of Epistemology," *The Thomist,* V (1943), pp. 246–55.

Smith, J. W., "Pragmatism, Realism, and Positivism in the United States," *Mind,* n.s., LXI (1952), pp. 190–208.

Smith, N. K., *Prolegomena to an Idealist Theory of Knowledge,* The Macmillan Co., London, 1924.

Tillich, P., "Reinhold Neibuhr's Doctrine of Knowledge," *R. Niebuhr: His Religious, Social and Political Thought,* ed., Kegley and Bretall, II, Library of Living Theology, The Macmillan Co., New York, 1956.

Turner, J. E., *A Theory of Direct Realism,* The Macmillan Co., New York, 1925.

Vancourt, R., *La théorie de la connaissance chez Maine de Biran,* Aubier, Paris, 1944.

Van Hall, G., *The Theory of Knowledge of Samuel Alexander,* Gregorian University, Rome, 1936.

Veatch, H. B., *Realism and Nominalism Revisited,* Marquette University Press, Milwaukee, 1954.

Von Mises, R., *Positivism: A Study in Human Understanding,* Harvard University Press, Cambridge, 1951.

Wild, J., "What is Realism," *The Journal of Philosophy,* XXXXIV (1947), pp. 148–58.

Williams, M. V., *Six Essays on the Platonic Theory of Knowledge as Expounded in the Later Dialogues and Reviewed by Aristotle,* The University Press, Cambridge, 1908.

Wolz, H. G., "The Double Guarantee of Descartes' Ideas," *Review of Metaphysics,* III (1950), pp. 471–89.

Wood, L., "Recent Epistemological Schools," *A History of Philosophical Systems,* ed. V. Ferm, Philosophical Library, New York, 1950, pp. 516–39.

Yolden, T. D. C., *Hume's Theory of Knowledge,* University of Texas Press, Austin, 1953.

Yost, R. M., *Leibniz and Philosophical Analysis,* University of California Press, Berkeley, 1954.

META-BIBLIOGRAPHY

B. Rand, *Bibliography of Philosophy, Psychology, and Cognate Subjects,* Vol. III, Part 2 of J. M. Baldwin's *Dictionary of Philosophy and Psychology,* The Macmillan Co., New York, 1905: "Epistemology," pp. 574–89.

Mandonnet et Destrez, *Bibliographie thomiste,* Le Saulchoir, Kain, 1921, pp. 796–875.

V. J. Bourke, *Thomistic Bibliography,* The Modern Schoolman, University of St. Louis, St. Louis, 1945, Nos. 2216–2741.

G. A. De Brie, *Bibliographia Philosophica, 1934–45,* Vol. II, Editiones Spectrum, Bruxelis, 1954: *"Theoria Cognitionis,"* Nos. 27557–28905, pp. 130–65.

L. Rougier, *Traité de la Connaissance,* Gauthier-Villars, Paris, 1955, pp. 435–42.

G. Varet, *Manuel de Bibliographie Philosophique,* Vol. II, Les Sciences Philosophiques, Presses Universitaires de France, Paris, 1956: "Epistémologie générale," pp. 647–62.

R. Klibansky, ed., *Philosophy in the Mid-Century,* 4 vols., La Nuova Italia Editrice, Firenze, 1958: "Epistemology, Publications in English," by David Pears, Vol. II, pp. 109–16; "Theorie de la connaissance, Hors des Pays Anglo-Saxons," par Gilbert Varet, Vol. II, pp. 119–38; "Linguistic Analysis," by Anthony Quinton, Vol. II, pp. 146–202; "Philosophy of Language," by Rulon Wells, Vol. II, pp. 139–45.

F. H. Heinemann, "Die Aufgabe einer Enzyklopädie des 20. Jahrhunderts," in the volume: "Philosophie" of the *Neue Europaische Enzyklopädie,* Stuttgart, 1959; cf. also "Theory of Knowledge," by Heinemann in the same *Enzyklopädie.*

L. Wood, "Epistemology," in *Dictionary of Philosophy,* ed. by D. D. Runes, Philosophical Library, New York, 1942, pp. 94–96.

"Gnoseologia," in *Enciclopedia Filosofica,* II, Istituto Per La Collaborazione Culturale, Venezia-Roma, 1957, pp. 813–40.

"Conocimiento," in *Diccionario de Filosofía,* cuarta edición, 1958, ed. by Jose Ferrater Mora, Editorial Sudamericana, Buenos Aires, pp. 266–69.

SELECTED BIBLIOGRAPHY (1939–1959)

Amerio, F., *Epistemologia*, Morcelliana, Brescia, 1948.

Areud, J. P., *Die Geschichte der Erkenntnis*, Thomas-Verlag, Zurich, 1948.

Ayer, A. J., *The Foundations of Empirical Knowledge*, The Macmillan Company, London, 1940.

——, *The Problem of Knowledge*, St. Martin's Press, New York, 1956.

Ballauff, Th., *Das gnoseologische Problem*, Vandenhoeck-Ruprecht, Göttingen, 1949.

Beck, L. W., *Synopsis; a study in the theory of knowledge*, Duke University, Durham, 1939. (Diss.)

Berger, G., *Recherches sur les conditions de la connaissance*, Presses Universitaires de France, Paris, 1941.

Blanshard, B., *The Nature of Thought*, 2 vols., George Allen & Unwin, London, 1939.

Bohr, N. H. D., *Atomic Physics and Human Knowledge*, John Wiley & Sons, New York, 1958.

Boll, M. et Pagès, J.-C., *Les étapes de la connaissance*, Hermann, Paris, 1953.

Brain, W. R., *Mind, Perception, and Science*, Charles C. Thomas, Springfield, Ill., 1952.

Bridgman, P. W., *The Way Things Are,* Harvard University Press, Cambridge, 1959.

Bruner, J. S., *et al., Contemporary Approaches to Cognition;* a symposium held at the University of Colorado, Harvard University Press, Cambridge, 1957.

Brunner, A., *La connaissance humaine,* Aubier, Paris, 1943.

Calogero, G., *La conclusíone della filosofiá del conoscere,* F. Le Monnier, Firenze, 1938.

Childe, V. G., *Society and Knowledge,* Harper & Brothers, New York, 1956.

Chisholm, R. M., *Perceiving: a philosophical study,* Cornell University Press, Ithaca, 1957.

Collin, R., *Les deux savoirs,* A. Michel, Paris, 1946.

Coninck, A. de, *L'unité de la connaissance humaine,* L'Institut Supérieur de Philosophie, Louvain, 1947.

Cornforth, M. C., *The Theory of Knowledge,* International Publishers, New York, 1955.

Cournot, A. A., *An Essay on the Foundations of Our Knowledge,* tr. M. H. Moore, Liberal Arts Press, New York, 1954.

Desmangeot, L., *Théorie de la connaissance,* Société d'édition d'enseignement supérieur, Paris, 1951.

Ducasse, C. J., *The Method of Knowledge in Philosophy,* University of California Press, Berkeley, 1945.

Earle, W. A., *Objectivity,* Noonday Press, New York, 1955.

Emiliani Roman, R., *Fuentes del conocimiento,* Cartagena, Colombia, 1951.

Feigl, H., *et al., Concepts, Theories, and the Mind-Body Problem,* University of Minnesota Press, Minneapolis, 1958.

Fireman, P., *Perceptualistic Theory of Knowledge,* Philosophical Library, New York, 1954.

Gevens, F. G. M., *De Materiele logica,* R. K. Jongensweeshuis, Tilburg, 1949.

Goodman, N., *The Structure of Appearance,* Harvard University Press, Cambridge, 1951.

Hartland-Swann, J., *An Analysis of Knowing,* George Allen & Unwin, London, 1958.

Hartmann, N., *Les principes d'une métaphysique de la connaissance,* tr. et préf. R. Vancourt, Aubier, Paris, 2 vols., 1945–46.

Heistermann, W. E., *Erkenntnis und Sein,* Maximilian-Verlag, Detnold, 1951.

Inter-American Congress of Philosophy (first, Port-au-Prince, 1944). *Travaux du Congrès . . .* consacré aux problèmes de la connaissance, Imprimerie de l'Etat, Port-au-Prince, 1947.

Isaacs, N., *The Foundations of Common Sense;* a psychological preface to the problems of knowledge, Routledge & Paul, London, 1949.

Jacques, E., *Introduction au problème de la connaissance,* Publications Universitaires de Louvain, 1953.

Johnson, M., *Science and the Meaning of Truth,* Faber and Faber, London, 1946.

Jones, A. J., *In Search of Truth,* Thomas Nelson & Sons, London, 1945.

Krikorian, Y. H. and Edel, A., *Contemporary Philosophic Problems, Selected Readings,* The Macmillan Company, New York, 1959: I, "Meaning," pp. 7–82; II, "Knowledge," pp. 83–229.

Lauer, Q. J., *Triumph of Subjectivity,* Fordham University Press, New York, 1958.

Lonergan, B. J. F., *Insight,* A Study of Human Understanding, Philosophical Library, New York, 1956.

Maritain, J., *Distinguish to Unite or The Degrees of Knowledge,* ed. by G. B. Phelan, Geoffrey Bles, London, 1959.

Martin, W. O., *The Order and Integration of Knowledge,* U. of Michigan Press, Ann Arbor, 1957.

Nagel, E., *Logic without Metaphysics,* The Free Press, Glencoe, Ill., 1956.

Negley, G., *The Organization of Knowledge,* Prentice-Hall, New York, 1942.

Pap, A., *Semantics and Necessary Truth,* Yale University Press, New Haven, 1958.

Péghaire, J., *Regards sur le connaître,* Fides, Montréal, 1949.

Régis, L.-M., *St. Thomas and Epistemology,* Marquette University Press, Milwaukee, 1946.

———, *Epistemology,* The Macmillan Company, New York, 1959.

Reiser, O. L., *The Integration of Human Knowledge,* Porter Sargent Publisher, Boston, 1958.

Simon, Y. R., *Prévoir et Savoir,* Edition de l'Arbre, Montréal, 1945.

Sinclair, A., *The Conditions of Knowing,* Harcourt, Brace and Co., New York, 1951.

Smith, A. H., *A Treatise on Knowledge,* Clarendon Press, Oxford, 1943.

Sprague, E., Taylor, P. W., *Knowledge and Value,* Harcourt, Brace and Co., New York, 1959.

Stark, W., *The Sociology of Knowledge,* The Free Press, Glencoe, Ill., 1958.

Werkmeister, W. H., *The Basis and Structure of Knowledge,* Harper & Brothers, New York, 1948.

Wood, L., *The Analysis of Knowledge,* Princeton University Press, Princeton, 1941.

INDEX OF PROPER NAMES

Rougier, L., 411
Ruja, J. H., 51
Runes, D., 412
Russell, B., 51, 56, 71, 72, 86, 87, 106,
  120, 141, 223, 233, 234, 236, 349
Ryan, E. J., 112
Ryan, J. A., 409
Ryan, J. H., 51, 409
Ryle, G., 346
St. John, 334
St. John of the Cross, 335, 339
St. Paul, 340
Salzi, P., 112
Sams, H. W., 181
Santayana, G., 349
Sapir, E., 170
Scheler, M., 397, 400
Schiller, F. C. S., 345, 399
Schlick, M., 247
Schneider, R., 399
Schrodinger, 278
Searles, H. L., 51
Sellars, R. W., 112, 349, 409
Sells, S. B., 284
Sheffer, H. M., 238
Sheldon, W. H., 350
Sherrington, C. S., 69
Shien Gi-Ming, 409
Sidgwick, H., 283, 350
Simmons, E. D., 145–169
Simon, Y. R., 55–95, 112, 201, 206, 207,
  209, 385, 415
Simplicius, 92
Sinclair, A., 415
Sing-Nan, Fen, 181
Sisson, E. O., 181
Smith, A., 283, 415
Smith, G., 181, 409
Smith, J. A., 59, 66
Smith, J. W., 409
Smith, N. K., 409
Smith, V. E., 146, 350
Smith, W., 51
Socrates, 90, 359
Solomon, J., 350
Solon, 4
Somerfeld, A., 278
Sora, M. M., 124
Sorel, G., 93
Spaulding, E. G., 291
Spinoza, B., 128, 330, 357, 358

Sprague, E., 415
Sprenger, 398
Stace, W. T., 350, 371, 372, 373, 374,
  375, 376
Stallo, J. B., 264
Stark, W., 415
Stebbing, L. S., 116, 120
Sterling, J. H., 350
Stern, S. M., 203
Stevinus, 255
Stöhr, A., 10, 12, 14
Stone, H., 281
Stout, G. F., 117, 118
Strong, C. A., 112
Strong, E. W., 350
Stuart, H. W., 350
Suárez, 65
Swabey, W. C., 112, 350
Swammerdam, 9
Taine, H., 65, 391
Tarski, A., 101
Taylor, A. E., 345
Taylor, P. W., 415
Taylor, R., 350
Tennyson, 214
Thales, 8
Thomas, I., 181
Thompson, M. H., 350
Thompson, S. M., 42
Thompson, W. R., 30, 276, 277
Thro, L., 181
Thucydides, 4
Tillich, P., 409
Tonquédec, J. de, 206
Toohey, J. J., 51, 350
Trager, G. L., 171
Trethowan, I., 350
Tsanoff, R. A., 350
Turner, J. E., 409
Turning, A., 350
Tusquets, J., 112
Tymieniecka, E. J., 51
Vancourt, R., 409
Van Hall, G., 409
Van Riet, G., 146, 350
Varet, G., 411
Veatch, H. B., 20, 31, 185–199, 409
Verbeke, G., 350
Vier, P. C., 350
Voegelin, C. F., 171
Von Mises, R., 409

SUBJECT INDEX

Abstraction, 33–36, 66, 133, 142
  degrees of, 146–69
Activity
  immanent, 43, 61, 62
  transient, 61
American Indian, 170 ff.
Analogy, 335 ff.
A posteriori, 221
Apprehension, 124
A priori, 221
Beatific vision, 340 ff.
Being, 122–30, 329 ff.
  composition of, 194 ff.
Bipolarity of concepts, 21
Cartesianism, 57, 126
Category, 171 ff., 357
Certitude, 305
  empirical, 104
  experiential, 97
Change, 28, 59
Compatibility of systems, 104

Concept, 35, 62, 71, 186 ff.
  of God, 337
Consistency, 108, 272
Contemplation, 340 ff.
Contradiction, 64, 309
Creativity, 396–402
Criteriology, 3, 80
Demonstration, 325
Differentiation of sensation, 70
Dreams, 64
Empiricism, 32, 105, 138–44, 371–78,
  379–84
Encounter, 395 ff.
Entities, 57
Epistemology, 5, 184
Error, 83, 291–316
Essence, 31, 127–36, 186, 329 ff.
Ethics, 5, 15, 16, 283–89
Excluded middle, 235–37
Existence, 65, 123, 126–36, 187, 188, 189,
  204, 330–33

origin of, 74 ff.
and certainty, 96 ff.
truth of, 83 ff.
Senses
deception of, 84 ff.
Sensible species, 75
Separation, 133, 165 ff.
Signification, 197
Skepticism, 19 ff.
Species, 74 ff.
Subjectivity, 273 ff.
Suffering, 12 ff.
Symbolism of physical knowledge, 273
Theoretical physics, 245–79
Theory, 92 ff.
Thought-thing, 115–20, 206

Time, 173 ff.
Transcendentals, 320–22, 336
Transitivity, 43
Truth
definition of, 202
kinds of, 217–30
meanings of, 231–44
problem of, 201
Unity of knower, known, 44, 45, 67, 68, 87, 88
Universals, 25, 137–44, 229, 303, 322, 323
Verifiability, 234, 243, 377
Vérités de fait, 221 ff.
Vérités de raison, 221 ff.
Verum sequitur . . . 200 ff.
Weltanschauung, 10, 172
Whorfian hypothesis, 170 ff.